CULTURE MATTERS IN CHINA-INDIA RELATIONS

Interaction, Perception and Tradition

CULTURE MATTERS IN CHINA-INDIA RELATIONS

Interaction, Perception and Tradition

Zhang Yang

PENTAGON PRESS LLP

First published in 2023 by

PENTAGON PRESS LLP
206, Peacock Lane, Shahpur Jat
New Delhi-110049, India
Contact: 011-64706243

Typeset in Times New Roman, 10.5 Point
Printed by Aegean Offset Printers, Greater Noida, U.P.

ISBN: 978-93-90095-79-7 (HB)

www.pentagonpress.in

CONTENTS

ACKNOWLEDGMENTS

This work is an outcome of my continuous thinking and research in the studies process at the University of Delhi and the Jawaharlal Nehru University, India. The experience of doing post-doctoral research in the National Museum of China and the Chinese Academy of Social Sciences inspires me greatly to publish it as a book.

In writing this book, I have received the support of numerous resourceful individuals. Thanks to those who supported and helped me, I was able to accomplish it. I am grateful to all of them but thank only a few by name.

To begin with, I am grateful to my M.Phil./Ph.D. supervisor Prof. Srikanth Kondapalli for guiding me throughout my work with his patience and knowledge. I thank the faculties and staff from the Centre for East Asian Studies who helped me to start, continue and finish my work. Notably, Dr. Ritu Agarwal and Prof. Varaprasad Sekhar Dolla who suggested and guided me to improve my research skill. I am indebted to Dr. H.S. Prabhakar and Prof. Srabani Roy Choudhury for their valuable suggestions and comments during the course of my work. Dr. Sandip Kumar Mishra, who encouraged me to continue what I had abandoned before presenting my synopsis. Dr. Jitendra Uttam who has advised me to expand my vision. Thanks to the external faculties from the School of International Studies who read my synopsis and gave me beneficial suggestions. Criticism can make research life hard and hopeless or make research opinion better and stronger. Debates with Professors in JNU were an essential point in my research life. Although many of my opinions or views of my research were seriously challenged during the conversations, after I read the works of various professors and discussed with scholars and friends, the foundation became stronger.

Special thanks to my two co-advisors Zhang Zhihua, Research Fellow of National Museum of China and Meng Qinglong, Research Fellow of Chinese Academy of Social Sciences for their patient guidance and insightful suggestions for my post-doctoral research.

Thanks to Prof. Yin Xinan from Sichuan University, Mr. Lei Ming, Director of Confucius Institute, Mumbai, and Prof. Tansen Sen from City University of

New York, Dr. Gopa Sabharwal, Vice Chancellor of Nalanda University, Prof. Pankaj Mohan and Ms. Naomi Nelson from Nalanda University. I am also thankful to Prof. Avijit Banerjee from Cheena Bhavana; he guided me on the sources available on this subject.

I appreciate Prof. Shang Huipeng, in whose class in Peking University and by whose works I benefited a lot. I also appreciate Dr. You Guolong who was always ready to give me suggestions and guidance.

I am grateful for Prof. Zhang Shulan, who invited me for a book project and gave me a chance to improve my research and writing skills and my understanding of Indian culture and society. Informal talks are crucial for research. Talking with diplomats and scholars during breaks in conferences was also quite helpful. Thanks to my seniors who were very generous with their time and opinions.

I am really thankful to JNU's Central Library, National Library of China, Parliament Library, Nehru Memorial Hall administrators, and Oxford University librarians, for the source material I accessed in the above libraries and the ready assistance of library personnel in accessing it. I am also indebted to the Juxtapose Project team for their support and encouragement.

This research also benefits from interviews and seminars. I sincerely thank the scholars, managers, and employees from China or India who gave me much useful information to improve my research. Especially, Dr. Shen Kaiyan of Institute of Economics, Shanghai Academy of Social Sciences kindly spared time to patiently listen to my research and answer my questions regarding China-India economic relations and the role of culture in the Indian economy. Her views again strengthened my conviction in this research. Her understanding of the importance of culture in the Indian economy expanded my vision. Thanks to Prof. Yan Xuetong, Prof. Xing Yue, Prof. Zhang Lihua (Tsinghua University), Prof. Anil K. Gupta (Indian Institution of Management); and three professors from Varanasi—Prof. Hriday Ranjan Sharma, Prof. Rajaram Shukla, and Prof. Rajneesh Kumar Shukla. I express my thanks for the support of my high school and college friends and relatives during my fieldwork in Beijing.

The discussions with Prof. Yin Xinan, Prof. B. R. Deepak and professionals in Beijing and New Delhi were also extremely helpful in my research. I thank them for their encouragements and supports. All my friends in China and India or new friends who are studying in Europe also contributed to my work. I cannot list all their names but will always remember their help.

My seniors and friends from Centre for East Asian Studies have always been a source of strength. My seniors, batch mates and juniors carefully read and gave a critical feedback on this book; they were always ready for discussion and help. My ex-hostel mates, who were busy preparing for exams, patiently and carefully replied to all my questions about India and encouraged me with suggestions and advice.

Last, but not least, my desire to work on the role of culture in China-India relations would not have ultimately taken the form of a book without the encouragement and support of my late grandfather, my parents, my late brother and other family members who gave me moral support. I dedicate this work to them. Without their support, I could not have come such a long way.

Abbreviations

BCIM-EC	Bangladesh-China-India-Myanmar Economic Corridor
BGEI	Bilateral Goods Export and Import
BRI	Belt and Road Initiative
CASS	Chinese Academy of Social Sciences
CCCI	Chindia Chamber of Commerce and Industry
CCTV	China Central Television
CPEC	China-Pakistan Economic Corridor
CSR	Corporate Social Responsibility
DIPP	Department of Industrial Policy & Promotion, Ministry of Commerce and Industry, Government of India
ENS	Express News Service
EOI	Embassy of India, Beijing, China
EPW	Economic & Political Weekly
FDI	Foreign Direct Investment
FICCI	Federation of Indian Chambers of Commerce and Industry
GLOBE	Global Leadership & Organizational Behavior Effectiveness
GOI	Government of India
HCP	Hiralaxmi Craft Park
HZSTEEL	Hangzhou Iron & Steel Group Co., Ltd.
ICBCMB	Industrial and Commercial Bank of China Limited, Mumbai Branch
ICWA	Indian Council of World Affairs
IANS	Indo-Asian News Service
IAPS	Institute of Asia-Pacific Studies
JSPL	Jindal Steel & Power Limited
MDNERGOI	Ministry of Development of North Eastern Region, Government of India

MEA	Ministry of External Affairs, Republic of India
MFA	Ministry of Foreign Affairs, the People's Republic of China
MOCPRC	Ministry of Commerce of the People's Republic of China
MTPA	Million tons per annum
MHL	Metallon Holding Limited
MoU	Memorandum of Understanding
NNM	Nava Nalanda Mahavihara
NBS	National Bureau of Statistics of the People's Republic of China
NCERT	National Council of Educational Research and Training of India
PSH	Psycho-Social Homeostasis
PRC	People's Republic of China
PM	Prime Minister
PTI	Press Trust of India
RoI	Republic of India
RSS	Rashtriya Swayamsevak Sangh
SDSTEEL	Shandong Iron & Steel Group Co., Ltd.
SJM	Swadeshi Jagaran Manch
TAR	Tibet Autonomous Region
TNN	The Times News Network
TWT	The Washington Times
UNCTAD	United Nations Conference on Trade and Development

Introduction

"The spirit gives rise to the desire for self-esteem which is satisfied by excelling in activities valued by our peer group or society and by winning the approbation of those count feeling good about ourselves. The drive for self-esteem is extremely powerful and people and states alike can pursue it at the expense of wealth or security."

—**Richard Ned Lebow**, *A Cultural Theory of International Relations*

China and India have had interactions through cultural exchanges in the last two thousand years. Chinese *Gongfu*, language and preservation of Buddhist records are the medium of the Chinese government to improve relations with India. Indian Buddhism was introduced into China in the late Western Han dynasty and the early Eastern Han dynasty. The exchange of Buddhism occupies the most prominent position in the spiritual and cultural exchange between China and India for more than 2000 years (Xue 2017: 29, 30).

Greek philosophers considered three universal drives: appetite, spirit (*thumos*) and reason (Lebow 2015). These three drives are also shown in cultural exchanges. The curiosity and admiration for another culture are the embodiment of desire, which promotes the deepening of cultural exchange. For example, the exchange of Buddhism is accompanied by various desires. The initial curiosity of Emperor Ming of the Han dynasty who dreamt of the "Golden People" started a historical chapter of China officially sending envoys to Tianzhu (West Heaven, ancient India) to ask for Buddhism (Xue 2017: 29). There was the "desire" of eminent monk Xuan Zang of the Tang dynasty for Buddhism. After going through difficulties and obstacles, he retrieved Buddhist scriptures from India.

The important content of cultural exchange is spiritual exchange, and the carrier of spiritual exchange is culture. Spiritual communication can make people or countries win praise, so as to produce a good sense of self and to meet the needs of self-esteem. Self-esteem can lead to powerful motives and even make people or countries sacrifice wealth or security for it (Lebow 2015). "Reason" is "a drive in its own right" and "attempts to discover what makes for the happy life and to constrain and then educate appetite and spirit alike to cooperate with it toward this end" (Lebow 2015:1).

The governments' participation in cultural exchanges have injected more "reason" into the exchanges between the two countries. The governments of the two countries formulate exchange plans according to their own cultural policies, which are official guarantees for systematic and in-depth exchanges between them. Of course, the exchanges between individuals or non-governmental organizations are more about "appetite" and "spirit", making the exchanges between the two countries dynamic and lasting.

India strongly influenced China through Buddhism. These exchanges made impacts on the Chinese language, thought, culture and society. One of the most important Chinese festivals, the Lantern Festival (*Yuan Xiao Jie*), was influenced by two Indians who "brought the Indian 'diwali' (festival of light) spirit to China" (Tan 2002:133). Chinese celebrate Lantern Festival with lamps, which is considered a result of diwali's impact (ibid.), continues till date.

As neighbouring countries, China and India have historical friendly exchanges but also disputes. It is necessary to have good relations with one's neighbour. The Chinese say, "*Yuanqin buru jinlin*" (the far relatives are not as good as the close neighbour). The neighbour is quite influential in this sense. It is important to analyse what achievements and disadvantages of the cultural dialogue between the two countries are so that relations can be improved.

China's leader, Deng Xiaoping, underscored the importance of China and India for Asia as a whole. He stated when meeting Prime Minister Rajiv Gandhi in 1988 that without the development of China and India, the Asian Century could not be realised. The Asian Century could not be built until China, India and other neighbouring countries developed. There are many challenges and disputes within Asia. To improve relations between Asian countries, there is a need for mutual understanding and respect which sets a stage for cultural exchanges. To improve the bilateral relations China and India have to do the same. Cultural dialogue could play a very important role.

China and India have increasingly significant parts to play in the world, as both have big markets and huge developmental potentials. China and India have chosen different ways to develop the countries. There are both challenges, even conflicts, and opportunities for cooperation between China and India. It is a good way to recognise one's own self by looking at the opposite side and how to reduce misunderstandings more over cooperate better. As the theory of cultural diplomacy explains, good relations come with understanding and respect. Cultural exchanges would strengthen the relationship between the two countries. What are the obstacles that come in the way of knowing each other? How widely should these two know each other? What is the most effective way to understand each other? Those are the things we should consider and change the perceptive when other topical issue occur in the world which may influence strategies of China and India.

For improve the bilateral relations, China and India should improve communication in different aspects. Cultural exchange programmes have a role to build bridges to connect Chinese and Indian thoughts, and people's emotions towards each other should not only be led by politics and economy which are the top priorities for the governments. It should be realised that culture is an invisible line that has linked different political systems and economic patterns throughout different periods of history. It is, and will be, the linkage of the two nations' emotions which can help achieve new heights for the people from the two countries and the world. Atal Bihari Vajpayee, the former Indian Prime Minister, visited China in 2003. He was the first Prime Minister visited China after 1993 and the first political leader from the BJP which is also the current ruling party in India. From 2003 to 2014, China and India signed many cultural MoUs and joint statements to improve the bilateral relations, which includes the building of the Buddhist memorial hall and cultural centres, holding cultural festivals, exhibitions, education-exchange programmes and China-India Friendship Exchanges Year, publishing of books on exchanges, starting a programme of translating classic literatures and so on. In contemporary times, the cultural exchanges are increasing under the new global context. What will be examined in Part I is how those exchanges influenced the relations between these two countries and whether they are based on strength and mutual trust.

To examine the role of culture in China-India relations, this research explores the impact of culture on bilateral relations of these two in Part II, especially the misunderstandings caused by cultural differences and the resulting conflicts that hinder relations. The question of inquiry is the characteristic of the cultures of the two countries and its influence on behaviour and thinking. This research examines the manifestation of the above factors in the economic field, especially the impact of culture on the economies of the two countries, and the misunderstandings caused by cultural differences and the impact of the cultural conflicts on China-India economic relations.

In the history of India, it was once the British colonists who did not respect the local culture, ignored the willingness of Indian soldiers to refuse to use bullets coated with lard or beef tallow, and instead suppressed such soldiers, which eventually led to a national resistance uprising (Ren and Li 2016: 89). Common misunderstanding or bullying might not awaken this kind of opposing force, but because of crossing the most fundamental cultural redline. Disrespect for culture could lead to catastrophic damage, but fully understanding cultural differences and respect for each other's culture could avoid conflicts. To understand the culture of others is the essential requirement for individuals or organisations' survival in a foreign country.

This research looks into how culture, which includes "customary and dominant beliefs, values [and ideas] that ethnic, religious, and social groups transmit fairly unchanged from generation to generation" (Guiso, Sapienza and Zingales 2006:23), helps to explain economic relations between China and India. Cultural similarities are always highlighted in the bilateral talks between China and India, even as the differences on the cultural front remain prominent. Cultural differences are the leading cause of misunderstanding between the two nations, which led to a different degree of cultural conflicts. This is not quite China-India specific and has been found to be a factor elsewhere as well. Samuel P. Huntington predicted that "the great divisions among humankind and the dominating source of conflict will be cultural" instead of "primarily ideological and primarily economic" (Huntington 1993: 22).

Although the idea of the clash of civilisations has been controversial since it was introduced, it has recurred among the government officials of the USA in 2019. It is considered a competition between China and the USA: "[...] is a fight with a really different civilization and a different ideology and the United States hasn't had that before" (Gehrke 2019). Chinese national leaders have denied the "clash of civilisations" theory (Xi 2019) and pointed out "[...] human civilisation will die out because of a lack of exchanges" (Aneja 2019). The debate between China and the USA showed the importance of civilisation and provided a reference for China and India. This research agrees that "Various civilisations are not destined to clash" (Aneja 2019), but considers that culture has differences that could cause different degrees of uneasiness and form different degrees of cultural conflicts and further affect bilateral relations, though it does not necessarily lead to a violent confrontation.

The above cultural constraints remain despite the fact that, historically, there are instances of strong interaction in the field of culture and economy between China and India. For instance, in ancient times, via the Silk Road, goods and culture circulated greatly and improved ties between these two civilisations. Buddhism was the primary catalyst for China-India trade (Sen 2005). Even now, Buddhism is the primary linkage when it comes to cultural and people-to-people exchanges between China and India. Chinese fishing nets (*Cheena vala*) were introduced by Chinese explorer Zheng He, and still attract tourists to Kochi, Kerala, South India (Sen 2004:243 and Ge 2014:792). Indian tea was introduced from China by the British, and later, Indians got into the habit of imbibing it. Moreover, Indian tea such as Darjeeling tea and Assam tea are now becoming popular in China. More recently, the reopening of Nathu La in 2006 after 1962 can also be seen as evidence of the cultural and economic interaction between China and India.

As mentioned above, modern China and India have many cultural linkages mostly because of Buddhism. Yet, domestically, Confucian culture has been more influential than Buddhism in China just like Hinduism in India. It is, therefore, crucial to understand that while the ties between these two nations are not limited to Buddhism, it is necessary to understand the dominant beliefs and values that influence their economic behaviours in the contemporary period.

In 2000, the Government of China officially initiated the "Go Global" strategy to encourage its enterprises to invest abroad. After joining the World Trade Organization (WTO) on 11 December 2001, China soon surpassed the USA to become India's largest trade partner in 2007. Clearly, along with the fast growth of the Chinese and Indian economies over the last decades, the bilateral economic relations have grown as well. India is China's biggest trade partner in South Asia and a crucial partner on the international stage, while mainly representing the interests of developing countries. Nevertheless, being the two emerging economic powers in the world, the China and India could reach a much higher level in the field of economic cooperation. Except that politics has a strong bearing on the China-India relations, cultural misunderstandings and disrespect are also significantly affecting their perceptions towards each other, thereby influencing the deepening of bilateral relations.

Not that there has been no progress. Moderately, without doubt, perceptions in China and India towards each other are changing positively. Still, compared to China-India traditional ties and dramatic economic development, they fall far short of realising the full potential of the two ancient civilisations. In other words, it is not yet easy, especially for the ordinary people of these two different civilisations, to understand the values of each other, which were developed to deal within their societies. It is crucial for people from these two countries to decipher the cultural values since there is the influence of those values on how China and India behave on the stage of globalisation. In brief, it is inalienable to their own identity and characteristics, which have a bearing on their negotiations, interactions and behaviours. This research examines the ignored impacts of culture on China-India relations in order to promote the smooth development of relations and to accelerate the process of cooperation.

1.1 Early and Current Research

Cultural Relations

There has been a long tradition of cultural exchanges between China and India, which began in ancient times and has continued to date. Besides, helping the two nations in understanding each other better, these exchanges have also immensely contributed to the world. For example, Buddhism was born in India and spread to China before it declined in Indian society. China contributed to pass on Buddhism to the East Asian regions and even the world. Chinese monks travelled to India and not only brought the Buddhist sutras with them and translated the sutras into Chinese but, in this process, they contributed to preserving Indian history and culture with their efforts. So while, India is still time-honoured for being the birth place of Buddhism, Buddhism is no longer the foremost religion of India and it was only because of cultural exchanges with China and other countries outside India that Buddhism is not losing its vitality and identity. China remains the top country with the largest number of Buddhists in the world (Pew Research 2020). Because of the joint Indian and Chinese efforts of many generations, both cultures are expanding and booming. The well-known Indian scholar of Sino-Indian studies, Prabodh Chandra Bagchi, in his work *India And China: A Thousand Years Of Cultural Relations* (1927), reviewed the spiritual affinity of India and China, explained the process of how Buddhism was introduced in China and continued to describe the similarities and differences between the two cultures and how they promoted the exchanges and booming of culture.

In Tan Yunshan's works, *Cultural Interchange Between India and China* (1937), *India's Contribution to Chinese Culture* (1942), *The Spirit of Indian and Chinese Cultures* (1949), he evaluates the cultural exchanges from the Chinese perspective. Ji Xianlin had a similar idea. In his book, *The History of China and India Cultural Exchanges* (2008), he describes China and India as a "match made in heaven" to be neighbours. He writes that human beings created four civilisations, and China and India form half of them. In human history, the cultural exchanges between China and India have been commendable. Ji held that in two thousand years, China and India learned from each other and contributed in developing each other's culture. Till now, Chinese and Indian still benefit from it. The cultural exchanges have had a positive influence on the bilateral relations.

Along with choosing different paths for modernisation and different domestic situations, there are some differences between Indian and Chinese approaches to some issues. From Rabindranath Tagore's visit to China in 1924, we could see some indications of these differences. His visit can be seen as a dialogue between Indian and Chinese civilisations. Tagore epitomised Indian culture. As Asia's first Nobel Prize winner, he got respect and recognition from the Western world. His visit to China was under this momentum. However, there were two different kinds of attitudes towards Tagore's visit. One group of Chinese people respected his achievement and the other group thought his idea was inopportune. Kalidas Nag, who came to China with Tagore, mentioned in his article "Tagore in Asia", that the poet met Chinese youth in Shanghai, Beijing, Hankou, Nanjing, etc., but they sent out a discordant sound.

What is the behind the divided attitudes towards Tagore's visit? Did the visit prevent further exchanges between China and India? Tan Chung in his work *Tagore and China* (2011) has explained the historical significance of Tagore's 1924 China visit. He pointed out the dialogue between Chinese and Indian artists since 1924, which he calls 'a forgotten dialogue', and mentioned the Sino-Indian Studies at Visva-Bharati University. The establishment of Cheena Bhavana (1937) in Visva-Bharati can be seen as a high tide of cultural exchanges between China and India. It strengthened the idea that the exchanges can be of long standing.

Although, there were some discordant sounds, they did not reduce the significance of Tagore's visit, and it also did not prevent the aspiration and determination of Tagore to build linkages with China as mentioned in the website of Cheena Bhavana, "Cheena Bhavana was formally opened as a research department by Rabindranath Tagore on April 14, 1937, with lofty ideals of strengthening the age-old cultural ties between India and China."

The wise men of China and India built the foundation of the long-term development of China-India relations. In the history tide, many generations of Chinese and Indian scholars, politicians, artists, businessmen, etc., have continuously reviewed the history and tried to use new postures and attitudes to achieve new heights together.

Huang Xinchuan, in his article, "Tan Yun-shan: A Cultural Envoy between China and India (In the Footsteps of Xuan Zang: Tan Yun-shan and India", wrote "the Sino-Indian cultural interaction was unique in the history of world cultural interaction. All the great inventions and creations, both spiritual and material, of the Indian people were introduced into our country with blossom and fruition." There are some scholars who paid important attention on the affect of Buddhism on the other side of exchanges. For example, Tansen Sen, focused on the research of India-China interaction. In his article "From Buddhism to Commerce: The Transformation of Sino-India", he puts forth that Buddhism promoted the initial India-China relations, but the exchange related to Buddhism reduced during the Song dynasty while commerce-related exchanges increased.

Besides, there has been a significant effect on different fields due to the exchanges between India and China. In the book, *The Argumentative Indian: Writings on Indian History, Culture and Identity* (2005), Amartya Sen devotes one chapter to explain in detail that the interactions between India and China started due to trade, but then Buddhism became a catalyst. The extensive contacts that were also formed between India and China were through science, mathematics, literature, linguistics, medicine, music, etc.

In the article "Indian Approaches to Modern China: A Social-Historical Analysis (1972)", Krishna Prakash Gupta analysed the changing process of the Indian attitude towards China. He analysed the attitudes of different Indian intellectuals towards China in different periods. There is an asymmetry in the approaches of India and China towards each other. India wanted to form a joint front with China and, most of the time, had a positive image of China, as it was influenced by the Hindu philosophy that believed in pluralism. However, China has been influenced by Confucian Sinocentrism and Communist ideology and has perceived only distinctions and conflicts.

The cultural exchanges stopped during the China-India border clash in 1962; however, there were some different points of view for the clash, Indira Gandhi began the process of normalisation of bilateral relations on January 1, 1969. She said in a statement that conflicts with China need to be solved through talks. Because of a new recognition of the clash and the international scenario, both Indian and Chinese scholars appealed that China and India should positively improve their bilateral relations. Some also mentioned that there was a new need for positive China-India relations. In the book, *Making Sense of Chindia: Reflections on China and India* (2007), Jairam Ramesh coins the term 'Chindia'. He focuses on the economic cooperation between China and India. He mentions the spiritual affinity shared through Buddhism. Tan Chung, in his article, "India and China: A Saga of Sharing a Historical Heritage (2002)", uses the cultural perspective to analyse the countless ties between India and China. He calls on India and China to realise that they were developed countries even before the Industrial Revolution began. India and China should work together and become the new light of the world. They should look at each other directly and not through the Western perceptive. To know each other is also to re-understand and rediscover their own cultural heritage. In another other book that Tan Chung edited with Geng Yinzheng, *India And China: Twenty Centuries Civilisational Interaction And Vibrations*, they expressed their conviction that civilisations do not clash. Tan Chung's discourse on Geng's historiography highlighting the beneficial results of India-China civilisational interaction, which the author terms "Sino-Indic ratna" permeates China's political, social and cultural development.

In 21st century, the world stage needs China and India that are described respectively as a rising power and an emerging power. Will these two nations work together for new achievements or enter the trap again? It depends on whether they establish a favourable communication approach and atmosphere. The loose communication environment has made further interaction between China and India difficult. Books by a few Indians, who stayed in China for a couple of years, show this reality. In the book *China: A Search for Its Soul: Leaves from a Beijing Diary* (2009), Poonam Surie, shares her experiences in China, and her journeys through Beijing, Yunnan, and Xinjiang. She found that there are inextricable links between China and its important neighbour, India. She explored the cultural and historical commonalities and differences between the two countries. Pallavi Aiyar, the author of *Smoke and Mirror: An Experience of China* (2009), writes of the time when she worked in China for eight years as an English teacher and then she joined the Indian media to report the news from China. She also compares the developments in China and India. Chinese scholar Yin Xinan wrote a review of this book and pointed out, "We can find that she has deep misunderstandings to China's political system, she takes a negative attitude toward contemporary China when she observes and thinks problems based on political or ideological prejudice, but she also praises China's rapid economic development and the improving living standard of the Chinese people....Aiyar's observation on China can be regarded as a mirror reflecting Sino-Indian media communication or even Sino-Indian relations." Reshma Patil, who stayed in

China for three-and-a-half years, wrote a book titled *Strangers Across the Border, Indian Encounters in Boomtown China* (2014), in which she describes that the ordinary people of China have very limited knowledge about India and her interactions with people of China from different fields. Indians introduced China through their perspective. On the other hand, Chinese scholars also are groping at how India looks at China. Yin Xinan (2010) settled the Indian recognition of China from ancient to modern times in his work *The Indian Images of China*.

The new idea also developed on the soil of China and India, the West Heavens. An initiative for cultural exchanges was developed jointly by the Institution of Visual Culture, China Academy of Art and Hanart TZ Gallery, which presents that to think about India, to be close with India are essential for self-recognition of China. The initiative aims "to foster closer understanding of India through contemporary art and scholarship, and develop cross-cultural dialogue based on visual culture and notions of Asian modernity". The West Heavens invited many Indian scholars to speak in China, to bring and to expand their ideas to China. A work of West Heavens, *India-China Summit on Social Thought* (2014), Indian scholars, edited by Chang Tsong-Zung, Kuan-Hsing Chen and Gao Shiming, invited Indian scholars from different backgrounds like Sarat Maharaj, Ashis Nandy, Homi K. Bhabha, Partha Chatterjee to lead a large-scale interaction in the Indian and Chinese realm of thought. To explore the reasons for this new ideology between China and India, like "Chindia" and West Heavens, is also an aim of this book and to examine whether great imagination will lead China and India enter a great new age.

Culture and Conflict

One of the major concerns of this research is the negative influence, namely, conflict that may be caused by culture. In this regard, the argument of Samuel P. Huntington is relevant to a certain extent. In his article "The Clash of Civilizations?" (1993:22) and his work *The Clash of Civilizations and the Remaking of World Order* (1996), Huntington first predicted that "the great divisions among humankind and the dominating source of conflict will be cultural" instead of "primarily ideological or primarily economic". He considered that "[...] the principal conflicts of global politics will occur between nations and groups of different civilisations. The clash of civilisations will dominate global politics", and suggested that there were eight major diverse groups including "Confucian, Hindu and Islamic, etc., and 'international cooperation between them is the best safeguard against war" (Huntington 1993, 1996).

Jonathan H. Turner (2005:87) explains the reason of conflict, and considers "A conflict caused by differences in cultural values and beliefs that place people at odds with one another". In *Sociology*, Alexander Grewe (2005) gave a detailed explanation on the process of conflict by pointing out "the conflict as one that occurs when people's expectations of a certain behaviour coming from their cultural backgrounds are not met, as others have different cultural backgrounds and different expectations". In the article "Culture and Conflict", Michelle LeBaron (2003) described culture mentioning its causation with conflict. He describes different cultures as "underground rivers that run through our lives and relationships, giving us messages that shape our perceptions, attributions, judgments, and ideas of self and other". LeBaron stated, "though cultures are powerful, they are often unconscious, influencing conflict and attempts to resolve conflict in imperceptible ways".

In order to understand the cultural conflict in economic relations, one evidence can be found in an academic work saying that the analysis of the clash between different cultures should not be taken lightly. Wu Changqi pointed out in his work *The Internationalisation Strategy of Chinese Enterprises* (2014) that cross-border/international Mergers and Acquisitions (M&A) has become one of the primary methods for the FDI of Chinese enterprises to enter markets abroad (Wu 2014:7). When he analyses the influence of national culture and organisational culture on the strategic choice and performance of cross-border/international M&A, he quoted from scholars like Nahavandi and Malekzadeh (1988) that the cultural clash between the two sides of M&A may prompt demission by major managers and core staff and group boycott (Wu 2014:145). John W. Berry (2005) pointed out that "during acculturation, groups of people and their individual members engage in intercultural contacts, producing a potential for conflict, and the need for negotiation in order to achieve outcomes that are adaptive for both parties."

Culture and Economy

It is considered that economic life could not be divorced from cultural life. In a study of the interconnectedness of economic life with cultural life, Francis Fukuyama, in *Trust: the social virtues and the creation of prosperity* (1995) pointed out the culture linked with the central issue of international competition, politics and economy, and the economy bears a direct influence of culture on internal peace and international order. He mentioned the work *Adam Smith in His Time and Ours* by Jerry Z. Muller (1992) that culture, including moral value and social customs, is considered a necessary part for understanding economic behaviour,

> "economic life is deeply embedded in social life, and it cannot be understood apart from the customs, morals, and habits of the society in which it occurs. In short, it cannot be divorced from culture." (Fukuyama 1995:13)

Moreover, Adam Smith portrays economic motivation as highly complex and embedded in broader social habits and mores in his work *The Theory of Moral Sentiments* (Fukuyama 1995:18). Inevitably, the "social habits" are created by culture. Although some humanity transcends cultural borders, for instance, "rational self-interested calculation" (Fukuyama 1995:18-19)[1], this research focuses on summarising the cultural dimensions "inside the border" which influenced economic relations.

In *The Wealth and Poverty of Nations: Why Some are So Rich and Some are So Poor*, David Landes (1998) has pointed out the cultural influence on economic development from a historical perceptive: "If we learn anything from the history of economic development, it is that culture makes all the difference (Here, Max Weber was right on)". He explained the "expatriate minorities—the Chinese in East and Southeast Asia, Indians in East Africa, Lebanese in West Africa, Jews and Calvinists throughout much of Europe, and on and on"—as the "coming from outsiders" that would have to make cultural changes, which he believes is better than "deploring changes". (Landes 1998: 516-517). Landes considers "criticisms of culture cut close to the ego, injure identity and self-esteem". The opinion could be conducive to understand the competition between local enterprise and outside enterprise; the "outsiders" sometimes more successful than the local brand in the market when they can seriously and acuminously deal with the "criticism" and adapt the local (consumer) culture for surviving with more challenges. Jan Truszczynski (2010), the Director-General for Education and Culture, European Commission, pointed out the impact of culture on the economy from the perspective of the European Union. He argued that in the challenging time of economic and financial crises, the capacity of culture had proven contribution to combat social exclusion and promote economic development, and that culture would play a crucial role in the implementation of the Europe 2020 strategy for an economically strong and socially inclusive European Union.

To analyse the effect of culture on the economy, it is necessary to enhance the understanding of one branch of economics—cultural economics—which studies the relations of culture to economics. The categories of cultural economics include the following three, firstly, "cultural dimensions of economic activity (the design or marketing of any product or service)". Secondly, "a particular subsection of economic activity which is concerned with cultural products and activities (such as fine arts such as music, film and fine art)" (Pratt 2007). Thirdly, the culture influences on economic outcomes, which is one of the main concerns of this research,

> "Economic discourse here is not simply a matter of beliefs, values and symbols but rather a form of representational and technological (i.e., 'cultural') practice that constitutes the spaces within which economic action is formatted and framed." (Gay and Pryke 2002:2)

---

1 It is considered that "The power of neoclassical theory rests on the fact that its model of humanity is accurate a good deal of the time: people can indeed be relied on to pursue their own selfish interests more often than they pursue some kind of common good. Rational self-interested calculation transcends cultural borders" (Fukuyama 1995:18-19).

These aspects are helpful to understand the policy making of national leaders such as the Belt and Road Initiative of China and the Act East Policy of India.

Meanwhile, business negotiations, cross-cultural management, organisational behaviour, business communications, etc., were respectively analysed regarding the cultural influence on the economy in the academic field. Guiso, Sapienza and Zingales (2006) defined culture as "those customary beliefs and values that ethnic, religious, and social groups transmit fairly unchanged from generation to generation" and restricted "the potential channels of influence to two standard ones—prior beliefs, and values or preferences. This definition provides an approach that can identify a causal effect from culture to economic outcomes" and "enhance our understanding of economic behaviour". It was pointed out that after "better techniques and expanded data have made it possible to identify systematic differences in people's preferences", economists began to "apply their analytical frameworks and empirical tools to the issue of culture and economic outcomes" (Guiso et al. 2006:23). Besides, the relations between culture and economy were examined through the perspectives of economic performance (Casson 2006), economic development (Streeten 2006), economic behaviour (Henrich et al. 2005), and market and economic institutions (Bowles 1998).

In the book *The Religion of India: The Sociology of Hinduism and Buddhism*, German economist and sociologist, Max Weber (1916) has examined the influence of Hinduism and Buddhism on social activities and economy. Weber argued the economic development is slowed because the influence of the traditionalism of the Varna system (social classes, author's note) supported by *dharma* and that the 'spirit' of the Varna system worked against the development of capitalism (Weber 1916, Bendix 1997). In his work, *The Religion of China: Confucianism and Taoism*, Weber (1915) analysed how the values of Confucianism and Taoism influenced the economic pattern. Sriya Iyer of the University of Cambridge (2018) explored the history of religious conflict in India from 1955-2006, how religious organisations in India provide services and links among income inequality, demographic characteristics, socioeconomic status, and religion in India. She has elaborated this in her book *The Economics of Religion in India*.

In the book *Guanxi (The art of relationships): Microsoft, China, and Bill Gates's Plan to Win the Road Ahead*, the authors, Robert Buderi and Gregory T. Huang, mention, "In China, there's no such thing as a purely business relationship. Instead, to be successful in business, you must blend formal relationships with personal ones. *Guanxi* refers to the delicate art of building and nurturing such ties." They further pointed out "Its [good *guanxi*] four basic principles can be roughly translated as trust (respect and knowledge of others), favour (loyalty and obligation), dependence (harmony and reciprocity, mutual benefit), and adaptation (patience and cultivation)." (Buderi and Huang 2006:6-7). Besides, there are scholars who have different views on the relation between culture and the economy. Teresa L. Cyrus (2015) considers "cultural distance does not affect trade, while trade reduces cultural distance."

It was pointed out "As to economic development, culture may act as a brake or filter but is seldom likely to be the original source of change" (Jones 2006:270-271; Zoninsein 2007:135-136), meanwhile,

> "culture as a determinant of economic life... [but] culture is contingent, intrinsically labile, inherited, unstable, barely conscious, related to personal matters, lacking in permanent foundations, and is not derived from explicit choices by those making economic decisions...culture is shaped as a residue of past decisions subjected to slow and gradual change and is impacted by current material incentives, priorities and choices. [...] Custom, traditions, beliefs, and values combine with economic choice to produce existing culture" (Zoninsein 2007:135-136).

Eric L. Jones defines "pure culture", in his *Cultures Merging: A Historical and Economic Critique of Culture,* "as an unconsciously assimilated pattern of beliefs, habits, expectations, values, ideals, and preferences absorbed mainly from families and the surrounding society's influences" (Ibid.).

Samuel Huntington has emphasised the influence of culture on economic development,

> "[Yet] the major differences in political and economic development among civilizations are clearly rooted in their different cultures" and "The predominant patterns of political and economic development differ from civilization to civilization. The key issues on the international agenda involve differences among civilizations." (Huntington 1996:29)

Different beliefs in India have resulted in the performance of economic activities. According to Pritam Singh, the ancient Brahman caste of Hinduism has always had a tradition of contempt for physical labour, but Sikhism advocates labour and encourages believers to become self-reliant. The Sikhs have thus become a model for a new generation of Indian peasants. (Singh, Pritam 2016: 375).

By citing the example of the fastest-growing countries and regions during 1991-2001, i.e., China [including Hong Kong and Taiwan], Japan, Singapore and South Korea, Kristoff and Wudunn argued that "Chinese may be the most economically successful ethnic group in the world" as the above countries and regions "either have a large Chinese population or have been heavily influenced by Chinese culture" (Kristoff and Wudunn 1994: 392). Moreover, it could also support the idea that Chinese ethnic populations have greatly contributed to economic growth by considering the situation in the Philippines and Indonesia where the Chinese constitute 1.5 per cent and 2 per cent of the population, respectively, and were responsible for 35 per cent of the sales of locally-owned firms and 70 per cent of private domestic capital (Ibid.).

In addition to this, James K. Sebenius and Cheng (Jason) Qian from Harvard Business School believe that culture plays a very crucial role in negotiations. In the paper "Cultural Notes on Chinese Negotiating Behavior", Sebenius and Qian (2008) argued "better understanding the key elements of Chinese culture to which Chinese negotiators attune their business mentality and manners" would "decipher the Chinese negotiating style and bring about mutually beneficial results". They pointed out "unique Chinese cultural elements such as complicated local etiquette, obscure decision-making process, and (heavy) reliance on interpersonal relationships (instead of legal instruments) all add to the complexities of Sino-foreign business negotiations, and can make the process tiresome and protracted." They believe "over the past two thousand years, Confucianism and Taoism have shaped the design of China's political, educational, and economic systems, and influenced the behavioural and thinking patterns of the Chinese people" which has ingrained among the Chinese the following characteristics:

1. the focus on relationships (*guanxi*. Author's note, similarly hereinafter),
2. reliance on moral (*daoyi*) influence over the legal practice,
3. respect for hierarchy and expectation of reciprocity,
4. face-saving (*mianzi*),
5. (different understanding of) trust and ethics.

Besides, *Guoqing* (national conditions) was also analysed as they believe "it is the milieu in which Chinese business culture evolved" which show up:

- A centrally controlled political system with a "Socialistic" market economy,
- Multilayered governance of business,
- The dominance of state-owned enterprises.

In their conclusion, they suggested reform of Chinese Business Culture to adopt international best practices:

- Efficiency-oriented control,
- Materialistic world view,
- Awareness of international business rules and cultural differences.

The "Global Leadership and Organizational Behavior Effectiveness" (GLOBE) Research Program was conceived in 1991 by Robert J. House of the Wharton School of Business, University of Pennsylvania (Hoppe 2007). Two volumes were published: *Culture, Leadership, and Organizations: The GLOBE Study of 62 Societies* (2004) and *Culture and Leadership across the World: The GLOBE*

Book of In-Depth Studies of 25 Societies (2007). The scholars of GLOBE research program empirically established nine cultural dimensions, i.e.,

1. Power Distance,
2. In-Group Collectivism,
3. Institutional Collectivism,
4. Uncertainty Avoidance,
5. Future Orientation,
6. Gender Egalitarianism,
7. Assertiveness,
8. Humane Orientation,
9. Performance Orientation.

The above dimensions were "to capture the similarities and/or differences in norms, values, beliefs—and practices—among societies" (Hoppe 2007). They build on the findings of Hofstede (1980), Schwartz (1994), Smith (1995), Inglehart (1997), and others (Ibid). The definition of culture used by the GLOBE research project is "shared understandings made manifest in act and artifact" defined by anthropologist Redfield (1948), "which examines culture as practices (acts or 'the way things are done in this culture') and values (artifacts because they are human made and, in this specific case, are judgments about 'the way things should be done')" (House et al 2004: XV). The GLOBE researchers examined "how is culture related to societal, organizational, and leadership effectiveness". House (2004) pointed out "all experts in international business agree that to succeed in global business, managers need the flexibility to respond positively and effectively to practices and values that may be drastically different from what they are accustomed to".

Some scholars used the data from the GLOBE research program to analyse the effect of cultural difference on the economy. A Chinese scholar who was in Tsinghua University (Beijing), Jiang Lu (2008), and her colleagues analysed "The Cultural Difference of China and India and Its Influence on Attracting FDI".

Importance of the Culture towards Nations' Relations

In addition, there are other academic works regarding the relations of culture with international relations and international order, which could be helpful to understand the role of culture towards the economy and politics. The cultural factor could be a double-edged sword. Obviously, it would benefit the relations of nations and economic cooperation if the culture of others is clearly understood and respected. According to Patricia M. Goff (2013), "good relations can take rest in the fertile ground of understanding and respect" and "cultural diplomacy rests on the assumption that art, language and education are among the most significant entry points into a culture". In *How Does Culture Affect Foreign Policy: A Case Study of U.S.A*, Xing Yue (2011) argued that nations choose cooperation with each other because of a common threat and interests; however, in order to establish stable and everlasting relations, it is necessary to understand and respect the culture of others. She illustrated the reason of the "unique relations" between some present great powers like the United States of America, the United Kingdom and Canada, and the nations of the European Union, is due to the relatively profound cultural basis.

Yan Xuetong (2016) argued China should establish an international order for its rise with the idea of *gōngpíng* (equity), *zhèngyì* (righteousness) and *wénmíng* (civilised) based on the thoughts of Confucianism: *rén* (Benevolence), *yì* (Righteousness), *lǐ* (Rites) which he believes could surpass the US idea of an international order, i.e., equality, democracy, liberty. Jayant Sinha and Sanjeev Sanyal in their article (2016) illustrated that "it is possible to build an intellectual framework for policy and governance based on our [Indian] civilisational values" as they considered "an Indian state rooted in our [Indian] cultural matrix will be able to better harness the energies of the Indian people".

Cultural Comparison between China and India

Summing up the above, the aspects of the cultural effect were stated from different perspectives. Among those aspects, the cultural difference could be one of the most important points in economic cooperation, which might create misunderstandings, distrusts and even conflicts. When considering the cultural differences between China and India, lots of works have been done in this area. The representative works will be exhibited as below. In Shang Huipeng's works *Chinese and Hindus, A Comparative Study of Cultural Traditions* (2015) and *An Outline of Psychoculturology, the Comparative Study of Literate Civilizations* (2013), the differences in Chinese and Indian (Hindu) cultures were systematically examined including the different values towards relationships, supernature, politics, etc. Jay Taylor (1987) broadly compared "the Indian and Chinese societies and the factors that have shaped their approaches to modernization" and examined "Chinese and Indian attitudes towards religion, art, authority, science and so on". Lokesh Chandra and Daisaku Ikeda (2011) summarised the difference in the spiritual tradition between China and India in different dimensions such as the Chinese attaching importance to "ethics in society" while India paying more attention to "transcendence of being". These differences systemically analysed by scholars could be a significant foundation to be cited for understanding each other's behaviour.

Some scholars have summarized Confucianism's shaping of contemporary Chinese values into ten characteristics, including: Morality is more important than law, community is more important than the individual, spirit is more important than material, responsibility is more important than rights. Besides, people's livelihood is more important than democracy, order is more important than freedom, this life is more valuable than the afterlife, harmony is more worthy than struggle, civilisation is more valuable than poverty, family is more important than class (Chen 2015).

China-India relations

It is essential to know China-India relations from a historical perspective. In Tansen Sen's book, *Buddhism, Diplomacy and Trade—The Realignment of Sino-Indian Relations, 600-1400* (2004), the role of Buddhism and trade in China-India relations were systematically analysed. He focused on the changes in Buddhist and commercial interactions between India and China and examined the transformation of Sino-Indian relations from a Buddhist-dominated to trade-centred exchanges between the 7th and the 15th centuries. In the book, *Indians in China 1800-1949*, Madhavi Thampi (2005) shows that there already existed commercial intercourse with China in Mumbai. Due to this intercourse with China, Mumbai gradually formed a commerce community and became a trade centre. Unfortunately, opium had catalysed the process.

Due to economic interests, positive options are the mainstream towards the economic relations of these two most prominent emerging economies. Jairam Ramesh (2005), appeals to sideline the border issue for the sake of economic cooperation. Rodrik and Subramanian (2004) argued "Some of the motivation for this is plain silly, rooted in a martial conception of economics, and portraying India and China as in some zero-sum game rivalry. Economic growth in China and India and increasing trade by and between them will, of course, be mutually beneficial and positively reinforcing." The Chinese scholar Liu Zongyi from the Shanghai Institute for International Studies stressed that "geo-economics rather than geopolitics," should rule India-China ties. He pointed out "with India resolving the General Sales Tax (GST) issue, Chinese companies will now have more opportunities to invest. We cherish these opportunities" (Aneja 2016).

In the book of Pakistani writer Ahmed Rashid, *Pakistan on the Brink: The Future of America, Pakistan and Afghanistan*, he argued China no longer treats India as its enemy owing to the $74 billion bilateral trade (Chaulia 2012). Although "Beijing was an 'all-weather ally' of Islamabad", the Sino-Pakistani trade is only $ 9 billion (Ibid). It made the author's recall the idea of Cordell Hull, the US Secretary of State during World War II and a champion of commercial liberalism, "If goods do not cross borders, then armies will" (Ibid). In this sense, economic cooperation between China and India could ease the tension caused by political disputes.

Against the background mentioned above, the bright prospect of economic relations between China and India means that these two nations are going to have growing interactions. So it would still be further necessary to analyse their economic relations through a "more cautious analytical approach" which is a difference of cultural economy with the mainstream finance and political economy (Gay 2007:346).

Literature Gap

There are three main gaps in the literature. Firstly, the interaction of cultural exchanges with bilateral relations, the cultural policy and the role of cultural exchanges during the crisis period.

Secondly, lack in the understanding of the impact of culture on China and India economic relations. Although existing literature on Chinese and Indian culture has an in-depth interpretation of culture, the literature of economic thought, meanwhile, has a detailed introduction of culture influence on the economy. It does not have a systematic and detailed analysis of the impact of culture on economic relations. In other words, there is hardly any analysis of the cultural impact on economic relations between China and India. This study attempts to analyse the impact of culture on the bilateral relations, to find the roots of ideas from the traditional classics such as the *Analects of Confucius*, *Bhagavad Gita*. It filters the cultural factors that influence the relations between the two countries, considering that not all of the cultural factors affect the thought or the relations between China and India.

Thirdly, lack of taking into account the factor of cultural conflict in the interaction between China and India. There is already an analysis of the cultural differences between the two countries in the literature, but there are few interpretations of the differences that cause cultural conflicts, and less is the study of cultural conflicts that impact the interaction between the two countries. The "Clash of Civilizations" proposes that Chinese Confucian culture and Indian Hindu culture are two cultures that are more likely to cause conflicts. It can be said that the influence of culture is not negligible while examining the reasons behind the unsmooth relations. The control of military conflicts is common in today's international relations. Especially between China and India, the border conflict between the two countries is still within the control of the diplomatic dialogue. The cultural conflicts are more diverse and recurrent. Among military, political and cultural conflicts, the conflicts caused by culture, compared with "structural contradictions", are more challenging to be discovered or considered tough to solve. At the same time, it can be avoided by perfecting or increasing mutual understanding through effective communication, thus reducing the possibility of misunderstanding. Therefore, this study attempts to discover the cultural conflicts of interaction, and then to establish a basis for enhancing mutual understanding and promoting smoother relations at different levels between the two countries.

1.2 Definition, Rationale and Scope of Part I

Cultural exchanges have developed at different stages in different periods. Past experiences set the path along which further cultural exchanges will proceed. Cultural exchanges always mentioned in governmental talks; sometimes, cultural exchanges are very important card to play before a political or economical cooperation. However, are those exchanges really taken seriously by the government? Has the government tried to exchange the essence of mutual culture? The degree and way in which cultural exchanges influence bilateral relations should be thought over seriously. The importance of cultural exchanges for the present and the future of these two nations should be discussed in order to build a better and deeper mutual perception as well as peaceful and constructive bilateral relations.

Part I focuses on and examines the influence of cultural exchanges on bilateral relations. Culture is an umbrella term, which includes music, films, arts, education, etc. This research will not divide culture into different branches but will treat its different aspects in unity. It will focus, examine and analyse the achievements from 2003, the year when former Prime Minister Vajpayee visited China, when there was an increase in cultural exchanges between China and India, to 2014, the year of president Xi Jinping's visit to India when he signed many agreements regarding prospective book fairs, sister city, and other cultural exchanges.

Part I is based on two crucial hypotheses. The first is that cultural exchanges between China and India have improved the bilateral relations of the two nations and the second hypothesis is that perceptions in China and India have positively influenced the leaderships' perspectives.

Some of the crucial research questions addressed in Part I include: Are the cultural exchanges successful in improving China-India relations? Why do the leaders want to expand cultural exchanges? What is the context of the cultural exchanges in early the 21st century? What are the advantages and disadvantages of emphasising the role played by Buddhism in China-India relations? Why were organisations like West Heavens and others that are focusing on China-India studies established? What is the new ideological dialogue between China and India? Does the concept of Chindia and institutions like West Heavens hold any importance in the current context of cultural exchanges? Were Indian and Chinese cultures united and built a new Asian Image? Is Indian culture influencing China as Buddhism did in the past? Or is China reversing the influence? In order to find answers to these research questions and to test the hypotheses' descriptive, applied and analytical methods of research were used. The aim of this study was to analyse the internal connection of cultural exchanges and China-India relations in contemporary time. The study includes the proper examination of the history of cultural exchanges between these two nations by analysing relevant events. Meanwhile, this research also refers to the cultural exchanges between India and other countries and regions of East Asia. The research attaches special importance to the use of dialogue between Indians and Chinese from different walks of life to emphasise the individual idea of cultural exchanges and the influence exerted by such exchanges upon individual ideas.

The two main segments of Part I are the influence of cultural exchanges on China-India relations and their contributions. For Part I, the independent variable is China-India relations; the dependent variable is territorial disputes, the influence of cultural exchanges and the Taiwan and Tibet factors as intervening variables.

Part I has used both primary and secondary sources. The primary sources include government documents, White Papers and statistics, interviews, archival materials, documents of embassies and ministries, historical records of institutions, historical sites, etc. Part I is based on the works of scholars from India, China and a few Western scholars and on several government documents. The interviews were conducted with people in India and also in China through Internet and face to face. The secondary sources are various academic works, journals, documentaries, literature, websites, online sources, newspapers, magazines, articles and data from relevant institutions, etc. Part I uses both qualitative research and quantitative research. It is based on the inductive method.

Part I is organised in four chapters. The first tries to locate the achievements of cultural exchanges between China and India and the overall cultural relation between them in the early 21st century with the outline of the attitude of the world towards Indian and Chinese cultures. It also tries to identify the changes in the global perception, the gradually changing role of China and India, the predicament of Western culture to understand the global context of China-India cultural exchanges.

The second chapter deals with perceptions in the contemporary period. It summarises the perceptions in both countries reflected in the speeches of national leaders, media reports and analyses of scholars during the eight high-level visits and the changing attitude about China-India relations in contemporary time. The third chapter focuses on the Policy of Cultural Exchanges of China and India. It presents the policy of cultural exchanges of these two countries, and examines how it influenced China-India relations, and the similarity and differences of the policy between these two countries towards each other. This chapter also introduces the programs and MoUs that were signed during 2003-2014.

The fourth chapter is the conclusion. It concludes with how achievements influenced the perceptions which, in turn, shaped government policy on cultural exchanges between India and China. It also draws attention to the fact that perception and policy built on cultural exchanges would shape future achievements in the cultural exchanges between China and India.

1.3 Definition, Rationale and Scope of Part II

The definition of culture in Part II is mainly drawn from the ideas of previous research, i.e., culture is "ordinary, in every society and in every mind". It meant both 'a whole way of life' (culture in the anthropological sense, synonymous with everyday life)" (Williams 1958), "the shared way of life of a group of people" (Berry et al. 2002:2), and "those customary beliefs and values that ethnic, religious, and social groups transmit fairly unchanged from generation to generation" (Guiso, Sapienza and Zingales 2006:23). Further, the religious beliefs and values (Hinduism) are considered as the most important part of culture in Part II, while the views of Gunnar Myrdal (1968:103) on religion "the institutional arrangements and modes of living to which sacred status has been given by a complex of beliefs and values" and the latter which "give legitimacy to the models of behaviour shaping social life" (Harriss-White 2003:133) are also focuses.

In short, culture is studied as a thought, value and idea, which was developed to deal with issues within a region, group or society. In other words, some aspects of one's culture are difficult to be understood by outsiders, without knowing the history, geography and so on. The cultural difference could cause misunderstanding, distrust and conflict. In Part II, culture means the dominant beliefs and values of ethnic, religious, and social groups including Chinese and Indian mainly influenced by Confucianism and Hinduism, yet these are mainly about the core values and hardly related with religious rites (Hinduism).

Culture and Civilisation

Two views are helpful to understand the difference between cultures and civilisations. Anthropologists believe cultures are "characteristic of primitive, unchanging, non-urban societies" and civilisations are "more complex, developed, urban, and dynamic societies" (Huntington 1996:41). It is helpful to understand the level of cultures and civilisations located. From this perspective, civilisations are more developed than cultures and are at a higher level. Differently, 19th century German thinkers consider civilisation involved "mechanics, technology, and material factors" and culture involved "values, ideals, and the higher intellectual artistic, moral qualities of a society" (Ibid.). Part II agrees with the latter view on culture and considers culture is part of civilisation.

Conflict

In the theory of International Studies, the term "conflict" usually refers to "a condition in which one identifiable group of human beings (whether tribal, ethnic, linguistic, cultural, religious, socio-economic, political, or other) is engaged in conscious opposition to one or more identifiable human groups because these groups are pursuing what are or appear to be incompatible goals." (Dougherty and Pfaltzgraff 2000:189). Conflict does not necessarily manifest as a force confrontation, but rather a different form of expression. As pointed out by Dougherty and Pfaltzgraff (2000:189), "Conflict may be violent or nonviolent (i.e., in terms of physical force), dominant or recessive, controllable or uncontrollable, and resolvable or insolvable under various sets of circumstances."

Culture conflict in Part II means the conflict caused by using one's culture to understand others when the expectations of certain behaviours are not met (Grewe 2005). It probably could result in negative perception, passive cooperation and cancellation of cooperation as well. Researching on conflicts is mainly to avoid or reduce conflicts, and are conducive to cooperation. This is also the significance of the IR discipline.

Economic relations, Commercial behaviour, Organisational culture and Trade policy

Economic relations are defined as "Internal and external relations that influence economic stability and growth" (Marques 2014). In Part II, it mainly includes trade, investment and economic cooperation and relevant economic activities. Commercial behaviour refers to the economic, behavioural tendency of the individual. In the Business Dictionary, the definition of organisational culture (also called corporate culture) is "the values and behaviours that contribute to the unique social and psychological environment of an organization" (*Business Dictionary* 2018). It includes:

> "an organization's expectations, experiences, philosophy, and values that hold it together, and is expressed in its self-image, inner workings, interactions with the outside world, and future expectations. It is based on shared attitudes, beliefs, customs, and written and unwritten rules that have been developed over time and are considered valid. [...] it's shown in (1) the ways the organization conducts its business, treats its employees, customers, and the wider community [...] (4) how committed employees are towards collective objectives. It affects the organization's productivity and performance, and provides guidelines on customer care and service, product quality and safety, attendance and punctuality, and concern for the environment." (Ibid.)

Organisational culture is considered a product of factors such as "history, product, market, [...], type of employees, national culture; [and] culture includes "the organization's vision, values, norms, [...] language, assumptions, environment, locations, beliefs and habits" (Needle 2004:239).

In Part II, the linkage between cultures (Confucianism and Hinduism) and organisational culture including, an organisation's expectation, philosophy, values and future expectations, will be examined by analysing the relevant information from the official websites of the companies in terms of the introduction of the founder, the vision and values of the companies. The definition of "trade policy" is "Laws related to the exchange of goods or services involved in international trade including taxes, subsidies, and import/export regulations" (*Business Dictionary* 2018b). It is also defined as "a government policy that directly influences the quantity of goods and services that a country imports or exports" (Mankiw 1991:690). In Part II, national policy mainly refers to the trade policy and the related policy in economic relations. The analysis of the relationship among culture, behavioural patterns, organisational culture and policies is to understand the behavioural patterns and cultural principles of the two countries in order to facilitate exchanges and achieve less or no-conflict in trade, more efficient in organisation management and rational in economic exchanges.

Rationale

In economic development, groups with different cultures have different performances. Cultural economy helps understand the relations of culture and economic outcomes. It displays "a more cautious analytical approach than mainstream finance and political economy" (Gay and Pryke 2007). In economic relations beyond groups, culture, because of the influence it wields on interaction, is still an influential factor. Thus, in economic activities of all sorts including inter-country ones, it has a reflection on commercial negotiations, cross culture management, business communications and so on.

Further, in case of a conflict caused by cultural differences, it could be an unavoidable obstacle in cross-culture interactions. It may happen frequently and profoundly influence perceptions towards each other. Moreover, it is almost always ignored and evaded, thus often causing a change in the entire business strategy and even the process of investment, cross-cultural management, and so on. Most critically, it imperceptibly causes problems and makes people from different cultures bear with it helplessly and generates negative perceptions towards each other.

Along with the rise of China and India, the prospect of economic relations would set to speed up, and so would the engagement between China and India. Alongside, the confidence is growing in both China and India and both governments want to revive their cultures. Somehow, when it comes to these two civilisational nations, if the mechanism of contacts to understand each other is not established rationally and their culture insufficiently understood mutually, bilateral disputes would increase.

Part II tries to assess how far China-India economic relations could have picked up if cultural issues were managed well. It focuses on how culture affects the economy, what are the main cultural differences between China and India, how the cultural differences cause conflict and what are its influences on the China-India economic relations. The aim is to enhance mutual understanding and trust to improve bilateral relations.

Scope of the Study

The proposed research of Part II covers the period from 2000 to 2017. In 2000, China's government officially initiated the "Go Global" strategy [Zǒu chū-qù zhàn-lüe] to encourage its enterprises to invest abroad. China's overseas investments since then increased dramatically from $ 3 billion (1991) to $ 35 billion (2003) (*People's Daily* 2004). The China-India trade volume also witnessed considerable improvement which was $ 2.91 billion in 2000 (MOCPRC 2011:472) and reached $ 84.54 billion in 2017 (MOCPRC 2018).

Part II focuses on the impact of culture on the economic relations of China and India as reflected in the economic activities mainly in Beijing, Shanghai and New Delhi and Gurugram (Haryana) where the author conducted interviews and with the concern of the entire economic interaction in terms of trade, investment and economic cooperation of the two nations. The cultural analysis of China and India mainly focuses on the dominant traditional culture (Confucianism and Hinduism) and the core values of these two cultures are emphasized as mentioned below.

Part II is not a pure study on economics but an interdisciplinary study. In it, cultural industry is not included, which is defined as "industries which produce tangible or intangible artistic and creative outputs, and which have a potential for wealth creation and income generation through the utilisation of cultural assets and production of knowledge-based goods and services (both traditional and contemporary)". (Tenkayala et al. 2014)

Part II is based on two hypotheses. The first is that economic relations between China and India are affected by their cultures as they influence their commercial behaviour, organisational culture and national policy. The second hypothesis is that the cultural differences between China and India have caused cultural conflicts which, in turn, have hindered their economic cooperation. Part II is empirical. It uses both primary and secondary sources. The primary sources include government documents, White Papers and statistics, interviews, archival materials, the documents of ministries, embassies, etc. Online interviews and face-to-face interactions were carried out in India and China. The secondary sources are various academic works, journals, documentaries, literature, websites, online sources, newspapers, magazines, articles and data from relevant institutions, etc. Part II is based on the works of scholars from China, India and the West and mainly uses qualitative research.

It is based on the inductive method. Part II is descriptive, applied and analytical. The aim is to analyse how culture influences China-India economic relations in contemporary times (2000-2017). It includes the proper examination of the effect of culture on the economy, the cultural differences of China and India, the economic relations between these two nations, the cultural conflicts caused by cultural differences and the impact on China-India economic relations. The two main parts of Part II are culture and economic relations. The independent variable is the culture of China and India with an emphasis on Confucianism and Hinduism, respectively. The dependent variable is China-India economic relations, and the intervening variable is commercial behaviour, organisational culture and national policy. Part II looks into Psycho-Culturology and the data and outcomes of GLOBE research projects were used to assess this study.

Part II is organised as follows. Chapter 5 considers Psycho-Culturology and moral realism. Chapter 6 explains the aspects that culture influences on the economy in China and India and describes how culture influences commercial behaviour, organisational culture and national policy. Chapter 7 analyses the core values of Confucianism and Hinduism and their impact on economic thought and behaviour, and identifies the cultural differences between China and India. Chapter 8 explores the fields of trade, investment and economic cooperation between China and India and examines the cultural influences on them. Chapter 9 assesses the cultural influence on economic relations in seven dimensions at three levels and the impact of cultural conflicts caused by cultural differences on their economic relations. Chapter 10 concludes the research by bringing together the findings from all the other chapters with discussions that conflict is good or bad; the aspects of cultural differences that could be conducive for economic relations. It also contains some reflections on how mutual cultural understanding could promote economic interaction.

PART I

Cultural Interaction, Perceptions and Policy

CHAPTER 1

THE ACHIEVEMENTS OF CULTURAL EXCHANGES BETWEEN CHINA AND INDIA

This research aims to understand the role of culture in China-India relations. This chapter examines the achievements of cultural exchanges between these two countries. To build good relations between the two nations in various fields, it is important to maintain political relations by frequent high-level contacts, and to increase economic cooperation between them. Increase in political and economic contacts will encourage cultural exchanges between these countries. The general aim of cultural exchanges between two nations is to build mutual understanding between them. They also help in building cooperation in socio, political and economic areas. Cultural exchanges promote bilateral relations resulting in forgetting past perceptions of threats and developing a more positive perception of each other. A positive perception will accelerate the process of better mutual understanding between these two countries. Thus, cultural exchanges are the fundamental method to practice the exchange of ideas, which gives value to further multicultural identities. It is also a vigorous approach to promote international relations on the cultural front rather than only with politics. In this case, at a certain level, cultural exchanges are the essential factor to promote two-nation relations.

1.1. Cultural Exchanges in China-India Relations

China and India are two ancient civilisations with a long continuous history. Geographically, they are neighbours as well, facilitating contacts between the two countries (Ji 2008:1). China and India have had cultural exchanges since historical times. The edicts of Emperor Ashoka (268-32 BCE), who ruled the Mauryan Empire (324/321-187 BCE), reflect an extension of Buddhism in the direction of China and Central Asia (Sen 2014, Embassy of India, Beijing, China). Indian Buddhist monks Kashyapa Matanga and Dharmaratna came to China and translated the first Chinese Buddhist sutra in the 1st century. The Chinese pilgrims, Fa Xian (342-423 CE), Xuan Zang (600-664 CE), and Yi Jing (635-713 CE) went to India to learn Buddhism (Tan 2014:288, Xue 2014:296, Wang 2014:304).

Definitely, there are several achievements* in the cultural exchanges between China and India. Those ancient cultural exchanges and events of cultural cooperation made the two nations draw closer for the future. There were also old achievements that portray the bilateral relations more closely in contemporary studies. For instance, the Xuan Zang Memorial Hall was built with the support of the governments of China and India to commemorate his contribution to communication between the two nations. On the other hand, India's great poet, Rabindranath Tagore, whose poems are very popular in China, also visited China twice, and built the Cheena Bhavana (Institute of Chinese Language and Culture) in Visva-Bharati University, India. The following are case studies of cultural exchanges: 1) Xuan Zang's encounter with Memory Hall (in Rajgir), and 2) Cheena Bhavana (in Shantiniketan).

1.2. A Case Study of Xuan Zang Memorial Hall

Xuan Zang was a Buddhist monk who travelled to India during the 7th century. He had travelled through many countries before entered India and studied in Nalanda University for five years from 631 CE. The places he travelled in India were Bengal, Orissa, Andhra Pradesh, Tamil Nadu, etc. (Xue 2014). His experiences are written in his well-known work *Da Tang Xi Yu Ji* [Great Tang Records on the Western Regions]. Even now, his stories are not only very famous in China, he was also well recognised in India by political leaders and scholars. In China, CCTV and many other TV programmes broadcast his experiences in India, namely, "Xi You Ji (Journey to the West)" (Qiao 2006), which is composed based on the *Da Tang Xi Yu Ji* [Great Tang Records on the Western Regions]. Xuan Zang plays an important role in both Chinese and Indian history in terms of cultural exchanges between China and India. Former Prime Minister (PM) of China, Zhou Enlai (1956) said the, "Chinese people consistently admired Indian cultural tradition and creative talent. Therefore, Chinese people should modestly learn from India like what forefather Xuan Zang did before" (Chen Ruisheng 2006:4).

Moreover, Xuan Zang provided the base for improving China-India relations. Most importantly, his ideas became a bridge for an 'unbreakable bond' between these two nations as described by current Indian PM Narendra Modi (Press Trust of India 2015). PM Narendra Modi recognised Xuan Zang's role to link himself with China, "He has a personal connection with China as he hails from a village

---

*Achievement here means "the process or fact of achieving something". The two selected cases are famous and representative in the circle of China-India cultural relations. The author had done fieldwork in these two places.

in Gujarat's Vadnagar, which famous Chinese traveller Hiuen Tsang (Xuan Zang) also visited" (Ibid).

It is true to say that Xuan Zang has played a crucial role in building the China-India relationship. The most prominent example is reflected in the website of the Nava Nalanda Mahavihara, which says, "The Xuan Zang Memorial Hall symbolizes the age-old ties between the two great civilizations of India and China and is a befitting tribute to Indo-China friendship. The essential components of the creative works to shape it in a Memorial Museum were carried out subsequently" (NNM 2014). The Xuan Zang Memorial Hall provides a platform for Indians to know about Chinese passion and emotions towards Indian Buddhism.

The former deputy director-general of State Administration for Religious Affairs of China explained the intention to rebuild the memorial hall. He stated, "The reason we rebuilt the Xuan Zang Memorial Hall is because we wanted a window which can show the tradition of China-India friendship and also provide a platform to improve the cultural cooperation, specially the Buddhist cultural exchanges between China-India" (*China Religion* 2007).

The process of building the Xuan Zang Memorial Hall is shown below in order to clearly review the building process. In 1956, Bhikkhu Jagadish Kashyap, the Founder-Director of Nava Nalanda Mahavihara

> ... first proposed the establishment of a Memorial Hall as a symbol of India-China friendship dedicated to Xuan Zang to pay homage to his spirit of freedom and quest for knowledge, and to strengthen the friendship between the India and China (*NNM* 2014).

The governments of China and India supported the construction of the "Memorial Hall". In 1957, former PM of China, Zhou Enlai, visited India to discuss the programme of building the "memorial hall" with Nehru (*China Religion* 2007). For many reasons, this programme of building the "memorial hall" was prolonged and it was only in 1984 that the construction of the Xuan Zang Memorial Hall was completed. Further, in 2003, approximately ₹ 30 million was donated for the construction of the Hall by the Indian government (*NNM* 2014). The floor area of the main building is 4.5 hectares; 47.5 hectares of land was given to Nalanda University near the hall in order to build a New Nalanda University Cultural Village. During 2005, the National Religion Bureau of China for the remembrance of China-India friendship started the repair project. A Chinese delegation visited India from 19 to 25 December 2005 and discussed the programme with the Indian government (*China Religion* 2007). It was decided to complete the project before the end of 2006 and on 12 February 2007, it was jointly inaugurated by dignitaries from India and China (*NNM* 2014). Both the Chinese and Indian government have spent resources such as people, materials, finance, and vigour for the establishment of the Memorial Hall.

1.2.1. The Influence of Xuan Zang Memorial Hall

A structure will be built to judge the influence of cultural exchanges on the bilateral relations. According to Guan Shijie (2015), there is a system of standards to test the influence of cultural projects. Here we will highlight four standards to measure the influence of cultural exchanges on bilateral relations in terms of the Xuan Zang Memorial Hall: 1) Existent or Non-existent, 2) Positive or Negative, 3) Durable or Transient, and 4) Significant or Insignificant.

EXISTENT OR NON-EXISTENT

Firstly, the Xuan Zang Memorial Hall made an "existence" of source for cultural exchange. This "existence" provided the possibility for further connections with future generations. It also provided a platform for people to travel, to learn about Xuan Zang and to understand his experiences during the visit. The existence of his visit would have been incomplete without the building of the "memorial hall". In terms of non-existence, the translations of Chinese classic literature into Sanskrit, 50 Buddhist sutras and seeds of flowers were lost in the Xindu He (Shindu River, aka Indus) while returning to China (Ji 2008:54).

POSITIVE OR NEGATIVE

How can we define positive or negative aspects of the "memorial hall" in terms of cultural exchange? During its construction, negotiations were long winding between China and India but both were positive towards preserving the ancient culture. The interest on both sides brought them to cooperate with the same ideas. For some, this story of Xuan Zang might be a tale that leads to disbelief and creates scepticism for contemporary scholars to conduct research. For instance, Sen pointed out that Xuan Zang called some ancient Gujaratis "stingy by custom and deceitful in disposition" (Sen 2014). Although the above quote is just a very small point in the stories of Xuan Zang, it may have a negative impact on the thinking of people towards this programme.

DURABLE OR TRANSIENT

The influence of the Xuan Zang Memorial Hall may be durable or transient. First, the cultural relation was built by Buddhism (or Buddhist culture in religion) as a carrier of 'ideas, interest and ideology' for cultural exchanges (Wendt 1999). It promoted the benign development of bilateral relations. Compared with other forms like oral histories and written documents, the existence of the Xuan Zang Memorial Hall shows the mature belief of interactive culture between the ancient people that will definitely help future generations to understand Xuan Zang and his experiences with Indian culture.

SIGNIFICANT OR INSIGNIFICANT

There are two points of view in understanding the significance of the memorial hall. Historically, it was Xuan Zang's personal desire to visit India because monks were not allowed to go abroad privately as the Chinese authority was concerned that the Western area was non-tranquil (Xue 2007:60; Xue 2014:297). However when he came back from India to China, he was very famous and welcomed by the Chinese authorities. Xuan Zang influenced their ideas. And now, there is official action to build a memorial hall and influence the ideas of the common people.

From these four gradations, the Xuan Zang Memorial Hall forms an influence on China-India relations. The influence is positive, durable, and significant which contemporary scholars cannot deny.

At the level of cultural exchanges, from protection to the promotion of history, the Xuan Zang Memorial Hall has shown its role to facilitate a positive influence and the formation of multiple relations between China and India. However, the cultural exchange rests only on historical legacy for many people. In an article titled "China and India: the Necessity of Recognition to Each Other", Zhang Li argued that the lack of knowing each other resulted in many misunderstandings. Exchanges between intellectuals has a very crucial role on this; it is an important catalyst to break the ice between China and India. "The political condition of the Indian nuclear test of 1998 brought both China and India into hard times. It was only the Track Two diplomacy, with the character of scholars' dialogue, which brought the bilateral relations to normal soon" (Zhang 2006). Intellectuals who know the other's national conditions, culture, and language promoted the changing of the cognition and opinion towards the other, especially those who have had the experience to stay in the other country. "Direct contact and communications neither restricted them from seeking existing conclusions from some Western scholars, nor simply march or transplant the cognition towards China, and thus avoid many prejudices and demonised recognition" (Zhang 2006).

As a place to cultivate intellectuals, how far does an educational institution play the role? An effective cooperation programme on cultural and educational aspects may benefit generations; however, it takes long time, and financial and material resources to complete the process. The role of Cheena Bhavana (Institute of Chinese Language and Culture), located in Visva-Bharati University, has a greater impact comparing with Xuan Zang Memorial Hall in China-India relations. Cheena Bhavana was established in 1937 and has developed into a comparatively mature and influential institution in contemporary times.

1.3. A Case Study of Cheena Bhavana

Cheena Bhavana was founded by Rabindranath Tagore and Tan Yunshan at Visva-Bharati University with help from both China and India. This mutual assistance of China and India in building Cheena Bhavana in 1937 was for "strengthening the age-old cultural ties between India and China" (Cheena Bhavana 2015). The Cheena Bhavana also played an important role in bringing China and India together to set up the "Xuan Zang Memorial Hall" to develop

Chinese studies. The cultural exchanges programmes between China and India that were organised in Cheena Bhavana will be briefly reviewed for the period of 2003 to 2014. The information of the review is based on interviews, which the researcher undertook with the faculty including the Dean of Cheena Bhavana, Avijit Banerjee, during fieldwork in January 2015.

Avijit Banerjee started teaching in Cheena Bhavana in 2003, where he has been witnessing development like seminars, exhibitions, Chinese Movie festivals, Spring Festival celebration and other activities, which were held to discuss, learn and exhibit Chinese culture. Moreover, an agreement was signed between Visva-Bharati University and Yunnan University, which opened the door for visiting students to be sent every year from each side. According to that agreement, two Chinese teachers from Yunnan University come to teach in Cheena Bhavana. According to Bannerjee, library staff from Yunnan University come to arrange books and donate teaching material, which become the source material for Chinese departments of other Indian universities. Activities like The First Xuan Zang Cup Chinese Language Contest was held and the number of students increased eight times from 20 (1991) to 150 (2015) in the academies (Banerjee 2015).

The effect of Cheena Bhabana could be summarised as below. Firstly, Cheena Bhavana created an influence in the area of China-India cultural exchanges from 2003 to 2014. It gave a platform for deepening interest in exchanging ideas. However, its level of influence is not as promising as it was supposed to be. From the beginning of its establishment, there are two main objectives in the General Rules of Visva-Bharati Cheena-Bhavana: Article II:

> The objective of this department (Cheena-Bhavana) shall be to establish and promote cultural exchange between China and India, for which purpose it will provide facilities for Chinese scholars to study Indian languages, literature, history, religion, philosophy, etc., as well as for Indian scholars to study Chinese language, literature, religion, philosophy, etc. (Tan 1957:20)

In the current stage, the situation is already relatively perfect and mature for Cheena Bhavana to provide facilities for Indians to study about China. Chinese scholars like Liang Qichao (Tan 1957:18), Jin Kemu, Buddhist master Tai Xu, etc., had studied at Visva-Bharati University where they conducted research on Indian culture and language. This experience gave them a deep understanding of society and this helped in disseminating the ideals about Indian culture in China. Similarly, it is quite effective that Cheena Bhavana has provided a platform for Indians to know about China. According to Patricia M. Goff (2013), Cultural Diplomacy springs from two premises—

> First, that good relations can take rest in the fertile ground of understanding and respect. Second, cultural diplomacy rests on the

> assumption that art, language and education are among the most significant entry points into a culture.

Therefore, Cheena Bhavana gave an opportunity for Chinese visiting scholars to understand art, language, and education in further promoting the cultural exchange programme. In China, it might be a different case, where most Chinese scholars are unaware of Indian culture, which leads to asymmetric perceptions. Thus, the cultural exchange has included introducing Indian culture to the Chinese counterparts.

Secondly, Cheena Bhavana has positive and negative effects on culture exchanges. Those educated elites who are interested in China will inherit and develop the achievements of cultural exchanges, and continue the tradition of exchange of ideas. Cheena Bhavana also provided an equal platform for common Indian students to study about China. Culture exchange goes beyond the understanding of "Hindi-Chini Bhai-Bhai" by inclusion of culture in the educational system. Sen (2014) says some Indian and Chinese researchers "blindly and deliberately implant and generalise the viewpoint of China-India relationship" without understanding the ground reality. Some only criticise the relations (China-India) in a pessimistic way, i.e., they are more nationalists than the objective scholars. They tend to focus more on political propaganda to affect the relations than on academic research. Both positive and negative influences may include rational influence. Some Indian scholars propose the 1962 border conflict should not be treated emotionally or influence too heavily on cooperation in other aspects.

Thirdly, an institution like Cheena Bhavana has influence across the world by producing ideas about cultural exchanges, which have a long durability. Like in Greek history, Socrates created Plato and Plato created Aristotle in maintaining the educational system. The institution serves for the long run, except from the destruction caused by war. For example, invaders like Bakhtiyar Khilji who came with 200 horsemen (Chandra 2004:41), to India in the 12th century led to the destruction of Nalanda University (Nalanda University 2014). The influence of Cheena Bhavana could be significant. Non-governmental institutions like Cheena Bhavana took the role of construction of ideas. It also holds the role of reminding and provides a platform to constantly review and disseminate this affection.

Before the establishment of Cheena Bhavana, Mahatma Gandhi wrote a letter to Tagore (Tan Yunshan 1957:16) thus: "May the Chinese Hall be a symbol of living contact between China and India!" Gandhi wrote:

> "We want cultural contact between the two nations. Yours is a worthy effort. May it bring fruit!" (Tan Yunshan 1957:16).

Jawaharlal Nehru, who was unable to join the opening ceremony of Cheena Bhavana due to sickness, also expressed his desire to enhance the cultural exchanges between China and India. Nehru's letter read out by his daughter Indira Gandhi during the inauguration stated:

> "I gave my word gladly and with the full confidence, I would join in the great ceremony, great in the memories of the long past that it invokes, great also in the promise of future comradeship and the forging of new links to bring China and India nearer to each other. What a long past that has been of friendly contact and mutual influences, untroubled by political conflict and aggression! We have traded in ideas, in art, in culture, and grown richer in our own inheritance by the other's offering" (Tan Yunshan 1957:16).

The establishment of Cheena Bhavana raised the confidence of the leaders of the two nations in promoting cultural exchanges as well as cooperating in other fields. During the 20th anniversary of Cheena Bhavana, Jawaharlal Nehru commended the contribution of this institution towards cultural exchanges. Jawaharlal Nehru, who was also the Chancellor of Visva-Bharati University said:

> Twenty years ago, the Visva-Bharati Cheena Bhavana was started. It was intended to promote contacts between India and China and to encourage the study of the Chinese Language in India...the friendship of these two great countries has continued and will, no doubt, continue. The roots of that friendship go back thousands of years, and it has withstood many storms and stresses during the past because of those deep roots...Cheena Bhavana at Visva-Bharati has quietly and unobtrusively continued its work to increase mutual understanding (Ibid: 3).

President Rajendra Prasad was also deeply influenced by the extension of cultural exchanges between these two nations. He stated:

> It is in keeping with the age-old tradition of friendship between India and China that the Cheena-Bhavana at Visva-Bharati should be progressing and gaining in popularity. Such contacts, which the background of ancient cultures and friendly relations inspire me, I think, the surest way of creating understanding and mutual goodwill among nations (Ibid: 2).

From the discourse of the national leaders on the Indian side, it showed that supported Chinese cultural knowledge had importance in India and its influence grew from a non-governmental institution to the idea of national leadership. It facilitated the development of evolution of bilateral relations. When Chinese President Xi Jinping visited India in September 2014, he conferred the "Five Principles of Peaceful Coexistence Friendship Award" to Cheena Bhavana (Meng 2014) showing affirmation of the role of Cheena Bhavana to promote bilateral relations through an educational institution like it.

1.4. A Brief Analysis of China Town in Kolkata

China Town is located in the city of Kolkata in West Bengal. Overseas Chinese in India have made an immense contribution to the spread of Chinese culture in India, especially in terms of Chinese food, which has become a part of their daily lives. This is an attempt to study the present condition, situation of cultural exchange and the position and role of overseas Chinese in China-India relations. The overseas Chinese who have settled in the city of Kolkata have concentrated themselves in two areas and they are of Guangzhou, *Kejia* (Hakka) and Hubei descent.

The first two groups are engaged in the leather, food and drinks and hair-dressing industry whereas Chinese from Hubei are mostly engaged in dentistry to earn their livelihood (Miao 2015). Therefore, the first two ethnic groups are close to Chinese cultural customs and folk beliefs. In the process of investigation and research, especially in the past, in the aspects of architecture of dwelling place, interior decoration, food habits, temple beliefs retain a strong Chinese flavour. They have kept the Chinese cultural characteristics intact, and preferred self-conservation.

However, there are a few manifestations of integration with Indian culture. Chinese temples open not only for Chinese but also for Indians. The Chinese statue of Buddha is draped in the sacrificial cloth as in Indian custom. Moreover, a Chinese dwelling place had an Indian temple. A part of overseas Chinese was influenced by Hinduism. The Hubei Chinese integrated closely with Indian society because management in the dentistry industry had no choice but to spread all over India. As a private clinic, and a group serving upper class society, the integration of the Hubei Chinese with Indian society is even deeper. The influence of Indian culture is great. Overseas Chinese often receive invitations to participate in activities like celebration of festivals in the Chinese Embassy and Consulate, and national leaders sometimes visit them.

Nonetheless, the overseas Chinese could receive more appropriate value in the process of China-India high-level exchange visits and formulation of cultural exchange projects. As groups living in a foreign country, overseas Chinese are familiar with customs, politics, and the economy. They are a pillar of strength for cultural exchange and ought to attach sufficient importance and stimulate the groups to play an important role.

1.5. The Role of the Cultural Exchanges between China and India in the 21st Century

In the current phase of globalisation, what is the role of cultural exchanges between China and India? There are many intellectuals who have appealed to unite China and India in culture and politics, like Rabindranath Tagore, and Tan Yunshan. In the dialogue between the British historian, Arnold J. Toynbee, and Japanese scholar Daisaku Ikeda, which was recorded in the book, "*Forecast 21st*

Century also called Choose Life" they argued their expectations towards Chinese culture and Indian culture (specially the influence of Buddhism), which was not highlighted but has an important role in the construction of the former's culture in the 21st century. Another work, *Chindia* (coined in 2007 by Jairam Ramesh), considered that 'China and India' have a spiritual affinity shared through Buddhism, which should promote economic cooperation. From the 'Power Transition' theoretical perspective in the field of international relations, scholars like Kugler (2001) et al., says that though China and India seek common points while reserving differences, it would be more beneficial for them to peacefully raise and stabilise the international order.

Again, the concept of the 'Asian Century' was proposed with respect to British Century for the 19th century and American Century for the 20th century (Deng 1988:281). On the one hand, the trend showed to take up a dominant position in world economy from the economic performance of Asian countries. On the other hand, Western culture, which holds the leading role in the world, is not able to solve the many contemporary issues that have motivated more conflicts. The material culture made daily life convenient while making light of spiritual life. Both China and India are good on export of cultural, spiritual consumer goods, like Chinese Gongfu and Qigong (a system of deep breathing exercises), etc., as good as Indian Yoga and other religious culture from Hinduism and Buddhism and so forth. Moreover, there are many ideas about yearning for peace in the core of both Chinese and Indian cultures, for example, *He Wei Gui* (Harmony is most precious), *Tian Xia Da Tong* (The world is a great unity) in Chinese and *Vasudhaiva Kutumbakam* (The world is one family) in Indian and so forth. The potential leadership of world peace by China and India which is mentioned in Nehru's message and written before the establishment of Cheena Bhavana in 1937 played the prominent role—

> China and India, sister nations from the dawn of history, with their long tradition of culture and peaceful development of ideas, have to play a leading part in this world drama, in which they themselves are so deeply involved" (Tan Yunshan 1957:11).

Although it is historically a fact that both China and India had the experience of colonial master rule and revolted against it, except the historical parentage when Nehru wanted to bring China and India closer in history. The contribution of Buddhism in constructing the international leadership should not be neglected. It should be the most suitable example to show that culture mingles peacefully most of the time in history. The blend of Chinese and Indian culture exported the peaceful idea together to the world. The speeches of the leaders of the two nations show that they pay much attention to the role of Buddhism in China-India relations. These ideas show the contribution of China and India to world culture and peace as well as the possibility of China-India cooperation in the world.

The former Indian Prime Minister, Atal Bihari Vajpayee, proposed to construct an Indian temple inside the White Horse Temple when he visited China in 2003. He said: "This temple is the first building to build the contact between China and India. I wanted to show my regard to the pioneers who built this contact" (Chen 2003). Vajpayee wrote in the visitor's book of the temple, "The former Indian president, Smt. Pratibha Devisingh Patil, came to White Horse Temple to present a souvenir to the temple". Buddhism is also always mentioned by the current Prime Minister of India, Narendra Modi. During his interaction with Chinese leaders, he said, "Buddhism is a very strong bond between China and India" (PMO 2014). Similarly, Chinese national leader Wen Jiabao spoke at the Indian Institute of Technology (IIT) when he visited India in 2005. Former Prime Minister Wen Jiabao referred to "The story of Xuan Zang about his experience of travel to India, which is widely known in classic literature '*Journey to the West in China*' " (Ma et al. 2005). In 2006, former Chinese President Hu Jintao mentioned that Chinese Buddhist monks Fa Xian and Xuan Zang came to India to take the Buddhist sutras, and that Kumarajiva and Budhidharma brought Buddhist sutras from India to China. These are historical facts that connect the people of the two nations (Hu 2006). Again, in 2010, Wen Jiabao said, "Indian Buddhism enriched Chinese culture" (Wen 2010). In 2014, China's President Xi Jinping described the Buddhist exchanges in the history of people's contact between China and India as "*Nongmo zhongcai*" (thick and heavy in colours). He mentioned that the '*Sutra of Forty-two Chapters*' translated by Kasyapa Matanga and Dharmaratna (also called Gobharana) (who came to Luoyang, China, from Tian Zhu, as India was called in ancient times) was the earliest translation of Buddhist sutras in China. Xuan Zang travelled west (India) and brought Indian culture back to China" (Xi 2014). Those works showed the importance of Buddhism in constructing relations between these two nations from the perspectives of national leaders. The culture of non-violence was constructed during the period of Indian Buddhism, which spread from China to other countries. Cultural exchanges constructed the base for good relations and increased the stability factor not only in the region but also in the world.

It could be a reference that the cultural exchanges between China and India influenced other cultures in the world. The contribution of cultural exchanges led to introspection of the relations between China and India. Why were these exchanges formed so strongly in Mahayana Buddhism through Chinese culture? The exchanges between Chinese and Indian cultures promoted the ideas to different neighbouring cultures like Japan, South Korea, etc. The foundation was built through the forms of Buddhism for those countries to have further connection.

1.5.1. "Forecast 21st Century" with a Base Point in Buddhism

How did Buddhism unconsciously influence international relations? What kind of vision does Buddhism provide for China-India relations? How will Buddhism shape the 'relations' of these two nations in the 21st century and produce the potential to influence the world? From the following analysis, we may get some idea. The idea forms the book by Arnold Toynbee and Daisaku Ikeda *Choose Life*, also known as *Forecast 21st Century or Choose Life*, based on the dialogue between historian Arnold J. Toynbee and Japanese scholar Daisaku Ikeda; it will be used as a reference for analysis.

In the dialogue between Toynbee and Daisaku Ikeda, it was predicted that China and other Asian countries would "create an axis round which the unification of the whole world would be achieved" (Gage 1976:230). Daisaku Ikeda explained further,

> "The undercurrent of Buddhist philosophy common to all the peoples of Eastern Asia deserves attention because its future influence can be great. Though its visible influence today is small, Buddhist thought has cultivated and enriched the spiritual life of East Asian peoples for centuries and enveloped their histories in an aura of peace."

East Asia is known as 'ripe with rivalry' but there is still the possibility of peace. Ikeda emphasises Buddhist thought to decipher the producing process of peace and its potential to contribute towards world peace—

> East Asian culture, which was reared under the influence of Buddhist philosophy and which inspires repose and a sense of wonderful harmony between man and nature, has inspired in the peoples of this part of the world a mighty urge to live. It seems to me that philosophy and religion, especially Buddhism, will be the fields in which the peoples of Eastern Asia can make the greatest contributions to peace and civilisation (Gage 1976: 230).

From his perspective, Ikeda was talking about East Asian Buddhism. However in a long-run perception, the origin of influence building is India. Thus, China played a crucial role in the spread of Buddhism and makes it suitable with East Asian culture. Although Buddhism did not obviously affix any tag to China or India, it was Indian in origin and the Chinese took part in spread it. It mixed with the local culture and with huge and deep influence in the economy, politics, and culture. Cultural exchanges promoted the similarity of value and world outlook among different regions and different cultures. They built the foundation to reach a consensus on other issues. This foundation of Buddhism also built the geographic connection that also can be a conference for other cultures to seek a view to solve regional conflicts.

Toynbee says,

> It is very difficult to conquer and unite by violence in the atomic age today which way used atomic device to unite extensive area in the earth. Meanwhile, the peaceful reunification, which I predicted, must

> constantly crystallise and enlarge by using the principal axis of geography and culture as its centre. I foreboded this principal axis will be in East Asia instead of USA, Europe and USSR (Toynbee 1983:283).

The East Asia mentioned by Toynbee as constructed by Chinese, Indian and other neighbouring countries is the foundation of cultural similarity. In the new age, culture will probably play a leading role on the peaceful reunification of the world in the future.

From the prediction of this dialogue, a perspective caused by culture is offered to solve the problems of the world. It could be said that China and India shaped this region in peace, which has the possibility for the cultural cohesion and to form a unity as the cultural parentage. In this 21st century, the so called Asian century, Buddhism may come to play the role it did in the Silk Road in ancient times to link and unite different countries and encourage them to carry out more cooperation as a "catalyst" and positive factor to reduce conflicts (Sen 2005:166).

The historian, Toynbee, emphasises the role of China in his analysis. India was not on the front line and played more roles in the background. Buddhism has the potential to play a positive role in the new pattern of world development. So to speak, it is the contribution of China and India. It may be said that the important achievement of cultural exchanges is in influencing the world.

1.5.2. New Demand to China-India Cooperation

Besides the cultural influence of Buddhism, there are other cultures like movies, which have played an important role in the promotion of cultural exchange. Movies like *Three Idiots, Life of Pie, Slumdog Millionaire*, etc., have played a crucial role in understanding the culture of the field. Similarly, actors like Jackie Chan and Jet Lee are very famous in India for their roles in action movies. This type of image has not only touched the leaders but the local people also in imagining the fields. The achievement of cultural exchanges between China and India provides a viewpoint, a channel for world development. On the basis of the cultural blend, a more positive way would be to initiate dialogue in the limited time and space and set up an example to lessen conflicts.

In the article of "Power Transitions and Alliances in the 21st Century", Kugler et al. (2001) says China and India need to cooperate. Meanwhile, the bad relations will cause very serious consequences with the inducement of border conflicts. According to this article, "Power transitions can create conditions either for a challenge or a reinforcement of the status quo. Power transition between satisfied nations ensures peace and continuation of the status quo. Conversely, dissatisfaction increases the probability of war dramatically" (Kugler et al. 2001:5-29). From the Power Transition perspective, the authors predicted "challenges to US dominance primarily will emerge from Asia in the 21st century.

China and India are identified as the potential contenders because of their overwhelming population base and potential for economic growth" (Kugler et al. 2001:6). Accordingly, if China and India will be united, it will be more beneficial for world peace and stability. It may cause conflict if the border issue cannot be solved. However, China and India will unite, which lesser conflicts and build bilateral trust to promote peace. The new demand from different institutions is needed for understanding and promoting mutual trust.

1.6. The Constraints in Cultural Exchanges

There are constraints in cultural exchanges such as political distrust, language, border disputes, etc. Regarding political distrust, it influenced the establishment of Confucius Institutes as well. Agreements for three Confucius Institutes were signed between China and India but only one is working at present. The first Confucius Institute was in Jawaharlal Nehru University (JNU), the agreement for which was signed in 2005. It was revived recently in 2015. The second one is in Vellore Institute of Technology (VIT). The MoU was signed in 2007 and the institute started running in 2009. The third one is in Mumbai University, it started running in 2012. Because of lack of Chinese teachers and other disagreements, the first and last mentioned Confucius institutes are not in working condition. It is mainly because Chinese language teachers are still having difficulty in getting work visas for India (Lei 2015). The negative role of political distrust on the opening and working of Confucius Institutes in India becomes apparent as one compares the number and working of Confucius Institutes in India with the Taiwan Education Centre. While only one of three Confucius Institutes in India, i.e., the one in Vellore is working, all the four Taiwan Education Centres, located respectively in Jindal Global University, Amity University, Jamia Millia Islamia, and IIT Madras in India are working well.

It also needs to be noted that scholars from both China and India lack knowledge of each other's native language. Language limits the information on both sides which will cause further misunderstandings. These constraints are also caused or influenced by the border dispute which has limited the level of cultural exchanges between these two countries.

CHAPTER 2

PERCEPTIONS IN CONTEMPORARY PERIOD

When the heads of states or governments of China and India visit each other, they sum up the progress of the Sino-Indian relationship and make plans for the future. This chapter will summarise the perceptions* in both countries reflected in the speeches of the national leaders, media reports, and analyses of scholars during the visits. The durations of these visits are the best time to observe and analyse the attitude of the two governments towards each other and the direction of the overall policy. In this chapter, the periods during the key visits have been selected to analyse the perceptions from China and India towards each other and the attitudes on cultural exchanges at different levels. From 2003 to 2014, a period of 11 years, there was a total of eight top-level visits. These were by Prime Minister Atal Bihari Vajpayee in 2003 and by Prime Minister Manmohan Singh in 2008 and 2013 from India as well as of Premier Wen Jiabao in 2005 and 2010, of President Hu Jintao in 2006, of Premier Li Keqiang in 2013 and of President Xi Jinping in 2014 from China (Embassy of India, Beijing 2014).

To judge the impressions of various sections about the visits, this chapter will analyse the following: (1) important speeches made by the leaders during their visits, a detailed analysis in order to test the impact of public perceptions on the leaders' perspectives; (2) joint declarations signed by the two governments; (3) news reports during the visits. From the Indian side: *The Hindu, The Indian Express* (English) and *Navbharat Times* (Hindi) and from the Chinese side: Xinhua Agency, *People's Daily*, etc.; (4) experts' points of view from reference journals like India's *Economic & Political Weekly* (EPW), *China Report*, *India Today,* China's *South Asian Studies* and *Phoenix Magazine*, etc.

---

* This chapter defines perception as "political cognition, the ways in which we think and reason politically". See Houghton, David Patrick (2009), *Political Psychology: Situations, Individuals, and Cases*, New York: Routledge: 115.

2.1. Atal Bihari Vajpayee's Visit to China in 2003

At the invitation of Chinese Premier Wen Jiabao, Indian Prime Minister Atal Bihari Vajpayee visited China from June 22 to 27 in 2003. The two sides signed the Declaration on Principles for Relations and Comprehensive Cooperation between the Republic of India and the People's Republic of China to confirm the development of a long-term constructive and cooperative partnership. Before this, Vajpayee had visited China as the Indian Minister of External Affairs in 1979, which then gave an impetus to rebuilding the fractured relations between China and India (Cai 2007). However, Vajpayee's 2003 visit was a landmark, attached with greater importance in relation to the Chinese government, because major leaders of China's central government interacted with Prime Minister Vajpayee.

In this context, the importance of Prime Minister Vajpayee's interaction with his Chinese counterpart can be analysed from different perspectives. On the political front, as reported by the Indian media, Vajpayee in his interaction with the then Chinese Premier, Wen Jiabao, seemed to adopt a tough stand on the question of appointment of special representatives for border talks. While Wen Jiabao called for a postponement, Vajpayee sought immediate appointment. Finally, with Vajpayee's staunch attitude, special representatives for the border talks were appointed. In contrast to the Indian media, the Chinese media focused its attention on highlighting the personal profile of Vajpayee than on reflecting his political attitude. *Xinhua* (Chen and Fu 2003) described him as a man full of human feelings and a renowned poet.

Vajpayee's strong position on the issue of Tibet too gained media attention and the Indian media appreciated his adherence to India's position on Tibet causing no harm to national interests in the negotiations on Tibet. According to *India Today*, the Indian side in a Cabinet Committee meeting before Vajpayee's China visit decided to "ignore both Sikkim and Tibet and concentrate on economics and border clarification" (Chawla 2003). It is noted that China agreed on all other issues of "education, renewable energy and culture" but "refused to commit on Sikkim". Maintaining this stand, Vajpayee in opposition to the Chinese insistence that "India should recognise Tibet as an inalienable part of [China]", stood for recognising that "only the Tibet Autonomous Region (TAR) was part of the People's Republic of China" (Ibid.). In response to Vajpayee's stand on Tibet, China too removed the name of Sikkim, as a different entity, from the website of the Chinese Ministry of Foreign Affairs on 8 October 2003 (Tang 2003).

Unlike his strong political attitude towards China, Prime Minister Atal Bihari Vajpayee's China visit had strong cultural underpinnings. In his speech at Peking University on June 23, emphasis was laid on China-India friendship drawing from the ancient linkages between the two countries. While inaugurating the Centre for Indian Studies at Peking University, Vajpayee recalled the ancient China-India cultural exchanges, and stated: "We are, of course, two of the world's oldest civilisations with contacts over at least two millennia. The Silk Route connected us through commerce, but also by facilitating the free flow of our music, our scriptures, and our literature." He further mentioned that Buddhism from India influenced millions in China and that maritime trade between the two countries promoted closer contacts and strengthened cultural exchanges, thereby, creating a confluence of the two cultures with that of South-East Asia (Vajpayee 2003).

Emphasising the need for the Centre for Indian Studies, Vajpayee suggested that it should not be limited to understanding history, languages and literature but also focus on modern Indian political, economic, and sociological studies. He said, "Academic exchanges and contemporary studies help to bridge the gap of information and perceptions." In doing so, he quoted the words of the Chinese sage, Lao Zi, who is regarded as the founder of Taoism. He said:

> "You can make your Centre fulfils Lao Zi's ideal of knowledge and understanding: Without stirring abroad one can know the whole world; Without looking out of the window one can see the way of heaven" (Bu chuhu, zhi tianxia; bu kuiyou, jian tiandao —Dao De Jing, Chapter 47).

In this regard, Vajpayee's remarks hold great symbolism and significance for they are a way to strengthen the cultural aspect of China-India relations. The Indian national leadership's citation of China's famous epigram is reflective of its attention to Chinese culture as well as its keen interest to know about it, and stimulate national interests about Chinese culture in India. There is a need for greater understanding among the Indian leadership about Chinese traditional culture to create a common basis for solving problems and as a way to understand their cultural differences; moreover, this contributes to the need for the understanding of Indian culture among Chinese leadership.

These high-level cultural exchanges help to promote the level and explore the potential of bilateral relationships. Besides the political and the economic aspects, cultural exchange too has a significant role in building ties between the two long-standing civilisational neighbours and promoting mutual understanding based on cultural linkages. Therefore, the 'culture aspect' is and should be taken as an important component in defining the China-India relationship. In this regard, cultural exchanges among the leadership on either side do play a vital role in contributing to a greater understanding of each other's perceptions.

Cultural exchanges between the two countries could enhance mutual affinity. Cordial dialogue between the two can help reduce the negative influence created by other countries. Keeping this in view, Vajpayee (2003) stated that, "If we [China and India] acted in concert, it would be very difficult for the world to ignore us". This positive attitude of Vajpayee continued to be further upheld by the leadership on either side. For when one side (India) issues a benign message, it normally causes the other (China) to respond positively and vice-versa. The positive perception between the two nations provided the basic condition to withstand forces that seek to create a fracture in the relations. In this way, exchange of perceptions can contribute to a deeper mutual understanding between the two countries and, thus, foster closer ties. Apart from bilateral ties, such exchanges can also enhance the unity of the two countries internationally. In considering the two countries to speak with one voice, the understanding of each other's cultures also put forward higher requirements. Hence, for China and India to "act in concert" it becomes imperative to expand the limits of their cultural advantage at all lengths, both at the leadership level as well as that of the common masses.

In this context, the comment of Vajpayee on China-India relations provided a basis for furthering ties as opposed to the persistent negative attitude. He said, "We should focus on the simple truth that there is no objective reason for discord between us, and neither of us is a threat to the other. These simple, but profound, principles should form the bedrock of the future India-China partnership" (Vajpayee 2003) Adhering to the need to expand cultural exchanges, the two sides signed a cultural MOU to establish each other's cultural centres in their respective capitals. Hence, such diplomatic moves opened up a new base for further cultural exchanges between the two countries (Embassy of P.R. of China in India 2004).

What is important to note here is that such behaviour on part of national leaders can help to thwart the negative influences that impact the ties, and contribute to rational and active relations. Besides, on controversial issues, the heads of the states need to safeguard the fundamental interests of their countries, which tends to negatively impact other aspects of bilateral cooperation. For example, the protracted border issue was once a major barrier in the cooperation process between China and India. However, with the joint efforts by both sides, a new mechanism to mutually resolve the issue by means of border talks by the establishment of a special representative mechanism gradually reduced the negative influence of the border issue on the cooperation between the two nations. This resulted in a change of mutual perceptions of each other.

2.2. Wen Jiabao's Visit to India in 2005

In 2005, Chinese Premier Wen Jiabao visited India from April 9 to 12, as part of his South Asian diplomatic tour. India was one of his stops besides Pakistan, Bangladesh, and Sri Lanka. During the trip, he delivered the keynote speech at the opening ceremony of the Asia Cooperation Dialogue held in Islamabad on April 6. Although India formed the last leg of the South Asian trip, the idea of his India visit was first proposed on November 2004, when Premier Wen met then Indian PM Manmohan Singh in Laos on the occasion of the Third India-ASEAN Summit. Premier Wen had expressed that "the India visit will be the most important event on my agenda next year, and 'I hope this will send a positive signal throughout the world" (Ram 2004). In international relations, the way leaders behave with one another plays an important characteristic in defining their relations with each other. As in 2003, then Indian PM Atal Bihari Vajpayee called for the two countries to "act in concert"—providing a positive impetus to the Sino-Indian relationship, likewise, Wen Jiabao in 2004 put forward a more confident vision of Sino-Indian relations. At the Third India-ASEAN Summit, he stated that the handshake between him and PM Manmohan Singh "will catch the attention of the whole world" (Ibid), thereby attaching a positive perception of China in the future direction of the Sino-Indian relationship.

What is noteworthy is that two months prior to Premier Wen Jiabao's India visit in April, the groundwork had already been placed. In an attempt to understand India better, China had sent six academic delegations to visit various Indian strategic, economic, and political institutes, think tanks, and universities in New Delhi in order to make a primary assessment of various Indian expectations from the upcoming Chinese Premier's India visit. Being the first of its kind, such an initiative on the part of the Chinese Government signifies the importance that China attaches to a prior understanding of India's interests and concerns towards China that would be useful in furthering the process of policy-making as well as preparing the groundwork for the Premier's visit to an important neighbour. In this context, Alka Acharya (2005) notes that this was a new Chinese initiative as there was no such attempt in India earlier.

Every high-level visit is limited by time constraints. Hence, to assess the success of high-level interactions cannot be done by scaling the positive and negative perspectives of the joint statement of the two countries or media perceptions. Rather, success can be rightly assessed in the manner that policies make substantial progress over time in terms of implementation. Generally, in every high-level meeting between China and India, the locus has been mainly on border negotiations, and advancement of political, economic, cultural, and other aspects of cooperation, the posture that China and India share in the international situation and the upgradation of the partnership to new levels and so on. In short, emphasising on the resolution of old contentious issues and promoting new areas of cooperation in the bilateral relations.

Keeping this in view, during Wen's visit, main emphasis was on the objective need for China and India to work together to safeguard the interests of developing countries in the international system. Any China-India interaction is often weighed down by Western perceptions and speculations, which negatively influence the bonhomie of the two countries. In order to avoid such negative influences, as reported in Guo Ji Xian Qu Bao (*International Herald Tribune*) Wen Jiabao intentionally wanted to avoid the destabilising 'US factor' in the China-India relationship (Wang 2015:3). Here, it is important to note that the international perception of China-India relationship is complex. The Western media often views the relationship mainly from a competitive aspect, whereby the disputes form the common theme. However, in recent times, there has been an emerging perspective based on the comparative aspects of China and India providing common ground of interaction. There is a growing interest among both countries to ignore the over-reliance on Western sources to look at each other. For example, the USA's sale of arms to India prior to Wen Jiabao's visit did not cause any detrimental effect on the Sino-Indian relationship as exemplified in the upgradation of the relationship from "comprehensive cooperation" to "Strategic Partnership" (Wang 2015).

However, the views of other countries cannot be ignored in the sphere of international relations. In contrast, China continued to enhance its diplomatic approach towards India. Whether it is China's unilateral change in attitude or affected by the international environment is an important point of deliberation. On the eve of Wen's visit to India in April, the then US Secretary of State, Condoleezza Rice, during her visit to India in March had proclaimed that India is emerging as not just a regional power but as a global power (Rice 2005). Following this, a senior US official in an interview to ATP stated, "It was the 'goal' of the United States to help India become a major world power in the 21st century" (AFP 2005). Based on these American perceptions of India, it is argued that China's strategic behaviour towards India is influenced by the USA's growing attention to India, causing China to shift its perception of India from being "an important country within South Asia" to "jointly working together at the Asian level" (Kondapalli 2008). These positive behavioural dynamics between China and India are reflective of the changing perceptions that constructively define the present Sino-Indian relationship.

2.2.1. Cultural Factors in Wen's Perception of India

Chinese Premier Wen Jiabao's India visit also had a cultural element drawn mainly from India's rich cultural heritage. Prior to his visit, in his interaction with an Indian reporter on China-India relations in the press conference post election, Wen answered by citing sentences from the Upanishads and added his own understanding. Wen interpreted the Sino-Indian relationship and defined it as "Would like us sheltered, would wish us protected, would like us to work together, would like us to gain cultural glory. Do not hate, forever peace, peace, peace". This view of Wen got widespread attention from India. Citing the importance of this behaviour of Wen, Alka Acharya (2005) stated that "the civilisational context of the India-China relations must not be lost sight of: *Ma vidvishavaih, om shantih, shantih, shantih*!"

During his India visit on April 12, Wen Jiabao delivered a speech at the Indian Institute of Technology, New Delhi. Presenting a positive attitude, he emphasised on the need of strengthening friendship and expansion of cooperation as the key objectives of his visit. With this objective in mind, in his speech titled "Join Hands to Create a Better Future", he majorly cited quotations of famous

Indian literary figures on friendly exchanges between China and India, from the level of culture to strengthen ties between China and India, as well as positioning a new relationship between them. He cited the words of Tagore: "My friends, I do not know the reason, but I just feel like back home in China, I always feel that India is a very close relative of China, China and India are very old and close brothers". He also analysed the cultural origin between China and India drawing from the famous Chinese tale of 'Journey to the West' which is based on the history of the Buddhist monk, Xuan Zang, who went to India to study Buddhism during the Tang dynasty, to show the mutual exchanges between China and India and its influence in current times. This cultural exchange between China and India holds great significance both for the common public as well as contributes to the vision of the national leaders. The story has stood the test of time and is an example of the influence of public perception on leadership. For example, citing Amartya Sen's attitude on Sino-Indian relations, Wen suggested that it has contributed to the leadership's vision, as he points out that India and China should learn from each other, rather than debate on who will surpass whom (Wen 2005). It provides a strong foundation for the influence and persuasion of discourses by national leader.

In Wen Jiabao's speech, one of the primary references was to Dr. Dwarkanath Kotnis, a classic Indian reference of every Chinese leader vis-a-vis India. Dr. Kotnis is a positive connecting link between China and India for his selfless contribution to the people of China during the Sino-Japanese War. In great adulation of this Indian doctor, China shares a positive sentiment towards India. In commemorating Dr. Kotnis' contribution, Wen quoted Soong Ching Ling (Song Qingling) who is famously known as "The sincere friend of the Indian people", and stated: "*Ta sheng qian shi zai wei wei lai er fen dou, wei lai ye jiang yin ci fu yu ta jiao xian zai geng chong gao de guang rong*" (He was fighting for the future in his lifetime; thus, he will be given more noble than the present glory in the future).

From these references by Wen, it can be stated that national leaders use such examples as historical linkages that define the friendly exchanges between the two countries, which resonate beyond the limits of time and space.

2.2.2. *Chinese and Indian Perceptions in Media*

Wen Jiabao's India visit invited variant media perceptions from both the Chinese and Indian sides. Drawing from the joint statement issued by the two governments, the Indian media emphasised, "While China wanted India to state that it opposed the secession of Taiwan, India only reiterated its one-China policy. On Tibet, China wanted India to condemn any "separatist" activity, which was politely declined." (Shukla 2005). It was also suggested that China and India need to solve the border issue and China should not give nuclear technology support to countries that were hostile to India. Besides, China must show enough recognition and respect to India in Asia and the world (Virmani 2005). There were concerns over China's "all-weather friendship" with Pakistan and its implications for India. In addition, there were some positive views that emphasised the need to learn from each other in many areas between China and India (Khanna 2005), as well as set aside the border dispute and others.

In 2005, the then Chinese Ambassador to India, Sun Yuxi, expressed confidence in the great potential of China-India cooperation when he stated: "If we can speak in one voice it will be the strongest in the world". Sun's statement was reported in the Indian media. In addition, he expressed his expectations for resolution of the Sino-Indian border issue by anticipating the "border to be a bridge for exchanges of friendship" (Khanna 2005). Chinese scholars had cited the editorial of April 11, 2005 in Singapore's *Lianhe Zaobao*, which said it is rare to have such an unusual close contact and harmony in political, economic, religious and cultural fields like China and India as two neighbouring countries (Wang 2005). However, there was a more critical view from India on indicating the scale of interaction between India and China in the contemporary period, unlike the scale of interaction among all large neighbours in the world such as Mexico and the USA or Germany and France or South Africa and its neighbours, India and China share a very limited interaction (Khanna 2005).

While Chinese scholars noted that despite India's concerns over the "China threat theory", during Wen Jiabao's visit the India mainstream media's positive perceptions superseded the existing negative perceptions of China. The Chinese Premier speculated that the people of these two nations hope to eliminate misunderstanding and create peace and prosperity in the new century by cooperation. Nevertheless, the Chinese reporter Tang Lu in New Delhi came across some unfriendly voices, "China occupied territory belonging to India", "It is also possible there will be a battle between India and China in the future". Who said these words was just a 14-year-old Indian teenager (Wang 2005).

While Chinese scholars perceive that both politicians and scholars have learned a lesson from history they recognise that peace will benefit both while strife will harm both, the two countries would like to see the normalised and faster development of bilateral relations. The consensus between the two sides laid the foundation of such a belief (Ma 2005). Although the two countries exhibit different characteristics and expectations, their continued tendency to promote the changing views of all sectors of society under the objective needs of a new situation reflect the greater positive linkage between the two countries.

2.3. Hu Jintao's Visit to India in 2006

In 2006, Chinese President Hu Jintao visited India from November 20 to 23. His visit came at the interface of the 2006 APEC meeting held in Hanoi; he visited Pakistan from November 23 to 26. This high-level meeting between the heads of state of China and India came with greater expectations on bilateral relations. The high expectations can be assessed from the then Indian External Affairs Minister Pranab Mukherjee who, prior to Hu's visit, set the stage by stating: "There is enough space. Both of us can grow and there is no need of being competitive; we can be cooperative" (Baruah 2006). Even in this positive state of affairs, Hu's visit also witnessed the anxiety that persisted between the two countries. As for China, there were concerns related to the Indo-US Nuclear cooperation as a counter balance against China; moreover, there were contentions regarding Chinese companies in India as they faced challenges in entering some regions due to India's security considerations, and so on.

With respect to China's concerns vis-a-vis India, India clarified China's fear about the Indo-US nuclear deal aimed at balancing China by stating that the civil nuclear deal is a "guarded support to India's quest for civil nuclear energy and rejected perceptions that the growing relations between India and the USA were aimed at containing it" (PTI 2006). Clarifying China's concerns against US involvement in India, the then Indian Foreign Minister, Pranab Mukherjee, said, "It's our firm conviction that friendship with one country is not dependent on friendship with another country" (Baruah 2006). That is to say that India's relations with China are not determined by India's cooperative links with the USA. In contrast, the long-term friendly relations between China and Pakistan and China's providing military assistance to Bangladesh and Sri Lanka does cause an unease in India vis-a-vis China (Xiao 2006).

2.3.1. Perceptions during Hu Jintao's Visit

The mainstream media's major concern was centred on the unresolved border that perennially limits the scope of China-India relations although leaders of both countries, especially India's, increasingly emphasised that cooperation should not be stopped due to the contention at the border. Upholding this view, the then Indian External Affairs Minister, Pranab Mukherjee, in an interview reiterated the Indian government's position by responding that: "there could be difference of views between two countries, but that did not mean they could not cooperate in other areas. India and China could move ahead in trade and economic development." He further stated that the mechanism of special representatives would contribute to the gradual and peaceful settlement of the border problem (Baruah 2006). Thus, it is clear that despite the negative influences of the border issue, there exists a positive perception that both China and India should adopt a policy of peace and prosperity in dealing with any issue of contention in bilateral relations through dialogue and mutual exchange rather than any kind of conjecture.

Here, it is important to note that during Hu's India visit, the existing positive Indian attitude on the border was faced with certain setbacks. What is significant is the fact that Chinese President Hu Jintao's India visit coincided with China's announcement of a unilateral ceasefire and withdrawal of forces as happened on

November 20, 1962, bringing back memories of the 1962 debacle. The Chinese Ambassador to India, Sun Yuxi, strongly alleged that the region called "Arunachal Pradesh" under India's control which China calls "Southern Tibet" entirely belongs to China. This statement created a sudden stalemate in the relations resulting in the cancellation of the Special Envoys meeting scheduled to be held before the high-level meeting (Xiao, 2006). Similarly Chinese Foreign Minister Yang Jiechi made another contentious political remark on denial of Chinese visas to "Arunachalis", by pointing out that "The 'mere' fact of populated areas was insufficient reason for China to give up its territorial claims." This Chinese position on the border was perceived as an infringement and, thereby, seen as a violation of the 2005 Agreement signed between the two countries. This is so, as according to Article VII of the 2005 Agreement on Political Parameters and Guiding Principles, it states that "the two sides shall safeguard due interests of their settled populations in the border areas" (Jacob 2008: 63).

The prickly border issue implies the risk factors that challenge the 'trust' between China and India. Here, Srikanth Kondapalli (2008) notes that with the rapid growth of their economy and military, China and India "must no longer have mistrust and misunderstanding", as he proposed that China and India require to adopt a constant dialogue mechanism in order to avoid the serious challenges caused by mutual distrust and border issues while, former Indian Ambassador to China, C. Dasgupta, forecast that India's distrust of China may lead to China's retaliation, including an increase in aid to Pakistan, limit the development of Indian enterprises in China and other actions. Further, he added that China should not look down upon India, for only then would it eliminate India's guard against China (Xiao 2006). Hence, these varying perspectives on the border defined the dynamics of the China-India relationship during Hu Jintao's 2006 India visit.

Besides the border issue, the other major concern was based on the challenges faced by Chinese companies in doing business in India. In this regard, Chinese Ambassador Sun Yuxi in an interview to PTI pointed to the existing influence of bilateral distrust. He said that unlike companies of other foreign countries, Chinese companies faced discrimination in India and were not allowed in some areas (PTI 2006). The trade deficit between China and India is argued to have plagued the Indian government, but the Chinese government also suffered similar problems as "150 Indian companies invested in more than 2,000 projects in China while only 50 Chinese companies did so in India". In response to this phenomenon, an Indian expert on China trade, Srivastava, notes that before persuading India and convincing it to open up the market, China first needs to alleviate India's concerns regarding its national security. For example, with regard to Huawei, it raised India's vigilance when Huawei provided consulting facilities services for the Chinese military along with doing small business with the Indian military (Xiao 2006). These concerns raise security alarms in China-India relations.

2.3.2. China's Perception on Cultural Exchanges

One month before Hu's visit to India, the Sino-Indian Cultural Exchanges Seminar (Zhong Yin Wen Hua Jiao Liu Yan Tao Hui) was held in the Institute of Asia-Pacific Studies (IAPS) at the Chinese Academy of Social Sciences (CASS). Its report exemplified the views of the South Asian research community in China on Sino-Indian cultural exchanges as culture plays a special role in bilateral relations. This is evident from the fact that in the Sino-Indian Friendship Year, the exchanges are mainly centred on cultural activities. Cultural exchanges consolidate the political and economic relations between the two countries. In the setback period of China and India, the exchanges were not interrupted, which act as the "firewall" of exchanges between the two states. Such mutual learning makes it more conducive to understand each other through their own cultural "soft power" (Lan 2006).

Nevertheless, due to the relatively weak comprehensive national strength of the two countries, full-fledged cultural exchanges between the two countries suffer a significant deficit, which seems to persist for a long time. This is an important issue in the cultural cooperation between the two countries. There is a need to promote the status of culture by strengthening political and economic cooperation. It should be a part of the national strategy to develop the comprehensive national strength by means of cultural exchanges. In this regard, some academics have proposed attaching importance to the study of the role of traditional culture in the process of Indian modernisation, in particular 82 per cent of population was Hindu out of 1.09 billion (2005) Indians. Hinduism has a strong practical significance in Indian politics and culture and has not received enough attention by the Chinese. Reasonably, it affected the political, economic and other aspects in deep exchanges. The current focus of cultural exchanges between China and India is just based on Buddhism. However, only about 0.8 per cent of the Indian population is Buddhist (Lan 2006). Cultural exchange is an important need to foster political, economic and other aspects of support, but it also needs to provide a powerful auxiliary to political, economic and other aspects. Only then will it be established as a solid foundation for mutual trust between the two countries.

2.3.3. Perception of 'China Threat'

Before Hu's visit, a May 27 media report noted that the fear and mistrust of the past of many countries are being replaced by appreciation for China. It can be clearly seen from the changing attitude of India towards China. There is an increasing belief in India that China is an opportunity, not a threat (Xinhua Net 2006). However, here 'not a threat' does not signify that China can be completely trusted but rather can be cooperated with in some respects. In this view, the

Chinese media's analysis of the agreements signed between China and India on investment, promotion and protection on November 21 showed that Chinese companies met with a warning by the Indian security committee. Chinese media stated that the Indian security committee considers Chinese companies would pose a huge threat for India if these companies work on expanding airports in Indian major cities, as airports are considered "national security sites" (Xiao 2006). On the day of Hu's visit, it was reported by Indian television channels that there was a fear of Chinese companies undertaking spying activities in India. Such scepticism was denied by Indian officials on the ground of just being restriction for the project and the location but not aimed at any country specifically. The Chinese media reported that India no longer recognised China as a "threat" although the Indian media quoted the security committee warning that Chinese companies close to India's "national security site" could be "a huge threat". These complexities create an imbalance in Sino-Indian relations based on the nature of their diversity and variability.

In respect to such perceptions on the "China threat", Chinese scholars point to Indian Prime Minister Manmohan Singh's expression of China and India's belief that "the prospects for the common development of China and India is bright" (Wang 2009: 366). While Sino-Indian relations are developing in the process of normalisation, Indian scholars have identified "little doubt", as they argue that though India and China "have acquired a fair degree of political comfort", they are "merely conflict-free, though suspicion-prone". It is not a temporary establishment between China and India and, therefore, impossible to eliminate in the short term. Hence, Sino-Indian relations need the process of dialogue which should be "meaningful, substantial and in real earnest" (Acharya 2006).

2.4. Manmohan Singh's Visit to China 2008

In 2008, Indian PM Manmohan Singh visited China from January13 to 15. During the high-level meeting between the leaders of the two countries, Manmohan Singh and his Chinese counterpart, Premier Wen Jiabao, held talks and signed an agreement on "A Shared Vision for the 21st Century of the Republic of India and the People's Republic of China" on January 14. Apart from Wen, Singh, during his visit also met the then Chinese President, Hu Jintao, and Chairman and Party Secretary of the Standing Committee of the National People's Congress, Wu Bangguo. One of the significant features of Singh's China visit is his speech at the Chinese Academy of Social Sciences (CASS) on January 15 that primarily reflected his perceptions on culture, communication and expectations from Sino-Indian bilateral relations.

2.4.1. Manmohan Singh's Cultural Perceptions of China

One of the central aspects that defined Manmohan's Singh's 2008 China visit is his vision of a collaborative role played by China and India in Asia in particular and the world at large. Having an optimistic view, Singh pointed that "there is enough space for both India and China to grow and prosper while strengthening our cooperative engagement" (Singh 2008). Adding to the scope of engagement based on expanding the economy between the two countries in recent years, as well as on linkage built from multilateral organisations, Singh further emphasised on the historical aspect that the "two great civilisations flourished for centuries side by side, interacting and influencing each other" (Singh 2008). As bilateral exchanges continue to penetrate all areas, hence, to maintain this positive influence, it is imperative to deepen and improve the exchanges keeping a long-term perspective.

Against the backdrop of common challenges faced by China and India in terms of extremism, Singh proposed that China and India should "demonstrate the benefits of moderation and peaceful co-existence" as non-state entities are a result of "intolerance and narrow understanding of identity". With recurrent terrorist attacks in the two countries, Singh suggested that it was wise for both China and India to act together to fight against terrorism. In this context, Singh posited the vision of an "Asian way" based on peaceful co-existence, which implies the two civilisations have common aspirations and exhibit great potential to contribute to world peace. To produce the resultant force from the two civilisations, the two governments should work together and that would require intellectuals, thinkers, and academics to work closely "through a free flow of ideas and sharing of different perspectives" to "build upon the edifice of our civilisational links" (Singh 2008).

In his speech, Manmohan Singh cited Ji Xianlin's idea and considered that it was a very insightful summary. He stated that "It is history as well as reality that China and India, these two great cultural circles, had learnt from each other, influenced each other and promoted mutual cultural development" (Ibid). From this perspective, it can be attributed that research scholars provide adequate perspective on the understanding of relationships between two countries, influencing the perspectives of the national leadership. For example, Ji Xianlin found similar spellings of the word 'sugar' in several different languages and how it was associated with the nomenclature of several countries. He explored the cultural exchanges among China, India and other countries tracing the history of sugar (Ji 1986:153; Ji 1998). He found there were many cultural similarities between China and India led by his passion and spirit that do not ignore any details. His research is not only highly respected in China, but also got compliments from the Indian government. This can be exemplified in the fact that after Singh's China visit, the Indian President announced awarding Ji Xianlin with the high honour of an Indian Padma Bhushan award (IANS 2008).

2.4.2. The Proposition and Development of "Chindia"

The concept of "Chindia" was coined and first used by Indian scholar Jairam Ramesh on April 18, 2005 in his article published by the *Wall Street Journal* and later advocated by a renowned scholar on Chinese history, Sino-Indian relations and cultural exchange, Tan Chung (Ramesh 2005; Yin 2014). Tan translated "Chindia" as "*Zhong Yin Da Tong*" in Chinese and tried to set off a "Chindia" movement in the academic arena. Besides, Chinese scholar Wang Dehua developed this idea and conceived '*Long-xiang Gongwu*' (Dragon-Elephant Tango) as an "analogy for the idea of 'Chindia'" (Tan 2008: xviii). Tan Chung along with many scholars from China and India wrote articles and published books to promote this concept which initially aimed at economic cooperation and later let to a lot of different ideas (Tan 2007). Some scholars considered that "Chindia" was a cultural symbol with less than two years of existence. It was seem not to be handled by the government but as a peaceful exchange of spiritual values and material goods between people. Upholding this spirit of bonhomie, Madhavi Thampi (2007:310) posited that the government should eliminate the political obstacles in people-to-people contacts. Some scholars believed that Ramesh's conception of "Chindia" aimed to describe the rich, long and complex relationship between China and India, while it was argued that the relationship between China and India should not be limited to Buddhist cultural exchanges, but rather seek to understand the status and role of Chinese and Indian cultures in the world from a wider range (Qiu 2007:440). In this perspective, some scholars such as B. R. Deepak (2007) proposed that the solution to the Sino-Indian border issue can provide the premise to actualise the construct of "Chindia".

"Chindia" has been supported under the cultural umbrella in both China and India. Despite its positive understanding, the idea has also attracted various speculations. In this view of thought, Pallavi Aiyar considered "Chindia" as a fantasy while Gautam Das thought that to compare India and China is relatively useless as it hurts the feelings of the Indian and Chinese public. It is only applicable for catching the eye and enhance advertising value. There are individuals who strongly believe that China and India have been "years of civilisation opponents" (Yin 2014:189) while most military sources, media reports, and political and scholarly views did not promote the idea as it was seen to be a typical idealistic doctrine. The negative understanding of "Chindia" resulted in criticism of the Ministry of Home Affairs and the attitude of the security sector in India regarding defence against China in May 2010. The founder of "Chindia", Jairam Ramesh, faced a political siege by public opinion and ultimately had to apologise for the trouble (Yin 2014:256-273). This created an obstruction in the promotion of the "Chindia" concept but later Tan Chung revived it by stating that China and India should learn from each other, and that they should mutually recognise the achievements of each other's civilisation to truly and deeply understand each other. Hence, it was argued that it needs time to reach the "Chindia" ideal and required cultural exchanges in an ideal state; only then more people will come together to support "Chindia" (Tan 2011; Yin 2014). What is more important to note, comparing with Tan's promotion of the concept of "Chindia", is that Jawaharlal Nehru's view after the 1962 Sino-Indian border conflict, wherein Nehru, in his speech at Vishva-Bharti University, stated: "We do not go to war with China...... Chinese people are not our enemy" (Tan 2008a). Nehru's remarks exemplify his complicated inclination towards making peace with China.

2.4.3. The Concept of "Chindia" in Chinese Perceptions

The concept of "Chindia" has been a very popular jargon used in China's mainstream media such as the *People's Daily*, Xinhua News Agency, etc., in describing China-India cooperation during Singh's visit. Sceptical about the feasibility of this unified construct, some scholars have argued "Chindia" to be an impossible utopia. While believing in the potential of China and India based on their historical friendly exchanges, some scholars posit that the deep similarities between the cultural heritage of China and India contribute to greater cooperative linkages. In this context, the theoretical basis of "Chindia" is grounded on the harmony theory and cultural values of both China and India. It is also interpreted as an emotional construct originating from the two thousand-years history of friendly cultural exchanges between China and India. However, in contemporary times, the people-to-people contacts between the two countries is weak and limited as compared to the ancient exchanges, thereby, their understanding of each other stands to be superficial and poor. In order to fill this gap, it is believed that both countries need to promote their friendship and deepen the understanding between their people. This also contributes to the creation of a conducive environment to solve conflicts and promote peaceful settlement of disputes. In this view, Wu Yongnian (2008) points out that "Chindia" should not only put China and India together emotionally but should also embody the seeking of a new, non-confrontational model and mutual respect in international relations in the international community.

Some scholars believe that the effect of "Chindia" could not reach beyond the scope of the two countries due to their clash of interests in the international sphere. For example, once the voting rights of China was expanded in the IMF, the right of India became narrow. India wants to increase its iron ore price while China is the world's largest importer of iron ore. The tightness between the two countries has improved significantly, but the progress of cooperation in the international context is slow. Both sides need to come up with a broader international vision to inject new vitality in the bilateral relations. With such existing contentions, "Chindia" should not just be a slogan and expand cooperation in one area, but needs to facilitate comprehensive development in diversified areas (Ye 2008).

2.4.4. *Border Issue: A Bone of Contention in India's Perception of China*

One of the major factors that contribute to shape India's perception towards China is the protracted border issue. The relationship is often weighed down by the unresolved sovereignty issue at the border. In this vein, the border problem remains to be the primary highlight in Indian mainstream media, wherein India raised concerns over China's 'incursion'. As Indian Foreign Minister Pranab Mukherjee admits concerns over Chinese incursions, he says there is "no need to panic". He contends that "mechanisms which were established to address these border problems are doing well, so nothing need to be worried". When questioned about the increasing frequency of incursions, Mukherjee pointed out that "It is not unusual (but) it has not suddenly increased (ENS 2008)". Such Chinese activities along the border have resulted in strengthening of India's negative perception of China. In this regard, what Indian scholars argue is that any such action from the Chinese side can result in a strong reaction in India. It becomes important for China to pay attention to this characteristic, so that both sides can have an objective position to deal with the issue and be familiar with each other's problems. Although the two sides stand for peaceful resolution of the border problem as agreed to in the 2005 Agreement, having different notions of "interest" in their respective cognitive systems can cause disputes to lead to a great stir in the development of China-India relations (Jacob 2008).

2.5. Wen Jiabao's Visit to India in 2010

Chinese Premier Wen Jiabao visited India from December 15 to 17, 2010, on an invitation from Indian PM Manmohan Singh. It was his second visit since he took office as Chinese Premier in 2005. Since then, both Wen and Singh have met ten times in the past six years and established a personal rapport based on their close contacts and the operationalisation of a hotline agreed for "enhancing mutual understanding necessary to de-escalate tensions and reduce misperceptions" (Kondapalli 2010). Their personal equation also contributed to fostering multilateral cooperation between China and India based on their consistent views on various issues at large (Ibid.). Since each high-level visit contributes to deeper exchanges, Wen Jiabao considered his India visit as an opportunity to have "in-depth exchange of views and strategic communications" with Manmohan Singh and other Indian leaders with the objective of deepening friendship, expanding practical cooperation and increasing people-to-people exchanges (*The Indian Express* 2010). Wen Jiabao's India visit came at an opportune time as 2010 marked the 60th anniversary of Sino-Indian diplomatic ties. The positive atmosphere of Sino-Indian ties provided an impetus to Wen's India visit in all aspects.

2.5.1. *The Continuous Extension of the Ideas Exchange between Leaderships*

Chinese leaders like to use the word "great" to describe the people of India. It also attracted the attention of the Indian media which was directly quoted in a news headline: "India a great neighbour, says Wen Jiabao" (*The Indian Express* 2010). "When we two nations communicate heart to heart, I believe the world will pay attention and listen" (Wen 2010). The ideology started by the two leaders continued to be expanded from top to bottom. When the two countries reach a consensus, it will form influence in the international arena. The two leaders exchanged ideas at one point. The words from the national highest point will produce a different effect in the two countries with different regimes. Relatively speaking, the presentation of this view in China would perhaps play a greater role than in India; at least, it will attract more attention in the social vanguard who are concerned about the trends of national leaders to understand the attitude of the Chinese government towards India and have an impact on more public views towards India in China.

There is a gap between national leadership and the public at the point of understanding each other; because of the lack of adequate understanding about each other, people do not have such positive attitude as leaders do. In India, they once saw China as a 'threat' that later evolve into a 'challenge' (Tang 2010). The views of the public may not change as fast as the leadership. However, the positive attitude of the leaders to their neighbours will gradually affect a change among the people.

2.5.2. China's Cultural Perceptions of India

During his 2010 visit, Wen Jiabao in his speech at the Indian Council of World Affairs (ICWA), New Delhi, cited references from the Indian classics providing a guiding thought to India's cultural heritage. Drawing from the Upanishads, he stated: "The truth is paramount and the common ground of understanding". Upholding this philosophical thought, Wen applied it to explain the reason behind the growing consensus between China and India. As he said, it is premised on the common understanding of "truth": "independence, autonomy, and self-reliance are the soul of a nation. Only by being open and inclusive can a country be prosperous. The world has enough space for the common development of China and India. There are sufficient areas for Sino-Indian cooperation." It is clear that the growing consensus is reflected in terms of treating each other as "old friend", and the build-up and cooperative behaviour led to trusting each other by the two nations in international affairs. It also forms the basis for the "the traditions deeply rooted in the Chinese and Indian traditional culture and the long history of exchanges" and the "correct understanding of the world situation as well as the profound understanding of the national interest". The very nature of this growing consensus can be seen in Wen's own words when he states: "Only by being open and inclusive can a country become prosperous", thereby making this approach a common adaptation on either side to strengthen ties (Wen 2010).

In this note, Wen Jiabao's interpretation of Sino-Indian ties is dominantly shaped by the Chinese understanding of Indian culture based on elite beliefs, media perceptions and the ideas of common people. Besides customarily mentioning the common links of Buddhism and Tagore, Wen also stated the role of the Silk Road and Ji Xianlin in his speech for the first time. Ji Xianlin, a Padma Bhushan awardee by the President of India in 2008, inspired ideas of Indian officials and attracted the attention of the Chinese leadership. This reflects the role of scholars in shaping perceptions. Ji Xianlin who has been widely recognised in both China and India once posited that "The long history and deep impact in the history of exchanges between China and India is rare in the history of world civilisation." His idea also influenced the view of the leaderships. It provided proof for the leaders in their speeches and preserved many cultural memories in the two thousand-year history of friendly exchanges between the two countries. It mentioned the rich association between the two countries. Based on these perspectives, Wen believed that leaders on either side could discern bilateral relations in historical depth when they "get wisdom and courage from each other's rich cultural accumulation" as compared against the backdrop of a rich historical legacy; "big setbacks" such as the 1962 border conflict in Sino-Indian relations perhaps eventually become a "brief page" (Wen 2010).

Apart from the cultural influences of his speech, Wen's cultural perception of India was also driven by his behaviour when he paid homage at the memorial of Gandhi reflecting China's admiration and respect for India's 'Father of the Nation'.. This Chinese behaviour is attributed to the "precious support" given by Gandhi during the Chinese liberation, which is a constant reminder of India's China link among the Chinese leadership. In this way, such historical interactions between the two civilisations expanded the horizons and generated a positive effect. It also built confidence for national leaders to continuously enrich bilateral relations so that the two civilisations could "cast new glories of oriental civilisation" (Ibid.).

Popular art also contributed to Wen's perceptions of India. During an interaction with Indian filmmakers, Wen reacted by his impromptu singing of the famous theme song from an Indian classic movie *Awara* thereby reflecting another positive element of India in Chinese minds. Since popular art has a unique role in promoting cultural exchanges between the people of two countries, it was suggested that both China and India should promote exchanges and cooperation in the area of films. The influence of movies on people's thought is very strong-and can positively or negatively influence perceptions of the other. In this aspect, the movie *Awara*, which was screened in the 1950s and 1970s in China, became a cultural connect between China and India (Zhang 2014). It can be stated that the practitioners in various fields actually play a more effective link in the cultural areas of China and India. *Awara* directly established the connection between the life and thought of the Chinese and Indian peoples.

Wen Jiabao also visited the Tagore International School (TIS) which has exchange programs with the Shanghai Jinyuan High School. The two schools provide distance-learning courses for bilateral cooperation on Yoga, calligraphy and other cultural programs. Tagore International School is very close to many Chinese schools on exchange programs. In the interaction with students from TIS, Wen talked about Indian cultural exchanges, calligraphy, the impact of Tagore on China and taught simple Chinese leaving the enlightenment of cultural exchange in the minds of the students. All these instances of Wen Jiabao's India visit reflected the strong cultural aspects that guided his diplomatic tour. There is a strong sentimental rhetoric based on cultural practices that defined every aspect of Wen's perception of India.

2.5.3. The Imbalanced Perceptions of the Media

The misrepresentations in media negatively influence the relational index. For example, during his visit, Wen referred to Tagore at the Tagore International School wherein he had said that Chinese writers such as Bing Xin, Liang Qichao, and Xu Zhimo's writings were influenced by Tagore. However, the Indian media's misrepresentation of facts by reporting Bing Xin as Lu Xun who actually made negative comments when Tagore visited China created a perceptual gap in the relations (Bhatt 2010; Yin and Zhang 2001). When the two leaders reached consensus on a number of cooperative agreements, the key Indian media concerns revolved around issues that had not been addressed, such stapled visas to people from Jammu and Kashmir, terrorism emanating from Pakistan and India's aspirations to become a Permanent Member of the UNSC, and so on. The media also misrepresented the Chinese Premier's outlook towards India's free press. Wen said he "understand[s] that the press in India had freedom but it should play a role in promoting friendship" (*The Indian Express* 2010). This is the big difference between public opinion in the Indian and Chinese media. The Chinese media paid more attention to emphasise the positive side while the Indian media mostly pointed out the contending problems in the relationship. Nevertheless, it was also conducive to see clearly the problems, such as *The Indian Express* reported that Karan Singh refused the China friendship award in order to avoid unnecessary problems. The Indian media also pointed out that China provided flood data to India on a payment of Rs. 12 lakh per annum. In contrast, India provides similar flood warnings to Pakistan and Bangladesh "free of cost as a goodwill gesture" (Ibid.). It even reminded that for the first time India made no reference to the 'One China' policy as mentioned in earlier summit-level meetings as a response to Beijing's "silence on J & K" (Samanta 2010).

Regarding the Chinese media, a survey by Global Net showed that in 2001 more than 50 per cent of netizens considered China-India relations as a 'Dragon-Elephant Fight' and 20 per cent believed the idea of a 'Dragon-Elephant Tango'. To discard the asymmetrical media perceptions created by misrepresentation of facts, it is imperative for both the Chinese and Indian media to exchange communications in order to minimise the perceptual gaps and, thereby, positively influence the quality and scope of their reports. In this context, Lan Jianxue stated that it should extend the balance of the information; only then will the rationality of the report be improved and hostility reduced between the people (Wu 2010). Similarly, Tansen Sen (2012: 296) argues that "the Indian media must devote resources to cover China not through sensational news reports, but by presenting insightful views and factual information".

In the Hindi media, it was reported that China celebrated the opening of a key tunnel to Tibet before Chinese Premier Wen Jiabao's visit to India. It raised India's concerns over the sensitive issue of the border problem with China. It concluded with the note that China's steadfast move may actually instigate India to develop its infrastructure in 'Arunachal Pradesh' (*Navbharat Times* 2010). Maintaining a positive view on the China-India relationship, *Navbharat Times* stated that though the high-level visits between China and India were mechanical they linked the societies of both the countries through people-to-people contacts that would will surely contribute to an emotional bonding between China and India. (बैंकिंग, आईटी और मीडिया, तीनों ही क्षेत्रों में भारत के पास चीन को बेचने के लिए काफी कुछ है और ये तीनों ही कारोबार कूटनीति से ऊपर उठकर आम आदमी के स्तर पर भारत और चीन के जुड़ाव की जमीन तैयार करेंगे। नेताओं का आना-जाना अभी भले मशीनी हो लेकिन दोनों देशों के समाज जुड़ेंगे तो भावना के लिए भी कुछ न कुछ जगह जरूर निकल आएगी।)

2.6. Li Keqiang's Visit to India and Manmohan Singh's Visit to China in 2013

The year 2013 marked an important phase in China-India relations with the mutual visits of the Prime Ministers of both sides. Chinese Premier Le Keqiang's visit to India from May 19 to 21 was reciprocated by Indian Prime Minister Manmohan Singh's China visit in October 22-24. It was the first foreign visit by Premier Le since he took office in 2013 and Prime Minister Manmohan Singh's last visit to China before leaving office. This mutual exchange of high-level leadership between China and India in 2013 is parallel similar exchanges between Premier Zhou Enlai and Prime Minister Jawaharlal Nehru in 1954, widely accepted on both sides as of "great significance" in laying the foundation of Panchsheel to define Sino-Indian relations based on peaceful coexistence.

2.6.1. Premier Li Keqiang's Cultural Perceptions of India and China

On 20 May 2013, Chinese Premier Li Keqiang, during his visit to India, published an article titled "A Handshake Across the Himalayas" in India's mainstream English-language newspaper *The Hindu* as well as the Hindi newspaper *Dainik Jagran*. Such an act on the part of the Chinese leadership was the first of its kind. It was an act of direct interaction with the people of the country and a strong means of public diplomacy to connect via the Indian national media. What is important to note is that Li Keqiang, in his article, mainly drew from the cultural linkages that formed the bond between China and India since ancient times. The primary reference was to Chinese Buddhist monks Fa Xian and Xuan Zang's visits to India and Indian monk Bodhidharma's visit to China, thereby making the earliest contribution to the religious cultural exchanges between China and India. In this way, Buddhism acts as a strong cultural connect contributing to greater friendship and historical exchanges between China and India thus, forming a primary reference point for the leaders and people of both the countries to exemplify the ancient roots to the contemporary relationship.

In his article, Li reminisced about his personal connections with India. He mentioned that during his service as the head of the China youth organisation, he had first visited in India about 27 years earlier, which left him with a strong impression of Indian culture and society. Drawing on his earliest India connections, Li shared his interest of reading the poems of Indian poet Rabindranath Tagore at a young age which left him with a deep insight of the friendship between Tagore and Chinese literary giants. Here, it is important to note that Li's reference to Tagore is suggestive of the way intellectuals play an important and positive role in the psyche of the people. It also denotes the Chinese national leader's perception of India through the writings of Tagore. Apart from Tagore, Li also mentioned about his interaction and gaining insights from the ideas of a Chinese Indologist at his Alma Mater in Peking University. Although he did not name the Indologist, it is generally conceived to be Ji Xianlin, who was the only Chinese Sanskrit expert and a Padma Bhushan awardee. Ji Xianlin was an important representative in the contemporary period who promoted Sino-Indian relations through cultural linkages. Ji Xianlin has been a popular reference point in the articles and speeches of the Chinese leadership visiting India, mainly since 2008 after he was awarded the Padma Award by the Government of India. His expression of understanding China-India relations as "created by heaven and constructed by earth" is repeatedly mentioned in the texts since 2010 after Premier Wen argued of shortening the distance and thinking about the position of bilateral relations. This constant drawing from insights of influential scholars proves that such representative ideas greatly shape leadership perceptions towards other countries.

It is a known fact that traditional culture plays an important role in defining the national identity and, so, greatly impacts a country's national ideology and behavioural norms. In this light, Li Keqiang's perception of China is greatly shaped by the Chinese way of thinking premised on the foundation of ancient traditional Chinese culture, of which, the teachings of Confucius from some 2000 years ago form the primary knowledge base. Confucius' famous proclamation "*Jisuo buyu, wushi yuren*" which means "Don't treat others differently than you would like to be treated" (Jiao and Stone 2014: 13), as well as the traditional thinking of "*Jiangxin xiumu*" which means "honouring promises and living in harmony" and "*Qinren Shanlin*" which means "benevolence and good-neighbourliness" form the core of Chinese traditional thinking that strongly shapes current thinking and the lives of Chinese people. In the current context, China was being perceived in the rubric of its 'rise' that drew greater attention and speculations from all over the globe on the manner in which China would rise. Under this pretext, Li Keqiang's article laid emphasis on alleviating the worldwide fears and concerns on China's rise. For there was a worldwide perception of China's rise as a threat to other countries, but what China was looking for is peaceful coexistence and common development. Here, Li's reference to traditional culture in alleviating the fears is argued on the grounds of acting as the guideline for relations with other countries in order to establish credibility, mutual understanding and tolerance among nations. Confucian thought contributes to China's self-discipline and presents other countries a peg to reflect China's benign intention and behaviour in international politics.

2.6.2. The Convincing Ability of Civilisation and Cultural Traditions

During his India visit in 2013, Chinese Premier Li Keqiang was invited by the Indian Council of World Affairs (ICWA), New Delhi to deliver a speech on 21 May 2013 under the theme "China, India must grasp fresh opportunities in strategic cooperation". Similarly, Indian Prime Minister Manmohan Singh during his China visit delivered a speech on "India and China in the New Era" on October 24 at the Central Party School of the Communist Party of China in Beijing. What is noteworthy is that while Li Keqiang highlighted the emotional quotient in defining Sino-Indian relations based on cultural ties, Singh ignored the cultural linkage between the two nations and focussed attention on the economic factors that determine the strengths of the relationship.

In dealing with the words of the "ancient civilisation", Li seemed more focused on highlighting the emotional strength of the word which can be used to solve the acute problems faced by common interests between the two countries, that is, the border issue. In order to broaden the vision of the two countries to treat problems, Li stressed that the two "ancient civilisations" have sufficient wisdom to solve problems while Manmohan Singh seemed very cautious to use words when he referred to the rapid economic growth with a special mention that both countries should also attach great importance to the protection of the fragile environment. Singh proposed that "both India and China are heirs to civilisations that value nature and have practised sustainability through the ages" (Singh 2013). He further stressed that in the face of challenges, both countries need to expand responsibility and connotation of the two "ancient civilisations". From the speeches of both the leaders, it is clear that they aimed at producing synergy in the relationship and shape the global image in a wider vision. Li Keqiang said that the ancient civilisations can "generate fresh vitality" reflecting on the cultural characteristics that can contribute to a shared vision. In the eyes of Chinese leaders, the cultural essence of the two countries lies in learning to deal with current "deep-seated problems and challenges facing mankind".

2.6.3. Shape Image and Mutual Principle by Culture

Based on the principle of peaceful development, the Chinese leadership wants to shape the path of Chinese growth and development. To promote this Chinese thinking, Premier Li in his speech quoted the teachings of Confucius, "*Jisuo buyu, Wushi yuren*" which means "Don't treat others differently than you would like to be treated". This statement by China's top leadership reflects China's benign intention in the phenomenon of 'China rise' to be "a staunch defender of world peace" based on the "deep insights" drawn from Chinese history. The usage of Confucius's teachings by the Chinese leadership projects China's national identity drawn from traditional culture. This identity has evolved with the passage of time as China has refrained from giving up the essence of culture practised some 2,000 years ago. In its attempt to have peaceful development, China draws on its ancient cultural norms. In this light, Li during his India visit promoted the idea that India should also learn to know about Chinese ancient culture in order to gain deeper insights into China's current thinking, both its interests and its actions in the international arena.

2.6.4. Perceptions and the Gap in Theory and Practice of Cultural Norms

In understanding the importance of 'culture' in the China-India relationship, it becomes imperative to probe deep into the query as to 'how cultural exchange at the leadership level contributes to the relationship?', 'how it can be used as driving force in defining the relationship' and others. In answering these queries, one needs to probe deeper into assessing whether the culture factor can add to China's advantage by promoting its benign image or will it result in negative outcomes due to the inconsistency in theory and practice of the cultural quotient. Hence, to avoid such consequences that result in misunderstanding of China's intentions based on the cultural aspect, it needs someone to stand up, explain and clarify. In this respect, it becomes a necessity for each country to accept responsibility for their own cultures and respective value systems.

There is a gap in the theory and practice of cultural understanding as promoted in the Confucius idea of "*Jisuo buyu, Wushi yuren*" which means "Don't treat others differently than you would like to be treated", which can be explained by the example of the "Tent Confrontation" that occurred between China-India at the contested border area on 15 April 2013. Clarifying China's stand on the matter, a spokesman of the Chinese Foreign Ministry said that China did not cross the border and had strictly abided by the agreements signed between the two countries (Xinhua 2013) while a well-known Chinese military think tank claimed the incident to be an accident, and not a deliberate move (Bagchi 2013). Apart from these viewpoints, a Chinese media report quoted the view of the deputy director of the China Institute of International Studies, Professor Dong Manyuan, who attributed the accident to the influence of the historic emotion from the Nehru era, in which India has always perceived China as an enemy since the 1962 border conflict. In this context, in the last 60 years after the founding of the P. R. of China, 90 per cent of China's land disputes have been settled through negotiations. With this positive view, it is anticipated that the China-India border dispute can be resolved through communication (Yuan 2013). However, such a positive mediation between China and India seems problematic as both sides hold diametrically opposite perceptions as exemplified in the "Tent Confrontation", when China failed to give a clear interpretation, while India reported it as China's "invasion", hence, projecting the clash of viewpoints on the two sides.

This disjuncture in perceptions can be assessed from the opposing viewpoints. It was reported that China's action was in protest against India's "construction of some temporary posts and bunkers at Chumar and Fukche near the LAS in Eastern Ladakh over the last four to five years" (TNN 2013; Lee 2013). However, after 20 days of negotiations, the two sides reached an agreement to settle the military standoff whereby the Indian side agreed to dismantle the bunker at Chumar. In addition, the Chinese side also asked the Indian side to demolish listening and video facilities along the Line of Actual Control, prevent Ladakh nomadic herders from entering Chinese territory, and others (Goswami 2013). With such mediation, the "Tent Confrontation" ended through negotiations between China and India on May 5 (Bukhari and Bhattacharjya 2013). In the aftermath of the resolution of the standoff, the Indian army built a road in the disputed region in August 2013, which directly led to another military standoff between China and India that thus acted as a destabiliser in the relations during Chinese President Xi Jinping's visit to India in September 2014.

Therefore, from the above incidental mishaps between China and India, it is clear that both sides have the responsibility to convey accurate information and clear explanations as only then will there be a possibility of establishing a positive perception of each other and deal efficiently with the situational crisis, elevating the potential of the bilateral relations as both sides can maximise their benefits from each other by adopting mutual cooperation instead of being suspicious of each other. For example, the 1962 border conflict has negatively impacted India's image of China in the aftermath of the signing of the "Five Principles of Peaceful Coexistence" among Burma, China and India in 1954, while China attributed the causality of the conflict to India's occupation of Chinese territory in the "Southern Tibet" region, which India calls "Arunachal Pradesh". Hence, from these varying perspectives, it is clear that there is a strong perceptual gap between China and India based on opposite cognitive perceptions of each other towards each other.

2.6.5. Played down the Cultural, Economics in Command in Singh's Talk

Indian Prime Minister Manmohan Singh during his 2013 China visit delivered a lecture at the Central Party School of the Communist Party of China. It attracted a wide audience comprising the executive Vice-President of the Central Party

School, He Yingting and Chinese Foreign Minister Wang Yi, along with more than 500 participants from the Party School (Zhou 2013) whom Singh recognised as key actors in playing a decisive role in shaping China's future development, which will be of great significance for Asia and the world. In this case, choosing the Central Party School as the forum to address the Chinese audience received significant attention from both Chinese and Indian media identifying the relevance of the choice of location. Professor Su Hao from China's Foreign Affairs University pointed out that it signifies the importance China attached to Indian Prime Minister's China visit (Ma 2013). Similarly, the Indian media also shared the same view on the primacy attached to Singh's visit based on the high stature of the Central Party School in China as it has trained a large number of senior Chinese leaders (Ma 2013).

In his speech, PM Manmohan Singh described the Sino-Indian relationship as that of being "unique in the world". He stressed that the two countries are "two continuous ancient civilisations" and "neighbours having a long history of cultural, spiritual and economic ties". With limited focus on the shared cultural linkage, unlike his Chinese counterpart, Li Keqiang, PM Singh put greater emphasis on the existing economic equation between China and India. Understanding the Indian demand, Singh pointed to India's critical challenges and proposed areas of opportunities for cooperation between India and China. He highlighted eight areas of cooperation: infrastructure, urbanisation, China's manufacturing and India's service sector, energy security, food security and resources, conducive international economic environment, climate change and common challenges. In this regard, Singh suggested that India needs China's expertise and investment in these sectors and that both countries can learn from each other and thus form a win-win cooperation to face the challenges. With a positive outlook, Singh (2013) posited that China and India can together contribute "for enhancing the security and stability of the two nations in different levels; all it needs is a cooperative, inclusive and rule-based security architecture. It is also in their mutual interest and more effective cooperation. India and China should share an enterprise that stronger connectivity will lead more stability and prosperity."

While a majority of the Indian mainstream media and public still have speculative emotions about China, Singh, in contrast, contended that both countries cannot use "old theories of alliance and containment" as it is "no longer relevant" in order to deal with each other. He believed that the two countries cannot be contained and that they should not seek to contain others. Singh called for greater emphasis on the achievements of great cooperation between the two countries. This perception of economic engagement in bringing the two countries together is widely accepted by some scholars in India as well as forms a majoritarian view of the Chinese scholarship. Prioritising economy as a key factor, Singh stated that "the most dynamic area" is "economic" in bilateral relations as exemplified in the fact that China is one of India's largest economic partners. He also clearly indicated that India's strategic partnerships with other countries are defined by primarily its economic interests, needs and aspirations, in which case China too shares a "similar approach". Therefore, for a common destiny and closer cooperation between China and India, Singh proposed "seven practical principles of engagement", which entail mutual respect, peace and tranquillity in border, trans-border rivers, trade imbalance, high level of strategic communication and consultations, cooperation on regional and global issues and harnessing the full potential of cooperation in all aspects, especially mentioning the economic area. Besides, in his final assessment of the China-India relationship, Manmohan Singh called for greater contacts and familiarity between the people "in every walk of life" to tap the full potential of the relationship. Therefore, unlike Li Keqiang, for Manmohan Singh the crux lay in prioritising economics over culture as an important contributing factor in shaping the Sino-Indian relationship.

Comparing the speeches of the two Prime Ministers in the same time frame, reflects the existing asymmetry in their perceptions. It therefore, represents the characteristic of the bilateral relations and reflects the strategic equation of the two countries and mainly denotes the status of the two countries in each other's policy framework.

2.6.6. The Views of Chinese and Indian Media on the Two Visits

CHINESE MEDIA

In assessing both the high-level visits of 2013, the Chinese media paid more attention to the consensus reached between the two countries and on the development of relations based on more harmonious views while the media emphasized on the impetus given by the visits to the positive growth of the bilateral relations. Presenting a positive attitude, the Chinese media captured the positive report of the Indian media and then actively voiced it from China. For example, even on the tensions at the border, the Chinese media maintained a positive tone, drawn from the Indian media's point of view, which suggested Premier Li Keqiang's visit to India as "very timely" against the backdrop of the military standoff at the border between the two countries. In this light, Li's visit was termed as a 'landmark visit' and a 'historic event', clearly denoting the importance that both China and India attach to each other in bilateral relations (Wu 2013).

While reporting the events, the Chinese Foreign Ministry's report which was also reproduced by the *People's Daily* stated: "The Indian media had a number of highlighted reports that said Li Keqiang's visit will be to get rid of the historical burden of China-India relations; it will provide an opportunity to open an innovation situation". To highlight the Indian perceptions, the Chinese media drew from the views of reporters, editors from various popular media forums such as *First Post*, *The Indian Express*, *The Herald*, *Outlook*, *Economic Times*, *Hindustan Times*, *Political Rights* and others to reflect Indian expectations from Li Keqiang's visit, the good faith to resolve the border issue and the positive attitude towards India-China cooperation. The Indian media also highlighted the declaration of the two countries of 2014 as the "Year of Friendly Exchanges" to strengthen the exchange of youth and media with the thought that it would help cultivate public support to expand India-China relations. Adding to the mood of knowing India better, Li Keqiang made a reference to the famous Bollywood film "*Three Idiots*" signifying India's popularity in China. At the same time it also exhibited the influence of Indian movies on Chinese psyche that shaped the leadership's perception at the social level drawn from his understanding of Indian society and culture from different angles (MFA 2013; Niu 2013).

During Prime Minister Manmohan Singh's visit in October, *Xinhua* and other Chinese media also quoted the report in the Indian media such as *Rediff*, *Times of India*, and *The New Indian Express*. The report said that Singh's speech at the Central Party School was welcomed by Xi Jinping who received the foreign guests as an old friend of former Prime Minister Wen Jiabao who had hosted PM Singh. This special personal "courtesy" was highlighted (*Xinhua Net* 2013). In the eyes of the Chinese media, the *Indo-Asian News Service* (IANS) also expressed the need for China and India's strategic partnership in a changing world situation, which pointed out that considering China as an opponent would not get China's respect and friendship.

2.6.7. Relations with Other Countries should not affect China-India Relations

Because of the susceptibility and advantage present when an event happens, there are some perceptions that were highlighted in the media report which may be ignored from other sources. Manmohan Singh pointed out that China and India's development of relations with other countries should not become each other's concern (Zhou 2013; Gao 2013). In an editorial the *Global Times* had a more detailed description of the situation and referred to some fundamental problems of Sino-Indian relations in a different tone. China and India were both benefitted by treating their disputes rationally unlike with Japan and the Philippines; even the presence of heightened nationalism among Asian countries. Both sides had such a positive attitude towards any sensitivity between the two countries that they aimed for win-win results rather than suffer the consequences. The author mentioned the lack of understanding, interest and respect about India in Chinese society. The research was not serious. The Chinese do not want to oppose the Indians' strong self-esteem. It contains a huge risk to negatively impact the surrounding environment of China. Negative news is plaguing Sino-Indian relations but this was not just the responsibility of the media. The government needs to play a guiding role to create an interest in public opinion on both sides and guide the media concerns about good things (*Global Times* 2013).

In short, the Chinese media summarised a more positive message so that it made the people from China's political and academic spheres to seek good cooperation with positive forces from India, more intuitive, and build confidence. The disadvantage of the Chinese reports is not conducive to get comprehensive information for understanding. China's mainstream readers may consider that all Indians are friendly to China. When they interacted with Indians, it would cause obstacles in dialogue. In the Sino-Indian exchange program in India, some scholars had this experience. Chinese scholars who made short-term visits to India held the overly optimistic thinking that slight friction causing the situation was not pleasing to see.

2.6.8. Chinese Perceptions in Media on October Visit

The views of some Chinese scholars in colleges and universities were referred to by the media. Their integrated concerns included the cooperation of China and India in the international system, relaxation of restrictions on visas, border issues, bilateral trade and a new pattern of relationship between the great powers and so on. Their overall views were optimistic and confident to resolve the border issue and trade deficit. The assistant dean of the School of International Relations, Renmin University of China, Jin Canrong, the president of the Chinese Association for South Asian Studies, Sun Shihai, etc., all expressed an optimistic attitude on Sino-Indian relations in the Chinese media. Jin said the two countries were still treated with discrimination in the current international system. They nations needed to join forces to achieve a greater voice in international organisations like the World Trade Organization (WTO), the World Bank, the International Monetary Fund (IMF), etc. The two countries need to strengthen investment and control the small contradictions. On the border issue, Sun Shihai also proposed the two sides need to have a new agreement as a supplement (Chu and Gao 2013; Ma 2013; Zhang 2013). The Dean of the Institute of Contemporary International Relations in Tsinghua University, Yan Xuetong, also said the two countries wanted to control the border issues affecting bilateral relations and prevent the deterioration of relations. The border issue can be said to be a trigger to worsen relations between the two countries (Chen 2013). Although it was not directly referenced, the border issues seem to contain a big risk and need to be controlled through effective ways; this seemed to be the subtext of the Chinese scholars. It is really not easy to find a mutually acceptable conclusion. It also needs to have wisdom and courage to control this potential risk. Professor Su Hao from the China Foreign Affairs University suggested finding a new entry point for cooperation and put forward the need to strengthen the institutionalisation of the border issue (Ma 2013). The director of the Institute for South Asian Studies, Yunnan Academy of Social Sciences (YASS), Prof. Chen Lijun, believes that improvement of people-to-people contacts is the way to change the present situation of lacking mutual trust between the two countries. China and India should promote people-to-people exchanges and achieve greater development of transportation, visa facilitation, as well as tourism, trade and the like (Li 2013).

Chinese scholars and stakeholders raised their expectations on China-India relations and touched on the problems that needed to be solved. The interaction between China and Pakistan has always been of grave concern for India. It is one of the key factors that influences China-India relations, especially from the Indian side. However, the situation has been changing, at least in the views of Dr. Zheng Jiabin (Jabin T. Jacob), the then deputy director of the Institute of Chinese Studies: the role of Pakistan has fallen in China-India relations. He also mentioned that the visit of Singh reflects China and India's different global outlooks and interests with the USA. With the growing friendship between the two countries, it must also reduce the effect of other countries on China-India relations. China and India should increasingly form their own independent diplomatic relations without any external influences.

Yet, whether the relations between these two will be smooth as anticipated by the leaders of the two countries is not an easy task to reach a balance in bilateral relations. This query forms the present debate on China-India relations as Professor Madhu Bhalla, from the Department of East Asian Studies, University of Delhi, raised the point that China attempted to make India play a lower and dominated role in bilateral relations, as reflected in the border dispute, the trade deficit, Pakistan-India relations as well as different competition in the Asia-Pacific region, which made India feel particularly uncomfortable (You 2013). It seems difficult to believe that China wants India to play a dominant role as portrayed from the speeches of Chinese leaders, Chinese media reports, and analyses of scholars. However, the dominant impression of India among the Chinese people lacks a positive perception deficit. It is of decisive relevance that the Chinese people get very limited positive news about India. The media of these two nations are different in their approach and thinking. As the Indian media showcases China's rapid development and social issues, similarly the Chinese media can also perceive the promotion of India's position in the world and its status of international reputation. However, the actual reports are mostly negative. It was not because of any single aspect but caused by the entire diplomatic system having the influence of political, social and cultural characteristics.

2.6.9. Is the Settlement of Border Issue a Prerequisite?

In the eyes of different Indian communities, there was another major trend to believe that the settlement of the border issue is still a prerequisite for better cooperation with China in other areas. Indian Foreign Secretary Sujatha Singh and China expert Sujit Dutta based on New Delhi expressed the border issue as an important factor in bilateral relations and that solving this problem would be conducive to other areas of cooperation (Chen 2013). Some scholars believed that the problem between China and India was just being controlled. In fact, the situation has not changed. An Indian scholar from the Institute for Defence Studies and Analyses (IDSA), New Delhi, pointed out that although Sino-Indian relations have expanded greatly, the two have just managed the complications and the difficult relationship as the deep-seated distrust has not reduced (Cheng 2013). The Chinese media quoted from *The Telegraph* (Calcutta) which said that the border issue was not so simple and optimistic; even if PM Singh could sign the border defence cooperation agreement with China, it will likely become the most significant and most enduring diplomatic achievement of Singh's visit. Nevertheless, there are Indian scholars who believe that this agreement was not much of a breakthrough and rather proposed that India must show its defence strength along the LAC to achieve stability. Some argue that there is a sense of using violence to solve the problem. Chinese experts are of the view that only time will help to solve the problem and that the agreement is conducive to rebuild mutual trust which needs to continue to accumulate (Phoenix 2013; Cheng 2013). Thus, it seems that Indian scholars have very balanced perceptions regarding China-India relations as appearing in the Chinese media, having both positive and negative views.

The Indian side did hold a positive view. Sanjay Bhardwaj, an Indian scholar from Jawaharlal Nehru University who conducted the academic exchanges in Kunming, said that the two countries have a good basis for cooperation, and that during the visit of the Indian PM, the border issue would be a major topic of discussion but will also promote all-round cooperation between the two countries including BCIM (Li 2013). Furthermore, the Chinese media quoted a number of positive reports from the Indian media about PM Singh's visit to China, as *Times of India* reported Xi Jinping's making a rare courtesy for PM Singh. However, some media such as *The New Indian Express* criticized that dinner cannot be used to measure the success or failure of diplomacy.

2.6.10. The Continuation of the Dr. Kotnis Family: Government-to-People Contact

Dr. Kotnis has always been a special reference point of contact between China and India. During Li Keqiang's visit, meeting Dr. Kotnis' family was high on the political agenda. This is a symbolic practice on the part of China as it reflects the Chinese government's gratitude towards the Indian friend's help during the crisis of China (Wu et al. 2013). It is believed that Dr. Kotnis has been an important inspiration for Chinese society, wherein people have been influenced to engage in medical or other work for Sino-Indian friendship. In this way, Dr. Kotnis has become a positive factor between the people and the governments of the two countries. As one of the five members who was sent by Jawaharlal Nehru to provide medical support to China during the Chinese Anti-Japanese War, Dr. Kotnis has continued to play a significant role in the bilateral relations. The decision made by the Indian government to support China at that time is the origin of this government-to-people contacts between China and India and, thus, encourages the Chinese government to maintain close contact with Dr. Kotnis' family for many generations. This act on the part of China clearly reflects China's gratitude towards India and, thus, such exchanges contribute to a deeper bond between China and India.

2.6.11. The Report of Li and Singh's Visits in Indian Media

During Li Keqiang's visit, the border issue remained a major concern in the Indian media. In assessing India's perception of China, a survey launched by Observer Research Foundation pointed that "83 per cent Indians view China as a major security threat" and that 63 per cent would like to strengthen relations with the neighbouring country (PTI 2013). There were several positive reports in the Chinese media on Li's India visit while the Indian media played a role highlighting the contentious aspects of India-China relations based on the border issue, trade gap, flood data, and others (PTI 2013; Parsai 2013; *The Hindu* 2013). The Tibet issue is an important and sensitive issue between the two countries on which a consensus has been reached based on broad principles but still tends to be problematic. Since the Kashmir issue was outlawed, Tibet too found no mention in the joint statement. However, on the issue of Tibet, both Chinese academics and Indian officials believed that making no reference to the Tibet issue did not mean that India would change its policy on it. There is an accepted consensus that the Indian government will not allow anyone in India to do any anti-China activity and that practical actions will prove the stands of both sides (Krishnan and Dikshit 2013). This statement stands valid as all incidents of Tibetan protests are kept under tight control by the Indian police during every Chinese leader's visit to India (PTI 2013). On Li's interaction with Dr. Kotnis' family, the Indian media reported it as "talkative Chinese Premier seems to be relatively easing tension" (*The Hindu* 2013; Samanta 2013).

During Indian PM Manmohan Singh's visit to China, the question of the unresolved border again occupied the attention of the Indian mainstream media with special focus on the issue of stapled visas as granted by China to the people of "Arunachal Pradesh". Some Hindi media also carried reports on the theme of the border issue and expressed little hope (Kumar 2013; *Navbharat Times* 2013). In contrast to the Indian media, China attached great importance to trade and cooperation, with some reflecting the harmonious attitude of the Chinese government towards easing the nervous tensions with respect to the Indian public.

2.7. Xi Jinping's Visit to India in 2014

Chinese President Xi Jinping paid his maiden visit to India after taking office from September 17 to 19, 2014. Prior to his India stopover, he visited two other Indian Ocean island nations—The Maldives (the first Chinese head of state to visit it) and Sri Lanka (the last Chinese occasion of head of state to visit it was in 1986). Xi Jinping's visit to India is significant as it is the visit by a Chinese head of state after an hiatus of eight years since former President Hu Jintao's India visit in 2006 (Wang 2014). What is significant to note is that breaking protocol, the newly-elected Indian PM Modi received Xi in his home town, Gujarat, rather than in New Delhi, thus adding a personal touch to the diplomatic ties. Prior to Xi's visit, Modi had already expressed his high expectations from the visit and its impact on Sino-Indian relations. He strongly stated that the relationship will grow from "INCH" ('India-China') to "MILES" ('millennium of exceptional synergy') and that the unique chemistry between the two leaders "can make for a defining moment" (TNN 2014). Xi Jinping suggested that China and India should be partners in bilateral, regional relations around the world and thus, they should further consolidate the strengths of their relationship by elevating it to that of a "strategic and cooperative partnership for peace and prosperity".

In this respect, the bonhomie between Xi and Modi was greatly appreciated and highlighted by China's official media, the *People's Daily*, which hailed Xi and Modi's personal interaction and called it "Hometown diplomacy" and "Friendship diplomacy" that would deepen the strings of public diplomacy between the two countries. The personal equation between the leaders of the two countries can be traced from the VI BRICS Summit held in Fortalez, Brazil, in July 2014, where Xi and Modi had their first interaction and reached a consensus on many aspects concerning the development of friendly relations between the two countries. In this note, some Chinese scholars indicate that the closeness of the two leaders needs friendly sincerity between them and good relations between the countries (Zeng and Li 2013).

Adding to the positive overtones of the high-level visit, Xi Jinping's article titled "Towards an Asian century of prosperity" was published in the Indian mainstream newspaper, *The Hindu*, and in the Hindi newspaper, *Dainik Jagran* on September 17. Invited by the Indian Council of World Affairs (ICWA) Xi, on September 18, delivered a speech titled "In Joint Pursuit of a Dream of National Renewal". Here, what is important to note is that Xi Jinping, both in his article as well as in his speech, emphasized on the cultural aspect visa-vis thriving exchanges and bilateral relations.

2.7.1. "China's Energy" and "India's Wisdom"

Prior to his maiden visit as Chinese President to India in 2013, Xi Jinping had once visited India 17 years ago. As reflected in his article, he had great appreciation for India in looking at the trajectory of India's growth and development in the past 17 years since his first visit. Pointing to the positive indexes of Sino-Indian relationship in terms of a phenomenal bilateral trade figure of US$ 70 billion, over 820,000 mutual visits in 2013, cooperation on international issues and the negotiation on border issues, and others, Xi posited that the bilateral relations between China and India had become one of "the most dynamic and promising" bilateral relations of the 21st century. Since both China and India are in a period of reform and development and their aspirations are the same, therefore, it provides them with an opportunity to complement each other (Xi, 2014). That is to say, both have complementary advantages for each other in the areas of infrastructure, manufacturing and others. China is called the "world's factory" which reflects "China's energy" and India is called the "world's back office" reflecting "India's wisdom" in the fields of IT, pharmaceuticals and other industries. In this regard, both China and India have a huge potential to drive sustainable growth in Asia's economy. In this context, Xi also agreed to Indian PM Modi's view that "China and India are two bodies with one spirit" and highlighted the existing consensus between the two countries on issues of peaceful environment for development, fair and just international mechanism and rules, and others. Thus, it is in the best interest of the two countries to deeply exchange views, strengthen the friendship and work together to promote the early arrival of the Asian century.

Apart from an interest-centric approach, the speeches of Chinese state leaders always reflect some features of cultural sensibilities (Samanta 2013) based on praising the history, culture and people of the visiting country in order to narrow the distance between them. There is always a continuity in terms of drawing from the erstwhile expectations of their own former leaders to express their inheritance of the bond of friendship over successive generations that define the closeness of the relationship. There is always a reiteration of the expressions that have characterized the relationship over the years. In the course of exchanging cultural views many new ideas are shaped. Like Chinese Premier Li Keqiang's reference, President Xi Jinping too cited Gandhi's words that China and India are fellow travellers sharing weal and woe in a common journey. Providing a new perspective on the relationship of the two countries, the leadership proposed the idea that "China and India are two bodies with one spirit" as proposed by Indian PM Modi in his communication with Xi Jinping. That is, China and India have the same spirit of forging ahead in the sphere of international politics, both regionally and globally, and that calls for a new era in global politics.

2.7.2. Partnership at Different Levels

Owing to the cultural connect between China and India, Xi too recalled the historical exchanges between China and India. In reviving the ancient links, Xi advocated the promotion of the ancient human spirit and reproduce the spectacular circumstance of exchanges and mutual learning. By mentioning India's history, Gandhi's thoughts, and Tagore's poetry, Xi revealed his emotions on India and formed a model of establishing linkages between the two countries among the people in terms of ideology (*CCTV News* 2014). The aspects of early exchanges between China and India are often cited in reference to scholarly exchanges such as Kasyapa Matanga and Dharmaratna, who came to Luoyang, China, from Tianzhu (ancient India) in 67 AD and translated the earliest Buddhist sutras; Xuanzang, who came to India and took Indian culture to China; Zheng He, who came to India six times in his seven voyages and so on. India has always had a cultural impact on China in terms of dance, astronomy, calendar, literature, architecture, sugar technology, and others. China has influenced India in terms of paper-making, silk, porcelain, tea, music and so on. These ancient links have constantly been a common theme in the speeches of the Chinese leadership. Besides, there is a significant reference to the support of the two countries for each other's national independence and liberation, especially in relation to Dr. Kotnis' help to China during the Sino-Japanese war. There was acknowledgment of India's early recognition of New China with the birth of the People's Republic of China in 1949 and India's support for China's legitimate seat in the United Nations, the foundation of Five Principles of Peaceful Coexistence between the two countries and others. Hence, in reviewing the emotional connect and India's steadfast progress in recent years, Xi stated that China-India relations have moved "far beyond bilateral ties to have a broad and global impact " and thus, should be partners at bilateral, regional and global levels.

2.7.3. The Chinese Culture in Xi's Perceptions

In drawing the cultural linkage between China and India, Xi commented that there some interlinkage existed between China and India regarding peace. He drew similarities between the Chinese concept of *Tianxia Datong* (Unity of the world) to that of the Indian conception of *Vasudhaiva Kutumbhakam* (the whole world is a family) and *Jian Ai* (universal fraternity) to that of *Ahimsa* (non-violence). He also highlighted that China is a big country that is good at learning by using the Confucian doctrine to prove it, and thus, the objective to seek peace is at the core of Chinese culture which deeply and continuously influences China's diplomatic ties with other countries. In this context, Xi notes that the young people of both the countries could get wisdom from the ancient civilisations of China and India and, thereby, strengthen the spiritual communication between the two countries like what Tagore said to remain in the heart of China with spiritual exchanges to create a better future.

2.7.4. The Positive Perceptions from Chinese Media, Academics

The Chinese media consistently conveyed, with its positive reporting style, the success of President Xi Jinping's visit and quoted the Indian media's affirmative reports as *The Hindu* described this visit as an historic opportunity. Chinese scholars such as Ye Hailin, Secretary-General of the Centre for South Asian Studies, Chinese Academy of Social Sciences and Jiang Jingkui, the then Director of the Centre for South Asia Studies at Peking University, considered that the relaxed atmosphere at the time of the visit exemplified the positive interest of the two countries to develop good relations.

Jiang Jingku, in his interaction at the Strengthening Nation Forum organized by *People's Daily* on September 19, stated that China and India had very close contacts till the late Qing Dynasty when China's national strength weakened and gradually the contact declined. Furthermore, the decline of Buddhism in India also caused the Chinese people to lose interest in India and thus created the gap in the understanding of India. However, in modern times, the leaders of both the countries have increasingly worked for closer ties, which has led to the steady development of bilateral relations. This is especially visible after Vajpayee's visit to China in 2003, which led to the affiliation of Tibet and Sikkim in each other's geography. It reflected that both sides respected each other's sovereignty and promoted a peaceful relationship. It was based on common grounds even in the presence of differences. There is recognition among the Chinese that India has important strategic significance for China and that it is an indispensable country in China's diplomacy which is reflected in the interaction between the two countries at various forums such as BRICS, G-20, SCO, and others. In this light, it is argued by some that China needs the participation of India and other South Asian countries if China wanted to develop the Silk Road Economic Belt and the 21st Century Maritime Silk Road (Xie and Wei 2014). Fu Xiaoqiang, the South Asian Studies expert at the China Institute of Contemporary International Relations, argues that China and India need to strengthen their commonalities and reduce the differences, when China sees India at a more prominent strategic position. In this light, China and India should strengthen cooperation in the areas where they have more consensus like economy and, thus, accumulate strategic mutual trust and lay the foundation of peaceful resolution of their differences. Even the international sphere demands cooperation between the two countries for the greater good.

Nevertheless, India has also expressed its concerns towards China (Mohan 2014) mainly on China's investment in the Indian Ocean Region to build ports, which has been pointed out by the US defence contractor, Booz Allen Hamilton, as that of China's "String of Pearls" strategy (TWT 2005). China has opposed this allegation based on the claim that it is practising a balanced diplomacy by adopting the peripheral diplomatic idea of "*qin* (closeness), *cheng* (earnestness), *hui* (benefit) and *rong* (inclusiveness)". This idea was proposed by China's President, Xi Jinping, in 2013 to pay more attention to develop relations with South Asian countries after the peripheral diplomacy conference of the Central Committee, Communist Party of China. Rejecting the allegation, Chinese Ambassador to India Le Yucheng said that China does not have a so-called "string of pearls" strategy. It is accepted on both sides that the two governments have attached great importance to Sino-Indian relations and that China and India are at an important stage of reform and development. In this context, the unity between China and India is seen to have huge potential to benefit the people of the two countries, Asia and the world. Fu Xiaoqiang proposed that China should develop a "community of interest" with India to expand its cooperation with South Asian countries and that engage in greater cooperation with India to reduce India's concerns regarding China. Former Ambassador to India, Zhou Gang stated that the two countries had recently carried out important diplomatic activities that are reflective of their enhanced mutual trust towards each other. This is exemplified in the fact that since 2013, China has become India's largest trading partner with bilateral trade accounting for US$ 65 billion. In this respect, it is believed that China's "Silk Road Economic Belt" and "Twenty-first Century Maritime Silk Road" are inseparable from "India's wisdom" (Liu 2013; Xie and Wei 2013).

In the case of China and India, there is a coexistence of both consensus as well as differing interests and concerns. In this respect, it becomes important for the two sides to not only communicate on these various aspects of major concern, but also requires joint efforts to eliminate the problems caused by lack of understanding of the other. This needs an attitude on either side to learn from each other and develop relations by accepting each other's faults and gaps. Jiang Jingkui suggested that China should learn from India's awareness of traditional culture as the Chinese tradition and spirit can only be reflected by paying more attention to traditional culture.

2.7.5. The Perceptions of Indian Media

Apart from the introduction of Xi Jinping's journey and cooperation, the Indian media repeatedly reported about the border confrontation that occurred during Xi Jinping's visit and expressed the view that China's "incursions" were attempts to end India's dominance in the Chumar area of Jammu and Kashmir and therefore the 'Chinese Army pushed in more troops into Indian territory'. Compared to other news about the Chinese leader's visit, there appeared a variety of comments, giving both positive and negative impressions of the visit. Denoting Xi's visit to India as negative, one of the perceptions that emerged was that Modi had made the same mistake like Nehru by emphasizing on the notion that "Never trust the Chinese and Americans. Build better ties with Japan and Russia"; such impressions exemplify the distrustful image of China (PTI 2014). Simultaneously, there also were reports that pointed to the confidence of the Chinese and Indian leaders in the peaceful settlement of the border issue through negotiations and their conformity to jointly safeguard the security and stability in the border area. The Indian media also quoted the evaluation of the Chinese media on this visit highlighting the significance of Xi's visit in defining China-India relations. For example, there was a special report with reference to Xi Jinping's meeting with Dr. Kotnis' relatives in New Delhi, adding special mentions of earlier visits of former Chinese heads of state to Dr. Kotnis' family (PTI 2014).

The Indian media's actions is seen to represent as if it was holding a magnifying glass and examining the terms of the agreements signed by China and India, pointing at the solution of India's core interests such as border issues and outlining the economic constraints based on trade deficits. In contrast to the Indian media reports, the Chinese media paid more attention to highlighting the positive factors between the two sides such as attaching greater importance to economic cooperation, and others. On the matter of contentious issues, unlike the

Indian media, the Chinese scholars prompted that the Chinese public keep up with the pace of the Chinese government to reach the correct the understanding of India, which played a harmonious role in the relationship. The interests of the two countries kept playing in the hands of officials, academics, the media and so on. The interests may cause tensions but the problem would be solved only by constant interaction and discussion until an acceptable conclusion was reached between the two sides. In this vein, it therefore presents China and India with a test of their wisdom and patience as well as the habit of thinking, in a way to deal with the problem between the two ancient civilisations. Thus, it is clear that the leaderships' perspectives, media reports, opinions of scholars and others have played a vital role, acting as different forces in shaping Sino-Indian relations.

2.8. Summary

In the overall analysis of the perceptions based on the eight high-level visits between China and India from 2003-2014, it is clear that there has been a difference in the attitude and thinking of one towards the other. The bilateral relationship between China and India has undergone significant changes based on the changing patterns of the international environment, their respective growth and development vis-a-vis the other and a combined influence of politics and economy along with varying perceptions of the leaders, the media, academia and so on. In this context, it is clear that the relationship has constantly developed and expanded when the two governments initiated significant adjustments vis-a-vis the other at different levels of bilateral relations.

It is visible that there have been momentary pauses in the flow of the bilateral relations due to reduced cooperation resulting from differing perceptions. In this process, sometimes public perceptions may show a phenomenon of mutual condemnation for a short time. It is noteworthy that during these pauses, in essence, the different sectors of the two sides were not necessarily mutually hostile but that the system had not been well established in stages and that the speed of resolution of issues was slow as compared to that of the rapidly rising tensions. Therefore, it becomes imperative for both sides to act rationally and probe deeper into the roots of the problems rather than being critical of each other. On the one hand, the response of all sectors will help the establishment of a more perfect diplomatic system, while on the other, the two sides should learn from the mechanism that has been established in some areas to guide the resolution of differences in other areas as a pre-mechanism for mutual exchange and cooperation.

There is also a need to provide an atmosphere and platform where differing views can coexist in an amicable way. The actual participants generally hold a better understanding of all aspects of the case which can help them to identify problems and propose effective measures to solve problems. It will be advantageous to continuously take different perspectives in order to avoid problems. For, if not, there is a greater possibility of negative perceptions to impact other areas of common interest and, thus, cause an inflexible and passive situation. For instance, the visas issued for economic purposes is a greater cause for concern than the academic visas. It has been constantly promoted that there is a need to improve the relevant systems for there is a need to maintain the balance in all aspects in order to achieve reasonable overall development.

In this light, the exchanges and perceptions of academics act as a core factor in promoting mutual understanding and thus deserve more attention. Academics have a deeper understanding of the real situation and contribute to the shaping of effective perceptions. And that, most importantly, in many instances, their perceptions have positively influenced the leaderships' attitude and decision making. In this way, such factors play an important role in bilateral relations. Academics continuously promote the succession and development of the relationship as well as develop fresh perspectives to adapt to new situations. However, at the same time, there are many views that are often short-lived or less cited, or are probably too advanced, too emotional or not suitable for the nation's current interests. Here, it is necessary to continuously explore different points of view, particularly through the media to contact different people and learn unusual views from various participants in the field. It will be more conducive to identify the problems and thus find potential ground for cooperative exchanges, which will further help to develop the boundaries of bilateral relations. However, it is found that the perceptions of some Chinese scholars hold implicit information that needs greater clarification and inference while the views of Indian scholars appear to be direct and multifaceted. Hence, these existing differences should be carefully taken into account in assessing the varied perceptions between the two countries.

It is therefore a practical need to strengthen the media exchanges between the two countries and adapt to each other's characteristics. The Chinese media is more inclined to report positive aspects in defining the nature of the bilateral relationship, calling for greater attention to be paid to the positive aspects while the Indian media is primarily focused on issues that limit the relationship and thus in some way limit wholesome engagement, as a result of negative perceptions. Thus, since the media plays an important role in creating perceptions, it is therefore necessary in the best interests of both China and India to encourage greater cooperation and exchanges between the media of the two countries in order to achieve comprehensive facts over faulty perceptions.

CHAPTER 3

THE POLICY OF CULTURAL EXCHANGES BETWEEN CHINA AND INDIA

China and India have cultural exchanges based on previous achievements and extended to new areas from 2003 to 2014. The main purpose of cultural exchanges is to share the spiritual wealth of the two countries, so that there is understanding on both sides, beneficial for attaining their goals and promoting bilateral relations. Improved bilateral relations cultivate positive images of both countries in the neighbourhood and the world. With an evolving international environment and the domestic conditions of the two countries, their perceptions of each other are transforming. The increasing cooperation has impelled China and India to seek deeper levels of cultural exchanges and proactive policies for better relations. Due to diverse cultural and political systems, the policies of cultural exchanges of the two countries have different emphases. In this chapter, the influence of the foreign policies of China and India on their cultural exchange policies, the main items of their cultural exchange policies and the actual exchange programs will be analyzed, so that we can explore the different emphases of the cultural exchange policies of the two countries as well as the influence of the policies on their bilateral relations.

3.1. Policy Making of Cultural Exchanges

China's policy of external cultural exchanges is made by the Bureau for External Culture Relations under the Ministry of Culture, People's Republic of China. The bureau also signs cultural cooperation agreements between China and foreign countries, carries out annual executive plans and plans for cultural exchange programmes as well as conducts liaison work with the cultural departments in Chinese embassies abroad, instructs China's overseas cultural centres and the foreign cultural centres in China and does publicity work in foreign countries (Ministry of Culture, PRY 2015). Moreover, there is a Department of Policies and Regulations under the Ministry of Culture that makes policies for cultural work.

India's cultural exchange policy-making institutions differ substantially from China's. There is no mention of policy-making in the mission statement of the Ministry of Culture, Government of India, but "to promote cultural exchanges at international level" is one of its functions. Its mission also includes "entering into cultural agreements with foreign countries". It is worth noting that "promotion of institutions and organizations of Buddhist and Tibetan studies" is one of the eight missions for the Ministry of Culture (Ministry of Culture, GoI 2015). However, India's Ministry of External Affairs is responsible for all aspects of external relations and one of its functional divisions is to look after policy planning (MEA, GoI 2015). Thus, there is an overlapping of responsibilities between the two ministries. Moreover, one of the objectives of the Indian Council of Cultural Relations, an autonomous organization of the Government of India, is also "to participate in the formulation and implementation of policies and programmes relating to India's external cultural relations" (ICCR 2015).

3.2. Influence of Foreign Policy on Cultural Exchanges Policies

China's cultural exchanges with foreign countries are a part of its overall diplomacy. "*Bixu tong dang he guojia duiwai zongzhengce baochi xiangyi zhi*", i.e., it must be consistent with the general foreign policy of the Communist Party and the state (Fan 1993). China's Constitution states that "*Zhongguo jianchi duli zizhu de duiwai zhengce...heping gongchu wuxiang yuanze...fazhan tong geguode waijiao guanxi he jingji, wenhuade jiaoliu*", i.e., China adheres to an independent foreign policy and the Five Principles of Peaceful Coexistence and develops diplomatic relations as well as economic and cultural exchanges with other countries (PRC 1982). Thus, we must understand China's cultural exchange policies in the context of its overall foreign policy principles.

The Ministry of Foreign Affairs (2015) specifically states:

> *Zhongguo waijiaode zhuyao renwu shi weihu guojiade zhuquan, anquan he fazhan liyi, wei quanmian jianshe xiaokang shehui, jiakuai shehui zhuyi xiandaihua yingzao lianghaode waibu huanjing, jiji tuijin shijiede heping yu fazhan shiye*
>
> The main task of China's diplomacy is to safeguard the sovereignty, security and development interests of the country, to create favourable external environment for building a moderately prosperous society and accelerate the socialist modernisation, and actively promote the work of world peace and development.

There are different perspectives for developed countries, neighbouring countries and developing countries in China's foreign policy. For the developed countries, it is to continue to

> *Jiaqiang zhanlue duihua, zengjin huxin, shenhua hezuo, tuoshan chuli fenqi, tuidong xianghu guanxi changqi wending jiankang fazhan*
>
> Strengthen strategic dialogue, enhance mutual trust and deepen cooperation, properly handle differences, and promote long-term stable and healthy development of mutual relations (MFA 2015).

For neighbouring countries, it is to

> *Jixu guanche yulin weishan, yilin weiban de zhoubian wai jiao fangzhen, jiaqiang tong zhoubian guojiade mulin youhao he wushi hezuo, jiji kaizhan quyu hezuo, gongtong yingzao heping wending, pingdeng huxin, hezuo gongyingde zhoubian huanjing*
>
> Continue to implement the good neighbour policy, to strengthen friendship with neighbouring countries and pragmatic cooperation, actively carry out regional cooperation and jointly create a common regional environment for peace and stability, equality, mutual trust and win-win cooperation (MFA 2015).

For the developing countries, it is to

> *Jiaqiang tuanjie hezuo, shenhua chuantong youyi, kuoda wushi hezuo, tigong lisuonengjide yuanzhu, weihu fazhanzhong guojiade zhengdang yaoqiu he gongtong liyi*
>
> To strengthen unity and cooperation, deepen traditional friendship, expand pragmatic cooperation and provide assistance within its capacity, and uphold the legitimate demands of developing countries and common interests (MFA 2015).

India is a neighbouring country of China as well as a developing country. Combining these two identities of India, we can infer the features of China's foreign policy towards India; these are *Youshan xiangchu* (friendly coexistence), *Jianli huoban guanxi* (to build partnership) and *Shenhua chuantongde youyi* (to deepen traditional friendship). In the aspect of cooperation, it should carry out or expand pragmatic cooperation and regional cooperation (*Wushide hezuo he quyude hezuo*) and provide whatever assistance (*Tigong lisuonengjide yuanzhu*) in order to achieve the following objectives—establish win-win cooperation in the surrounding environment and maintain the legitimate demands and common interests of developing countries. These guidelines have been reflected in cultural exchanges between the two countries. For example, Buddhism is the main medium of the traditional friendship between China and India. The two countries established "comprehensive cooperation" relations in 2003 and upgraded it to "strategic and cooperative partnership for peace and prosperity" in 2005, which reflected *Youshan xiangchu* (friendly coexistence) and *Jianli huoban guanxi* (to build partnership). China provided financial support to the Nalanda University project led by the Indian government, which reflects *Wushide hezuo he quyude hezuo* (pragmatic cooperation and regional cooperation), and *Tigong lisuonengjide yuanzhu* (provide whatever assistance) and so on.

China's foreign policy emphasizes that strategic dialogue, improving the mutual trust and cooperation level as well as to build long-term stable and healthy relationships with developed countries. So, India will be treated differently from developed countries. For developed countries, more emphasis is on *Changqi wending jiankang fazhan* (long-term stable and healthy development) and *Zhanlue duihua* (strategic dialogue) in order to enhance mutual trust and the depth of cooperation. The policies were summarised very briefly but the difference can be seen literally. There are specific policy expressions for different sets of countries.

In India, its foreign policy is considered as "an enabling instrument for securing a peaceful and tranquil environment for the transformation of its society and economy" (Bhasin 2013: XI). For achieving goals of its foreign policy, India seeks to use "soft power and diplomacy by scrupulously avoiding the use of any coercive power in its relations with other countries" and the use of coercive power is advocated only when it is challenged by non-state actors and other non-conventional sources (Bhasin 2013: XXV). Besides, India has started highlighting its "neighbour first" policy since the formation of a new government in 2004 (Chand 2014). Yet, even earlier, it had given the highest priority to its neighbours as a peaceful periphery is essential for India to achieve her multifarious developmental goals (MEA, GoI 2015). According to External Affairs Minister, S.M. Krishna (2012), India has given special priority to relations with its immediate neighbour, China.

Hence, the foreign policies of both China and India are focused on economic development, for which a peaceful and stable environment and good relations with other countries are compulsory. Through cooperation and exchanges, they seek to expand their influence and better achieve their own goals.

3.3. Different Aspects of Cultural Exchange Policies

The Ministry of Foreign Affairs of the People's Republic of China has made policy papers for the European Union (2003 and 2014), Africa (2006), and Latin America and the Caribbean (2008). The policy papers declare the goals of China's policies for these regions and countries and state its cooperation blueprint for the next five to ten years. Its first foreign policy paper, published in 2003, was for the EU, the first by the Chinese government since the founding of New China (Feng 2004). These policies described China's relationship with the countries, highlighting the significance of the Five Principles of Peaceful Coexistence. Currently, there is no particular policy paper of China for India.

From the differences of China's policy on cultural exchanges towards the EU, Africa and Latin America and the Caribbean, we understand the different focus of China for developed and developing countries. For Africa, Latin America and the Caribbean, there are substantially similar contents; e.g., some stated goals are

> *Luoshi shuangfang qiandingde wenhua hezuo xieding he xiangguan zhixing jihua, baochi shuangfang wenhua zhuguan bumen jingchangxing jiaowang, jiaqiang shuangfang wenhua, yishu jigou, zhuanye renyuan jiaoliu hezuo. Genju shuangfang wenhua jiaoliu he shichang xuqiu, jiji yindao he tuidong shehui gejie kaizhan duozhong xingshide wenhua jiaoliu huodong*
>
> To implement the cultural cooperation agreements and associated implementation plans signed between the two sides, to maintain frequent exchanges between cultural administrations, to strengthen culture, art institutions, professional exchanges and cooperation. Under the demand of market, actively guide and encourage the community to carry out various forms of cultural exchange activities (MFA 2006; 2008).

Nevertheless, China is more meticulous regarding cultural exchanges in the policy paper on the EU compared with the papers on Africa and Latin America and the Caribbean. In the 2003 paper on the EU, it stressed on *Kaifangde zitai* (open attitude) and *Duocengci he quanfangwei* (multi-level and all-round) cultural exchanges, including with the EU, the EU member-states and governments, civil groups, businesses and at other levels.

To facilitate the Chinese and European people to know each other's excellent culture, it is clearly mentioned that China will gradually establish Chinese cultural centres in the capital of the EU headquarters and member-states and that it welcomed the EU to establish cultural centres in Beijing. It had encouraged the co-hosting of high-level cultural exchange activities and establishing new models of cooperation to develop cultural industries and explore the establishment of China-EU cultural cooperation consultation mechanism and co-sponsor a 'China-EU Cultural Forum'. It emphasised the role of China-EU on advanced level people-to-people and cultural exchange mechanisms. For student exchanges, the target was to reach 300,000 people in EU-China annual two-way exchange of students. Regarding scholars' exchanges, language training cooperation and dialogue on educational policies, the two sides will set up research centres in their respective regions of the EU and its countries and it decided to do a series of cooperation activities in the realm of higher education. The two sides launched the "EU-China Year of Cultural Dialogue" and promoted cultural cooperation to a long-term mechanism. The two sides held a dialogue of cultural policy as well as shared the experiences of exchange of cultural industries, cultural heritage and contemporary arts. There are also details on the exchanges and cooperation of the media where they put forward specific requirements for a cultural aspect, such as to present a comprehensive and objective picture of each other's culture, to produce documentaries and publish books and news articles that reflect each other's history, culture and customs, to cooperate in making films and TV programs and jointly hold film and TV exhibitions, festivals, book fairs, etc. A Youth Exchange programme has been initiated on an advanced level of people-to-people and cultural exchange dialogue mechanism and youth policy dialogue mechanism as well as specialised platforms for the exchange of youth organisations. When compared, the policy papers of China between developing countries and developed countries, it is easy to see that there are more detailed and clear plans for developed countries while it is vague for developing countries. The China's Policy Paper on the EU was prepared earlier than others.

In September 1978, the State Council issued a document that the Ministry of Culture had taken charge of cultural exchanges with foreign countries. In 1982, it was written into the Constitution of China by the fifth session of the fifth National People's Congress that cultural exchanges with other countries must be developed (Cai 2009). Former Minister of Culture Cai Wu (2009) stated that China's cultural work with foreign countries has gradually extended into four major areas: cultural diplomacy, cultural exchanges, external cultural propaganda and cultural trade. He pointed out that the government's initiative of having an "Exchange Year" and "Culture Year" is a part of cultural diplomacy. The promotion of Chinese culture festivals, establishment of cultural centres in embassies and film festivals are within the scope of cultural external cultural propaganda. International business, copyright trade, film and television trade, creation of international cultural trading platforms and businesses belong to the category of cultural trade. For cultural exchanges, activities are carried out on the basis of agreements on cultural cooperation and implementation of plans on cultural exchanges between governments, including celebrating an international year of artistic themes, festivals and other activities as well as cultural cooperation at bilateral, multilateral, regional, and international levels that introduce the cultural products of other countries, and promote China's cultural products. In addition, Cai (2009) pointed out that the protection of cultural relics and heritage at the international level is also included within the scope of Chinese cultural exchanges. Therefore, programmes based on agreements of cultural cooperation and implementation plan on cultural exchanges will be given priority in this chapter. Moreover, because the 2013 joint statement of China and India also mentions the programmes of cultural exchanges including the exchange of youth, media, cultural heritage, education, sports, publications, mass communications, etc., those aspects of the statement relevant to cultural diplomacy, cultural propaganda, etc., as defined by the former Minister of Culture, Cai Wu, will be also thoroughly analysed.

In addition, according to the two characteristics of foreign policy proposed by Xing Yue (2011), the scope of cultural exchange policy will be explored. First, because the country's foreign affairs are confidential, almost all countries do not fully disclose their foreign policy. Second, at times, there are many differences between the content of policy documents and practical implementation as the government wants to obtain the support of the people at home and avoid opposition of the international community. Therefore, the following analysis will focus on the actual behaviour of the government, namely, cultural exchange activities, cultural cooperation agreements between the two governments, the implementation plan content of cultural exchanges effectively pursued by the governments of China and India, to estimate and interpret the tendency of their policies.

3.4. The Main Cultural Exchanges Programmes, 2003-2014

The Religious Affairs Bureau of Luoyang in China planned to build an "International Buddhist Monastery Hall" in the western side of the White Horse Temple in 1997. During Indian Prime Minister Atal Bihari Vajpayee's visit to China in 2003, the director of the Foreign Affairs Office of Luoyang city, Fang Shuangjian, proposed to the Indian Embassy to build an Indian-style Buddhist hall in the White Horse Temple. It attracted the interest of the Indian government. Later on, officials of China and India continued to discuss the details for this programme (Fang 2009; Zhang and Qiao 2014:173). Finally, in an unprecedented gesture, the Indian government provided financial support of 50 million rupees to build this Indian-style Buddhist hall inside the White Horse Temple (Fang 2009). The White Horse Temple is the first government-run monastery of China, historically proposed by Emperor Ming of the Han dynasty for Buddhist monks from India, Kasyapa Matanga and Dharmaratna, who had used a white horse to bring Buddhist sutras to China (Fang 2009). During Chinese Premier Wen Jiabao's visit to India in April 2005, the two countries signed a memorandum on "India's Indian-style Buddhist Hall in White Horse Temple in Luoyang, China" which was part of the joint statement. The hall was completed in 2010 when Indian President Pratibha Patil came to China to participate in the opening ceremony.

From the building process of this Indian-style Buddhist Hall, it can be seen that promoting the spread of Buddhist culture in China is also related to the policy of China on cultural exchanges. Since China wants to promote Buddhist exchanges, the Indian side has a better chance to do so. In modern India, Buddhism is a minor religion, so it promotes only a limited understanding of India. However, China's policy-makers should keep in mind that India seeks to promote "institutions and organisations of Buddhist and Tibetan studies" as it is one of the eight missions for its Ministry of Culture (Ministry of Culture, GoI 2015). So, China should not ignore the role of Buddhism, but simultaneously try to balance cultural exchange policies by expanding them to other trends in modern India.

The Government of India also supported the establishment of the Centre for Indian Studies in Peking University during Vajpayee's 2003 visit. The centre was a response to the contribution of Cheena Bhavana at Visva-Bharati University, where the Indian Prime Minister is the University Chancellor; so, in 2003, Vajpayee was in that position. The Indian government deputed two faculty members from India to the Centre and donated one million rupees annually for the first five years. An annual scholarship was offered to a student of the Centre to study in an Indian institution and also an annual prize to the first-ranking student of the Centre for a three-week visit to India. Besides, the Tan Yun Shan Award was proposed by Vajpayee "in memory of that modern-day pioneer of India-China cultural understanding" (Vajpayee 2003).

During Chinese Premier Wen Jiabao's visit to India in 2005, he put forward cultural cooperation as one of four aspects to reflect the relations of "strategic partnership for peace and prosperity" between the two countries. In 2005, the two countries celebrated the 55th anniversary of Sino-Indian diplomatic relations. "Indian Culture Month" and "Chinese Culture Month" were held in China and India, respectively, while the year 2006 was proposed as the "China-India Friendship Year". China and India decided to initiate mutual recognition of academic qualifications. The two sides also decided to carry out regular youth exchange activities. China invited 100 Indian youth to visit China in 2005. Besides, the Chinese People's Institute of Foreign Affairs signed a memorandum of understanding on exchanges and cooperation with the Indian Council of World Affairs.

In 2006, China's president, Hu Jintao, made six recommendations for the purpose of developing bilateral relations during his visit to India. The fourth point was about cultural exchanges, which included the promotion of cultural exchanges and consolidating the basis of friendship, expansion of culture, education, tourism, religion, news, sports and other fields of friendly exchanges, jointly running the 2007 "China-India Tourism Friendship Year" activities as well as expansion of air links, simplifying visa procedures and other measures to promote personnel exchanges. The Chinese government invited 500 Indian youths to visit China in the next five years. In the Joint Declaration of China and India, the two leaders committed to the pursuit of ten strategies, including the promotion of cultural relations and nurturing non-governmental exchanges and establishment of the Indian Buddhist Hall in White Horse Temple, Luoyang, and repairing the Nalanda Xuan Zang Memorial Hall. Among the other items discussed were the digitisation of the Chinese Buddhist sutras and reconstruction of Nalanda University. It was also decided to cooperate in the celebration of festivals such as "Festival of India" and "Festival of China", academic exchanges, educational exchanges, youth exchanges, tourism, civil exchanges, etc. To promote academic exchanges between China and India, the two sides agreed to encourage the establishment of the "China-India Exchange Foundation" (Embassy of PRC in India 2006). A protocol was signed on the establishment of consulates at Guangzhou and Kolkata. This initiative was a great boost for cultural exchanges as Cheena Bhavana turned into a major beneficiary of the Guangzhou consulate when Chinese teachers got help from the consulate in resolution of their visa issues, so that they could teach at Cheena Bhavana. Meanwhile, the consulate in Kolkata and Cheena Bhavana have organised many Chinese activities that have promoted Chinese teaching extensively (Acharya 2006; Banerjee 2015).

During Indian PM Manmohan Singh's visit to China in 2008, the two leaders signed a common vision for the 21st century of reaching a consensus in many aspects. Singh considered strengthening exchanges to reach a better understanding of each other as the first and most important task for future development: "First, we need to narrow the cognitive distance between India and China, we should make efforts for a long-term proper understanding of each other, not only to understand each other's culture and history, but also to understand the current developments. We should strengthen cultural exchanges to eliminate misunderstanding and prejudice. We need the academia, the media, non-governmental professionals and arts conducted for broad, comprehensive dialogue". Exchanges are not broad enough and not conducive for eliminating misunderstandings and prejudices, communication needs to expand and there is need for more profound exchanges. In addition, "The two sides believe that in the new century, the Five Principles should continue for developing friendly relations and creating conditions for peace and development of mankind. To achieve the basic guiding principles, cultural and religious tolerance and dialogue among civilisations and people would lead to overall peace and stability in the world. The two sides appreciate all efforts to promote among civilisations and interfaith dialogue". From 2006, the two sides agreed to promote the establishment of a Sino-Indian exchange fund and this time it was clearly established. "The two sides will continue to organise exchange visits between hundreds of youth. The two sides also agree to launch a five-year programme for mutual exchange of youth delegations. In this context, the Chinese side invites five hundred youth from India over the next five years". This merely mentions China, but not the Indian side. The two countries jointly hosted the 2010 "Festival of India" and "China Day". The year 2008 is the 70th anniversary of the Indian medical team to China. These two countries established a joint medical team (Cao 2008) of 10 members from both countries that will conduct a free clinic to help vulnerable groups in India and China. The medical team held joint regular annual events (Wen and Wu 2008).

During Wen's visit to India in 2010, the two countries announced the year 2011 as the "China-India Exchange Year." Visits of 500 young people was listed as one of the priorities. At this stage, youth exchanges were institutionalised. The government will invite young people to visit each year. This has been recognised as an important link between the two countries to promote mutual trust, as clearly stated in the Joint Communique. The two sides agreed to continue the youth exchange visits between the two countries over the next five years. In this publication, there is reference that only China will invite 500 Indian youth from various segments of society to visit China in 2011, without reference to the Indian side "to encourage both social groups, youth, media, academics, think tanks, artists and cultural figures to carry out more large-scale exchanges." China donated $ 1 million to support reconstruction of Nalanda University and this initiative in 2007 was mentioned during the Singapore East Asian Summit as the first initiative of "Asia talks to each other" (Sabharwal 2015). Asian countries, including Japan, Singapore and others, state-funded support to the Government of India and this was established in a bill relating to this university that scholars of China and India as well as those of other nationalities will be included as board members. Among scholars, it was seen as a new platform for exchange of ideas. Nalanda University in India and other Asian governments are involved in an important cooperation project of modern times. The cooperation project has international specialties and is not just limited to China and India, but will also provide reference to India and other multilateral cultural and educational cooperation (Ibid.). In addition to the Nalanda project, Premier Wen asserted that "encouraging local governments to strengthen exchanges between the two countries will play an active role in non-governmental friendship organisations." The two sides will "jointly set up India's outstanding students' exchange programs; implementation of the project will be determined by negotiations between the parties."

The two sides signed an agreement covering a number of areas like arts and culture, heritage, youth, education, sports, journalism, publishing and mass media. A "Cultural Cooperation Agreement 2010-2012 Implementation Plan" (Niu 2010) first proposed compilation of an encyclopaedia of India-China cultural contacts. Officials and experts from both sides formed a Joint Compilation Committee. In addition to the ancient cultural exchanges based on what has been achieved, the two governments also stressed on "educational exchanges" including "learning from each other to promote the importance of the national languages and their expansion." Both sides use language as an effective tool for encouraging interaction by various means such as the establishment of language institutions. The Indian side showed a more positive side, and the "India Secondary Education of the Central Committee" will, from the next semester (April 2011), start "Chinese as a foreign language to be included in the school curriculum in India." Hard work has been carried out in India compared to the "Confucius Institute" as it is difficult because teachers' visas are approved by the Indian government. The Indian government has done much and it is bold and pragmatic and with China's growing influence in the world, the importance of learning Chinese is also increasingly recognized by the public. China says the decision is "welcome" and "will provide support in Chinese language teacher training and language teaching materials".

During Chinese Premier Li Keqiang's visit to India in May 2013, the interests of the two countries for the development of "strategic partnership for peace and prosperity" in the five areas of cooperation reached a new consensus. Both sides confirmed that they are important partners, rather than competitors. Humanities exchanges are one of the five aspects of cooperation; both sides will "exchange and expand cultural exchanges of the two ancient peoples", and deepen cultural ties, as well as celebrate ties amongst youth and other areas. The two sides identified 2014 as a Year of Friendly Exchanges to celebrate and mark the 60th anniversary of the Five Principles of Peaceful Coexistence [Panchsheel]. The Joint Statement between the two countries put a greater emphasis on the important role of youth exchanges and media exchanges and cooperation between the two countries. It also decided to continue organising exchange visits of youth delegations as agreed to by the foreign ministries. It visualised the organisation of the "Indian Media Forum".

Indian PM Singh's visit in October, highlighted the need to promote greater people-to-people contacts and exchanges. Youth affairs and media and other areas such as art and culture, cultural heritage, education and sports, publications and mass communications were included in the Program of Cultural Exchange for the years 2013-2015, and it was proposed to support the establishment of sister-city relationships on a pilot basis; the first list of sister cities were Delhi and Beijing, Bangalore and Chengdu, Kolkata and Kunming.

In contrast, Li Keqiang's visit highlighted cooperation and more emphasis on the cultural aspects of the richer Chinese teaching and breakthrough on border exchanges: "The two sides encourage Chinese Hanban teaching cooperation with India Secondary Education of the Central Committee of Chinese". In 2010, a summit was proposed and in April 2011, to promote the implementation of the Central Committee of Secondary Education in India; the two sides agreed to consider the opening of the Nathu La Pass border trade. China will allow Indian Kailash Mansarovar pilgrims to visit China in the Tibet Autonomous Region and provide more facilities. In addition, the two governments signed in advance before the work was completed. They agreed in 2014 to complete the Encyclopedia of India-China Cultural Contacts which was mooted during Wen Jiabao's visit to India (Encyclopedia of India-China Cultural Contacts, 2014:xi), and to expand new cooperation, the two sides agreed for the Mutual Translation and Publication of Classic and Contemporary Works which included 25 books of Classic and Contemporary Works from each side (Deepak 2013:2). This will provide a more favourable basis for understanding in both countries.

During Xi Jinping's visit to India in 2014, based on the deep civilisational linkages, the two sides agreed to launch the "China-India Cultural Exchange Program" and "India-China Cultural Initiative" that included Buddhism exchanges. The two countries held the "India Tourism Year" and the "China Tourism Year". China will assist the Indian side in propagating the tourism related products of the 7th century Chinese monk Xuan Zang in India in 2015 and 2016. An Indian Buddhist art exhibition was held in China in 2014. The two sides also signed a program of cooperation at all levels, such as the 2015-2019 annual 200 youth visits, establishment of the Ministry of Culture ministerial consultation mechanism and strengthening exchanges between the museums and other cultural institutions of the two countries. In addition, Guangdong Province was established as a sister province of Gujarat State, Shanghai and Mumbai and Guangzhou and Ahmedabad as Partner Cities (not covered by the India-China Cultural Initiative). A contemporary Indian art exhibition is to be held in China in 2015. China will also hold similar exhibitions and, in addition, it will also serve as guest of honour at the 2014 International Film Festival of India and as a partner at the 2016 International Book Fair in Delhi. The two sides will strengthen exchanges and cooperation in film, radio and television, and jointly shoot audiovisual projects. They will also need to support each other's other Hindi and Chinese language teaching. China has decided to open through the Nathu La Pass, a pilgrimage route for religious exchanges between the two countries to facilitate pilgrims.

3.5. The Differences of Policy on Cultural Exchanges

During the 2014 visit of high-oriented cultural exchange programs between the two countries, the bilateral cultural exchanges focus of the project was concerned with Buddhism, and has continued to put forward more comprehensive projects, from the construction of an Indian-style Buddhist hall, to cooperation on the establishment of Nalanda University, repairing Xuan Zang's Memorial Hall to improvising translations of Buddhist scriptures and their digitisation. In 2014, China put forward in support of Buddhism, Indian tourist products and routes of publicity. Reflecting the policy, China invited India to spread Buddhist culture and China provided various forms of support, and so on. Also, in this period, the two countries, in their respective embassies and universities, carried out a number of activities to commemorate Tagore, Yoga, Indian festivals, Bollywood, Buddhism and other themes (MEA GOI 2012). China's cultural policy will also affect cultural trends in India, such as an Indian-style Buddhist hall is one of India's Chinese policies of engagement and response. There are also private activities affecting national policy, such as Peking University establishing the Centre for Indian Studies, which is in response to the establishment of Cheena Bhavana by Tagore and Tan Yunshan. These projects are in the tradition of friendly exchanges between China and India and the establishment of bilateral relations, especially as culture and education are conducive to further deepen mutual understanding and such positioning enriches the connotation of bilateral ties firmly. The two leaders also continue to promote the exchange of visits and the final implementation of the projects under discussion, for example, the proposed agreement to establish a "China-India Exchange Fund" in 2006, was instituted by 2008.

Exchange projects between China and India reflect the different emphasis of their policies. Chinese leaders advocate the promotion of China-India relations and more cooperation from the perspective of traditional culture, emphasising the identity of the two countries with ancient civilisations. However, in reality, India opened more cultural centres in China in different forms to spread its culture, such as cultural centres, Buddhist architecture, 2015 Yoga Centre, Gandhi research centres, etc., and they are not limited to one form. India did not put Hinduism as the mainstream Indian society to make a special focus on the obvious. It is worth noting that Buddhism in India is not in the mainstream, but still the Indian Ministry of Culture has focussed on Buddhism and to protect it, the Indian government feels that other nations also need to promote Buddhist cultural exchanges. According to China, the resource strengths of India have to be focused on the development of exchanges and projects in India, such as in the Buddhist context, focus needs to be put on the translation aspect of literary classics. Exchanges between the two countries attach great importance to the exchange of youth, but the number of exchanges is limited. Anniversaries of bilateral cooperation are the main opportunities for the two countries to expand cultural exchanges, such as during the anniversary of Panchsheel, there is a series of friendly tourist activities.

The principles of foreign policy between the two countries are to influence cultural policy. India's foreign policy thinks through soft power and diplomacy to achieve their purpose. China seeks to be a friendly neighbour and help neighbouring countries for their development meanwhile expand its cultural influence. During the visits of Chinese leaders, the two countries signed an agreement in which cooperation between the two sides has mainly been that of equal exchange, or help promote the culture of India, in addition to the promotion of Chinese in middle schools, which is not as positive as the establishment of cultural centres of the Indian government. In the cultural context, China has provided more input while India has benefitted from the output. If the two countries can communicate at policy levels, it will be a mutually beneficial cooperation and places such as Bihar and others which are economically backward provinces but have a lot of Buddhist shrines can be adequately protected. The Government of India may consider joint development of these historical resources. China may be provided more support in teaching Indian culture in different forms, such as providing support to the Chinese, establishing private training institutions at all levels of Indian universities and establishment of more universities with university level cooperation not just limited to the Confucius Institute.

Cultural policy being influenced by the country's foreign policy is also reflected in the visa issue. Since 2006, the rules of economic visas have been relaxed (PTI 2006), visa problems have been optimised to solve: firstly, business visa of 60 days can be extended up to 180 days and entry can be increased from single to multiple in India. Secondly, employment visa for Chinese nationals can now be extended in India up to five years. However, in the cultural core areas of study visas, student visas do not seem to be relaxing and the scope of academic exchanges as compared to the economic aspects and the obstacles are even greater. From China to India, exchanges for the purpose of research are only a handful, and even they are refused a visa. It seems that Indian officials are concerned by national security while dealing with cases of Chinese, especially academic researchers who are in sensitive fields from then Indian perspective. There is also lack of feedback from academic circles and academic contribution against the figures of economic development. Academic exchanges between China and India should have been the most important part of the promotion of mutual understanding, but it is the weakest link at this stage. It also reflects the lagging academic exchanges and cooperation, but visas for economic purposes were easily approved. However, the two cities of Guangzhou and Kolkata established consulates-general in order to solve the visa problem and provide convenient conditions.

3.6. Conclusion

Overall, the foreign policies of the two countries reflect different cultural characteristics; in the actual conduct of exchanges, there is a more specific display of this difference and general policy formulation directly affects the degree of cultural exchanges. China, for developed countries, reflects a positive attitude but exchanges in India and the developing countries reflect the status of a secondary nation. This restricts the Chinese in shaping their image in India, while India is showing greater diversity of cultural input attitude and cultural projects.

From 2003 to 2014, the size of Indian cultural exchange has been growing, and the exchange between the two countries has become increasingly specific. More cultural exchanges, and the need to understand the international situation, bilateral relations, and develop appropriate plans on this basis, to facilitate the implementation of a cultural exchange program, as well as act as an auxiliary conducive to other aspects of the work are necessary. As with other aspects of cooperation, cultural exchanges also need to establish a feedback control mechanism conducive to solve problems formation of new ideas. The mechanism of establishing the need to understand each other's culture, ideas and policies, and make other in-depth analysis, is conducive to produce cooperation that is more effective. Single field professionals have in-depth perspectives, but there are limitations of their own field's unilateral vision. If the policy makers master a number of professionals, it helps in a comprehensive understanding of the overall situation and their actual participation in the exchange and effectiveness of staff feedback will thereby help in developing more effective exchange programs and not be limited to just one area or to a limited section. In short, calm thinking and passionate action will turn the problem into a solution. Unrealistic sloganeering and overly emotional connection or blindly criticizing each other, are not conducive to the interests and the exchange programs of the two countries. In the choice of policy, the two countries need to have values, history and culture, policy and other "soft power" of well-known professionals, and have an understanding of bilateral political, economic and military as well as international relations and other "hard power" of understanding to participate.

There are many restrictions as well. Academic people on different occasions have said that the visa issues are difficult to handle. For example, in 2014,an application by the International Research Institute of East Asian Studies, Jawaharlal Nehru University, to learn the majority language was approved by the Chinese. But scholars who study politics and international relations have a relatively low pass rate; the Indian side in this regard seems to have requirements that are more stringent. Buddhist scholars or international relations scholars have not been approved for visas or a long time elapses before visa approval, resulting in exchange failures. Information provided by an officer of the Indian Foreigner Regional Registration Offices (FRRO), says that some provinces in northeast India, such as Sikkim, allow holders of tourist visas to visit Sikkim for sightseeing only after approval from the Home Ministry, but Chinese nationals with student visas are not allowed at all (MDNER GOI 2015). For a deeper understanding of local realities, people have been restricted to a large extent due to the negative influence of policy formulation and its feasibility.

3.6.1. Buddhism in Cultural Exchanges Policy

As leaders in the growing cooperation on Buddhist terms, this area is an important link in the promotion of Sino-Indian relations. However, work that can have a real good impact on the exchange policy should be to develop effective communication programs so as to really achieve the effect of improved relations. One would need to be relevant, not only to understand each other's culture, but also take into account each other's aspects, such as the status quo in both countries, differences, political, economic and international environment for the purpose of comprehensive co-ordination. For example, after Modi came to power in 2014, there has been some revival in India's Hindu boom. There is also some resistance to the development of a New Buddhist Movement phenomenon in India. According to the 2011 Census, Buddhism in India is only 0.8 per cent (Government of India 2011). Should Modern Buddhism cultural exchanges be limited to specific groups? There is also a need to analyze specific issues, such as contemporary Indian Buddhists, 73.4 per cent of whom are concentrated in Maharashtra (58.3 per cent of the local population, most of whom being low-caste Hindus converted to Buddhism); Modern Chinese Buddhists are of many categories, such as Chinese Buddhism (Zen, Pure Land Buddhism etc.), Tibetan Buddhism, and Theravada Buddhism. Buddhism has played the role of a catalyst (Sen 2005) in the history of Sino-Indian relations, but in the modern political environment and changes in the great religion itself, if one wants to promote bilateral relations through cultural exchanges to understand and eliminate barriers, a detailed planning of the project is needed. The governments of China and India in the Joint Declaration proposed religious exchanges and cooperation, including the establishment of the Buddhist Hall in Luoyang, reparation of the Nalanda Xuan Zang Memorial Hall, digitization of Buddhist sutras and reconstruction of Nalanda University, to retrace Xuan Zang's voyage to India, and film co-production on Xuan Zang. It shows the interaction between China and India still largely relies on Buddhism, which in the modern Indian culture is a small but important part. To understand key aspects of Chinese culture a comprehensive policy formulation should be considered. While the two governments have been promoting bilateral ties through Buddhism, and also paying attention to increased publicity tours of Buddhist shrines, yet, the main components of social groups in India and China are not Buddhists. History and culture-related activities without religious restrictions, in addition to the believers, history buffs and religious enthusiasts priority should also be to expand the scope of communication. From cultural and historical perspectives, the reason why the philosophy of Indian Buddhism could become a part of Chinese traditional culture is because of the shortages of Chinese culture on certain issues. For instance, the most influential philosopher in Chinese native culture Confucian explained elaborately about *sheng* (living) but less about *si* (dead); he advocated, "You do not yet know about the living, how can you know about the dead?" What kind of shortage can be found today in Indian culture which can be made up from other cultures, thus, becoming more conducive to the development each other's cultures. If we can sort out these problems, a more detailed exploration of Indian cultural differences and mutual learning can be promoted, presumably targeted to form an effective link.

3.6.2. Youth Exchanges in Cultural Exchanges Policy

Youth exchanges have two very important aspects, one as a meeting point between the two countries and second for the development of youth leadership exchange programs. To achieve the desired results, it is required that the government diverts attention to youth and play a good role in cultural exchanges, understanding the essence of each civilization and culture and its strengths. Tan Chung (2008) noted that China's "younger generation lacks a spiritual pursuit". He commented, "In modern Chinese cultural life, everyone 'seeks temporary benefits', and nobody cares for the 'soul'." Chindia has lost its momentum and he said with emotion that it is difficult for the Chinese today to understand the great contribution that their predecessors have made to cultural exchanges between the two nations. His comments reflect that some aspect of the situation in China, rapid economic growth, has also spawned a number of other issues such as benefit-oriented, fast-moving consumers paying more attention to material life. In India, there is a contrast in the way that the culture is influenced by the world. These issues also deserve attention.

Continuation of cultural exchanges requires that people of the other culture take great interest in them so as to make the exchanges more valuable and more charismatic. Emphasis on discovery, selection of new members and talent to provide a platform to maintain the quality of communication; for example, Chinese Bridge players from India are young but how to make them play an influential role requires effective communication, such as the production of television programs to introduce their culture, movies, music, etc., through their language so as to promote deep, intuitive understanding of people of other cultures. These practices are reflected in China's approach to the EU's policy document for developed areas, or may be taken as a reference.

3.6.3. Language and Institutes in Cultural Exchanges Policy

Political and economic cooperation between China and India because of the trust deficit have raised a lot of questions about security concerns, and the trust deficit is closely related to the understanding and respect deficits; it requires mutual understanding and respect between the two countries, to reduce the limits of cultural barriers. Confucius Institutes in India are caught in a dilemma; although there are ten universities providing Hindi courses in China until 2013, Hindi in China is not popular among professionals. A quarter of the world's population involves the two countries, and as there are a lot of people who cannot communicate through language, communication errors caused should not be underestimated. How to clear the obstacles in this regard on both sides should be considered. Confucius Institutes in recent years have suffered a number of questions in regard to their own need for improvement. Other countries need to continue to understand the needs of the Chinese language, and then develop more optimal policies to mitigate problems caused by language.

Civil society organisations with strong initiatives have been set up mostly by people who have a sense of responsibility and bilateral cultural identity. How to make these non-governmental organizations play a greater role in promoting the two countries' relations should also be included in the planning of mutual understanding, which is one of the key ways to eliminate bilateral "trust deficit". Civil society organizations, such as the New York-based India China Institute, Shanghai's West Heavens, and the Juxtapose Project established at the University of Oxford and so on are beginning to play a role to build links between the two countries in the academia and arts. They are also organized in cooperation with official activities. However, civil society organizations have many inherent limitations, such as funding problems, as there are scholars to "invest in appropriate research institutes and programmes to study in the other country" (Sen 2012). Feedback to the vision of promoting leadership scholars and reasonable adoption would make communication more targeted and effective policy.

The then director of ICS, Mohanty, at the forum with the participation of Chinese Premier Wen Jiabao, put forward a plan for the purpose of "Peaceful Coexistence". He stated that the two countries should establish a "peaceful coexistence research centre" in order to "promote language teaching, communication and other fields of art and culture exchange." In media reports, researchers did not directly highlight some of the intractable problems yet to be solved, but introduced a new cooperative mechanism. The new formulation is no doubt that educational cooperation between the two countries put together is dominant on both sides, but both can be in an equal position to participate in the platform, as a community of interests to build a culture perspective. Wen took this very seriously and required that the authorities immediately promise to study it. There is still need for more researchers to promote this area; leading scholars are also required to make a positive impact. Before Xi Jinping's visit to India in 2014, the introduction of the Five Principles is a strong response to this and there is a need to continually build on the basis of this intelligence and civilize countries on the product (Zhao et al. 2010).

CHAPTER 4

CONCLUSION

4.1. Summarising the Main Arguments

This research analyses achievements in the field of cultural exchanges between China and India, public perceptions of each country towards the other and government policies on cultural exchanges from 2003 to 2014. The most representative achievements in cultural exchanges have been in India in the form of the Xuan Zang Memorial Hall and Cheena Bhavana. Each of these institutions represents two aspects of exchanges; the Xuan Zang Memorial Hall is based on Buddhist links between the two countries, while Cheena Bhavana is on cultural-linguistics links. Although the national leaders have rationalised the role of Buddhism in the 21st century as a linkage between China and India and Buddhist culture has emerged as an important symbol of China-India relations, the cultural exchange policies should not be limited just to Buddhism. This is because Buddhism is a minor religion in India, practised by only 0.8 per cent of the population. Even in China, it is limited to only 20 per cent of the population. Moreover, there are many constraints to the efficiency of cultural exchanges, especially the border disputes that have been a political irritant between the two countries. In comparison to cultural issues, political matters take precedence in the overall strategic vision of a modern nation. So, the role of cultural exchanges would be limited until the many core disputes are not resolved to the satisfaction of both countries.

The attitudes of the two countries towards each other have evolved through historical experiences. The ancient and modern cultural exchanges have influenced the national consciousness, in turn influencing actual bilateral cooperation between the two nations. The official positions of both China and India have been to consistently and continuously improve the bilateral relations, but we can observe inconsistencies in the stands of the three sectors in India dealing with China: government, media and scholars. While in China, the media and scholars follow the official line and provide all necessary assistance to the government, the Indian press and academia scrutinise and expose problems in the relations. The latter also view the relations in terms of cost-benefit analysis and highlight any apparent infringement of India's national interests. Since cultural exchanges are dependent on the views of people from diverse fields, a comprehensive view of China-India relations is necessary and that will improve the utility of cultural exchanges and promote further improvement in bilateral relations.

When we observe the characteristics and policies of China and India from 2003 to 2014, there are significant differences in the focus of the two countries. These differences arise due to their variant political and cultural outlooks. India is more active and strong in protection and dissemination of its culture, but China approaches the matter with restraint and in a utilitarian manner. These cultural attitudes influence the general policies of the two countries and their influence in the world. Cultural attitude is a critical variable that can affect the final results of any policy on cultural exchanges and determine whether a culture contracts or expands.

There are deep linkages between achievements, perceptions and policies and they influence one another. For instance, Buddhism is an important achievement in the improvement of relations between the two countries, so it reflects on the perceptions of the national leaders and the policies of the two governments. Nonetheless, the Indian media and academia have only acknowledged the Buddhist linkages with reservations. On the other hand, Chinese thinkers have warmly perceived the common Buddhist heritage. Therefore, the cultural impact on the Chinese side of the relations has been more obvious. Cultural exchanges have also been a great achievement in bilateral co-operation from 2003 to 2014. However, border issues impede the growth of closeness, especially on the Indian side, which is quite sceptical of the efficacy of cultural exchanges without the resolution of the core disputes. Both the countries have continued to try mitigating the impact of the border disputes through the appointment of Special Representatives to resolve them and cultural exchange programmes in the border areas. That said, perception does matter and for the cultural exchanges to be effective, the countries must make headway in political negotiations.

4.2. Testing the Hypotheses

4.2.1. The Influence of Cultural Exchanges on China-India Relations

From 2003 to 2014, cultural exchanges between the two countries have come closer and more rationalised. In 2003, the China-India relationship had been defined as "comprehensive cooperation" and in 2005, it was called "strategic partnership", which has continued till 2014. The connotation has been constantly evolving. Cultural exchanges are an important factor in defining the relationship between both countries. The achievements of the cultural exchanges between the two countries have been constantly emphasised by people from all walks of life in both the countries because they reflect the common development of China and India in the 21st century and the constructive role the countries will play in establishing a new world order. The cultural exchange project is a continuation of the traditional relations between China and India, e.g., Buddhist linkages and scholarly interactions. Indeed, the exchange activities have developed even further. Deepening cultural exchanges can even support the emergence of mutual trust that can reduce tensions created by border disputes. Certainly, the above conclusion is based on the normalization of political relations between the two countries.

Cultural exchanges in 2020 paled into insignificance due to the China-India border conflict, with most of the 70 events planned to celebrate the 70th anniversary of diplomatic relations between the two countries not being held as scheduled due to clashes in the Galwan Valley on 15 June 2020. Political relations between the two countries were at an impasse. India banned 59 and then 118 Chinese apps on June 29 and 2 September 2020, disseminating the view that Chinese apps were suspected of participating in activities that endangered India's sovereignty and (territorial) integrity, defence, national security and public order. Good political relations are the basis of cultural exchanges, and tense political relations greatly limit their progress, especially at the official level. Although people-to-people exchanges have not completely stagnated, they have been affected to a certain extent. In particular, the mutual resistance of ordinary audience groups will breed "fear", which will affect the effect and impact of cultural exchange. In addition, the COVID-19 pandemic has exacerbated the border-affected exchanges between the two countries, preventing the normal flow of people and hindering exchanges.

4.2.2. The Influence of Perceptions on Leadership Perspectives

While analysing the whole framework, we can see that the influence of scholars on the leadership's perspective is quite distinct and significant. The ideas put forward by scholars have provided important reference points for leaders to define the relationship between both the countries. Among the scholars, the most representative and influential two figures might be Xuan Zang and Ji Xianlin. Nonetheless, it is important to mention that the viewpoints of scholars do not always have a bearing on the leadership. For instance, the idea of Chindia had a limited influence. At the same time, a few scholars have neither made substantial contributions to the improvement of China-India relations nor have they helped in the resolution of the border disputes nor have they exerted any influence on the leadership. However, the viewpoint of the scholars to resolve the border issue at the earliest has drawn the attention of the leadership. The perception of scholars on various events has made different influences on the perspective of the leadership. Scholars who have made a positive influence on the leadership of both the countries have got their ideas approved, especially Chinese scholars who have been recognised by Indian officials to have affected the perspective of the Chinese leadership.

The influence the media makes on the leadership of both the countries is comparatively limited. In China, the leadership basically exerts an influence on the media. In India, the media mainly reports on the problems existing in the China-India relationship and focuses on whether India's interests are being safeguarded or not. This does not have a direct effect on the perspective of the Indian leadership. It has not let negative media reports adversely affect its attitude towards China. The positive influence of the Chinese media on the Chinese leadership has been manifested indirectly in some spheres. If Indian films are welcomed in China, then this can be a topic of conversation among the leadership of both the countries.

Besides exerting an influence on the leadership of its own country, the public has also exerted a positive effect on that of the other country. For example, Wen Jiabao (2005) had once mentioned Amartya Sen's viewpoint on the China-India relationship in a speech. Singh (2008) had cited Ji Xianlin's definition of China-India relations and had said that scholars play an important role in understanding each other. Besides, friendly personnel have also affected the perspective of China's leadership on China-India relations, especially family members of Dwarkanath Kotnis have played an important role in developing relations between China and India, Simultaneously, the awardee of the Panchsheel Friendship Award is a manifestation of influence over the leadership's perspective.

4.3. Research Trends

If one wants to analyse the effect of China-India cultural exchanges on the relationship of both the countries, then one needs to understand the historical origin of China-India cultural exchanges, the real state of affairs and simultaneously needs to be familiar with various problems involved in China-India relations. It is not an easy task to find scholars who can connect them. First, the China-India cultural exchange is long-standing and well-established. A rational analysis requires knowledge about language, history, culture, religion and other aspects. Ji Xianlin (2005:155) had once said that the history of human cultural exchange ought to be a specialized branch of learning. In reality, behind common things, often lies a hidden complex and twisted history of cultural exchanges. Second, a study of China-India relations require a thorough understanding of political theories and IR theories. Connecting both the spheres requires an inter-disciplinary approach and a solid theoretical base. Moreover, it requires exchange experience and comprehensive reflection. It is only then can one effectively analyse the effect of cultural exchanges on the relationship of both the countries. Creating a rational perception about one another and progressive systematization of cultural policies, thereby diversifying each other's culture lets the relations enter a virtuous cycle and establish a scientific diplomatic system. The influence of cultural exchanges on the relationship between two countries requires a systematic knowledge set up. This also requires dialogues between scholars from various disciplines, cultivation of passion in this domain leading to peaceful co-existence between both China and India and making Asia and the world prosperous.

PART II

TRADITION, ECONOMY AND RELATIONS

CHAPTER 5

THEORY: PSYCHO-CULTUROLOGY AND MORAL REALISM

5.1. Psycho-Culturology: Psycho-social Homeostasis (PSH) and Human Constant

In International Relations (IR), there is a debate about the efficacy of non-Western theories as Western international relations theories are not sufficient to analyse all non-Western countries. As a result, many IR theories from non-Western countries have emerged. Among them, several Chinese and Indian scholars have certain theoretical representations, such as Yan Xuetong, whose theory is called Moral Realism, Qin Yaqing who established the *guanxi* theory, and Amitav Acharya and so on. Apart from these, Shang Huipeng (2013:3) coined Psycho-Culturology based on Francis L. K. Hsu's doctrine, which is about the comparative study of literate civilisations. This theory is conducive to explain the different levels of economic behaviour in the cultural dimensions of China and India.

This research draws on Psycho-Culturology as the primary theoretical interpretation tool. Psycho-Culturology analyses Chinese and Indians from the psychological and cultural perspective at different levels (individuals, groups, etc.). Individuals under the influence of Confucianism and Hinduism are respectively objects of analysis in Psycho-Culturology, and the *Lun-ren* (*lun-jen*) and the Homo Hierarchicus (Dumont 1980) are used as the scientific names of Chinese and Indians (Shang 2013:70,71,78).

"*Lun*" literally means match, ethics, and order. *Wu-lun* (five human relationships in ethics) is the most critical relationship in the ethics of Confucianism between ruler and subject, father and son, husband and wife, brothers and friends. The relationship of father and son, which reflect the concept of *xiao* (filial piety), is in the front rank in the order of Confucian tradition (*Mencius V*) that shows the importance of the family more over kinship. The ethics and order of *Lun-ren* could reflect the awareness of humans and the orientation of the understanding on interpersonal relationships as well as the particular sequence of people in relation in Chinese traditional culture (Shang 2013:71). The *lun-ren*, which is dominant in traditional China, is the embodiment of the Confucian values system, and Chinese civilisation is considered as the most splendid fruit of the human being, basing on this *lun-ren* human constant (Shang and You 2010:334; Shang 2013:72).Homo Hierarchicus is "referring to the integration and division of Indian society according to the hierarchy principle, the existential state of the people characterised by strong interdependence" (Shang 2013:78). The commercial behaviour, organisational culture, and national policies are embodied in the behaviours of the *Lun-ren* and the Homo Hierarchicus at different levels (individual, organisational, national). There are similarities and differences in the two cultures, and the influence of cultural differences on economic relations is the primary analysis objective of this study.

There are two main essential parts in Psycho-Culturology: Psycho-Social Homeostasis (PSH) theory and human constant (Shang 2013:53-55). Psycho-Social Homeostasis (PSH) is a theoretical model for understanding the relationship between human psychology, behaviour, and culture as proposed by Hsu Francis L. K. This theory holds that "human is in a 'field' (*chang*) where human and human, human and object, and human and cultural norms interact with each other. It is a dynamic homeostatic system between psychology and society; this homeostatic system is divided into nine layers from the inside to outside" (numbers 8 to 0), and these nine layers include (Shang 2013:54-56).

The individual's psychology contains these levels. Individuals follow certain principles and interact with people, things, and cultural norms in each layer to maintain a dynamic balance. Different cultures have different homeostatic models. The analysis of different models is conducive to understanding the psychological and behavioural characteristics of different cultures (Shang 2013:57). Indian scholar Age Handa Bharat suggested that a point, which is called "*atman*" (soul, self) in Hinduism, should be added in the PSH model centre to explain Hindus better. This layer (8) is called superconscious (Shang 2013:54, 58-60).

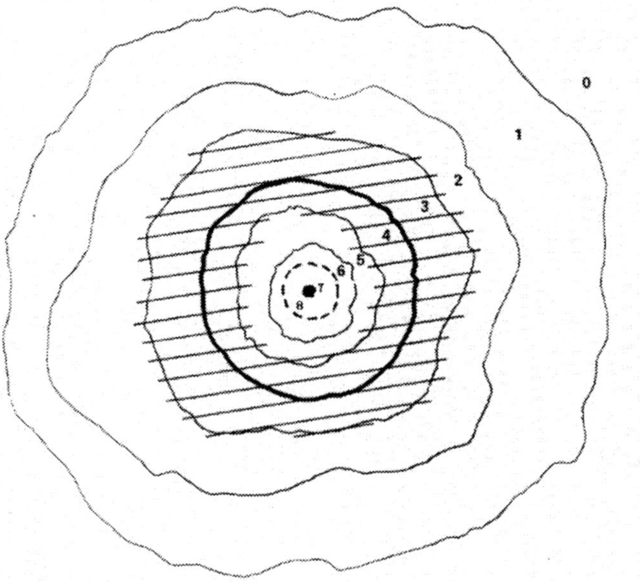

8. Superconscious, 7. Unconscious, 6. Preconscious, 5. Unexpressed conscious, 4. Expressed conscious, 3. Intimate society and culture, 2. Operative society and culture, 1. Wider society and culture, 0. Outer world

Psycho-Social Homeostasis (PSH) Model (Shang 2013:60)

7. Unconscious, 6. Preconscious: These two layers refer to the deep level of human consciousness and are the main psychoanalytic content of Sigmund Freud; 5. Unexpressed conscious: it relates to the hidden consciousness that is hidden in the heart of a person, only what he/she alone can realise, but the expression is restricted; 4. Expressed conscious: it includes ideas, feelings, emotions, as well as thoughts and beliefs, "it could interact with each other, being easily understood, accepted, or responded to", this layer is the most common sense of daily use; 3. Intimate society and culture: This layer includes "people who are strongly attached, items (the things of love) and the cultural norms (the obsession, including religious belief, ideals, norms to be followed, etc.)". This layer has also become a "life pack"; 2. Operative society and culture: including "useful": People, things and cultural norms, [people] generally do not bet on their emotions on this layer, it is role-based rather than emotional, such as teachers and students, manufacturers and customers; 1. Wider society and culture: Hsu (1973:4-14) refers to the people, goods and cultural norms are far away from life. Those are limited to just knowing and the impact is relatively weak; 0. Outer world: This refers to foreign culture, foreign countries, alien planets, and alien galaxies.

Human Constant

The fourth and third layers and the fifth and second layers constitute the "Human Constant", which is a "human system" and a general term for the mutual recognition and communication system between people (Shang 2013:60-61). The human constant in Chinese is called *lun-ren* (or *lun-jen*), *ren* (*jen*) means people, and the meaning of *lun* includes the "relationship between people", "orderliness", "order" (Ibid: 71). For *Lun-ren,* the kinship members are the main content and comparatively stable in the third layer of Psycho-Social Homeostasis (PSH) (Ibid: 72, 313). The human constant of the Hindu is Homo Hierarchicus (Ibid: 78). For Homo Hierarchicus, gods and priests are the critical content in the third layer of PSH (Ibid: 311).

The Human constant is divided into four dimensions: group dimension, exchange dimension, emotional dimension, self-cognition dimension (Shang 2013:64-66),

(1) The group dimension, which expresses the "method of human association", is the external image of the human constant. It includes the third and second layers in the PSH model, and relates to the first layer (Ibid: 65). It is used to analyse organisational culture and national policies in this research.

(2) The exchange dimension shows "how the individual interacts with others in a particular social and cultural context", and its content mainly belongs to the third and second layers in the PSH, and some of it involves the fourth and first layers (Ibid: 65). It is used in this research to analyse commercial behaviour. The exchange dimension outwards constitutes the group dimension, so it has an impact on the group dimension, and the group dimension affects the way people exchange (Ibid: 67)

(3) The self-cognition dimension refers to how the individual defines the self. It will be used to show how individuals, especially the national leader, realise self and the influence of their method of interacting with others. It is an essential factor as it influences the leader's mindset for policy-making.

The human is the carrier of culture, the subject of the group and the nation. The human constant is the basic system of human existence, representing the characteristics of "human", and the comparative study of the human constant as the basic operational unit can solve the psychological and cultural characteristics and behaviour patterns of the Chinese and Indians (Ibid: 70). The human constant is the status of human beings, a "probabilistic description". It describes the dynamic homeostatic process; "the possibility of a certain psychosocial dynamic homeostatic state tending to emerge in a particular cultural context"; Psycho-Culturology, which takes PSH and human constant as the two main research tools, could be considered as the new version of the national character studies (Ibid: 71).

5.2. Moral Realism (national behaviour: not only for profit)

The first deduction of Moral Realism is that "seeking profit is the first primary but not the entire motive force of national behaviour" (Yan 2016). Moral Realism supports the idea that not all national behaviour is motivated by profit. The non-seeking profit values are influencing national behaviour. The economic values of Confucianism and Hinduism include the seeking-profit value like *ren, zhi* and *manthan* (Chapter 7). Meanwhile, the non-seeking-profit value could also play a role in national behaviour, for instance, *yi*, *xin*, *karma* and *jugaad*. Thus, all those values, whether seeking for profit or not, need to be analysed in the national behaviour of China and India here on the aspect of their economic behaviour.

The core logic of Moral Realism is that the ideology (thought and ideas) of ways to achieve interest is one of the two factors to decide the external strategic choice of a nation (The other factor is the objective national strategic interests of nations) (Yan 2016). Taking the "ideology of way to achieve interest" as a reference, this research considers it as an essential factor influenced by traditional culture and plays a role on people's thought and behaviour in the aspect of the economy.

CHAPTER 6

THE IMPACT OF CONFUCIANSIM AND HINDUISM ON CHINA AND INDIA

6.1. Introduction

6.1.1. The Importance of Confucianism in China and Hinduism in India

Culture influences people's ways of thinking and behaviour that lead to different economic performances. By examining various ethnic groups, the situation of economic development shows the differences. Culture is "accorded a privileged position" as "it is seen to play a crucial role in structuring the way people think, feel and act [...]" (Gay and Pryke 2002:1), and "change the way they do things and how they see the world" (Mulgan 1997).

Culture is "those customary beliefs and values that ethnic, religious, and social groups transmit fairly unchanged from generation to generation (Guiso et al. 2006). In China, Confucian values are an essential foundation of Chinese civilisation (Shang 2013:72). In India, customary beliefs and values of religion are a significant part of its culture while Hindus account for 79.8 per cent of the population (GoI 2011). This chapter analyses the influence of Confucian culture and Hindu culture on the economic development of China and India, respectively, and use the research findings of Psycho-Culturology (Shang and You 2010; Shang 2013) to analyse the behavioural characteristics of these two civilisations. The economy performance at three levels will be examined, i.e., (1) individual (commercial behaviour), (2) organisational (organisational culture), and (3) national (trade policy). As a theory of interpreting behaviour, Psycho-Culturology analyses the behavioural characteristics of different civilisations (China, India, the USA and Japan) in four different dimensions including group, exchange, emotional and self-cognition (Shang 2013:64-67) that are conducive for understanding the behavioural characteristics in the three levels mentioned above. From the perspective of Psycho-Culturology, by considering the relationship among individual needs, social norms and cultural ideals, the cultural trends, individual behaviours and organisational characteristics of larger societies could be predicted and generalised (Hsu 1963), which is conducive to assess the impact of Chinese and Indian culture on the economy.

The Communist Party of China values Chinese traditional culture in the current period[1] and Confucian culture is an integral part of it. It was considered that "China's dynamism is as much a function of its burgeoning economy as of following Confucian ethics" and the traditional Confucian values such as harmony, hard work, austerity and peaceful development are emphasised in the official discourse (Nuri 2017). Hindu culture in India is either strongly enforced by the current ruling party, the Bharatiya Janata Party (BJP), which has an image "as a rabid Hindutva party" (Banerjee 2005:3116), or the other major, nationwide, secular, political party, the Indian National Congress (Congress), that needs to balance its pluralism approach and the reality that Hinduism is a majority (Sivaswamy 2018). For the Congress, which emphasises secularisation, it was believed that "[...] in the Indian context, secularism just means pluralism," "absence of religion [...] would never work" (Ibid.). The specific position of Hinduism in India was pointed out as,

> "India and other developing countries cannot afford to have social structures impeding their potential for growth and development. While Hinduism's emphasis on higher concerns is admirable and has many positive social consequences, its effect on people's propensity for entrepreneurialism should be considered." (Audretsch and Meyer 2009)

The influence of mainstream beliefs on the country has a unique performance in India, and this influence is difficult to eliminate,

> "While it is not feasible to diminish the influence of Hinduism in Indian society, it may be possible to implement policies and programs that can counteract the specific effects it may have on economic decision-making." (Ibid.)

Therefore, the respective influences of these two cultures in the two countries should necessarily be examined.

---

1 It was summarised as "under the revolutionary thinking and action the Chinese Communist Party has experienced from the intensive opposition, fundamental denial to the rational view and high approval with the thinking as a ruling party in the new century" towards the traditional culture (Yang Fengcheng 2014:78). After the reform and opening-up policy, the attitude towards traditional culture gradually attributed to rationality and objectivity in China, especially since the 18th National Congress of the Communist Party of China (2012), Confucius and Chinese excellent traditional culture were highly praised (Li and Le 2014:9).

6.1.2. The Reviving of Traditional Culture and its Impact

The reviving of traditional culture is taking place currently in China. The Belt and Road Initiative (BRI) is the signal of China's rising confidence. The Silk Road was the commercial pathway to export China's products in ancient times while the new initiative is a promotional factor to export China's technology and capital in the modern period. It could also be seen as the influence of a Chinese value "*Tian-xia da-tong*" (world-state) (*CCTV News* 2018). *Tian-xia da-tong* is originally from Confucianism and mentioned in its classic work *Li Ji* (Book of Rites). Moreover, in the Confucian classic book, *Mencius,* Mencius, "the Chinese philosopher and sage, and one of the principal interpreters of Confucianism", also emphasised to "be disciplined when poor, and be generous to the people in the world when rich" [*qiong-ze du-shan qi-shen, da-ze jian-shan tian-xia*].

For India, it can be seen that the Modi government is increasingly promoting Hindu culture in domestic politics and even diplomacy such as Yoga promotion and khadi (Dutta and Dave 2017). It is a soft power promotion as well as a culture-based national behaviour. It could promote the influence and international image of India. The development of cultural factors could help the government get the support of the people when the government enables people to identify individuals and align with the goals and objectives of the nation in which they live (Gay and Pryke 2002:1). Against the background of China's rising and India's emerging, it is sensible to emphasise their own cultural identity. As mentioned above, culture does influence people's thinking and behaviour. The economic developments of the two nations are influenced by their traditional culture.

6.2. The Influence of Confucianism on China's Economic Development

6.2.1. Introduction

In this paper, Chinese influenced by Confucianism—using the concept of Psycho-Culturology—are classified as the "*lun-ren*" (*lun-jen*), which is their "human constant" of Chinese (Shang 2013:71). Confucianism influenced the concept of interpersonal relationship and the differential pattern in the relationship, exchange mode, which reflected in the commercial behaviour of the Chinese.

6.2.2. Individual Level: The Influence of Confucianism on Behaviour

6.2.2.1. *GUANXI:* INTERPERSONAL RELATIONSHIP

Guanxi (interpersonal relationships) is considered to be a critical factor in understanding China. It was considered that "*Guanxi* is one of the major dynamics in Chinese society. It has been a pervasive part of the Chinese business world for the last few centuries" (Luo Yadong 2007:1). In the late 1980s, with the rise of the East Asian Chinese economic circle, [...] *guanxi* became the core concept of understanding Chinese social behaviour (Shang and You 2010:325).

It was considered that "the relational orientation", which is different with Westerners, captures the most essential part of the Chinese people's behaviour and social psychology" (He Youhui et al. 1989:49-66). Psycho-Culturology believes that the psycho-cultural orientation of *lun-ren* is based on the "Ren-centred" (*Jen*-centred), and considers that "the interpersonal relationship is the most meaningful and valuable to pursue [among the relationships of human and human, human and nature, human and supernatural, individual and outer world]", so more psychological energy is put into it (Shang 2013:274).

Guanxi (or interpersonal relationship) is considered to be a value that has a significant influence on China. It is a product of Confucian cultural entity (*wenhua ti*) and practical entity (*shijian ti*), and a cultural element and background knowledge accumulated in long-term historical practice (Qin 2012:6). It is a concept that pursues the harmony between human.

The *Guanxi* factor plays a role that cannot be ignored in the development of China's economy. *Guanxi* means power, connection, and resources (Huang 1987:5-6) (March and Wu 2007:127). Due to China's top-down approach of resource allocation, "some people will use tactics such as '*zou hou-men*' [entering through the back door], '*la guanxi*' [establish underhand connections and exploit for personal gain] and '*gao guanxi*' [engage in relationship] to seek some favours from organisational leaders who control scarce resources" (Huang 1987:3).

This situation is not static. Along with the influence of Western individualism on the code of conduct and motivation of daily life, and the expansion of market functions which is providing many resources that are not controlled by the top-down, people can have more opportunities to establish a valid or fair relationship with strangers (Huang 1987:32). "The adoption of universal management rules" makes "people tend to build relationships with others on the basis of instrumentality or fairness"; the influence of "*renqing*" [favour] and "*mianzi*" [face], which are related to *guanxi*, began to weaken on some occasions (Ibid.). Besides, the development of *guanxi* has also evolved something that is rooted in Confucianism but is different from it. Scholars have pointed out that *guanxi* can be connected with Confucianism, but it is different, as Zhai Xuewei (2011:4) believes.

> "Western sociology, psychology and anthropology have extracted "*guanxi zhuyi*" [relationshipism] and "*rujia guanxi zhuyi*" [Confucian relationshipism], *guanxi* is a feature of Chinese and Chinese society, neither the Confucian statement nor expression of people and Chinese culture under the Confucian influence. *Guanxi* can be connected with Confucianism, but it can also be combined with the so-called '*Guanxi Xue*' [*Guanxi* Study] (referring to the art of cultivating good personal relations) of Chinese people. The practice of *guanxi* means that the routine is very snobbish and utilitarian; it is not directly affected by

> Confucianism. On the contrary, orthodox Confucian defenders cannot be *chi de kai* [popular] in officialdom."

The influence of *guanxi* is complicated in Modern China. The contemporary concept of *guanxi* is influenced by the thought of Confucianism but present factors that are not entirely consistent with tradition. What is certain is that Confucianism has to pay attention to the interpersonal relationship. It was pointed out "Confucianism's emphasis is on the relationship among people rather than on the relationship between people and the supernatural." (Tang Zongli 1995:270). It was suggested that "a strong relationship existed between Confucianism and China's large population" (Ibid: 269).

The Chinese value relationships. The famous argument of Fei Xiaotong (1988: 359) describes this feature of Chinese society,

> "The structure of Chinese society is like the ripple of a circle that occurs when a stone is thrown on the water. Everyone is the centre of the circle that his social influence has launched. The relationship is established when the ripples of the circle are affected".

The connection creates the relationship. The relationship is "the core concept of understanding Chinese social behaviour"; this characteristic, which Fei Xiaotong has described, is considered as the central part of the essence of the Chinese and Chinese society (Shang and You 2010:324-325). *Guanxi* (relationship) has positive factors that promote social harmony by connecting individuals and also has the potential negative impact of making individual behaviour irregular and unlawful.

6.2.2.2. Mianzi (Face) and Li (Gift Giving)

Mianzi (face) is another factor that is related to the thought of Confucianism, representing dignity and the need to be respected (Cheng 1986). It reveals the social status or prestige gained by an individual in social achievements (Hu 1944). In China, *mianzi* is often used and valued; it is also connected with power.

> "In Chinese society, '*Zuo mianzi*'(make face, paint job) is a means for individuals to show off their power; '*mianzi gongfu*'(face work) is to influence the resource distributors to change the way resources are allocated according to their intentions, it is a kind of power game that Chinese people often play" (Huang 1987:24).

Mianzi could be relevant to power, and the impact of power in a society cannot be ignored. There are examples to show that '*ai mianzi*' (saving face) behaviour is often reflected in Chinese society, such as "*mianzi gong-cheng*" [face-saving project] of government, which attaches importance to the external form, which could cause a certain amount of extravagance and waste. The specific performance is that individuals pay more attention to the packaging of goods for gifts. Sometimes there are even whopping price increases because of extravagant packaging in the market. Besides, the Chinese like to express their enthusiasm and attach importance to their guests by ordering more than necessary food for them, regardless of whether it is required or not, resulting in waste and '*you yu*' (surplus) representing the abundance of life. Although this situation is changing, along with the campaigns of social organisations and government such as 'Clear your plate' (*guang-pan'er xing-dong*), it is different for Indians. They pay special attention to food not exceeding demand. The Chinese may feel that Indians are "stingy" and misunderstand their saving spirit.

Besides, *mianzi* is also associated with gift-giving, such as for '*zheng mianzi*' (seeking for *mianzi*) and sending more significant gifts to overpower others; rejecting other people's gifts is also a '*diu mianzi*' (face loss) (Gransow 1993:9). Gift-giving related to *mianzi* is a manifestation of China's "*li*" (ritual) culture and is considered to be an essential driving force of China's economic growth:

> "Statistics of the China gift industry research institute show that gift consumption usually accounts for about 5 per cent of sales of the year-round retail industry. It can be estimated that the consumption of retail gifts will reach 885 billion Chinese Yuan or more than last year's annual retail sales of 17.7 trillion Chinese Yuan" (Hilton 2013).

It is basic etiquette to buy gifts and visit relatives and friends in China during the Chinese New Year and other festivals. In social interactions, *jian mian li* (the first gift) is a kind of respect. Whether it is visiting people with high status or visiting elders, relatives and friends, it is a widespread phenomenon to meet with gifts. On the one hand, it is conducive to promoting social harmony. On the other hand, gift-giving for establishing *guanxi* also breeds corruption and undermines the management of state-authorised supervisory departments (Gransow 1993:11).

It is worth mentioning that the concept of *mianzi* presented above is not always acceptable to all Chinese. Some studies have shown that,

> "When an individual internalises modernised individualism into a part of personality traits, he/she generally ignores *renqing* (favour) and *mianzi* (face) when he/she deals with people. He/she generally does not feel the conflict of the '*renqing* (favour) dilemma.'" (Huang, Hu et al. 2010:28)

As pointed out, the Confucian moral binding force based on 'acquaintance society'[2] is weakening in the context of globalisation influenced by Western commercial civilisation (Xue 2015: 144). Modernisation is undoubtedly a non-negligible factor to eliminate traditional negative influences, but it does not mean that the impact of conventional thoughts could be reduced. How to "absorb the quintessence and remove the dross from the traditional culture" in development

2 *Shuren shehui* (acquaintance society), which is highly influenced by the concept of *mianzi* and *guanxi*.

is an endless theme. Although China is influenced by Marxism as well as Western culture, traditional culture, of which Confucianism is an indispensable and dominant part, is not waived as it is pointed out that the Party Constitution of the Communist Party of China promotes "the creative transformation and innovative development of Chinese excellent traditional culture" (CPC2017:13). It shows the design of the ruling party's selective practice of traditional culture in which Confucianism could continue to play a role in the development of China.

6.2.2.3. Ancestor Worship and Filial Piety

The worship of ancestors is considered to be the basis of Confucianism and sacrificing ancestors is considered a virtue; a social and moral obligation (Chen 2009). This is part of filial piety (*xiao dao*) along with fulfilling the filial duty to parents sometimes also including the relative kinship. Because of the emphasis on filial piety in Confucianism, there is a particular etiquette at funerals, which has social and ethical significance; the cost of the funeral is considerable and generally cannot be avoided. Supporting parents and conducting funerals for the deceased are seen as equally important (Chen 2009). Confucius's remarks are recorded in the classic work of Confucianism, *Zhong Yong* (*The Doctrine of the Mean*), "[...] to serve them now dead as if they were living, and now departed as if they were still with us—this is the highest achievement of true filial piety" [*shi-si ru shi-sheng, shi-wang ru shi-cun, xiao zhi zhi ye*]. It is reflected in Tomb-Sweeping Day (*Qing-ming* Festival), which is an essential traditional festival in China. The different attitudes of other schools like Mohism (Mo jia) to funerals made it lose its influence in China. Mo Tzu (Mo Zi)'s temperance in mourning apparel, coffin and mourning period is different from paying importance in Confucianism to the funeral. Confucius proposed three years of mourning, and Mo Tzu suggested only three months: "Once the deceased is buried, the living must immediately resume the production of wealth". It is also pointed out that Confucius's thinking can better meet Chinese people's needs (Chen 2009), thus becoming the doctrine of making a significant impact on China.

The customs derived from Confucian filial piety also have a profound impact on society and the economy. For example, many Chinese do not have a haircut in the first month of the Chinese lunar calendar. The Confucian classic, *Xiao Jing* [*The Book of Filial Piety*], mentions "Our bodies—to every hair and bit of skin—are received by us from our parents, and we must not presume to injure or wound them. It is the beginning of filial piety." Confucianism emphasises that the skin is given by parents and cannot be easily damaged. According to a legend of the Qing Dynasty, the Han nationality was reluctant to change their hairstyle and wear plaits to resist Manchu rule. Some people did not have a haircut in the first month of the lunar year, indicating nostalgia (*huai-jiu*), and passed it on to their maternal uncle who is supposed to die (*si jiu jiu*) if he has a haircut in the first lunar month (Liu 2006; Zhang Sisi 2015). This custom has been passed down to this day, and no haircut has become an expression of respect for the maternal uncle. It is widely held by the people that a haircut in the first lunar month will cause the death of the uncle; so many people do not have a haircut in this period. According to a report, "the number of customers in a barbershop in the first lunar month is about one-third less than usual" (Liu 2006), and many people still follow this custom in Chinese society.

6.2.2.4. Against Excessive Frugality and Emphasising Wealth

In the pursuit of material things, Confucianism has a different concept from Hinduism that promotes frugality and wealth. Chen Huanzhang (2009) pointed out in his book, *The Economic Principles of Confucius and His School,* that

> "The Confucius system is an advanced civilisation, not a primitive one. Therefore, he does not pay special attention to frugality in his economic theory. On the contrary, he proposes preventing excessive frugality."

Chen Huanzhang (2009) believes that Confucius's selection of poems in *Shi Jing* [*The Book of Songs*] reflects "Confucius's economic principle against parsimony" and believes that,

> "Consumption is the purpose of the economy, and production is only its method. If we do not consume products in economical ways, we will destroy the purpose of production, and there will be no economic progress".

Extreme frugality may even cause people to develop "narrow thinking, brutal temperament, wretched personality, no ambition, unhappy life, ungenerous social interaction, a fulsome social situation" (Ibid.).

Chen Huanzhang's interpretation of Confucianism reflects that Confucius does not propose extreme frugality. In addition, Chen (2009) also pointed out that Confucius did not completely ignore material enjoyment and put forward the aesthetic principles of consumption, but later the followers of Confucius in the Song Dynasty have "paid too much attention to the inner character, almost completely ignoring the external welfare", [...] and made "the material progress of China to stagnate".

The emphasis on material consumption and wealth are essential aspects of Confucianism that differs from other civilisations. Max Weber (1951:237) has pointed out that

> "Confucianism and Confucian mentality, deifying 'wealth', [...]. In no other civilised country has material welfare ever been as exalted as the supreme good. The oldest document of Chinese political economy is a tract by the Confucian Ssu-ma Ch'ien (*SimaQian*) on the 'balance of trade' [*maoyi pinghe* in *Shiji, ping huai shu*] in which the usefulness of wealth, including economic profit, is emphasized".

This philosophy has prompted the Chinese to create wealth. Because agriculture is the primary way of life for the ancient Chinese, poor conditions are considered to be an essential reason for Confucius to pay attention to people's economic life (Chen 2009). China's backwardness and poverty have also made the ruling party of modern China take economic construction as the centre of its reform, and the people have generally responded to it. It has formed a situation in which the people now attach importance to wealth and material consumption, and the favourable influence is to promote economic development.

6.2.2.5. Bao: Exchange as Trustworthiness Credit

Many societies have the concept of "*bao*" [return, repay, reward], yet the "*bao*" of the Chinese are more prominent in practice and have their own characteristics. Gouldner (1960) argues that the norm of "repay" is ubiquitous in human society and is the fundamental moral law recognised by any culture (Levi-Strauss 1965; Malinowski, 1926; Huang, Hu et al. 2010:15). However, the norms of "*bao*" that Chinese society values are different from other cultures. This mutual reward "is not a general transaction between autonomous actors, but a kind of obligation of an individual in a particular social context (Huang 1987:31)". The concept of "*bao*" in Chinese culture is also related to "*renqing*" (favour) and "*mianzi*" (face):

> "The content of '*renqing*' (favour) includes the position of the individual in the network of differential relations (*cha-xu xing guanxi*) and his expectation of how long the relationship will be maintained. Moreover, these will affect the obligation of '*bao*' (return); the concept of *mianzi* is also an influencing factor of accepting or rejecting; the consideration of factors such as *bao* (return), *renqing* (favour) and *mianzi* (face) are stronger parts in the thought and behaviour of the Chinese (Huang 1987:31)".

From the perspective of Psycho-Culturology, the exchange dimension of the human constant of *lun-ren* reflects the interaction mode between the individual and others (Shang 2013:65). It is in favour of understanding the commercial behaviour of the people. For example, the dominant mode of exchange of *lun-ren* is the "exchange as trustworthiness credit", that is,

> "[...] 'lending' and 'borrowing' under the premise of mutual trust and expectation of return; it is not an equivalent exchange, but is accompanied by '*en yi*' (spiritual debt) and '*renqing*' (favour), '*en*' (grace), '*bao*' (reward), '*renqing*' (favour), '*li*' (rites), '*guanxi*' that are the keywords for expressing this exchange mode" (Shang 2013:73).

It can be seen that the *lun-ren* society pays attention to the concept of '*bao*' (reward), which is formed based on these "key words". These key words are also important factors in understanding the *lun-ren* society.

The *lun-ren* has three different types of exchange dimensions. Firstly, "in the family group, people spontaneously oblige and voluntarily repay according to the principle of family ties" (Shang 2013:73). The embodiment of commercial behaviour is to provide convenience and benefits for the family group. Even if it is an official business, it may appear that it is done according to a private principle instead of the formal principle. Thus, it is the expression of '*en qing*' (loving-kindness) that makes the market have a factor of affection rather than a fair market. Secondly, "among acquaintances and friends, it is to release and receive good intentions based on the principle of *renqing* (favour)" (Ibid.), which includes the concept of *li* of '*li shang wang lai*' (courtesy demands reciprocation) and the influence of emotional commercial behaviour. However, it is weaker than the family group. Thirdly, strangers have a "transactional exchange relationship characterised by 'fairness'" (Shang 2013:73). It is a type that is conducive to fairness in commercial behaviour. Yet, the *lun-ren* society belongs to acquaintance society, so this type is less than other cultural communities. However, with the improvement of the political system and the economic model, as well as the increase of the immigrant population brought about by urbanisation, the proportion of good transaction-type exchange relations has increased.

In brief, the objects of exchange for *lun-ren* are initially divided into three categories: family group, acquaintances and friends, as well as strangers. Because of their interdependence, attaching more importance to relationship and the characteristics of "acquaintance society" of *lun-ren*, the first two exchange methods have become the mainstream; that is, in commercial activities, *lun-ren* tends to "oblige and repay" and "release and receive good intentions". Undoubtedly, it contributes to the harmony of society, but forms a constraint on a fair exchange. It is more evident in towns and villages, but relatively weak in large cities. With urbanisation, the characteristics of "stranger" society began to appear in large cities and promoted the increase of "fair" exchange relations. For economic relations between China and other countries, it is mainly acquaintances, friends, or strangers; that is, the "*renqing* principle" and "fair exchange" are implemented separately. With the institutionalisation of the economic and trade systems, the fair exchange relationship is on the rise. In short, if the traditional practice of Confucian culture is controlled within a reasonable range, it is conducive to harmony between individuals. If it exceeds the moderate range, it will easily breed corruption and cause extravagance and other adverse effects. Indeed, the grasp of reasonable range control is not an easy task; it needs to be adjusted continuously with practice.

To summarise the individual level, the influence of Confucianism on commercial behaviour is reflected in the concept of *guanxi*, *mianzi*, *li,* and filial piety against excessive frugality, emphasising wealth, and *bao* (reward). These concepts are inter-related and present a new feature in the process of modernisation. The factors of individual business behaviour need to be understood and cannot be ignored.

6.2.3. Organisational Level: The Influence of Confucianism on Organisational Culture

Confucian culture has an impact on the formation of Chinese business organisations. Except for "an outcome of rational decision-making by an autonomous state", the economic action of China was viewed as "a result of cultural patterns ingrained in Confucianism and other elements of traditional culture" (Chai 2003:1). It was argued that,

> "Cultural norms can provide points of convergence for rational actors in situations of strategic uncertainty" and "will be particularly important at those points in history when new institutions are being formed, and can lead to distinct institutional forms" and "Once created, however, the institutions themselves can structure incentives in a way that leads to self-perpetuation" (Ibid.).

Besides, Confucian norms of action were argued to have played a significant role in the design of new institutions during the early stages of capitalist development in China (Chai 2003:3-4).

Specifically, the influence of Confucian culture on an organisation can be seen in its classification. Chinese business organisations are divided into four types: 1) Patrilinealism or Patriarchicalism, 2) Paternalism, 3) Market despotism, and 4) Monopoly or Oligopoly Market (Cheng Weiyuan 2003:22). Confucian cultural thoughts wield more influence on the first two. It is worth noting that these four types are sometimes mixed and appear thus in Chinese business organisations. The first two types will be analysed separately and distinctly.

6.2.3.1. *WU-LUN* RELATIONSHIP OF CONFUCIANISM AND PATRILINEALISM

Patrilinealism (*Fu-xi zhi*) is referred to as "father passes the ownership and management of the business to the son who has a direct blood relationship with himself, not to the professional manager"; the patriarchal family business is typical throughout the world, especially in the Han Chinese society (Huang 2010: 247). The father-son relationship is one of the most important relations in the *wu-lun* (five human relationships) of Confucianism (Ibid: 245), which is notably different from the most crucial relationship in Hinduism or Christianity, i.e., the relationship with the supernatural or the creator. From the perspective of the universe, Confucianism pays more attention to "a simple and clear fact: one's life is the continuation of the physical life of the parents", which leads to the concept of 'filial piety' (Huang 2010:245). The "*fu-zi you-qin*" (intimacy should exist between father and son) in *wu-lun* (five human relationships of Confucianism) (Mencius) is reflected in the inheritance of the enterprise of Patrilinealism.

Some Chinese adopt 'equal inheritance' (*zhu-zi jun-fen zhi*) to maintain the company's success, i.e., "the corporate group moderator usually sets up a sub-enterprise for each son" (Ibid). This is more obvious in some parts of the mainland of China, Taiwan, and Hong Kong. In particular, employees are often members of the family in small and medium-size enterprise (SMEs) or have some blood relationship with their business owners (Orru, Biggart, Hamilton 1997). In the patrilinealism enterprise, "the grassroots employees and the operators may not necessarily have blood relationship", but "the employees in the same enterprise will be treated differently because of their close relationship with the business owner, forming a so-called '*cha-xuge-ju*' (the differential mode of association or differential pattern); and in the family business, it "needs to rely on *guanxi* (relationships) to support long-term overtime and exhaustive work" (Huang 2010:247). The emotion between the business owner and the employee could reflect '*jun-chen you-yi*' (righteousness should exist between the sovereign and subject) of *wu-lun*, that is, the "*yi*" (righteousness) is to maintain the relationship between business owner and employee, and the emphasis is on "*yi*" (righteousness). This relationship is different from the "individualism" and "spirit of contract" of European and American companies, and it is an "identity relationship" (Chen and Qiu 1984:459-484). It can be seen that the personal relationship in the Patrilinealism enterprise can be interpreted from the perspective of Confucian culture.

Patrilinealism enterprises are more evident in India than in China nowadays, the difference in China is that bosses and workers work together and workers are treated as family members in Chinese Patrilinealism enterprises (Xie 1989:48), which is difficult to achieve in India with caste awareness. Such Chinese companies often depend on "people's hard work" rather than a rationalisation of the system (Chen 1994:59-60). This tendency is a manifestation of the culture of "*yi*" (righteousness). Business owners use the Confucian relationshipism (Huang 2010: 239) to unite employees and form a sense of responsibility under the *guanxi*. One manifestation is the enshrinement and worship of *Guan Gong* (*Guan Yu*) in a Chinese enterprise, while *Guan Gong* (*Guan Yu*) is known by reading the Confucian classic, *Chun-qiu* (Spring and Autumn Annals), and is a representative figure of loyalty and righteousness. However, if the company does not have institutional incentives, and relies on "hard work of labour and employer", it is difficult to maintain during the period of expansion (Huang 2010:248). During expansion, the boss usually will "share his profits and losses to bind with workers" (Ke 1993). Confucianism on organisational culture has positive effects on a Patrilinealism enterprise, such as increased cohesion and cost reduction. It cannot be ignored that if it is entirely dependent on 'Confucius relationship', including *fu-zi you-qin* (intimacy should exist between father and son), *jun-chen you-yi* (righteousness should exist between the sovereign and subject), etc., it will also limit the development of enterprise organisation.

6.2.3.2. The Confucius Concept *Qin-Shu Zun-Bei* and Patriarchicalism

The concept of "the 'close or distant' (*qin-shu*) and 'superior or inferior' (*zun-bei*)" of Confucianism, part of the concept of '*li*' (rites), also affects the formation and internal operation of the organisation, including the source of leadership and employees. A typical representative is the township enterprise of Patriarchicalism (*zu-zhang zhi*). Patriarchicalism and Patrilinealism belong to the first of four categories of enterprise organization, which is based on cultural anthropology, divided by Cheng Weiyuan (2003:22). Both types have the following characteristics:

> "The employees and leaderships in the enterprise are more or less having some kinship, which is often referred to by sociologists as traditional 'social solidarity', that are the most common corporate paradigms of the Chinese, and their internal operational rules are deeply influenced by traditional Confucian ethics, [...] the working conditions are relatively 'lack of labour law guarantees' and to some extent are considered to be "rarely interfered with by the state" (Huang 2010:246).

The difference between Patriarchicalism and Patrilinealism is that in the former, the rights of the family or tribe may be in the hands of the father or the male elders, and the norms in Patriarchicalism are "derived from tradition and personal loyalty to the patriarch" (Huang 2010:248). This point is reflected in the organisational culture of Huaxi village of Jiangsu Province, China, which claims to be the richest village in China and is known as the "Number one village under the sky" (Xu 2013:66). The outstanding performance of the economy makes it famous in China and abroad. The organisational culture of Huaxi village reflects the role of the mindset of "*bao-en*" (requite favours) and the psychology of idolatry, which has contributed to "the absolute respect and obedience of the villagers to the patriarchal figures" (Xu 2013:68). The authority of the patriarch is produced from "common life and dependence, and therefore will not be restricted by law" (Weber 1978:1006-1007). Most of the patriarchal enterprises are "friends and relatives or who are introduced by friends, relatives and employees as 'guaranteed workers' through internal admission" (Ke 1993). Blood relation is not a necessary condition for Patriarchicalism. This is also the difference between Patriarchicalism and Patrilinealism (Huang 2010:249).

It cannot be denied that by calling itself a model socialist village, Huaxi is deeply influenced by socialism (Huaxia Xinghuo 2007:47-53). Meanwhile, when township and village enterprises develop to a certain extent with the participation of external labourers, this corporate organisational culture is not only influenced by Patriarchicalism (Huang 2010:249). Yet, a typical example of Patriarchicalism, township, and village enterprises is Huaxi village that is presided over by "the local leader with authority, and the main source of the employees is with family and regional 'solidarity'" (Vogel 1989). It is influenced by Confucian culture reflected by the mindset of "*bao-en*" (requite favours) of the villagers (Xu 2013:68), and the concept of filial piety (Huaxia Xinghuo 2007:53) and *mianzi* (face) (Zong 2013:69) of the leader especially as quoted by Huang Guangguo (2010:242) from *Zhong Yong* (The Doctrine of Mean, chapter 20),

> "*Ren* (benevolence) is the characteristic element of humanity, and the great exercise of it is in loving relatives. *Yi* (righteousness) is the accordance of actions with what is right, and the great exercise of it is in honouring the worthy. The differing levels in loving relatives should have a degree of close or distant, and venerating the worthy should have a hierarchy that will produce *Li* (rites)".

This shows that

> "Confucianism advocates that when individuals interact with anyone else, they should measure the relationship between each other from two social cognitive dimensions, i.e., 'close or distant' (*qin-shu*) and 'superiors or inferiors' (*zun-bei*): the former refers to 'close or distant' of each other's relationship, and the latter refers to the 'superiors or inferiors' of the status of both sides (Huang 2010:243-244)."

According to this Confucian point of view, the 'superiors or inferiors' determine "who is the resource dominator" and the 'close or distant' determines the "resource allocation or transaction method". It can be seen that the formation of the Patriarchicalism organisational culture can be traced back to the Confucian culture concept, especially the authority of organisational leadership and the formation of organisational personnel relations.

6.2.3.3. Paternalism and State-owned Enterprises

Private enterprises run by the Chinese are considered to be mostly on Patrilinealism or Patriarchicalism patterns, while some state-owned enterprises are considered to be Paternalism (Cheng 2003). Paternalism is a concept of Sociology, referring to the "benevolent family system", "traditional authoritative obedience, and the provision of employee benefits" (Huang 2010:249). Such enterprises involve everything regarding workers, including work, leisure, religious activities, etc.; employees also rely on the enterprise both economically and in general life (Ibid.). This is a manifestation of Confucian cultural society based on *renqing* (favour) and *guanxi*. "*Jiang mianzi* (thinking of face), *kan renqing* (considering favour), and *pin guanxi* (contending with *guanxi*)" are called the old state-owned enterprise style and are very popular in present-day state-owned enterprises. In order to establish a modern enterprise system, state-owned enterprise managers implement national laws and company regulations for reforms by replacing the *guanxi* with rules and replacing the *renqing* (favour) with institutions (Hu 2018).

Paternalism enterprises have the following characteristics: they are "excessive tolerance by the state" and "not only enjoy various privileges, but also are tolerated for losses under the preference of the state" such as the early state-owned enterprises in mainland China (Li, Jiang and Zhang 1992); "have the support of the government's monopoly of the market and are protected for a long time"; [...] employees have more than enough life support and lack of motivation, making it difficult for traditional paternal authority to manage slack employees and reflect the influence of *renqing* and *guanxi* (Huang 2010:249-250). Such Paternalism enterprises still exist today. The *renqing* and *guanxi* make it likely for managers to ignore costs and risks and expand blindly; and "easy to cause un-orderly sprawl, overstaffing, and loss of state-owned assets" (Wang 2017). It presents the unique organisational culture of state-owned enterprises in China and also a manifestation of *guanxi* culture. Because of the emphasis on *renqing* and *guanxi*, this organisational culture of Paternalism has been promoted.

6.2.3.4. *Renqing, Guanxi* and Regional Organisation

From the perspective of Psycho-Culturology, the organisational level of the *lun-ren* society influenced by Confucian culture has two crucial influences on economic development. Firstly, the formation of an organisation is based on kinship or blood relation, such as in organisations of Patrilinealism and Patriarchicalism. As mentioned in the analysis of Psycho-Culturology,

> "In the *Lun-ren* society, relatives and organisations with kinship characteristics provide the highest level of sense of security. People lack the inner impulse to seek close contacts outside the organisation of kinship, so their ability to establish non-relatives and non-regional groups is comparatively weak."

Secondly, the influence also reflects the characteristics of the *lun-ren* that tend to establish "regional business groups". In the history of China, a number of regional merchant groups have been formed, such as Shanxi merchants (*jin-shang*), Anhui merchants (*hui-shang*), Shaanxi merchants (*shaan-shang*), Fujian merchants (*min-shang*), Guangdong merchants (*yue-shang*), Jiangxi merchants (*gan-shang*), Suzhou merchants (*su-shang*), Zhejiang merchants (*zhe-shang*), Shandong merchants (*lu-shang*) and other groups divided by provinces and are known as China's top ten business groups. So far, many regional groups are still active, and they have received attention due to outstanding performance in economic development, such as the Guangdong and Zhejiang merchants (Zhejiang merchants are relatively famous among regional businessmen in the cities of Ningbo, Wenzhou, and Yiwu). The formation of regional groups is closely related to regional culture, and each region is more or less influenced by traditional culture, including the concept of emphasising *zhong-yi* (benevolence and righteousness) and integrity in Confucian culture. Among the business groups mentioned above, Anhui, Jiangxi, and Shanxi merchants are more influenced by

Confucian culture, while Anhui and Shanxi merchants are the two most powerful and influential business groups (another is Guangdong merchants) (Li 2016).

The formation of regional business groups reflects the strong ability of the *lun-ren* to establish regional groups. Compared to other civilised societies, it is most underdeveloped in China (at least in traditional China) with the sub-group (social organisation) that is entirely non-kinship, non-regional, and artificially established for a particular purpose (Shang 2013:122, 125, 129). More groups are formed by kinship and regional connections, which are more substantial and prominent, reflecting the characteristics of *renqing* and *guanxi* in organisational culture.

In summary of the organization level, the influence of Confucian culture is reflected in the culture of corporate organisations such as Patrilinealism, Patriarchicalism and Paternalism. *Renqing* and *Guanxi,* as well as regional associations, are also related to the characteristics of *lun-ren*. In the process of modernisation, organisational culture has taken on various forms; especially modern enterprises with non-traditional influences have gradually increased. Still, the different levels of management within the organisation are influenced by Confucian culture, and in the development of the enterprise, to a certain extent, it must face the business environment formed by Confucian culture. In addition, combined with the analysis of 6.2.2 individual levels, the cultural characteristics of individual commercial behaviour extend to organisational culture, such as *renqing*, *guanxi*, *mianzi,* etc., showing that the influence of Confucian culture runs through two levels, and the analysis of the individual level is conducive to understand the influence of the cultural influence in the organisational level.

6.2.4. National Level: Confucianism Impact on Policy

Culture and economy have distinct socialist characteristics in modern China, but the influence of traditional culture, especially Confucian culture, can still be seen. Culture is treated as an essential part in national policy as culture construction belongs to one-third of the five-sphere integrated overall plan for building socialism with Chinese characteristics (the five parts, in sequence, are the construction of economy, politics, culture, society and ecological civilisation) (CPC 2017:4). China has developed a socialist culture and socialist market economy under the leadership of the Communist Party of China (CPC 2017:2, 5). The party constitution maintains, "It shall be firm in consolidating and developing the public sector of the economy and shall remain steadfast in encouraging, supporting, and guiding the development of the non-public sector" (CPC 2017:5).

Nevertheless, China's culture and economy still has its own characteristics and is rooted in tradition. In other words, Chinese tradition still influences China's culture and economy. Traditional culture also has an impact on the economy. Scholars have pointed out that the Confucian civilisation can still play a role in economic development; "Objective facts prove that Chinese culture, in which Confucian civilisation is the important representative, can also provide the spiritual impetus for economic development" (Jin and Zhang 2018). It was also argued that "Confucius and his school have much to say about the morals of the public administration and market institutions in a more macro level" and Confucian business ethics has interaction with economy (Lam, 2003:153). The following is an analysis of the impact of Confucian culture on the economy at the national level.

6.2.4.1. Great Harmony of Confucianism and Socialism

The reason for China to adopt socialism could also be found in its linkage to its traditional cultural beliefs, especially Confucianism. It was pointed out by Wang Huning (1995:53), who later became a Chinese national political theorist and a current member of the CPC's Politburo Standing Committee (China's top decision-making body), that Confucian ethnics could be linked with Socialism like Protestantism is connected with Capitalism. Besides, China's excellent traditional culture, in which Confucianism is the central part, was linked with socialist culture in Xi Jinping's speech at the 19th NCCPC (National Congress of the CPC),

> "Socialist culture with Chinese characteristics is derived from China's fine traditional culture, which was born of the Chinese civilisation and nurtured over more than 5,000 years" (Xi 2017:33).

From the perspective of Psycho-Culturology, the human-centred[3] (*ren-lun*-centred or *Jen*-centred) is the psycho-cultural orientations of the *lun-ren*, which makes the *lun-ren* regard the "complete harmony between people" as a cultural ideal (Shang 2013: 274). The influence of this cultural ideal on the Chinese includes: "Chinese understanding of Karl Marx's 'communist society' is still '*shi-jie da*-tong' (Great Unity or Universal Harmony)", and current Chinese society has the concept of "harmonious society" and "harmonious world" (Shang 2013: 275). The "universal harmony" and "harmonious society" are derived from Confucianism.

The psycho-cultural orientations of the *lun-ren* are "human-centred" that help to understand the characteristics of national behaviour. As the interpretation of Psycho-Culturology, the individual and group (organisation) in the *lun-ren* society are "not a binary opposition, but a relationship of enlargement and reduction in differential pattern"; similarly, individual and nation are connected but in a differential pattern (Shang and You 2010:458, 460). These reflect the continuity of the individual's behavioural characteristics with organisation and nation. The psychological and cultural characteristics have caused this "isomorphic mapping" relationship. The national form of China is influenced by

3 Roel Sterckx (2019:xi) also pointed out, "Chinese thought is predominantly human-centred and practice-oriented."

the human constant of Chinese *lun-ren* (Ibid: 452). It can be seen that the influence of culture is linked from the individual level to the national level.

The focus of "human-centred" is "how to deal with the relationship between people", and the ultimate status tends to "complete harmony between people". This ideal is mainly reflected in the "*da-tong*" (universal harmony) society described by Chinese Confucianism (Shang 2013:274), which is recorded in the chapter *li-yun* of the Confucian classic, *Li-ji (Book of Rites*):

> "When the Great Way (highest morality) is practised, the world is for the public; those with virtue (the worthy) and those with ability are chosen and used; People value trustworthiness and cultivate harmony with each other. Thus people do not treat only their parents, but also care for others. They foster not only their children but also nurture others. The aged will be taken care of till the end of their lives; the able-bodied will find proper employment; the young will be well raised and educated; widowers or widows, orphans, the childless and the disabled will all be given ample maintenance. Males will have proper work, and females have their homes. People will loathe waste but will not keep properties only for themselves. They will hate not going all out on their jobs, but will not work only for their own gratification. Therefore people will not engage in intrigue or trickery, nor will they engage in robbery, theft, and rebellion. Thus, though people will leave their houses, they will not close their doors. This is what I mean by an ideal society of great harmony."

It shows "people follow the principle of mutual dependence, live together in harmony, and everyone is taken care of" (Shang 2013:275), following the Confucian great harmony ideal to pursuit harmony among humans. It could be said that to a certain extent, the great harmony thought of Confucianism matches "from each according to his ability, to each according to his need (Marx 1875)" of Communism, i.e., Scientific Socialism.

6.2.4.2. Economic Equal and World Peace

The economic principles of Confucius are considered for "the equalization of the whole world", "the world can never be equalized unless the economic life of the whole world is equal" and "Confucius regards the whole world as an economic unit" can be seen from the Confucian classic, *Da Xue* (Great Learning) (Chen 1911:140). It is believed that the vision of a world-state (*Tian-xiada-tong*, or Great Unity under heaven) and world-peace of Confucius derived from "the evils of feudalism, with its constant wars" which "impressed Confucius profoundly". (Ibid: 145)

> "In the Spring and Autumn, Confucius records about four hundred wars within the period of two hundred and forty-two years and

> condemns them all, for war is contrary to the principle of humanity" (Chen 1911:142)

Chen pointed out that "the doctrine of peace is harmonious with economic principles" which makes "the life of man more valuable than the land". In the *Analects of Confucius*, Confucius "attaches the chief importance to the life of the people" (Ibid: 143). This is why Confucius believes that the equalisation of the economic life of the whole world is a precondition for the equalisation of the whole world. To a certain extent, it shows that Confucianism uses economic equalisation to achieve means of avoiding war, thus achieving equalisation of the world. In the Confucian classic, *Da Xue* (Great Learning), "equalization of the world" is considered to be simplified into two: "employing the best men, and administering wealth" (Chen 1911:140), and it pointed out that the fundamental principle of the world economy is the principle of reciprocity (Ibid: 141).

The diplomatic initiatives formulated by the Chinese government today are also in line with these ideas. On the fifth anniversary of the Belt and Road Initiative (BRI), Chinese president Xi Jinping pointed out that,

> "The BRI is in line with the *Tian-xia Da-tong* concept that the Chinese nation has always upheld, in line with the Chinese people's view of the world of *huai-rou yuan-ren* (cherishing men from afar) and *he-xie wan-bang* (harmony among all nations)" (*CCTV News* 2018).

China has formulated a national policy centred on economic construction and got general acceptance from the people, which is consistent with this economic concept and peace concept in traditional Chinese thought. Considering "economic construction as the central task" is the centre of China's national policy, it could be helpful to explain that influence by this policy, to be rich became a quest of the majority of the Chinese. The national policy "take economic construction as the central task" is accepted by the Chinese people, and rooted and developed well in modern China.

The economy is a decisive factor in the thoughts of '*ping tian-xia*' (the equalisation of the whole world) of the ancient world, and "economic determinism" still occupies a prominent position in modern China's policy. "Economic construction as the central task" is regarded as the guiding ideology of foreign policy which theoretical logic is considered that "to compromise for peace, to ensure economic construction by peace, and to alleviate social conflicts by economic construction" and is currently the most influential (Yan 2013). However, the scholar has pointed out that this kind of economic pragmatism will become more and more challenging to be the guiding ideology of China's foreign policy and the reasons include that more and more conflicts of economic interests will hinder China from establishing friendly diplomatic relations (Ibid.). The domestic affairs of China need to be transferred from 'economic construction centred' to the establishment of a fair, just, and civilized society, and foreign policy has to shift from pursuing a peaceful environment conducive to economic construction to shaping a peaceful environment conducive to economic construction, and shaping an international environment conducive to national rejuvenation (Ibid.).

6.2.4.3. *Guanxi* and its Infinite Extensibility

As mentioned above (2.4.1), the impact of the characteristics of the *Lun-ren* also extend to the national level. Psycho-Culturology believes that the self-cognition of the *Lun-ren* is considered to be "mutual reliance type" (*xiang-hu-yi-lai-xing*), that is, "defining the self in the *guanxi* (relationship) between human beings", "if there is no *guanxi* (relationship), there is no self", which causes the *Lun-ren* to

> "care more about how others see himself or herself" (*hao mian-zi*, i.e., 'be sensitive about one's reputation'), more need to maintain close relationship with familiar others, but also need to maintain status and gain benefits from this intimate relationship" (Shang 2013:245-246).

This could not only explain the behavioural characteristics of the individual but also be conducive to understand the behavioural characteristics of the nation. Projects launched by the nation of *Lun-ren* often tend to be "comprehensive", covering a wide range, focusing on building relationships, "maintaining status and gaining benefits" in intimate relationships, which is displayed in China's interactions with Pakistan and African countries. Psycho-Culturology defines the "altruism" of *Lun-ren* mainly in "the circle of acquaintances and close relatives in personal life" (Shang 2013:249). Similarly, the individual's behavioural characteristics extend to the national level. In the close circle of intimate and close relations, such as China, when dealing with countries such as Pakistan, Russia, and Africa countries, "altruism" shows to a certain extent. At the same time, under the influence of the concept of modern international relations, China is not only influenced by the traditional *guanxi* but also seeks to establish new types of national relations such as a strategic partnership. While maintaining the traditional *guanxi*, political mutual trust, economic win-win, mutual cultural exchanges, and cooperation in security have become the embodiment of the practical spirit of establishing relations between China and other countries (Darbey 2018). Promoting the interests of the country and also to help other countries improve their self-development is also an essential part of economic and trade policy (Ibid.).

Also, China's *guanxi* (relationship) concept has an "infinite extensibility" (Zhai 2011:2-3), which also has an impact on China's diplomacy,

> "The relationship and power of the Chinese have an essential feature in theory and practice, that is, they are infinitely extended in time and space: first, the blood relationship...there is no end; secondly, the

> geographical relationship can be gradually enlarged until the *tian-xia* (world)...
>
> "If there is no boundary in the relationship, it will lead to unlimited power in the network of relations. It is diffuse, extensive, transferable, and circulating. It is a trait of the Chinese and the society of China that are willing to be *bao-rong* (inclusive), *da-tong* (open), *rong-tong* (accommodating), *guan-tong* (connected), *bian-tong* (flexible), and *shen-tou* (infiltrating)." (Zhai 2011:2-3)

Psycho-Culturology also explains the "infinite extensibility" behavioural characteristics of *guanxi*. The psycho-cultural orientation of *Lun-ren* is *Ren*-centred orientation. The characteristics of the self-recognition dimension of the *Lun-ren* are,

> "more emphasis on the mutuality of people, tending to be in the circle of interpersonal relationships (in layers 4 and 3 of PSH) and others, defining the self in the interactive relationship...'self' is not the centre of the world, 'self' and the world around is moving... 'self' is neither clear nor rigid" (Hsu 1985:32-35; Shang 2013:74).

This unclear self-emphasis or emphasis on *guanxi* (relationship) helps to understand this infinite extensibility, as well as the flexibility of public-private and group-self relationships and the ambiguity of boundary (Liu 2018:7). Specific performances include the fact that China's foreign aid is not only pursuing its own interests, the government is proposing BRI to pursue *tian-xia da-tong*, and the BRI project is also growing, from the initial 64 countries (Liu 2016) to 69 countries and international organizations that signed BRI cooperation agreements with China (An 2017). By the fifth anniversary of the Initiative in 2018, China had signed cooperation documents with more than 100 countries and international organisations to build the "Belt and Road" cooperation (*Xinhua Net* 2018); China's "Belt and Road Initiative" does not limit the category of participant countries the number of which is still growing.

6.2.4.4. Theory of "Differential Pattern" and BRI

By driving China's long-standing "family culture", Confucian scholars promoted the importance of Chinese traditional culture to the relationship of *Wu-lun* (five human relationships in ethics); Fei Xiaotong's *cha-xu ge-ju* (differential pattern or the pattern of difference sequence) theory, which emphasises the relationship between family and acquaintances, stems from the *Wu-lun* relationship (Liu 2018:7). From this perspective, the impact of this thought on national policy can be seen. Fei Xiaotong described the Chinese social differential pattern as "extending from the self to the other, expanding outwards in circles, just like ripples across the water, everyone defines the relationship between the self and the other by the distance with others". The Confucian culture's "*ke-ji fu-li*" (restrain ourselves for propriety) and "*xiu-shen wei-ben*" (self-cultivation centred) ideas have promoted the emergence of the self-centred relationship network (Liu 2018:7), that is, self-centred and self-cultivation as the first point and the basis for improving the external environment.

The theory of differential pattern, which is deeply rooted in Confucianism, is considered to be related to the initiative of the national leaders, the BRI, in the past few years (Liu 2018:9-10). The four main points of the differential pattern theory include (Ibid: 6):

> "the importance of the relationship between the family and the acquaintances such as the neighbourhood", "building the relationship network with self-centredness", "the relativity and flexibility of the relationship between the public and private, group and self", "focusing on cultivating effective relationships and commonalities".

The embodiments in the Belt and Road Initiative are (Ibid: 11-12): China's diplomatic discourse firstly takes Asian country as its identity, focuses on Asia, national leaders regard Asia as a big family; and diplomatic discourse highlights the relationship with neighbouring countries such as Pakistan, Afghanistan, the five countries of Central Asia, Mongolia, Russia, and India. The following public statements of the Ministry of Foreign Affairs reflect the dynamics and flexibility of the Belt and Road Initiative: The BRI belongs to China, Asia, as well as the world; the BRI is both regional and international, and the community of human destiny. In addition, the Belt and Road diplomatic discourse emphasizes cooperation and values the benefits and tolerance towards other countries, just as what Huang Guangguo described as "emotional relationship" as an essential level in the differential pattern. Once this "emotional relationship" was established, it will "do everything possible and give the other party more resources, support and tolerance for mistakes" (Ibid: 8).

Besides, the development path of the Belt and Road Initiative "has emphasis, level, and sequence", and takes the self as the core, and then extends to other economic corridors to form a relationship network, which reflects the differential order of the development path (Liu 2018:13), that is, the differential pattern, "extends itself to others, and expands outwards in circles". To benefit neighbouring countries as the first importance, then to expand from Asia to Europe, Africa, the Americas and the whole world reflects the differential order of China's diplomatic relations (Liu 2018:13).

It can be seen that the scholar's summary, such as the establishment of the theory of Differential Pattern, makes the origin of Chinese diplomatic thought from Confucianism obvious. The characteristics of Chinese diplomatic thoughts and discourses are also different from other countries because of the influence of this Confucian culture. The exploration of the root and texture is conducive to the understanding of China's national level behaviour, while the BRI is a typical representative of Confucianism affecting trade policy.

The ultimate ideal of the *Lun-ren* is to build a harmonious society, not only inland but also at the international level. The BRI proposed by the Chinese national leader has this characteristic. From the perspective of interests or realism, it is hard to understand similar behaviours of China. It is always assumed that China has some aggressiveness and the purpose of plundering resources. By further analysing the values of "human-centred", it can explore the original intention of this harmonious society design,

> "The values of *lun-ren-zhu-yi* (*lun-ren*-ism) tend to think that the relationship between man and nature is not a relationship between conquering and the conquered, but a harmonious relationship. People should adapt to nature. This is '*ren yu tian-dao he-xie yi-zhi*' (harmony between man and natural law) and '*tian-ren he-yi*' (harmony between heaven and human)" (Shang 2013:278).

This shows that the goal of expansion outside of the *Lun-ren* is not merely for the sake of benefit, but also for the establishment of a harmonious society, a concept influenced by Chinese traditional culture. Indeed, this cultural ideal also has both positive and negative impacts. The positive role is conducive to the harmony of society, including international society. The negative effect is that it may over-consume the energy of the nation. If the goal of building a harmonious international society is beyond the scope of competence, it may lead to an unsustainable situation and even face boycott from other countries that do not recognise this cultural ideal. It is essential for China, as a rising power, to prevent the 'premature advance' (*zhan-lue mao-jin*) (Yan 2017).

6.2.4.5. Negative Influence of Confucianism

Confucian culture benefits economic development but also hinders economic growth. Criticism of Confucian culture has existed both in China and abroad. During the May Fourth Movement, Confucianism was considered to be an "androphagous ethical code" (*chi-ren de li-jiao*), not to pay attention to science and social order but ethics and blind faith of authority (Lin 2012:30). Max Weber, the presenter of cultural determinism, believes that China's backwardness is its "long-term inability to escape from the influence of Confucian culture" (Lin 2012:31), because Confucian culture "emphasizes social harmony and the harmony between man and nature", but does not emphasize science and advancement; people affected by Confucian culture are more moderate and conservative" (Lin 2012:30). Also, Confucian culture has its drawbacks for the development of the economy, such as self-centred exclusivity. China's "Central Plains Centralism" (or Sinocentrism) once "made China strictly distinguish between 'civilization and barbarism', 'internal orthodoxy and foreign barbarism' and believe 'the latter needs to be educated' (Zhao 2016). This paradigm leads to the tendency of exclusionism and conservatism that 'stubbornly exist' in the Chinese economy and society (Ibid.).

The origin of conservatism can be seen in the analysis of Francis L.K. Hsu (1981) who pointed out that the Chinese is human relations-centeredness (or *ren-lun*-centred) of mutual-dependence, Chinese people benefit from the interdependence among kinship and are easy to satisfyfrom it, so they lack motivation for outward expansion, there is no large-scale immigration and the tradition of promoting Confucian culture (Shang 2013:274). Moreover, the identification of cultural values is not only difficult to change but also the root of prejudice (Shang and You 2010:11) which could make the thought exist stubbornly.

It is undeniable that in Confucian culture, thoughts such as attaching more importance to the relationship, sentiment, and favour and face-saving (*qing-mian*) have affected the progress of modernisation to a certain extent. On the one hand, many of China's problems of backwardness in modern times have been blamed on Confucianism. On the other hand, "countries with faster economic development after World War II are mostly countries and regions with deeper influence on Confucianism" (Wang 2015). Thus, the value of Confucian culture needs to be taken objectively and analysed case by case. It is not unreasonable to criticise the content of cultural incompatibility, but it cannot be generalised because the idea of restricting development does not contain all the content of Confucian cultural thought. Lin Yifu questioned the above criticism on Confucianism put forward by cultural determinism, because Chinese culture came down in one continuous line, and China was powerful and leading the world more than a thousand years ago (Lin 2012:31). Confucianism contains positive factors for economic development, such as the rational pursuit of wealth (*ren,* benevolence), the order formulated to a certain extent (*li,* ritual), the encouragement of learning (*zhi*), and the emphasis on integrity (*xin,* trust). Chinese traditional culture plays an essential role in China's development and its rise (Wei 2017).

Confucian thought contains influential factors of both sides, and how to extract the essence is a topic that continually adjusts to the changes of the times. Even in the rising era of China, economic pragmatism is not approved of and to bind economics and peace as the Confucius approach, is not applauded; the concept of "benevolence and righteousness" closely related to Confucianism is still used for advocating a new international order that is considered beyond the current order leading by the USA (Yan 2015:91). Inheriting traditional culture without blindness is conducive to development. Not to be self-enclosed and to establish relationships through diplomacy, trade, cultural exchanges, and not by force is a behavioural characteristic of Chinese culture that is different from many countries that seek development through force. Nowadays, 525 Confucius Institutes have been founded in 138 countries and regions around the world

(Hanban 2017). The Chinese government's development strategy of "going out" and the Belt and Road Initiative is all for outward development mixing political, economic, and cultural dimensions. In these national policies, the traditional influence is difficult to eliminate or avoid, and always has a fresh vitality in flexible applications.

Through an analysis of the national level, the origin of Confucian culture and China's national economic policy (centred on economic construction) can be seen, along with current important national economic initiatives (BRI) as well as the constraints of Confucian culture on China's development. Moreover, the influence of Confucian culture on an individual and organisational level is an essential basis for understanding the characteristics of the national level. However, at the level of economic relations between countries, the influence of the national level would be most obvious and direct. The analysis of the cultural dimension of the national level is more conducive to understand the specific content of cultural influence on the economic relations between countries.

6.2.5. Summary

To sum up, the influence of Confucian culture on the three levels of the individual (commercial behaviour), organisational (organisational culture), and national (trade policy) has both positive and negative factors for economic development. According to the above analysis, the impact on the individual and organisational levels seems to be more influential in the nation. Yet, the analysis of these two levels is conducive to understand the influence at the national level. The nation can play a balanced role and influence the developmental trends, both domestic and abroad. The role played by the national level, compared to the other two levels in the economic relationship between countries, is more direct in the cultural dimension. The influence of Confucian culture on the nation could be a key to analyse the economic relations between China and India.

6.3. The Influence of Hinduism on India's Economic Development

6.3.1. Introduction

According to the 2011 Indian Census, about 79.8 per cent of India's population is Hindu (GoI 2011). Some scholars point out that Hinduism is considered to be the hegemonic religion of India and has shaped the country's social and legal system after its independence, and affected other religions (Harriss-White 2003:133). The influence of Hinduism on the development of the Indian economy is extremely crucial and needs to be analysed.[4]

4 Besides, 14.2 per cent (2011) of India's population is Muslim. In the long-term practice process, Islam has formed a constant adaptation to development based on the economic concept of Islamic classics. The majority of Muslim economists still recognise that the sacredness of the Qur'an and the Sunnah is unquestionable. The Islamic economic thought

Hinduism has both positive and negative effects on the Indian economy. India's spirit of pursuing truth and argumentativeness promotes the intelligence of all classes of society; the polytheism belief promotes imagination, abstract logical thinking, innovative ability as well as inclusiveness; national pride makes them are unwilling to lag behind, promoting development; besides a spirit of thrift (Sun 2000:204-205). These are the positive factors of Hinduism that benefit India. Milton Singer (1972) concluded that,

> "industrial leaders borrowed selectively from Western industrial culture as well as from Hinduism. This enabled them not only to maintain a distinctive Hindu culture but also to define Hinduism, rather than secularity, as the cultural basis of Indian (capitalist) modernity", [...] and "showed Hinduism as being used as a force for change" (Harriss-White 2003:134).

It is further pointed out that,

> "religion was permitting a plurality of norms, one for private life and another for work. In the latter sphere, he found an abbreviated and relaxed religiosity where the religious foundations for ethical conduct were of active use to industrialists." (Harriss-White 2003:134)

Indian religions have values that are compatible with modernisation; meanwhile, some superstitions and customs have also contributed to India's poverty to some extent. The former Prime Minister of India, Jawaharlal Nehru, considered that a tremendous force of social inertia is responsible for India's economic backwardness (Myrdal 1968).

To be familiar with Indian culture would be conducive to understand its economic development. In particular, India's cultural heritage has been uninterrupted and ingrained, and with the improvement of national power, cultural confidence and national pride have also been strengthened. The emergence of cultural conflicts showed the resistance of Indian culture's radical defenders to foreign culture. Before the Western Valentine's Day in February 2010, some radical Hindu organisations issued warnings urging people to stick to traditional culture, and called on merchants not to sell Valentine's Day-related goods or hold related activities; young students were told not to participate in Valentine's Day activities, and the organisations threatened to fight such activities. Young students did not stop their celebrations and were fought by the radical defenders (Xue 2003:8).

---

of faith has its distinctive features influenced by its doctrine in terms of property system, commercial system, financial system, and taxation system. See Ma Yuxiu (2012), *An Introduction to Islamic Economic Thoughts*, Shanghai: Shanghai Academy of Social Sciences Press. Besides, many of India's consortiums are from Jainism.

Taking traditional belief as an essential factor in the economy, this section analyses the influence of Hindu thought on the three levels, i.e., individual (commercial behaviour), organisational (organisational culture), and national (national trade policy). The theory of Psycho-Culturology would be used to explain the characteristics of Hindu thought and behaviour in the economy to provide an overall interpretation of the impact of Hinduism on economic development.

6.3.2. Individual level: the Influence of Hinduism on Commercial Behaviour

Hinduism is a unique religion, and its characteristics of treating the world are summarised as "supernatural-centred" and "unilateral dependence" (Hsu 1963; Shang and You 2010:18). Caste consciousness, spiritual exploration, frugal spirit, exchange mode, and time concept influenced by Hindu thought affected the development of India at the individual level.

6.3.2.1. CASTE

The "inequality, different degrees of purity and exclusion" in Hinduism implies that "the economy is that stratification that is tolerated, with consequent severe limits to free competition and economic mobility"; these are seen as "inhibitors and obstacles", and "forces of inertia and irrationality" (Myrdal 1968:104,109; Harriss-White 2003:134). These ideas are influenced by "the basic ethics of Hinduism and the caste system (Qiu 2012:12)". Although in recent times Hindu ideologists have advocated the abolition of the caste system, and modern society has also largely overthrown India's caste barriers (Ibid: 25), castes still have a significant impact on economic development.

The Indian caste system originated in the ancient Indian period and "most castes originated as an occupational grouping. Even in the last part of the 20th century, caste determined the occupational status and training given to members within a family unit" (NCERT: 7). Hindu society is divided into four hierarchical castes (*varna*), from high to low, they being: Brahman (mainly priests, scholars), Kshatriya (mainly rulers, warriors), Vaishya (mainly merchants, traders and farmers), Shudra (mainly artisans, labourers, servants and slaves). In addition, the Dalits (or untouchables, *Harijan*) outside the four castes is traditionally engaged in the dirtiest menial work, and now called by the official euphemism of the British colonial period "Scheduled Caste" (SC) (Doniger 1999:186), which has been recognised as a "socially, economically weaker section of society. Therefore, the development and upliftment of the SC population has been a serious concern of the Government of India since Independence" (NCERT: 8-9).

As mentioned above, caste influences career choices that restrict free competition and economic mobilisation and reduces the intensity of competition. Competition is limited mainly within one caste hierarchy. Without free and large-scale competition, development can be significantly hindered. It was reported

(Biswas 2012) that more than half of 46 India's millionaires are from the traditional merchant caste hierarchy, such as Banias, Parsis and Sindhis, and many of them belong to the higher caste hierarchy Brahman and Khatris.[5]These are less lower caste, no dalit at all, and only one is Muslim on the above list of India's millionaires (Biswas 2012).Besides, the big families of Indian business circles, such as the G. D. Birla family, the Walchand Hirachand family, and the Kasturbhai Lalbhai family are considered to be Vaishyas (Song 2010:94).[6] It shows, on the one hand, that the hierarchic stratification of Hindu society has brought some stability factors to the Indian economy and capital, which was reflected, in the long history of business families or traditional business caste, as well as in the driving force and fertile foundation for continuous development. On the other hand, it has also led to a large gap between the rich and the poor.

Psycho-Culturology uses the concept "Homo Hierarchicus" proposed by the French anthropologist and specialist on the cultures and societies of India, Louis Dumont (1980) (Shang 2013:78-79), who maintained that the people of Hindu society were in the hierarchy or religion-based sequence (Shang and You 2010:355). Home Hierarchicus is used to refer to the 'Human Constant' of the Hindu in Psycho-Culturology (Shang 2013:78-79). This Human Constant considers that pursuing the supernatural is a significant method for the Hindu individual (i.e., Homo Hierarchicus) to gain Psycho-Social Homeostasis (PSH). In other words, the Human Constant of Home Hierarchicus is supernatural as a centre. In order to achieve PSH stability, Homo Hierarchicus tends to "religious transcendence and explore the soul", which causes individuals to easily dedicate themselves to various activities that could be close to the supernatural (Shang 2013:79), including "strictly following caste regulations, insisting on caste discrimination" and "various cruise, pilgrimage and sacrifice" (Ibid). This explains the characteristics of the Hindu individual in complying with hierarchic social stratification and dietary taboos as well as emphasising on spiritual exploration and so on.

6.3.2.2. Spiritual Exploration and Slow Development of Secondary Industry

Hinduism also influences the view of wealth, with emphasis on exploration of the spiritual world as one of its distinguishing features (Dong 2007; Zhang 2019). The characteristics of Hinduism have drawn the attention of economists who hold that the "*Atman* (true Self) that Hinduism advocates is the same as *Brahman* (the highest metaphysical Reality)" (*Advaita*) and *Moksha* (liberation), which makes

5 The latter is considered a mixed caste of Brahman and Kshatriya (Sharma 1975:279). Meanwhile, scholars have pointed out that although Khatris claim to be Kshatriya, most of their occupations are Vaishya (McLane 2002:131).

6 Song (2010:94) believes that the J.R.D. Tata family can also be traced to the Vaishyas, but the founder of the Tata Group came from a priest family of the Parsis (Lala 1981:3).

Hindus introspective, even escaping from reality and focusing on the spiritual world (Shen and Xu 2015). It was pointed out that "some Hindus leave their social world and material possessions, then engage in lifelong *Sannyasa* (monastic practices) to achieve *Moksha* (Ellinger 1996:69-70). The nature of Hinduism to emphasise on the exploration of the spiritual world and despise the material world, is not only reflected in the classic readings of Hinduism but also in the economic thought of the leader of Modern India. The Hindu classic, the *Bhagavad Gita,* says:

> "The Yogi who is satisfied with the knowledge and the wisdom (of the Self), who has conquered the senses, and to whom a clod of earth, a piece of stone and gold are the same, is said to be harmonised (that is, is said to have attained the state of *Nirvikalpa Samadhi*) "(Sivananda 2000:53; Dong 2007:80).

Milton Singer (1956:83) considers that "the Indian world view encompasses both material and spiritual values" (Kunkel 1965:268). Yet, emphasising the spiritual world is hard to avoid disregarding the material world. Besides, Mahatma Gandhi, who led India to independence once mentioned,

> "I suggest that we are thieves in a way. If I take anything that does[I do] not need for my own immediate use and keep it, I thieve [steal] it from somebody else...nature produces enough for our wants from day to day; and if only everybody took enough for himself and nothing more, there would be no pauperism in this world, there would be no man dying of starvation" (Gandhi 1947:284).

This reflects the factors of non-violence, asceticism and plain thinking in Indian culture, especially Hinduism. The tradition of India still lives deeply in its society. The level of behaviour that can be seen has different manifestations, such as the low cost of goods, temporary solutions in life, and frugal innovation. The ideological characteristics of the emphasis on the spirit contribute to promote social peace and stability and create a pleasant social environment for economic development (Sun 2000:204-205).

Scholars have pointed out that it is precisely because of these thoughts that India has not experienced a history of the general state from the primary industry to the secondary industry and further to the tertiary industry, but is directly influenced by the wave of 'de-industrialization' of the USA, and jumped from a farming civilization to a 'service industry' (He 1996:22-27). In fact, the proportion of India's secondary industry in the GDP rose from 13.6 per cent in 1950 to 24.7 per cent in the period of 1950-2007, not as the primary industry (from 56.5 per cent to 20.5 per cent) while the third industry (from 29.5 per cent to 54.7 per cent) has changed so much (He 1996:22-27; Bu 2017). In a sense, part of Hinduism belief could be considered as an underlying cause for the slow development of the secondary industry of India.

6.3.2.3. Frugal Innovation

Individual values and behavioural characteristics are shown in the language they used. The commonly used word in Hindi, "*Jugaad*", roughly translates as "an innovative fix; an improvised solution born from ingenuity and cleverness", and about "doing more with less" (Radjou, Prabhu and Ahuja 2012:4-5). Many images of India that are circulating in the Chinese network, such as many people squatting on trains and temporarily replacing mechanical parts with other items to keep equipment running, are related to this idea. Digging at the root of this idea will contribute to understanding the way Indians solve problems in their lives, Indian business practices and Indian market characteristics. The influence of *Jugaad* thinking is also reflected in the fact that there are many low-cost items in the Indian market. For example, India produces the cheapest products in the world such as Rs. 500 mobiles (Freedom 251), $ 25 water filters, $ 35 tablet PCs, $ 800 ECG machines, and $ 2,500 cars. Even the Indian Mars Orbiter Mission *Mangalyaan*, which was launched on 5 November 2013, is the cheapest in the world. Previously, Mars exploration launches in China and Japan failed, and the USA succeeded, but the cost was much higher than in India.

A large number of inventions have emerged in India in following *frugal* innovation to solve problems in life at little cost. Frugal Innovation is considered as a lifestyle of India (Zi 2013). One representative innovation is the electricity-free "refrigerator" invented by the Indian inventor, Mansukhbhai Prajapati. The "refrigerator" is cooled by evaporation, eliminating the need for electrical energy. There are also Rs. 100 cardiograms, Rs. 1,000 breast tests (Mashelkar 2017), and other low-priced products with features of daily necessities at low-cost. The innovators have not only gained recognition from the Indian government but are also gradually forming a network (Gupta 2016). People in various fields, including innovators, policymakers, and scholars, gradually systematise this field. This not only shows that this cost-saving idea is widely accepted and supported in India but also the contribution of Indians in saving energy and protecting the environment. Also, it will be conducive for foreign investors when they keep this characteristic of the Indian market in mind.

6.3.2.4. Food Culture: Vegetarian, Cow Slaughter Ban and Buffalo Meat Export

India's vegetarian culture and cow slaughter ban have a particular connection with Hinduism. Although Hindu scriptures do not specify vegetarianism, the idea of *ahimsa* (not killing) of Hinduism has subtly influenced the Hindus' choice of a vegetarian diet. Especially in some religious festivals, vegetarian customs are strictly observed by believers as well as many Hindus who are generally not pure vegetarian. There are many vegetarian celebrities in India, such as Mahatma Gandhi and current Prime Minister Narendra Modi. For these reasons, India is famous for being vegetarian. According to a survey in 2014 (Bose 2016), some states such as Punjab, Haryana, and Rajasthan, have around 65 per cent to 70 per cent vegetarians; whereas only about 2 per cent of the population is vegetarian in states such as Telangana, West Bengal, Andhra and Odisha; vegetarians over the age of 15 account for 29 per cent of the total population in India. Although it was reported that 70 per cent Indians eat non-vegetarian food, considering that the population of India was around 1.34 billion in 2017, it can be seen that the vegetarian culture is very influential among a large population in India.

Besides, India has a unique avoidance of beef culture. Most Hindus do not eat beef. It is reported (Bansal 2016) that more than 98 per cent of Hindus do not eat beef; there is a ban on slaughtering the cow in 24 states of India such as Uttar Pradesh and Haryana (TNN 2015). The population of Hindu beefeaters in the country has fallen from 18.9 million in 1999-2000 (2.51 per cent of the total Hindu population) to 12.5 million in 2011-12 (1.39 per cent of the total Hindu population) (Ibid.). Yet, 60-70 per cent of beef (generally buffalo meat) eaters are Hindus in the well-known public places in Lucknow and others; beefeaters include the high castes, but the fact is that they eat it secretly with relatives and friends as it is not allowed in their homes (Ibid.). From this point of view, the Hinduism to Hindus not to eat beef; those who do so generally cannot eat it in public.

Throughout India, according to data from the National Sample Survey Office, in 2011-12 (Bansal 2016), nearly 83.5 million people eat beef and buffalo meat,[7] although the population of such eaters in Delhi and Uttar Pradesh has fallen sharply. Beef is not entirely banned in India, but it has been a problem that cannot be ignored because it has caused conflicts. A Muslim man was lynched on suspicion of storing and consuming beef in Uttar Pradesh (BBC 2015), and a Muslim couple was attacked on suspicion that they were carrying beef in Madhya Pradesh (BBC 2016).

The demand for dairy products is high, and the market demand for meat products in India is small, which provides business opportunities for meat exports. India, as the world's largest dairy animal country, has 110 million buffalos, 133 million goats and 63 million sheep. The export of animal products has made a significant contribution to Indian agriculture, with the export of buffaloes taking up 89.08 per cent of the total export of animal products in India. Indian buffalo exports reached $ 4.037 billion in 2017-18 (mainly sold to Vietnam, Malaysia, Egypt, Iran and Saudi Arabia), while total animal product exports was $ 4.623 billion in 2017-18 (GoI 2018). India, which has $ 185 million (2017-18) of dairy exports, has also become the world's largest milk supplier, accounting for 20.17

7 The population distribution of beefeaters is divided by region. The southern provinces such as Andhra Pradesh, Tamil Nadu, Kerala and Karnataka have between 900,000 and 3.28 million beef or buffalo meat eaters. In Assam, Punjab, and Bihar, the population of such eaters is also growing exponentially.

per cent of world's milk products (Ibid.). Although the exports of India are composed entirely of buffalo meat, the ban on slaughter of cows could "bring an end to illegal slaughter and raise the price for buffalo meat thus proving to be beneficial for companies [...] engaged in legal slaughter and export of buffalo meat" (Iyengar 2015a).

6.3.2.5. Manthan and Exchange as One-side Benefit

The Hindu concept of *Manthan* literally means churning; the essence of the world is chaotic and churning in the Hindu world view (Sinha and Sanyal 2016). It will release both negative and positive forces in the agitation; only by bearing the negative forces and adapting the use of positive forces can one be invincible (Ibid.). Some Indian behaviours may be simply considered as keen on "getting a petty advantage" or "immediate interests", "insatiable", "maximise their interests" which are quite different from Chinese culture (Zhang W. J. 2018). Those behaviours, which could be called "gamesmanship" (Zhang 2017), can take on more favourable conditions; indeed, if the behaviour is irregular, it could cause a negative perception for the actor. This concept of "gamesmanship" can be further extended to understand the process of struggle until the end.

From this perspective, Hindus have a particular feature in understanding the world, i.e., chaos is the essence of the world. While facing chaos, they may be more comfortable and accustomed to it. On the one hand, it reflects the characteristics of the Indians' "optimistic attitude to life" which has a non-positive effect on development in terms of tolerance of chaos. On the other hand, it promotes the consciousness to avoid negative forces in chaos and take advantage of the positive forces. The use of positive power to fulfil immediate interests in the eyes of others is to get the best outcome between advantage and disadvantage, which is influenced by the Hindu value of *Manthan* ("churning"). Thus, "attain the immediate interests" or "maximise one's own benefit" could be a reasonable part of Hindu values.

The thought of *manthan* is different from the concept in Chinese culture, especially *li* (rites) or *lishang wanglai* (literally means courtesy demands reciprocity) (Zhang W. J. 2018) and *bao* (return, the exchange mode) (Shang 2013:171, 177-178). In this respect, Hinduism affects the Indians' exchange mode. As mentioned above, the dominant exchange mode in Homo Hierarchicus (or Hinduism) society is "exchange as a one-side benefit" which follows the rule of *dharma* (Shang 2013:177, 180). It is pointed out in Psycho-Culturology that Hindus are more inclined to "self of divinity" (*shenxing ziwo*)[8] (Ibid: 257-261).

---

8 Psycho-Culturology believes that individuals in Hindu society are different from individuals in Western religious society; the former pay more attention to the "spiritual self", pursue "self of divinity" (or Divine Self), and physical self is not considered the true self. This kind of "self of divinity" in Western religious society "only exists in a small

The analysis in Psycho-Culturology believes that the divine or the supernatural is essential in the PSH for Hierarchicus and the relationship between people in the secular world is *maya* (an illusion where things appear to be present but are not what they seem) (Ibid: 178). In this "one-side exchange mode", people from low levels could ask for benefit from people in higher positions; the exchange is uncoordinated, it is not necessary to return; the return may be repaid by another method under the law or *dharma* of the supernatural (Ibid.177-181), i.e., based on the supernatural *Dharma* and *Rin* (literally means debt) that is to return the supernatural *rin* based on *dharma* in order to get *Moksha* (liberation) (Shang 2013:178, 321). The "exchange as a one-sided benefit" is completely unequal as "the relationship between people, in reality, is illusory" (Shang 2013:177-178). The behavioural characteristics of Indians mentioned above including "getting petty advantage and immediate interests", "insatiable", "maximise their interests" is influenced by the value of *manthan*, the thought in Hinduism created the exchange mode of Indians, especially for the Hindus. The concept of *manthan* and exchange as a one-sided benefit causes behaviour to actively seek to develop their own interests, which sometimes could cause a negative image, particularly when interacting with *lun-ren* who emphasise on *li* and *bao*.

6.3.2.6. Unique Time Concept and Unpunctuality

The Hindu concept of time has a particular uniqueness (Qiu 2012:44). The *Vishnu Purana* of Hinduism records India's large-scale time system, such as Kalpa (4.32 billion years). The life of the Hindu god Brahma is about 311 trillion years (Ibid: 45). From the perspective of language, the unique time concept of Indians can be seen. The words "yesterday" and "tomorrow" in Hindi are the same as *kal* (कल). The "day before yesterday" and "the day after tomorrow" are the same as *parason* (परसों).[9] It is considered in language theory that language habits also affect people's thoughts and concepts (Chhokar 2007:992) (Bhoothalingam 2015). The language of India affects the Indians' perception of time. Many Indians are not "punctual". It is not uncommon that events are postponed. It creates a relaxed image of the Indian. The interpretation of this from a cultural perspective is related to the beliefs of Indians. As they have a different concept of time and large historical units of measurement (Qiu 2012:45), they believe in the past and the afterlife. Therefore, the small time units like minutes and seconds seem to lack attention. "Ten minutes" commonly said by Indian may take half an hour. "Come tomorrow" may not mean the work could be solved tomorrow. These time units sometimes do not refer to a specific time, but rather a kind of excuse for work that cannot be completed at present. However, along with the development of

---

number of believers". Western religious, social individuals are more inclined to have the characteristics of "extremely individual", see Shang (2013, 24, 74, 78, 80, 257.)

9 Through the tense of the verb, the Indian judges whether the word expresses the past or the future. That is to say, the past tense in the statement means "yesterday" or "the day before yesterday", and the future tense means "tomorrow" or "the day after tomorrow."

modernisation and internationalisation, this phenomenon of unpunctuality is changing in India. Still, the influence of traditional ideas is deeply rooted. This always affects labour productivity, which is not conducive to economic development. Unpunctuality is creating a negative perception in cooperation.

6.3.3. Organisational Level: The Influence of Hinduism on Organisational Culture

"Group" is considered to be "the most important social and cultural context in which people live"; The way to establish a group with others is an essential level for analysing different civilised societies (Shang 2013:84). "Groups that are artificially established in order to achieve a certain purpose effectively" are considered as "sub-groups" or "social organisations" (Ibid: 122). The sub-group or social organization in Hindu society is mainly represented by religious groups and affected by caste (Shang 2013:149). The analysis in this section takes the case studies of Indian commercial organisations, especially those dealing with China.

6.3.3.1. Hinduism and Commercial Organizations

In a broad sense, the influences of Hinduism on commercial organisations have two aspects; the method of concluding organisations and the organisational culture. Firstly, commercial organisations established and based on Hindu culture are everywhere, and the products of these commercial organisations account for a large share of the Indian market, such as books on philosophy, yoga, Ayurveda, food and medicine. Patanjali, which is operated by Yoga master Baba Ramdev and his partner Acharya Balkrishna, is an outstanding representative. The fast-moving consumer goods (FMCG) brand 'Patanjali' is one of the most recognised brands in India, which includes soap, toothpaste, hair oil, fruit and vegetable juices, Indian flour, biscuits, noodles, and the like, while another sub-brand of the group, Divya Pharmacy, manufactures and sells traditional Indian medicines, i.e., Ayurveda medicine. Up to March 31, 2017, the company's total turnover reached 105.61 billion rupees (Rs. 10,561 crore, equivalent to about 10.561 billion Chinese RMB), and has become the biggest local brand in India (Mitra 2017). The products produced by Patanjali are mostly related to diet and health and have a good reputation among Indians.. Besides, the Khadi brand, which is operated by the government, is also a brand with Indian characteristics formed by the Swaraj movement (self-governance) advocated by Mahatma Gandhi. It deals mainly with Indian textile products, Ayurveda medicines and food, and so on. The main products of another famous brand, Fab India, are also traditional Indian handlooms and daily necessities. The international chain brand, Good Earth, produces home accessories, clothing, essential oils and candles produced in combination with Indian meditation and yoga—all with Indian characteristics. In addition, in terms of catering, the vegetarian culture in India has led to a diversity of vegetarian diets, most notably served by Saravana Bhavan, a vegetarian restaurant in India that is inexpensive and has 10 categories of 350 dishes (Saravana Bhavan 2012), which are already spread throughout many first-tier cities in Europe, Americas and Asia through its branches. It is known as the world's largest Indian vegetarian chain. There are many vegetarians among the Hindus, and the demand for dairy products is heavy. Mother Dairy and Amul are dairy brands that Indians cannot live without in their daily lives.

Notably, the rise of Indian native Hindu brands has caused resistance to foreign goods. The founder of Patanjali Ayurveda Ltd., Ramdev, has publicly proposed "It is time to make India MNC-free" (multinational corporations) and "India should ban Chinese products and companies as China is not a friend of India" (Mitra 2017). Despite this, Patanjali was reported to keen to export to China in March 2017(Ibid.). Because the founder is a master of Indian yoga, the company has the characteristics of Hinduism. All the company's income is used for charity. The founder said that successor must also be a Sanyasi (Hindu monk) and will never hand over the business to a merchant (Ibid.).

Secondly, Hindu classics also influence the organisational culture of business groups. For example, the classic work, *Arthasastra* (Science of Material Gain or Science of political economy) that absorbed Hindu philosophy (Sharma 2005:186) elaborated on the ancient Indian economic thoughts and still has an impact on commercial organisations of India. The author, Kautilya, considers that *artha* (sound economy, prosperity) is the most crucial thing (Jose et al. 2011:175-176). Moreover, according to the *Arthasastra,* "The fundamental principle of economic activity is that no man you transact with will lose; then you shall not" is still passed down by Indian business groups. It is not only followed by the founders of the Murugappa Group as their basic principle and has been inherited for a century; this belief is still the guide of decision-making and defines its professional ethics (Murugappa 2018). This win-win concept is conducive to the growth of income in the long run and the improvement of trade. It reflects the spirit of equity that leads to economic development.

6.3.3.2. Commercial Caste and Entrepreneurship

The Murugappa Group, was founded and is owned by the Murugappa family. "The Murugappas belong to the Chettiar community, which is primarily based in Tamil Nadu and Kerala and is famed for its entrepreneurship" (Babu 2017). It was pointed out "much of Indian business enterprise has been associated with certain banking and trading castes and mercantile communities" (Kudaisya 2009:85) and "major entrepreneurs have emerged from communities with dominant cultures of banking and trading" (Menon 1985: 19-26 and Kapp 1963). According to Max Weber (1958), "caste inhibited occupational mobility, and the dominant emphasis within Hindu philosophy on *karma*—doing one's duty without concern for reward—offered little incentive for profit or material gain" and "entrepreneurial pursuits were the vocation of the hereditary trading castes and were hardly attractive to other sections of society" (Kudaisya 2009:85).

Yet, this view is opposed by many scholars (Singer 1956). Dwijendra Tripathi (1989, 2004), Sanjay Subrahmanyan (1996) and Harish Damodaran (2008) argued that "caste alone has not been the determinant in shaping business fortunes in South Asia", but "new ideas, knowledge and the adaptation of Western technology and managerial organization have been equally important"; Damodaran notes that "entrepreneurial groups have emerged from castes outside the hereditary mercantile order. Thus, it includes those from 'agricultural and allied backgrounds' and 'social castes' [...] their entry into industry is essentially a post-Independence phenomenon" (Kudaisya 2009:85-6).

However, the community of Chettiars, to which the Murugappas belong, has shown their "strong community networks" and "long histories of trading" (Ibid: 86). Besides, from the trajectory of the Chettiars, it should be noticed that their industrial presence not only related to capital and opportunity but also to the political and economic conditions (Ibid.). Although the influence is lessening, the caste still has an impact on the choice of industry. Especially, castes made the traditional group monopolize some particular industries and people to pursue the same occupation for generations (Shang 2013:147).

Besides, Psycho-Culturology pointed out that the "supernatural centre" oriented culture made Hindus form "surpass-kinship group, surpass-regional sub-group" (Shang 2015:276), and "political ruling mode of checking and balancing among various castes, sectarian groups" (Ibid: 271). While safeguarding the interests of various castes and groups, slogans such as "developing the economy is overwhelming" cannot be accepted as easily as in China (Ibid: 277). The cost of this is "endless debate, conflict, loss of order and discipline, slow decision-making", with a large part of the population disregarding economic backwardness as the primary problem of grumbling about the government (Ibid: 277). The dispute of interests of diversified groups with Indian characteristics has brought about disadvantages such as inefficiency, scattered forces, and large consumption of social resources in non-economic development issues, which have greatly affected the speed of India's economic development.

Hinduism influences the establishment of commercial organisations as well as organisational culture. It is the human constant and PSH of Homo Hierarchicus influenced by Hinduism impacting the establishment, management and development of organisations.

6.3.4. National Level: Hinduism Impact on Policy

Cultural confidence based on the influence of Hinduism is an essential part of its impact on India's national policy. Policies initiated in India, as well as India's attitude towards China's initiatives, can be traced to the influence of Hinduism.

6.3.4.1. Cultural Confidence: to be Dominant and Contain Foreign Forces

As mentioned at the beginning, firm beliefs and the values of Hinduism are essential parts of Indian culture, except that behaviour, thought, and strategic culture with Hindu characteristics also influence the economy. The cultural linkage established in the history between India and other South Asia countries also influences economic development. The cultural connection contributed by Hinduism made it easy for India to continue its relevance with those countries as a unity; past cultural relations were considered as the base for the Look East Policy and the later Act East Policy (2014). (Hussain 2017:147-155). Indian culture, especially Hinduism, created a deep connection with those countries and caused India to maintain the connection and pick it up again after a halt brought about by the Cold War (Ibid.).

India has a profound and far-reaching influence on the culture of South Asia. The cultural confidence of India towards South Asia affects India's economic and trade cooperation projects. An Indian scholar has pointed out that it is "more accurate to refer to it [India] as a cultural unit rather than as a political entity", and "the cultural unit in terms of the geographical area was almost always larger than what India is today" (Chhokar 2007:971-972). Apart from Pakistan and Bangladesh, which are separated from the Indian mainland, countries such as Nepal, Bhutan and Sri Lanka are deeply influenced by Indian culture. Indian civilisation is considered "one of the sources of mainland Southeast Asia, viz., Cambodia, Laos, Myanmar, Vietnam and Thailand" (Hussain 2017:147). India has deeply influenced those countries since ancient times. Compared to the political or military deterrence, cultural influence has contributed to India's position in South Asia. Against this background, India's cultural leadership in South Asia cannot be ignored, which is conducive to grasp India's perception when there are changes in the external economic situation in which other South Asian countries participate.

It was pointed out that the economic corridor in which India participates is not so smooth (Lin 2017).[10] The Bangladesh-China-India-Myanmar Economic Corridor (BCIM-EC) held its third meeting of the Joint Working Group (or Joint Study Group) in India in the second half of 2015; yet, there had been no progress (Lin 2017). In April 2017, the third meeting was held in Kolkata, India (ICS 2017). A scholar from an Indian think tank pointed out that India's attitude towards China's multilateral cooperative economic initiative is actually to observe and bide its time. Moreover, India's position in South Asia in terms of culture makes

10 Although Lin (2017) argued that the development of the economic corridor as long as India participates is not so active, he might mean the economic corridor that also includes China. It would be easier to understand this from the origin of regional cooperation, that is for increasing the influence of regional nations and decreasing external forces, including the transnational corporations and other non-regional nations.

India seem more willing to be in the driving seat. Not only regarding politics, economy, and military power as a measure of national strength, the regional cultural impact also created a sense of a commanding position for India. For example, an Indian diplomat believes that India has a significant influence on China, and since ancient times, China learned from India, while China's influence on India was limited. The splendid ancient civilisation created cultural pride and national confidence among the Indians, and it is an essential source of the ideology of India to be a great power (Long 2016:3). Moreover, this deep-rooted great power thought is often considered to be a foreign strategic thought of India, and it is mostly the basis for formulating foreign policy after India's independence (Sun 2000:2).

6.3.4.2. Homo Hierarchicus with Leadership Temperament and Independent Pursuit

Psycho-Culturology points out that there is a "self of independent type" (self-cognition dimension[11]) similar to the Human Constant of "rugged individual" of American society in the Hierarchicus society, as reflected in the priests and religionists of India (Shang 2013:252, 261). Besides, political leaders are also their representatives, emphasising self-cultivation. This type of self-cognition in Homo Hierarchicus society emphasises on the individual and is expressed in "they have a strong desire to directly relate the self to the 'absolute universal' (*jue-dui pu-bian*) (Shang 2015:113) and reject any intermediary" and also believe that "the universal truth is eternal; saving the soul of the individual can only rely on their own efforts without relying on others" (Ibid: 261).

The interpretation of Psycho-Culturology is largely meticulous, for further classification; this self-cognition can be classified as Homo Hierarchicus with leadership temperament, which also led to the emergence of many gurus in India, who think they have direct contact with the divine and form their doctrines and schools of thought; they are followed by ordinary Homo Hierarchicus. This type of political leaders are more inclined to pursue "autonomy" instead of "bandwagoning", such as Hind Swaraj (Indian Home Rule) emphasized by Gandhi (1909) during the Indian freedom struggle and the "Non-Alignment" movement advocated by Prime Minister Jawaharlal Nehru for the independence of foreign policy in the early days of independence.

So far, the strategic independent pursuit of India on whether to make alliances is based on national interests (Li 2017:8, 34). As pointed out by Samuel P. Huntington (1996: 209), India could strike a balance instead of bandwagoning towards China. The Look East Policy or the later Act East Policy pursued by India and other cooperation programmes involved countries like the USA, Japan, India

11 Self-cognition dimension is one of the four dimensions of Psycho-Culturology (Shang 2013:64-66).

and Australia coalition that tend to balance China. This can be considered as a combination of the Swaraj concept (traditional autonomous rule) and other concepts such as *manthan* pursuing self-interest and *karma* attaching importance to responsibility, or it can be said to balance the maintaining of the Hierarchicus leadership of the region in which it is located. From this, it can once again be seen that the influence of the Human Constant from the individual level to the national level is coherent. As pointed out in Psycho-Culturology, people under certain Human Constant will treat and deal with the "outer world" in a way that is compatible with their Human Constant (Shang 2015a:22). In this aspect, the influence of Hinduism on the national level is initiated by the individual. It reflects the influence of the national leader in the Human Constant of the Homo Hierarchicus on national policy.

6.3.4.3. Mandala, Strong Civilizational Entity and Hierarchy Principle

An analysis of national behaviour from the Psycho-Culturology perspective summarises that India is influenced by the following concepts: *mandala* (or Raja-*mandala*, the circle of states) formulated by Kautilya in *Arthashastra*, "strong civilizational and weak organisational entity" and the "hierarchy principle" related to the idea of the *Dharma* system (Shang 2015b:9-27). These concepts play their respective roles and influence each other.

It seems that India treats China paradoxically, but it has specific psychological and cultural roots. Firstly, combined with the characteristics of the *mandala* and the "strong civilizational and weak organisational entity" (Shang 2015), India regards the South Asian countries affected by Indian civilisation as a civilisational entity. China is a neighbouring country and therefore belongs to the enemy type following the *mandala* concept that neighbouring countries are enemies. However, because of the civilisational connection with India through Buddhism, China seems to be regarded as part of the civilisational entity. This has caused India and China to feel close to each other, making India tend to cooperate with China. The contradiction of a civilisational entity and organisational enemy has resulted in India cooperating with China but not comprehensively and freely. It shows India's hesitation on BCIM as analysed in 6.3.4.1.

Secondly, the "hierarchy principle" has caused India to treat its external civilisation inclusively and not wholly excluded, and thus the external forces formed an independent group in the hierarchy of India (Shang 2015b:22-24). Economically, even if it is seen as an "enemy" to a certain extent, China could step into the market of India notwithstanding the comparatively small trade volumes between these two neighbouring countries as well as the great economies. The hierarchy principle made India tolerate but limit the role of external civilisation like China. Despite a friendly approach from India, the vigilance towards China always exists.

Thirdly, the emphasis on "*dharma*" is reflected in the fact that spiritual products are an essential output and thus a factor in the establishment of the national position (Shang 2015b:16). "Asymmetric strategy" was used to describe it:

> "India advocates the establishment of India's advantages in a certain aspect based on national strength, to offset for its other shortcomings in regional and international affairs, and thus achieve the goal of India's equal position in regional and international affairs" (Ge 2015:71).

Therefore, India has an intervention within its civilisational entity as a spiritual exporter, especially in South Asia (as indicated in 6.3.4.1).

6.3.4.4. State Control and Obedience to Authority

"Ghosts from the past" is considered to still influence modern India given that "there is a powerful and ancient tradition in Indian economic thought that looks to the state for control of economic activity" (Dasgupta 1993:185-186). The acceptance of the people for national control of economic activities is reflected in the current economic development reforms in India. Although most economists and analysts consider demonetization "a bad policy that was badly implemented", this policy implemented by the Modi government received popular support (Khera 2017; TNN 2016).

Obedience to authority has made it is easier for the nation to implement its policies in Asia, which is considered not entirely possible in other parts of the world (Fukuyama 1995). In obeying authority, India has its own characteristic, especially with the influence of Hinduism in terms of the caste system. The main characteristic of Hinduism is the authority of the Brahman (Qiu 2012: 20-21). Although challenging the authority of a Brahman is considered a feature of the development of Hinduism (Ibid), it did not completely change the situation that the social resources of India are controlled by the upper castes. As it was pointed out, "caste politics determines access to public resources" (Munshi 2016), Brahman or upper castes are still the main dominant hierarchy in India.

It could explain the influences of Hinduism on people's compliance with authority from the Psycho-Culturology perspective. India's political and cultural traditions are influenced by the "supernatural-centred orientation", which has the following characteristics: "When social movements are 'connected with certain religious goals', individuals often show more significant emotional input and dedication in such activities" (Shang 2015a:254-255); traditional Hindus tend to treat politicians and other ruling figures as gods (Ibid: 260). Moreover, there are constant emergences of national leaders worshipped as divines in India (Iyengar 2015b; Apparasu 2018). The public recognises the leader's "truth" concept and will follow it loyally. When a popular movement is combined with some religious goal, the participants will have a strong emotional bond and incredible dedication, such as the '*Satyagraha* (holding onto truth) Movement' led by Gandhi (Shang 2015a:256-257), '*Hindutva*' (Hinduness) which is championed by the Hindu nationalist volunteer organization, the Rashtriya Swayamsevak Sangh (RSS) and later officially adopted as the ideology of the Bharatiya Janata Party (BJP) (Ramakrishnan 2004); all these reflect the Hindus' "emotional commitment and dedication". Therefore, one of the preconditions for Hindus to comply with authority are that those initiatives are recognised or linked to religious goals, and often get faithful follow-up and support. The cattle slaughter ban in India could also be taken as a representative example. The Swachh Bharat Abhiyan (Clean India Mission) was linked with Mahatma Gandhi by calling it the "best tribute India could pay to Mahatma Gandhi on his 150 birth anniversary in 2019" (PM India 2018).

However, state control and restrictions have a dual character towards economic development, and the negative effect cannot be ignored. As an economist pointed out, state control over development could also cause inefficiency (Dasgupta 1993:174) "[...] given the political administrative system in which Indian trade control policies were operating; 'delays and uncertainty together encourage corruption as a way of getting things done'" (Dasgupta 1974:116). Reducing "state control" could be a challenge for authority and the people living in a culture of respecting authority. In this sense, culture could be a constraint for economic development.

6.3.5. Summary

All in all, with the advancement of the modernisation process, although the influence of Hinduism has been weakened to varying degrees, the rate of weakening is slow, and Hindu philosophy is still an essential factor affecting India's economic development. Firstly, a follower of Hinduism has the following characteristics: stratification, emphasis on spiritual development, thrift, taboos in diet, fighting for benefits and avoiding risks, one-side benefit exchange, unique time concept, etc. Secondly, commercial organizations were also influenced by the following characteristics: commodities have traditional characteristics, wealth is stable in some groups, occupationalism, and trade exclusion. Thirdly, it influenced the country to have cultural confidence, independent choice, attach importance to the status of civilisation and practice asymmetric strategy. Hinduism has a positive impact on economic development, such as saving resources, imagining, stable wealth, exporting agriculture (meat and dairy products), fighting for interests, strong centripetal force in organization and self-motivation as well as the negative impact of income growth, structural development, domestic structural adjustment, and improvement of external economic conditions. The individual level has a more prominent influence, compared to its Chinese counterpart, in the economic relations between China and India. Yet, according to the analysis of this section, the most influential aspect could be the influence of Hinduism on the national level.

6.4. Conclusion

Based on the analysis in this paper, it can be seen that the cultures of China and India (Confucianism, Hinduism) have an impact on commercial behaviour, organisational culture, and national trade policy. Although the strength of the impact requires specific analysis of particular issues, it cannot be ignored. The impact of this cultural influence on the economic relations between the two countries can be summarised as follows.

Firstly, from the perspective of China, the impacts of culture on the economic relations between the two countries are the following. The characteristics of the nation-building *guanxi* (relationship), and infinite extensibility of *guanxi* are conducive to the development of economic relations between the two countries, and the concept of connecting economic equal with world peace as well as *Da-tong* thought are also positive factors. Based on the research of this chapter, the influence of Confucian culture on individual and organisational levels has a more visible impact. Yet, they are an important basis for analysing the national level. The impact of culture on bilateral economic relations could be mainly reflected on the national level in the context of this chapter. The individual and organisational levels are indispensable parts of the analysis as factors that help to understand the nation's behaviour. China attaches importance to economic development, believes that economic development can promote peace, takes developing the economy as the centre of domestic and foreign policies, and practices the concept of economic pragmatism. These differ from India that does not thoroughly agree with economic determinism and paying attention to the dignity and cultural status of big power, especially in the South Asia region. This difference has caused conflicts, such as the attitude towards the Belt and Road Initiative. It reflects China's concern about India on the CPEC and India's response,

> "The Kashmir issue is a legacy of history between India and Pakistan. We advocate that the two sides of India and Pakistan should properly resolve through dialogue and consultation and do not favour any party. China is bordered by Pakistan-controlled Kashmir, which is the only place we have to go in Pakistan. [...China is having] some livelihood and economic projects, but not aiming at third parties; China has no intention of intervening in disputes between India and Pakistan" (MFAPRC 2018).

It was emphasised that "China has an agreement with Pakistan that it will not back any side in the (disputed) claims on Kashmir" (PTI 2018). Nevertheless, India keeps on presenting consistent position,

> "Regarding the so-called 'China-Pakistan Economic Corridor', which is being projected as the flagship project of the BRI/OBOR, the international community is well aware of India's position. No country can accept a project that ignores its core concerns on sovereignty and territorial integrity" (MEA 2017),

While some media reports state that India could possibly cooperate with China in BRI after a year, the response from the MEA is the same,

> "Our position on OBOR/BRI is clear and there is no change. The so-called 'China-Pakistan Economic Corridor' violates India's sovereignty and territorial integrity. No country can accept a project that ignores its core concerns on sovereignty and territorial integrity." (MEA 2018)

This is undoubtedly a negative impact on the economic relations between the two countries. From the perspective of deep cultural concepts, the concepts of *guanxi* (relations), economy and peace, and *Da-tong* thought in Confucian culture have the most significant impact on Sino-Indian economic relations. The differences in ideas (whether or not they can be centred on economic construction) create conflicts.

Secondly, from the perspective of India, the impact of culture on the economic relations between the two countries could be summarised as below. The influences of Hindu culture on business behaviour affect the development of Chinese enterprises in India. For example, the product design needs to adapt to the Indian market. The management should consider the individual cultural characteristics of Hinduism, and the organisational culture needs to face the cultural differences. It is needed to balance and adjust the difference from the Indian caste pattern (hierarchy principle) and one-sided benefit exchange mode, with differential pattern and exchange as trustworthiness credit of the *lun-ren*. India's cultural confidence and intractable religious influence (even for the Congress Party, which advocates secularism and pluralism, has to forgo [their] reluctance to keep [their] belief private (Sivaswamy 2018)), which cannot be ignored by China. Hindu culture does cause discomfort for the Chinese in economic relations, such as the concept of time, vegetarian culture, and divine self, which causes some conflicts at the individual level. Even so, with gradual improvement and modernisation of the economic relations between the two countries, it seems the cultural impact on individual and organisation levels can be eliminated or minimised, especially given some of the culture-unrelated trade items of the two countries, which could be negligible in view of the research of this chapter. Yet, at the national level, characteristics such as cultural confidence, independent pursuit, *mandala*, and strong civilizational entity, have an essential role reflected in the Indian national behaviour. As mentioned in the above paragraph, the difference between Hindu culture and Confucian culture has caused cultural conflicts on some issues between the two countries in economic development, which has hindered the development of economic relations between the two countries.

CHAPTER 7

COMPARATIVE STUDIES OF CONFUCIANISM AND HINDUISM

The two ancient civilisations, China and India, had friendly interactions and cultural exchange for more than two thousand years (JCCEICCC 2014:3). An internationally recognised Chinese Indologist proposed that the "geo-civilisation narrative" should dominate in the bilateral relationship of China and India "rather than the geo-political or the geo-strategic discourse" (Anand 2015). However, the more the linkage and common ground of these two nations are highlighted, the differences between these two could not be ignored. Given the misunderstanding caused by cultural difference could be a threat to the relations; it is necessary to identify the cultural differences as well. It was warned that if the "civilizations exist today", the borders, centres and peripheries of the civilisations, even including "their provinces and the air one breathes there, the general and particular 'forms' existing and associating within them" are not known well, "catastrophic blunders of perspective could ensue" (Braudel 1980:210-211; Huntington 1996:39). Meanwhile, Samuel P. Huntington predicted that "India, along with Russia and Japan were to play the role of pawns between the US-dominated West allied with Israel, against the Chinese-Islamic challengers" (Nanda 2009:108).

The different cultural values of China and India could influence the development of the economic relations of the two nations macroscopically (e.g., policies, market features) and microscopically (e.g., economic behaviour). In this chapter, it will be selected and compared that the 'centre' of Chinese civilization, i.e., the core value of Confucianism such as *ren, yi, li, zhi, xin* as well as the 'centre' of Indian civilization, i.e., the core value of Hinduism such as *dharma, manthan, jugaad, karma.*[12] It was believed that the religious thought of India has close ties with economic activities from ancient times (Dehejia et al. 1993:145). From the perspective of Cultural Determinism, Confucianism has been argued to be responsible for the backwardness of China (Weber 2010; Lin 2012:30-31). However, it was pointed out that the reason why China was powerful and prosperous one thousand years earlier, could not be explained from this perspective, while Confucianism was the central ideology at that time (Lin 2012:31). Moreover, it is strongly believed that Chinese traditional culture has an essential role in the development and rise of China (Wei 2017). Roel Sterckx (2019: xii), a professor at the University of Cambridge, explained why Chinese traditional values are relevant for today's context. He pointed out most ideas of ancient China's masters of philosophy are,

> "offered as guidance to be lived, experienced and practised. [...] They reflect on how to live, function better and find harmony with the world. Yet, in putting lived experience above theoretical knowledge, their teachings touch the entire person, the brain as well as the emotions. That is why they are as relevant today as they are interesting for their past."

This chapter compares the core values of the two civilisations and analyses their influence on economic thought. Further, the impact of the values toward the bilateral economic relations will be discussed below.

7.1. Background: Civilisational Conflict and Economic Thought

7.1.1. Develop the View of Civilisational Clash

One of the most significant contributions of Samuel P. Huntington is that he provided "an easily grasped and intelligible framework for understanding the world, distinguishing what is important from what is unimportant among the multiplying conflicts [...]" by dividing the world in terms of seven or eight civilisations (Huntington 1996:36). This can be pursued, especially from the perspective of the USA and in the period when this world-famous work was published. It was emphasised in this work that "the conflicts that pose the greatest dangers for stability are those between states or groups from different civilizations" (Huntington 1996:36). Two more points might be highlighted in a deeper level of civilisational approach; firstly, civilisation might be divided into sub-civilisations and have conflicts among them. This happened in West Asia. Secondly, conflicts could be defused by diplomatic channels, which could be proved by examining the border dispute between China and India after 1962.

12 Confucianism is one of the most influential concepts in China. Hinduism is the dominant belief in India. The population of Hindus is around 79.8 per cent as seen in Census 2011 (PIB 2015).

The conflict between China and India can be understood in a better way from a civilisational perspective. It is notable that "the potentially most dangerous enmities occur across the fault lines between the world's major civilizations" (Huntington 1996:20).[13] Along with collision of national interests, different judgments towards the same issue could produce "enmities" and further conflict between the two major civilisations—China and India—especially when the gap of Comprehensive National Power is reducing between the two nations. Importantly, the border dispute between China and India, although solved peacefully in the last two decades, did influence economic relations between the two nations (See Chapter 8, 8.3).

Cultural differences would sharpen conflicts, especially the sources of disputes like economic issues. It was induced that "economic power and welfare, manifested in disputes over trade, investment, and other issues" is one of "the sources of conflict between humans throughout history" (Huntington 1996:208). More noticeable, "when states from different civilizations are involved [...] cultural differences sharpen the conflict" (Ibid.).

Moreover, while people are facing different cultures, they may have problems to understand them, which could cause a "cultural shock" (Oberg 1951). The reflection of cultural shock is deep mental anxiety, which could cause different issues in their life and work. They may have hostility or debarment to the people of the different cultures they are living in (Guan 1995:341). This is because lack of the necessary knowledge of the culture or appropriate skill to face the problem. Thus, it is crucial to understand the different cultures.

7.1.2. Two Civilisations: "Bandwagoning" or "Balancing"?

It was predicted that India could "generate balancing efforts" to the rise of Chinese power instead of "bandwagoning":

> "While bandwagoning may be more characteristic of Asian civilizations, the rise of Chinese power could generate balancing efforts from states in other civilizations, such as the USA, India, and Russia." (Huntington 1996:209)

Besides, the "balancing" role of India is reaffirmed in the current research. "The greatest scope for an expanded role for India is clearly in terms of its capacity to play a soft-balancing role to manage the rise of China." (Lee 2015:67). Given the attitude of India towards the Belt and Road Initiative (BRI) of China, it could be a robust supportive point to former scholars' prediction on India's balancing on the rise of Chinese power. Undoubtedly, the disputed territory between India and Pakistan in the China-Pakistan Economic Corridor (CPEC) is the biggest concern of India regarding the BRI. The plan, which India interacted with more closely,

13 These "fault lines" could appear in different understandings in the same civilisation.

including the Asia-Africa Growth Corridor (AAGC) initiated by India and Japan in November 2016, is seen as a balancing even "counter" to China's BRI (Special Correspondent, *The Hindu*, 2017).

In an environment where the philosophy of "Harmony in diversity" exists [*he-er bu-tong*], one of the primary responses of the Chinese from the government to academic levels towards India's balancing is to align China's BRI with India's "Act East Policy" or Project Mausam (Mawsim: Maritime Route and Cultural Landscapes) (Luo:2017; Hu 2015; Chen 2015; Tao 2015). The contrary opinion also exists as it is believed that "strategic connectivity between the Belt & Road Initiative and India's Project Mausam does not represent a viable policy option." (Feng 2016:44). However, it was reported by the Indian media that China wanted India to go slow on the Asia-Africa Growth Corridor and "persuade India and South Africa to merge the project with the BRICS platform and keep its rival, Japan, out of it" [as cited in *Global Times* in TNN (2017)].

7.1.3. Close Cultural Kinship or Two Conflictual Civilisations

"The close cultural kinship of the two societies" is believed to contribute to the peaceful shift between two big powers like Pax Britannica and Pax Americana (Huntington 1996:209). China and India do have a "close cultural kinship" in terms of Buddhism; this kinship created by Buddhism might not be strong enough to connect the majority of China and India, as Buddhism is not the dominant belief in either of the two societies as it was in the past. More notably, Hindu (India) civilisation and Sinic (China) civilisation are classified in the more conflictual category in different civilizations and the rise of China is believed to be "the potential source of a big inter-civilizational war of core states" (Huntington 1996:208, 245).[14] To reduce the risk of conflict between China and India and finding more common ground from their culture or beliefs, in a sense, is a far-reaching influential but very easily neglected option.

Value conflicts are considered unavoidable in intercultural communication. To understand each other's primary and essential values and explain them, which are different and may cause conflict, is one method of dealing with the conflicts of values (Guan 1995:176). In short, to compare and find out the similarities in Chinese and Indian cultures would contribute to the creation of a closer relationship between these two old Asian civilisations, and to realise the differences of the Chinese and Indian cultures could reduce the possibility of conflicts.

14 However, Fukuyama disagreed with Huntington's view that cultural difference could definitely cause conflict (Fukuyama 1995). Given the example of the interaction between Japanese and Western cultures, which paved the way for the Meiji restoration and the later industrialisation of Japan, he considers the competition that was created during the interaction between cultures always produced the creative change (Ibid).

7.2. Core Values of Confucianism and Hinduism

This research aims to examine how culture influences economic relations. To show evidence of the influence is not an easy task. The thoughts of Alastair Iain Johnston (1995:39-40) on the strategic culture of China could help make it more precise,

> "[...] to analyze the content of some most recent texts and some from the distant past, and assume that if there is congruence in preference rankings that strategic culture exists and has persisted up to the present. The longer the time across which this congruence stretches, the more powerful and persistent the strategic culture. Many of those who write from a strategic-culture perspective, especially on China, take this route."

The congruence, as mentioned above, could be a link from past to the present and evidence of the cultural influence. Johnston (1995:40) was also aware of the useful warning of McCauley,

> "What we cannot assume from the existence of two similar sets of beliefs at different periods of time is that they enjoy an unbroken existence. The 'same' beliefs can sprout from different roots, at different periods" (McCauley 1984:24).

7.2.1. The lun-ren and the Homo Hierarchicus

For the convenience of analysis, this research will use the conceptof *lun-ren* (伦人, *lun-jen* [Japanese]) which means the Chinese who have been influenced by Confucian civilization and attach importance to *wu-lun* (five human relationships in ethics, i.e., between ruler and subject, father and son, husband and wife, brothers, and friends); *Lun-ren* is the dominant human constant in the society of China (Shang 2013:71, 72). Hinduism was called "the core of Indian civilization" (Braudel 1980). "Homo Hierarchicus" was coined by French anthropologist and sociologist Louis Dumont (1966) and used to represent the Indian who is influenced profoundly by Hinduism in Psycho-Culturology (Shang 2013:78). Caste is highlighted in the concept "Homo Hierarchicus", which is used to describe Indians who follow the principles of Hinduism, and whose thoughts and behaviour are influenced by Hindu civilisation in this research.

It was believed that "a clear break" from tradition, including *karma, dharma,* frugality, idealism, transcendentalism, vegetarianism, religious tolerance and *ahimsa,* is found in India by examining the evidence that only 40 per cent of the population is vegetarian, lack of religious tolerance as seen "in the rise of fundamentalism in most religions of India—certainly in Hinduism, Islam and Sikhism", and a lot of violence in the past several years in the land of Gandhi and *ahimsa* (Sharma, Satya P. 1996:311). "Some of these radical transformations in the cultural ethos" are seen as "certainly outcomes of the process of globalization of the Indian economy" as well as a threat to political stability "in the 'largest democracy' of the world" including "the main danger", i.e., "the political swing to the Right and rising fascist tendencies" (Ibid 312). In this sense, there is a demand for the renaissance of the moral and cultural tradition for the unity and stability of India. Although culture is also in the process of evolution to fit in with modern development, some of the traditional beliefs are reviving, such as cow protection. Like a Chinese saying mentioned above, the dross should be discarded, and the essence should be selected. The core values of Confucianism, i.e., *ren yi li zhi xin* are called *Wu-chang* (the five constant virtues). A similar concept with *Wu-chang* and the essential values in Hinduism will be compared in the following section.

7.2.2. Rén (benevolence)

Confucius defined *rén* a few times in the dialogues between him and his disciples as recorded in *Analects*. One idea of *rén* is about self-control,

> "To subdue one's self and return to *lǐ* (rites, propriety) is *rén*. If a man can for one day subdue himself and return to *lǐ*, all under heaven will ascribe *rén* to him. [...] To practice *rén* is for a man himself, how should it depend on others? (*The Analects of Confucius* 12.1). Do not do to others what you would not wish done to you (12.2)".

Those values could be helpful to understand the character of modern China, which "will never accept interference by other countries in its internal affairs" and propose "the key principle governing the new international order should be non-interference in the internal affairs of other countries and social systems" (*People's Daily* 1990). It does not mean not to care for the rest of the world but to do so in a different way. The following points of *rén* may help explain China's foreign policy such us the "Belt and Road Initiative' which highlights cooperation and mutual benefits.

> '[*Rén* is to] cherish people.'(12.22).'He who can enact five things in the world is *rén*, [..., i.e.] *gong* (reverence), *kuan* (tolerance), *xìn* (trustworthiness), *min* (quickness), and *hui* (generosity)' (17.6).

Besides, to practice *rén* is not independent but linked with *lǐ*. When Yan Yuan asked Confucius what the items of *rén* are, he answered,

> "If it is not *lǐ* (rites, propriety), do not look at it; if it is not *lǐ*, do not listen to it; if it is not *lǐ*, do not say it; if it is not *lǐ*, do not do it.'(12.1) Still, *rén* is a high level ideal, and it will take time to practice *rén*, 'If a truly royal ruler were to arise, it would still require a generation [30 years, added by author] and then *rén* would prevail'" (13.12).

The Confucius idea developed in the period of the Pre-Qin Dynasty and during many generations in China's history as well the contemporary period. To inherit the most excellent tradition of Chinese culture is part of pursuing the road to peaceful development for the Chinese government (SCIOPRC 2011).

It was argued that ancient Chinese thinkers such as Guan Zi and Xun Zi had already classified the nature of the nation and realised that *wang quan* [humane authority] is better than *ba quan* [hegemon authority] (Yan 2015:89). Chinese scholars recognised that the humane value of China, theoretically, could create value better than the hegemon value of the USA (Ibid.). It was pointed out that the USA adopted two standards on issues such as the nuclear issue towards India and North Korea and recognition of democracy towards India and Iran, and does not strictly follow the so-called 'benevolent hegemon' (Kagan 1998:26; Yan 2015:90). Chinese scholars believed that *rén* and *yì* are the core values of humane authority and *rén* is closed to modern 'equity' while *yì* is closed to the meaning of 'righteousness' (Yan 2015:91).

Rén could guide the establishment of 'equity' as an international norm, and Moral Realism believes it is a better value than 'equality' to promote harmony among the international society (Yan 2015:92). 'Equity' means to care for small powers (similar to the concept of *Dharma* in Hinduism) and practice 'common but distinguishing responsibility' (Ibid). It has been practised in current international affairs; for instance, in the special concessions for developing countries in environmental agreements, such as the 1992 United Nations Framework Convention on Climate Change and the 1997 Kyoto Protocol (Ibid.). 'Equality', on the other hand, ignores the differences of strength and background, resulting in the law of the jungle (the weak is the prey of the strong) (Yan 2015:91). The USA-led international order is based on 'equality' or the law of the jungle, while China's traditional value '*rén*' could promote the establishment of a more equitable order (Yan 2015:91).

7.2.2.1. *RÉN* AND WEALTH

It was recorded in *Shiji* (Records of the Grand Historian, Merchants/Usurers Biographies 69) that the level of "*Rén*" was recognized by Bai Gui, a great merchant (*da huo zhi jia*) of the Western Zhou Dynasty, as one of the four basic examining standards that could serve him to do business, along with the qualities of *zhi* (wisdom), *yong* (brave) and *qiang* (manliest) (Nie 2012).

Sima Qian quoted the line "when there are adequate stores; they will know what decorum is; when the people have enough of food and clothing they will know what is an honour"[15] from the *Guanzi* (text) (BCE 723-BCE 645), and

15 The original words in Chinese *pinyin* are "*cang-lin-shi er zhi-li-jie, yi-shi-zu er zhi-rong-ru*".

explained the relationship between *ren*, *yi*, *li* and wealth.[16] The idea of Sima Qian is that when *Jun-zi* became wealthy, he will apply morals. *Ren* and *yi* would be attached to rich people. In this aspect, wealth became a condition to practice *ren* and *yi*. On the other hand, it was pointed out by Sima Qian "Who is not a hermit, stay in poverty and like to say *ren yi* is shameful",[17] In other words, poor people who are keen on current affairs and always talk about *ren* and *yi* might not be respected. *Ren* is also related to wealth. Wealth, in a sense, could be a condition to practice *ren*.

These ideas are different from what Indians think. For them the spiritual guru was always respected as full of knowledge and preachers of morality. Gautama Buddha and Mahatma Gandhi were not wealthy people but practised morality as an essential part of their underlying philosophy, for instance, the five rules of training (*Pancasila*) of Buddha's teaching and the non-violent resistance of Gandhi. Differently, when Confucius was in a weak position, he was not respected by many common people as recorded in "the biography of Confucius", *Records of the Grand Historian* (*Shi-ji*),

> "At the eastern gate there is a man, whose forehead looks like Yao's, neck like Gao Yao's, shoulders like Zi Chan's, yet the length to his waist is three *cun* shorter than Yu's. Haggard, he seems like a stray dog."[18]

Even Confucius' disciple doubted the one who lived in abject poverty. The response of Confucius shows his attitude towards poverty and morality,

> "When he [Confucius] was in Chen, their provisions were exhausted, and his followers became so ill that they were unable to rise. Zi Lu, with evident dissatisfaction, said, 'Has the superior man [*jun-zi*] likewise to endure in this way?' Then Confucius said, 'The superior man [*jun-zi*] may indeed have to endure want, but the mean man [*xiao-ren*], when he is in want, gives way to unbridled licence'." (*The Analects of Confucius* 15.2)

Confucius advocates that gentlemen [*jun-zi*] should endure poverty instead of being unbridled. In straitened times, the *lun-ren* pay more attention to self-cultivation while Homo Hierarchicus could preach his thoughts and gain respect

---

16 The original words in Chinese *pinyin* are "[...] *gu jun-zi fu, hao-xing qi de; xiao-ren fu, yi-shi qi-li. Yuan-shen er yu-sheng-zhi, shan-shen er shou-wang-zhi, ren-fu er ren-yi fu-yan*".

17 The original words in Chinese *pinyin* are "*wu yan-chu qi-shi-zhi-xing, er chang pin-jian, hao-yu ren-yi, yi-zu-xiu-ye*".

18 The original words in Chinese *pinyin* are "*dong-men you-ren, qi-sang si-yao, qi-xiang lei gao-yao, qi-jian lei zi-chan, ran-zi yao-yi-xia bu-ji yu san-cun. Lei-lei ruo sang-jia-zhi-gou.*" The English translation of the original Chinese is quoted from Zhang Hanmo (2018:95).

from others with his morality and wisdom. In the philosophy of the Chinese, "When you are poor, just improve yourself, when you are rich, then help the world"[19] is dominant. The attitudes towards the poor are different between these two civilisations.

This may also explain why people like Buddha were not born in other countries and why Indian philosophy is profound and abundant. In the markets of India, there are more brands, which provide cheap products such as Khadi, Patanjali, and the like. To care about the poor and to innovate for them is more evident in India (see the *Jugaad* part of this chapter) (There are also lots of cheap products in the Chinese market that benefit from its manufacturing advantage.) The Homo Hierarchicus is more tolerant and benevolent to the poor than the Chinese. The *lun-ren* aspires for still more material wealth than the Homo Hierarchicus.

7.2.2.2. *Ren* and Individual Behaviour: *Zhong* and Cautious Speaking

Confucius used to reply to Fan Chi who asked him about *ren* thus,

> "When positioning yourself, be respectful; when conducting jobs, be reverent; in treating others, be wholeheartedly devoted. Even when a person goes to the barbarians, [these qualities] may not be neglected." (*ju-chugong, zhi-shi jing, yu-ren zhong. Sui zhi yi-di, bu-ke qi ye.*) (*The Analects of Confucius* 13.19).

It shows that one meaning of *ren* for Confucius was to be *zhong* (faithful or wholeheartedly devoted) to others. However, *Zhong* could cause reliance on *guanxi* (relationship). When the *lun-ren* practice *zhong* and use this standard to judge the Homo Hierarchicus, disappointment could be caused, and even cultural conflicts could happen. As the *lun-ren* tend to be faithful to people and the Homo Hierarchicus are inclined to be faithful to the supernatural or truth, the two have a different attitude towards verbal promises and an exchange mode (See Chapter 6, 6.2).

Moreover, Confucius considered that "reticence" or "talk with caution" is part of *ren* (12.3; 13.27). Comparatively, the Chinese seem to be more silent while the Indians are more argumentive. It leads to different performances in cross-cultural management and global competition.

7.2.3. View on Wealth (artha) and Self-control (dama) in Hinduism

The word "*artha*" means wealth, value or price; it stands for economic value and a part of '*purusartha*' (object of human pursuit, the other three are *dharma, kama, moksha*) in Hinduism (Mohapatra et al. 1993:43-44). According to Hinduism, *artha* and *kama* ultimately cannot bring satiety, and the one who earns *artha*

---

19 The original words in Chinese *pinyin* are "*qiong-ze du-shan qi-shen, fu-ze jian-shan tian-xia*".

according to *dharma* would gain peace of mind and satisfaction (Ibid: 46-47). Influenced by the concept of Confucianism, *lun-ren* tend to make others productive after becoming rich, which means the alleviation of poverty. In Hinduism, "peace of mind and satisfaction" are essential and it is believed that "the more one runs, the less the satisfaction" (Ibid: 45). This value made the Hindus not only concerned about economic benefit and the rich take care of the poor instead of helping them become productive,

> "Our beloved leader, Mahatma Gandhi, stated that one must lead a simple life, with the minimum necessities of life. If someone earns money more than his requirements, then it is treated as a sin. In our society, if one does not get his food and shelter, that is a social evil being committed by a moneyed man towards him. So wealth must be as pure as crystal and as sacred as the Ganga." (Ibid.47).

It is also common sense in India that,

> "A person having more wealth is regarded as powerful and dignified in the modern age. It is difficult to live in this material world without money. Sometimes we pay more respect to a wealthy person than to a beggar." (Ibid: 45).

Meanwhile, there are many sages in India who "treated wealth as dust" such as Ramakrishna Thakur (Paramhansa).

Besides, there is a concept in Hinduism that means self-control that is *Dama*. It is believed that "It is the nature of mind to run after freedom. When the mind becomes free, it can do some evil work. [...] The mind is like a wild horse, and it is necessary to put a restraint on it." (Mohapatra et al. 1993:38). Moreover, *yama* also means self-control in Hinduism (Heim 2005:350). *Yama* is moral practices, "which Patanjali defines as five 'universal moral principles' or five virtues: non-violence (*ahimsa*), truthfulness (*satya*), abjuration of stealing (*asteya*), celibacy (renunciation, *aparigraha*), and lack of greed (chastity or continence, *brahmacharya*)" (Patanjali 400; Gupta 2006:385-386). The difference between Confucianism and Hinduism on this point could be summarised as self-control for the former is to being *ren*, the latter is for keeping away from evil.

7.2.4. Yì (righteousness)

Confucius considered *yì* (righteousness) as the rule of the *jun-zi*'s practice,

> "The superior man, in the world, does not set his mind either on anything or against anything, what is *yì* (righteousness) he will follow." (4.10)
>
> "The *jun-zi* (superior person) considers righteousness to be essential in everything." (15.18)

Confucius also appealed to pay importance to *yì* (righteousness) instead of profit,

> 'The *jun-zi* (superior person) comprehends according to *yì* (righteousness), the *xiao-ren* (petty person) comprehends according to profit.' (4.16)

Moreover, it was considered that *yong* (valour) is not valued without *yì* (righteousness),

> 'The *jun-zi* (superior person) holds *yì* (righteousness) to be of the highest importance. The *jun-zi* (superior person), having valour without *yì* (righteousness), will be guilty of insubordination; The *xiao-ren* (petty person), having valour without *yì* (righteousness), will commit robbery.' (17.23)

Both the *yi* of Confucianism and the *dharma* of Hinduism highlighted the importance of responsibility, yet comparatively, *yi* combines responsibility with bravery while *dharma* does not seem to do so. Based on the concept of *dharma*, the right-wing organisation, SJM, organised the boycotting of Chinese products. It is a "brave" action to challenge China, which is the second largest economy and most significant trading partner of India. However, without considering *yi* towards Chinese companies in India, which contributed to the growth of economic development and created job opportunities in India, the SJM protected the interests of the small and middle enterprises of India but created a negative element towards the interests of Chinese in India.

As mentioned above, it was argued that *yì* is close to 'justice' and could contribute to the establishment of a better international order than 'democracy' (Yan 2015:95). Democracy could only provide the legality of a nation's action but not justice (Yan 2015:94). The 2003 Iraq War received the approval of the U.S. Congress, making it legal from a domestic perspective, but millions of Americans protested against it because it was unjust (Ibid). According to the theory of Moral Realism, China would support a just international order that followed the concept of *yi*, which could reduce polarisation and create a win-win situation (Yan 2015:95). It could contribute to China-India relations as well.

7.2.4.1. YI AND INTEREST

In the classic literature of Confucianism, views on *yi* and profit helps in understanding the outlook on righteousness and benefit, Confucius said, "Exemplary persons (*jun-zi*) are persuaded by what is righteousness (*yi*); petty persons (*xiao-ren*) are persuaded by what is profitable." (4.16)

> "[...] If a man remembers what is righteousness (*yi*) at the sight of profit, is ready to lay down his life in the face of danger, and does not forget the sentiments he has repeated all his life, even when he has been in straitened circumstances for a long time, he may be said to be a complete man." (14.12)

The other view of Confucius on *yi* and benefit was recorded in "the war of Qi and Jin at An" of *Zuo Zhuan* (Commentary on the Spring and Autumn Annals), "[...] *li* (rites) is used to pursue *yi* (righteousness), *yi* is used to produce interest, interest is used to govern people, and these are the outlines of government affairs". It shows *yi* is the basis of interest; in other words, to produce benefit should consider *yi* first. Thus, interest is closely related to *yi* in the Confucian idea. Moreover, it was highlighted in *The Analects of Confucius* (9.1) that Confucius "rarely spoke about interest, he would rather leave it to destiny and *ren* (benevolence)".[20] Benefit is not the first concern; instead, *ren* and *yi* are more preferred in Confucianism.

The above reflect Confucius's views on the relationship between "*yi*" (righteousness) and "interest", that is, the relationship between the core meaning of Confucian civilisation "*yi*" and economic interests. To a certain extent, "righteousness being more important than interest" (*yi-zhu li-cong lun*) reflects one of the significant economic thoughts (Nie 2012:70-71) and the idea of righteousness and benefit (Wang 2017:14) in the Confucian concepts. The traditional value is still influencing the national leader's opinion, especially the idea of righteousness and benefit. Chinese President Xi Jinping indicated that,

> "*Yi* (righteousness) reflect one view of us, the idea of the communists and a socialist country. Some people in this world are getting along very well, and some people are getting along very badly; it is not a good phenomenon. True happiness is the general happiness of all. We hope that the world will develop together, we especially hope developing countries accelerate development. *Li* (benefit), is to abide by the principle of mutual benefit and 'win-win', not 'we win, and you lose', to achieve a win-win situation. We are obliged to help developing countries within our capacity. Sometimes we have to value justice above material gains, sacrifice profit to duty. We must not be mercenary and haggle over every ounce.
>
> For surrounding and developing countries, we must adhere to the correct view of righteousness and benefit. Only by adhering to the correct concept of righteousness and benefit can we do our work well and win the hearts of the people. Politically, we must adhere to fairness and righteousness, stick on the principle of equality, abide by the basic principles of international relations, oppose hegemonism and power politics, and oppose the harming of the interests of others for one's own ends and destruct regional peace and stability. Economically, we must adhere to mutual benefit and joint development." (Wang Yi 2013)

20 There are different translations on the line of 9.1 as Confucius rarely spoke about *yi* (interest), destiny and *ren* (benevolence) [on his own].The translation of Kang Youwei and Qian Mu is quoted in this research (Huan 2017).

Confucian civilisation has influenced the *lun-ren*'s attention to "righteousness" and even become a potentially important criterion in people's interactions.

7.2.5. Manthan

From the perspective of civilisational values, the acts of Hindus relate to a core value of Hinduism that is "*manthan*". The meaning of *manthan* is "churning". The worldview of Hinduism is explained by Member of the Indian Parliament and former Indian Minister of State for Finance Jayant Sinha and the Indian economist, Sanjeev Sanyal (2016),

> "The Indian, particularly Hindus, worldview is that the world is naturally chaotic as expressed in Shiva's *tandava*. While other societies try to identify an ideal equilibrium or Utopia and define success in terms of achieving it, Indians see churning as the natural state of the world. The churning releases both negative and positive forces, and success is measured by the ability to absorb the negative and adapt to take advantage of the positive."

Therefore, from the perspective of Hindu values, the understanding of the nature of commercial behaviour such as "gaining petty advantages" and "strongly pressing the price" is very different from the *lun-ren*. Also, the control of costs by Hindus involves the *jugaad* concept in their culture.

7.2.6. Jugaad[21]

As mentioned in Chapter 6, a rough translation of the common Hindi word *Jugaad* is "an innovative fix; an improvised solution born from ingenuity and cleverness" and reflecting the spirit of the Indians "doing more with less" (Radjou et al. 2012:4). Combining *jugaad* and *manthan* makes it easier to understand why Hindus use "gamesmanship". Tracing the ideological roots of behaviour helps to better understand the values behind the behaviour. An interpretation of values can better understand the reasons for such behaviour. Understanding each other's values is the basis of mutual respect, and mutual respect is more conducive to cooperation and dialogue.

The *jugaad* spirit influenced Indians widely and is reflected in different aspects of their life. For example, lots of lightly battered cars on the streets, simple entrance gates of famous universities, and even the Mars probe can be seen indicating that India has spent less than other countries to achieve success (Zi 2013). People of India may not use more sources when it is not necessary. Perhaps, it could be considered that the culture of "*mian zi*" (face-saving) is not so influential among Indians, at least they are not like some Chinese counterparts

---

21 Some points have been written in a conference paper "India's frugal innovation on China's Internet: Evaluation from a Cultural Perspective" by the author. Those were partly used in this thesis.

who pay much attention to the visible image. Moreover, inevitably, it is also related to India's politic system and social culture (Sun, Kang and Lin 2007; Mao Keji 2015). Still, by focusing on the cultural influence, stronger support could be found to understand the Indian way of solving problems in their daily life with innovations.

7.2.6.1. Frugal Innovation in India

Frugal innovation is a lifestyle of India (Zi 2013). If we look at the markets of India, we will find many cheap products or services, which are necessary for ordinary people and seem the cheapest in the world. Moreover, it is not only for the grassroots but also reflected in the development of science and technology in India. *Mangalyaan*, the Mars Orbiter Mission (MOM) of India, made India the fourth nation and the first Asian country to reach the fourth planet from the sun (Vji 2013). It is the least-expensive Mars mission to date, which cost USD 73 million, "less than an average Hollywood film" (Amos 2014). It was because of lower worker costs, home-grown technologies, simpler design and significantly less complicated payload than the National Aeronautics and Space Administration (NASA)'s Maven of the USA (Ibid.).

Undoubtedly, except for the cultural influence on the Indian's values, national conditions also play a role. For instance, India invests less than 1 per cent of its GDP on Research & Development while China spends 1.76 per cent; over 50 crore Indians live without constant electricity, including most of the people in the village of a grassroots innovator Mansukh Prajapati from the desert area of Gujarat (Radjou et al. 2012: 3,4).

The innovator Mansukh Prajapati, who first invented a Rs. 2,000 fridge made with clay called 'Mitticools', for which he "earned accolades from all over the world, including the President of India and *Forbes* magazine was named among the most influential rural Indian entrepreneurs, one of few to have made an impact on the lives of so many" (Radjou et al. 2012:3,4). Later, he founded a new factory, a 'mini' Industrial Revolution in pottery, launched in a remote Indian village and produced new clay products: non-stick frying pans that cost Rs. 100. Prajapati was called "true spirit of *Jugaad*", because he produced cheap and effective devices and created jobs, and he is "driving environmental and socio-economic sustainability in his community and ensuring the financial sustainability of his own business" (Ibid).

7.2.6.2. The Influence of *Bhagavad Gita*

In the *Bhagavad Gita*, the most popular of Hindu sacred books, the mystical experience of the Vedas is reflected in the form of ethical principles that "are not merely a matter of laws or customs" but "a sacred experience" (Saraswat 2005:4-5). Mahatma Gandhi preached the *Bhagavad Gita* philosophy, and said:

> "I find a verse here and a verse there and I immediately begin to smile in the midst of overwhelming external tragedies—and if they have left no visible, no indelible scar on me, I owe it all to the teachings of the *Bhagavad Gita*" (Muniapan and Dass 2008:408-420).

The principles of the *Bhagavad Gita* influence the Hindu's values and behaviour. Indeed, scholars suggest the principles of ethics from the *Bhagavad Gita* "can be assimilated in the management practices of global corporations from a non-sectarian perspective" (Ibid.).

The reason, why many Indians, especially the innovators mentioned above who do not treat money as their only or primary goal but to solve problems, take the responsibility of society (Mashelkar 2017; Li 2017), could be linked with the principles in the *Bhagavad Gita*.[22] Traditional thoughts do not only influence the solving of problems but also attitudes towards wealth.

Without understanding the value of its cultural dimension, it would be hard to understand India. It is necessary to pay attention to the culture, which still influences their values and behaviour. It could be meaningful in these times of the fragile environment to learn from India about innovation.

7.2.6.3. *Jugaad* Innovation and Environmental Concerns

Not only with considering the use of fewer materials, but taking into account the condition of the current situation, the *jugaad* spirit is quite valuable. A scholar on frugal innovation Anil K. Gupta, whose organization Honey Bee "has created a database of over ten thousand inventions of grassroots entrepreneurs who have created ingenious solutions to solve pressing socio-economic problems in their local communities", has added more vision to the value of *Jugaad* innovation which he prefers to call "grassroots innovation":

> "If China, India and other developing countries all follow the lifestyle of the USA, the available energy is not enough, and the environment will be destroyed. Most functions of the products are not used by the customers but paid for by them." (Gupta 2016)[23]

China and India are paying a huge price for their dramatic economic growth. They are two of the most polluted countries in the world and account for more than half

22 See Chapter 6, 6.3.2.2. The people, who believe in the ultimate goal to think, "a piece of stone and gold are the same", could not only think about interests. They could also link it with the Hindu concept of *karma* and rebirth.

23 See more in Rebecca Bundhun (2014), "The US and China serve as economic models for India", *The National Business*; Jeff Desjardins (2015), "China vs. United States: A Tale of Two Economies", Visual Capitalist. Desjardins argued, "The United States is a sophisticated and highly diversified economy that is based on services, finance, and consumption of the middle class. China has similar aspirations in the future, but right now, it is a resource-intensive growth engine making the transition from a manufacturing hub to a consumer-driven economy."

the world's pollution (Ross 2017). It was reported that "around 1.1 million people die prematurely as a result of pollution in India" (Ibid.). It is crucial to increase awareness and solve the problem of over-exploitation of resources. In this respect, the value behind Indian frugal innovation should be appropriately recognised to understand its market and China and India, as the two biggest developing countries should work together for saving the environment.

7.2.7. Indian Worldview and the Daily Sacrifice

Unlike other cultures where people prefer significantly costly innovations that target the rich instead of the poor, many innovations in India are for the poor (Sarma 2017). To help others, especially the poor, is part of Indian culture (Ibid.). In the Hindu tradition, the five *maha-yajnas* must be performed every day, including sacrifice to the beings, the men, the fathers, the gods and Brahman (Veda) (Kane 1941:696). The sentiments that prompted the performance of these five sacrifices influenced the thought and behaviour of the Hindu. It is believed that,

> "The whole world, human and non-human, is one creation and there must be the spirit of live and let live or give and take. Therefore, one must offer what one can afford to a guest and have something for all beings (including even such shunned animals as dogs, crows and insects). These feelings of devotion, gratitude, reverence, loving memory, kindliness and tolerance seem to have been the springs that prompted the Aryans of old to emphasize the importance of the five daily yajñas and to have led sutra writers like Gautama and legislators like Manu (11.28) to look upon them as *samskāras*, as ennobling the soul by freeing it from mere selfishness and elevating the body to become a fit vehicle for higher things "(Ibid: 698).

The thought, which is influenced by the five daily great sacrifices (*panca maha-yajnas*), form the psychology of Indians. The daily performance of sacrificing still exists in the daily life of the Homo Hierarchicus. The logic behind it is a necessary element to understand Indian culture. It shows the importance of nature and other beings in Hindu society.

Indeed, the behaviour, values, attitude and personality do influence economic development (Kunkel 1965: 257-277). It is necessary to pay attention to the culture behind the Indian economic phenomenon. Moreover, as an Indian scholar pointed out,

> "If India and China could energise the potentialities inherent in the complementary capabilities...India-China joint research programmes could invent a pollution-free car, a US$ 20 computer, a US$ 1,000 house, online education for the poor, etc" (Bhoothalingam 2015:119).

Positive cultural factors should be paid enough attention; at the same time, the negative factors should also get the same attention. It was argued that economic freedom and the attitude towards science and religion do affect economic growth (Lands 1998). Moreover, it was also pointed out by economists that an "invisible hand", i.e., price, plays a significant role in the market (Mankiw 2012). In a word, these factors are equally essential to take advantage of the traditional values and consider their base for modern development. It is neccesary to explore the origin of Chinese or Indian culture, instead of examining them just from superficial phenomenon in their societies.Only then can the dialogues be not only cross-cultural but also help to deepen understanding towards each other and develop a more suitable model for the development of both China and India.

7.2.8. Lǐ (rites): Guanxi, Renqing, Mianzi

The concept of '*lǐ*' is a crucial concept in the thinking and common sayings of the *lun-ren*, such as,

> 'In the practice of *lǐ*, Harmony is the key.' (1.12)
>
> 'If a man can subdue himself and return to *lǐ* for one day (rites, propriety), all under heaven will ascribe *rén* to him.' (12.1)

Lǐ also has linkage with other values like *rén* (benevolence), *yì* (righteousness), and *yong* (valour). For Confucius, '*lǐ*' could influence the function of other values,

> 'If a man is not *rén*, what can he do with *lǐ* ?' (3.3)
>
> 'The *Junzi* (superior person) in everything considers *yì* (righteousness) to be essential. He performs it according to the *lǐ* (rules of propriety).'(15.18)
>
> 'If you do not learn *lǐ*, you will not be able to establish yourself.'(16.13)
>
> '[...] He [*Junzi* (superior person)] hates those who are *yong* (valorous) but lack *lǐ*.' (17.24).
>
> Notably, Confucius pays importance to politics with *lǐ*.
>
> 'If a ruler loved *lǐ*, none among the people would dare to be disrespectful; if a ruler loved *yì*, none would dare not to obey; if a ruler loved *xìn* (trustworthiness), none would dare be insincere'. (13.4)
>
> 'When the ruler loves *lǐ*, the people are easy to employ'. (14.41)

Besides, for Confucius, one part of *lǐ*'s original meaning is related to the hierarchy of power. Different hierarchies have different treatments. For instance, only the *tian-zi* (emperor, Son of Heaven) has the right to perform sacrificial rituals on all the famous mountains and rivers under heaven; vassals only have the right to perform sacrificial rituals on the famous mountains and rivers of their fiefdoms.

> 'The *Ji Shi* (chief of the Ji family, a senior official of Lu State) was about to sacrifice to the Tai mountain. Confucius said to Ran You, 'You were unable to prevent this?' [...] (3.6).

Although Confucius's philosophy could not be fully practised during his time, his thoughts influenced Chinese generation after generation necessarily, to 'discard the dross and select the essence' while inheriting the traditional culture. According to Moral Realism, 'civilized', which developed from the concept of *lǐ*, could lie beyond the American insistence on 'freedom' (Yan 2015:97). Unlimited freedom leads to conflict, while civilised freedom tames the ambitions of unworthy powers (Yan 2015: 96).

7.2.8.1. Li and Means of Expression

Due to the influence of the values of *li* and *yi*, comparatively, the Chinese do not speak directly and openly. This characteristic is related to the culture of *renqing* and *mianzi*; it is believed in China that "you can cause someone to lose *mianzi*, esteem, or personal dignity by saying exactly what you mean or feel" which is a "difficult value to comprehend for people who believe in being direct and open" (Fu, Wu et al. 2008:884). Moreover, it is also believed that sometimes, more important things are what the Chinese did not speak out.

7.2.8.2. *Ren Zhi, Guanxi* and the Confucianism Root

It was pointed out that "the reason *guanxi* is so important is that China is a country 'ruled by people' (*ren zhi*) not by law, and the predefined nature of *guanxi* dictates the behaviour" (Fu, Wu et al. 2008:884). "92 per cent affirmed the importance of *guanxi* in their [Chinese citizens] daily life" according to a survey done by Gordon C. Chu and Yanan Ju who surveyed 2,000 Chinese from Shanghai and Qingpu (a rural county outside Shanghai), and "72 per cent preferred to use *guanxi* connections over normal bureaucratic channels to advance personal interests and solve problems" (Yeung and Tung 1996:58). Foreign businessmen who do business with the Chinese know "that companies wanting to get in on the ground floor in China need *guanxi* in addition to planning, funding, and a good product" (Murphy 1996).

The root of the importance of *guanxi* for the Chinese can be traced back to the *Analects of Confucius*,

> 'If a ruler loved *lǐ*, none among the people would dare to be disrespectful; if a ruler loved *yì*, none would dare not to obey; if a ruler loved *xìn* (trustworthiness), none would dare be insincere'. (13.4)

A ruler's virtues, i.e., *lǐ*, *yì*, and *xìn,* were believed to play the dominant role in governing the people. "The reliance on people rather than on the law would naturally promote the practice of *guanxi*, [...]" (Fu, Wu et al. 2008:884). It was pointed out that "*Guanxi* is typically seen as an outgrowth of the Confucian emphasis on personal relations" (Koehn 2001:421). *Guanxi* also means power; it was attributed to the local chief in many villages as "almost as powerful as God, but not so remote" (Kristoff and Wudunn 1994:96).

7.2.9. Wisdom: Zhì (right or wrong) and jñāna (momentary or everlasting)

Mencius added *zhi* and extended the *ren, yi* and *li* of Confucius to *ren, yi, li* and *zhi*. He said,

> "The sense of commiseration is the seed of *ren* (humanity); the sense of shame is the seed of *yi* (righteousness); the sense of respect is the seed of *li* (ritual); the sense of right and wrong is the seed of *zhi* (wisdom)." (Mencius c.300 BC).

Zhi was considered by a great merchant, Bai Gui, as recorded in *Shiji*, as the first and most important fundamental quality for merchants along with *yong* (valour), *ren*, *qiang* (Sima 2006). It was analysed as the merchant having the ability to analyse the trends in the market and adjusting the management strategy according to the changing situation (Nie 2012).

The extended meaning of *"Zhi"* is innovation, respect for knowledge and science, and follow the rule of the economy (Chen Jian 2011) in modern society. *Zhi* is also proposed by Chinese scholar Wang Yizhou to be practised in China's diplomacy in his work *A Wise and Benevolent Power: Creative Involvement in a Nutshell* (Wang 2018). There is a similar concept, *jñāna,* that means knowledge in Hinduism. It designates,

> "the sort of knowledge that is a total experience of its object, particularly the supreme being or reality. The cognitive experience of the supreme object sets the soul free from the transmigratory life and the polarities this imposes upon thought." (EB 2019)

In the *Bhagavad Gita*, *jnana-yoga* is the path for self-realisation combined with *raja-yoga* (Nadkarni 2017:266). "The emphasis on *jnana-yoga* is on using *buddhi*, the capacity to discriminate between the real and unreal, momentary and everlasting." (Ibid.) The difference between Confucianism and Hinduism on "wisdom" or "knowledge" is the discriminating object. As mentioned above, *zhi* in Confucianism is to discriminate "right and wrong", and "*jnana*" in Hinduism is to discriminate "real and unreal, momentary and everlasting".

Interestingly, there is no "right or wrong" in Hinduism (Singh 2019). It is believed that right or wrong is a relative concept, and there is no absolute right or wrong. This difference could cause different cognitions. The *Lun-ren* believes there is right or wrong while the Hindus believe that there is no right or wrong, but there is real and unreal, momentary and everlasting. The latter seems more detached and more grandiose. The former is more about reality and current judgment. It is precisely because of this that the *lun-ren* is more concerned about the present. Hindus have different understandings of the present, and they are more comfortable with the current situation and do not judge victory or defeat with momentary gains and losses. It is also reflected in the fact that Indians commonly treat themselves as anything that they believe to be their victory.

Economically, this can also help to understand the commercial behaviour of Hindu merchants. While they treat their interests, they will adopt different ways to achieve them. This kind of behaviour could cause inconsistency among the *lun-ren*. Most likely, Indians treat this as a sign of real or unreal profit, not right or wrong behaviour.

7.2.10. Xìn (trust) and Satya (truthfulness)

The Chinese scholar of the Han Dynasty, Dong Zhongshu, added *xin* (trust or being trustworthy) to the core concept of Confucianism, making *ren*, *yi, li, zhi* and *xin* the five constant virtues (*Wu-chang*) of Confucianism (Wang 2019:41). *Xin* "plays a central role in Confucian ethics" (Koehn 2001:415). The importance of *xin* is recorded in *The Analects of Confucius.*It is indicated by Confucius's disciples Zi Xia,

> "The *jun-zi* imposes labors upon his people only after earning their trust. Without trust, people will think him cruel. Only after earning trust does he remonstrate with a ruler. If he has not yet earned trust, the ruler will take it as slander." (19.10)

Confucius believed *xin* is more critical than armaments and grain in governance,

> "Zi Gong asked about governance. Confucius said, 'Provide people with adequate food, have adequate weapons, and people will have trust in you.' Zi Gong said, 'If one has no choice but to dispense with one of these three things, which would it be?''Dispense with weapons.' Zi Gong said, 'If one had no choice but to dispense with one of the remaining two, which would it be?' 'Dispense with food. Death has always been with us since the beginning of time, but when there is no trust, people will have nothing to stand on'." (12.7)

CULTURAL ROOT: NO CONTRACT BUT TRUST

It was considered that "[...] the Chinese historically have been loathe to rely upon contracts" as,

> "Confucian emphasis on trustworthiness makes reliance on contracts less attractive for several reasons. First, the use of particular contracts encourages parties to think of the contract as the basis for trust, the contract thus contributes to an atmosphere of distrust. [...] Second, reliance on contracts can prevent people from focusing on the larger picture and from being as mindful as they should be." (Koehn 2001:419,420).

Moreover, it was considered that "The Chinese continuously emphasize that all agreements should be based on friendship and goodwill, making finely detailed contracts unnecessary." (Mente 1994:121). The circumstances of not "relying upon contracts" still existed as mentioned above, especially for Chinese businessmen influenced by the Chinese "trust" culture. Yet, along with the legal system advancement in China, the contract is now a more necessary and reliable part of doing business.

Money Worship and the Decline of Xin

Chinese traditional culture could be influenced by modern thought, which could also shape the economic thought and behaviour of the Chinese. For instance, the famous "Cat Theory" of Deng Xiaoping which states, "It does not matter if a cat is black or white; as long as it catches mice, it is a good cat." Besides, it was considered that Deng Xiaoping's trip to south China in 1992 was linked with the embracing of capitalism and then triggered the so-called "*bai-jin zhu-yi*" (money worship) (Kristoff and Wudunn 1994:141). It made all levels of people from government officials, army staff and their relatives to the common people start doing business (Koehn 2001:423). The influence of ideas like "hard work and plain-living" (*jian-ku pu-su*) of Mao Zedong was reducing in the new generation. The Chinese market was developed to a new era and started to be filled with customers who turn their backs on the materialist way of life. Traditional values like *xin* have a period of decline when people only think about how to earn money.

Meanwhile, it is considered that traditional values set a high standard in a sense and are difficult to follow in modern times. The Chinese Confucian philosopher's views on *xin* are not considered practical in current society as people who follow these values must be cheated by the smart crook in the social, economic life (Ye Shengli 2004:17). There are phenomena without honest promises with different degrees in the individual, organisational and governmental levels in Chinese society (Wang 2006).

The government of China noticed the change happening in society and started to promote the importance of the value of *cheng-xin* (honesty). The State Council of China announced the "Planning Outline for the Construction of a Social Credit System (2014-2020)" in 2014 (SCPRC 2014) to promote honesty in society.

"Trust" in Organisational Culture of Indian Groups and *Satya* in Hinduism

Meanwhile, trust is also taken as an essential part of the organisational culture of Indian companies.[24] In the philosophy of an Indian water treatment technology company, it is written, "A partnership based on trust". They see themselves as a partner of their customers and "prepare optimized and customized concepts" (Wabag 2018a). The other 100 years old global group of India also sees "Leadership with Trust" as the base of their mission for their business in more than 100 countries across six continents (Tata 2018). Yet, it should be noticed that the origin of the two mentioned above, the former was founded in Breslau,

24 In this research, the Indian companies mentioned are mainly those doing business with or in China.

Germany (Wabag 2018b), the latter's founder belongs to a Parsi group (Lala, 1981:3), a Zoroastrian community (instead of Hinduism).

In Hinduism, one of the five virtues, *satya*, which means truthfulness, is believed to engender "mutual trust and love and binds individuals together" and "contributes to the welfare and harmony of society as a whole" (Mohapatra et al. 1993:39). There is different stress on trust in Confucianism and Hinduism. The concept of *xin* emphasised keeping promises and *satya* emphasised pursuing truth and create unity and harmony. The Hindu is more argumentive while pursuing truth and the *lun-ren* place more value on promises. This difference could also explain that the *lun-ren* rely more on interpersonal relations than Hindus. The latter could challenge authority for the sake of truth, and the former tends to keep the promise at any cost.

7.2.11. Dharma

The literal meaning of *dharma* in Sanskrit is "to sustain, to hold up"; In Hinduism, it means "the Sacred Law; a religious duty; customary rules of right conduct for members of a group; duty appropriate to one's *varna*; moral law" (Dasgupta 1993:188-189). The thought of *dharma* has an essential influence on Indians, and the implication of *dharma* in different aspects was emphasised dissimilarly in a different eras of India.

The author of *Arthasastra* (Science of Material Gain or Science of political economy in Sanskrit) Kautilya, considers "*artha* (sound economies) as the most important thing and *dharma* and *karma* are dependent on it." (Jose et al. 2011:175-176). This idea shows that *artha* is supreme and more critical than *dharma* and *karma*. Still, the ancient legal text of Hinduism, *Manusmriti,* recorded a different understanding of the importance of *dharma*. It mentioned that,

> "[...] the aggregate of *Dharma, Artha and Kama* (Trivarga, or three goals of human existence) secures welfare and happiness. However, desire (*kama*) and material wealth (*artha*) must be rejected if contrary to *dharma*." (VKO 2019).

Dharma became the most crucial thing in this text. Although views on the importance of *dharma* is different in the *Manusmriti* and the *Arthasastra*, these ancient texts have created the base for debating the connection between *dharma* and *artha* (wealth) in India.

Gandhi had a different approach to economic issues compared with mainstream tradition as "his extraordinary emphasis on the ethical aspect of economic behaviour", and he considered there was no distinction between economics and ethics (Ibid: 133). It was pointed out that "[...] Gandhian ethics constitute the essence of religion, the same two-way relationship holds as between economics and religion, and even more generally between economics and *dharma*" (Ibid: 134), and he considered that,

> "If *dharma* and economic interests cannot be reconciled, either the conception of that *dharma* is false or economic interest takes the form of unmitigated selfishness and does not aim at collective welfare." (Ibid: 134)

In a sense, Gandhi is consistent with the values of the *Manusmriti* that *dharma* should be a condition for material wealth (*artha*) or economic interests. In other words, economic interests should not violate the law of *dharma* or morality, and they should be good for the collective welfare. These values still exist in Indian society. The economic wing of the RSS, the SJM, believes the role of the state is "to protect the weak and to ensure that *Dharma* is adhered to" as "Bhishma said in *Shanti Parva* in the *Mahabharata*" and must be to,

> "defend the wealth and honour of the nation. Ordinarily, and except in order to protect national interests against foreign interests, the State must not be a trader; but must ensure that trade and commerce conform to *Dharma*" (SJM 2017b).

The traditional value regarding *dharma* is still implemented by the people influenced by organisations such as the SJM. Although the traditional value is, in a sense, in the process of evolution, it still influences the economic thought and behaviour of Indians.

Given that the behaviour is deeply influenced by values, and there are apparent cultural differences among values of different civilisations (Shang 2013:236), it is worth identifying and understanding the differences. The concepts of *dharma* and *yi* have emphasis on duty and not only obtain benefit for self. There is also a difference between these two concepts. It is difficult to conclude the difference. Yet, from the manifestation of the current understanding of the traditional value, it can be seen that the former tends to protect the interests of the weak and against foreign interests. The latter tends not to be concerned only about interests but also duty and create a win-win situation.

7.2.12. Karma: Prescribed Duty, without Attachment

Karma is another important concept in Hinduism. Derived from the Sanskrit root *kri*, '*karma*' stands for all the action from a person's body, speech and mind (Agarwalla et al. 2015:16). *Karma Yoga* means "to perform one's work with perfection" (Ramrattan 2009:43). The word 'yoga' means "a device or intelligent method" (Agarwalla et al. 2015:16). It is believed that "the ultimate goal of all beings is to free the soul from the cycle of births and deaths" in Hinduism, and *Karma Yoga* is "defined as a technique for intelligently performing actions such that the soul is no longer bound by the effects of the action" (Ibid; Mulla & Krishnan, 2010). It is pointed out that *Karma Yoga* is,

> "made up of three dimensions: a sense of obligation or duty towards others; an absence of desire for rewards; and a sense of equanimity which enables one to be neutral to environmental influences" (Mulla and Krishnan, 2007).

It can be seen that Hindus who follow *karma* pay importance to duty, absence of desire for rewards and be neutral. In "Chapter 3, Karma Yoga" of the *Bhagavad Gita*, it appealed to perform prescribed duties without attachment, control the "insatiable enemy", lust (Text 43) and approach self-realisation. Krsna taught that "[...] the ignorant perform their duties with attachment to results, the learned may similarly act, but without attachment, for the sake of leading people on the right path." (Text 25). Moreover, it suggested that "One should not come under the control of such attachments and aversions, because they are stumbling blocks on the path of self-realization" (Chapter 3, Text 34). The concept of karma could purify the follower not to be utilitarian. In this sense, it is similar to the concept of *yi,* which also appeals to not only think of benefit for self.

Moreover, it is believed that the doctrine of *karma* influenced people's "future orientation" regarding their next lives and "sometimes take the form of contributions to charitable and religious activities and institutions" (Chhokar 2007:990). It is different from Confucianism, which is more concerned about the current life. Confucius avoided answering the question of his disciple, Ji Lu, regarding the spirits of the dead and the gods and said, "You are not able even to serve man. How can you serve the spirits? [...] You do not understand even life. How can you understand death?" (11.12). He did not speak about prodigies, force, disorder and gods (7.21). In Hindu ideology, *karma* could dominate people's behaviour and destined caste groups (Cai 2017:269). It is mentioned in the *Gita* that,

> "It is far better to discharge one's prescribed duties, even though faultily, than another's duties perfectly. Destruction in the course of performing one's duty is better than engaging in another's duties, to follow another's path is dangerous." (Text 35)

Duties are divided in society and related to *karma.* It is similar to Confucian thought that behaviour should be suitable with one's social class; otherwise, it violates the *li* (See *The Analects of Confucius* 3.1, 3.6). Confucius also said, "If you are not in a certain position, you should not concern yourself too much about certain affairs." (8.14).

One difference between the two values is that *karma* emphasis on performing duty without attachment; it reduced the performance of the believer. According to the data of the GLOBE project, Indians got higher marks (6.05)[25] than the

25 The scope of the quantitative value is 1 to 7; 1 is the lowest, 4 is the middle, 7 is the highest (Jiang 2008, 34; Chhokar et al. 2007:20).

Chinese (5.67) in the "cultural value" or "*Should Be*" assessment of "Performance Orientation", yet, the Chinese got higher marks (4.45) in "cultural practices" or "*As Is*" (behaviour) of "Performance Orientation" than Indians (4.25), which means that Indians are more willing to perform well in work but in fact the Chinese could perform better. It could be an influence of the value of *karma,* i.e., to perform duty without attachment.

Karma emphasises performance of one's duty without attachment, which could promote performance without concerning returns. Confucian culture is human-centred, and the importance of interpersonal returns (*bao*) is attached (See Chapter 6, 6.2.5). In Hindu culture, the concept of returns is not only among human beings but in a bigger circle based on the concept of *dharma*. The exchange mode of the Hindu "exchange as one-sided benefit" is different from the *lun-ren*'s "exchange as trustworthiness" (See Chapter 6, 6.2.2.5). Thus, the Homo Hierarchicus concept of returns is different from the *lun-ren*.

Karma tends to be connected to the theory of reincarnation, and is suggested to be "more broadly interpreted to mean that every individual is responsible for his actions" (Sinha and Sanyal 2016). In the research of Corporation Social Responsibility (CSR), it is believed the law of *karma* (cause and effect) would,

> "motivate business people to carry out their responsibilities and duties to serve humanity. [...] '*Karma*' is then a concept of reward or punishment for the choice made by individual or corporations" (Muniapan and Satpathy 2013:182).

In this sense, the concept of *karma* encourages the Hindu to be responsible for their actions. It includes the actions of body, mouth and mind. The Confucian concept of *xin* has emphasis on the responsibility for one's verbal promises. *Karma* has more emphasis on the cause-effect and includes not only the current life but also previous lives and following lives. Comparatively, *xin* has more emphasis on the current life and worldly matters. It seems the concept of *karma* is grander in the aspect of period and *xin* has more restrictions on current and secular issues.

Moreover, the concept of *karma* could enhance the strain of historical memory. The Hindu is more inclined to be unable to shelve the dispute. For example, the Sino-Indian territorial dispute is considered by many Indians to be a problem to be solved before cooperation; and the *lun-ren* is more inclined to seek common ground while reserving differences. In the case of controversial issues, cooperation can still be carried out, at least not as strong as many Indians have reacted. For instance, China and Japan, the mainland of China and Taiwan, the settlement of disputes under certain conditions can be temporarily not a prerequisite for economic exchanges.

7.3. Conclusion: Cultural Difference, Conflict and Similarity

In summary, the core values of Confucian and Hindu civilisations still affect the thoughts and behaviour of the people to a certain extent, such as the influence of *ren* on the concept of wealth, personal behaviour (loyalty, cautious speech); the concept of *artha* also encourages people to pursue wealth and is linked to *dharma*. *Yi* is related to justice, and is more important than interests. *Dharma* influences the concept of economic interests and protecting national interests and weaknesses. *Manthan* influences the concept and behaviour of gaining from a chaotic world. *Li* affects the way Chinese people express themselves, how they do things, and how they value interpersonal relationships while the concept of *dharma* in Hindu culture emphasises religious duty, with the supernatural having the highest status. Meanwhile, there are synergies between the different values of each civilisation, such as *manthan* and *jugaad* jointly influenced low-cost concepts; *ren* and *yi,* respectively, and have promoted the advocacy and restriction of the pursuit of wealth.

These core values lead to different ways of doing and judging things in the two civilisations. Thus the differences are forming potential communication barriers and even causing cultural conflicts. For example, the *lun-ren* practice *yi* with the idea of interpersonal repaying and the Hindu tends to attribute benefits to divinity. The concepts of *zhi* in the Confucian culture and *jnana* in the Hindu culture reflect the importance attached to wisdom but have different focuses. The former values the judgment of right or wrong, while the latter attaches importance to the judgment of true or false, long-term or short-lived. These two different criteria are also one of the root causes of cognitive conflicts. The concept of *xin* in Confucian culture makes the *lun-ren* pay more attention to verbal commitments, which sometimes are even better than the role of contracts; but the Indian counterparts pay less attention to verbal commitments and pay more attention to the agreed content written on paper. This difference has caused some incompatibility between the Chinese and Indians in economic activities.

Preconceived values imperceptibly become the yardstick for judging others. In the interaction between the two civilisations, it is difficult to always get a consistent answer in understanding matters. A thorough study of each other's values would minimise misunderstandings and conflicts or set them to controllable limits. Adapting to each other and respecting each other's values is one way to avoid conflicts. Meanwhile, do not request but encourage others to draw closer to one's values (Guan 1995:176). That is to abandon what others do not like, and promote what others like, and even "cater to another's pleasure", to express one's good side. For those who cannot do this, they should strive to "seek common ground while reserving differences" even "seeking common ground in the difference", and find common ground on "controversial issues" (Guan 1995:176, 177). This aspect may not directly help solve the problem, but it can make each other consider the problem in the other's situation and will help ease the conflict and avoid further intensification. It also needs to gradually find ways to adapt to each other in the continuous running-in chronically, so that people from a different culture would become familiar with the other's behavioural patterns and thus adapt to each other. Indeed, the similarities of values are beneficial for building the foundation of communication; such as *ren* and *artha* emphasise on wealth, *yi* and *dharma* emphasis on morality and responsibility. The similarities could be the basis for building trust between the two countries and become the basis for dialogue in the bilateral relations, regional cooperation, as well as global governance.

CHAPTER 8

ECONOMIC RELATIONS AND CULTURAL DIMENSIONS

This chapter consists of three parts. The first will explain three areas of China-India economic relations: trade, investment, economic cooperation, enumerating data to have a general understanding of the overall picture of China-India economic relations, and then grasping the aspects of the impact of culture on economic relations. In these three areas, whether it is trade, investment, or economic cooperation, companies are playing their roles. Therefore, the second part of this chapter will analyse the companies of the two countries, in particular, the cultural factors that have an impact on the their businesses. The third part focuses on specific issues in economic relations, especially the factors that have a substantial impact on economic relations: border conflict and boycotting Chinese products in India, accordingly, to understand the conflicts in the economic relationship from the interpretation of a cultural perspective. In other words, it is to bring out the influence of culture on significant issues in economic relations and the problems that are affected by an insufficient understanding of cultural differences. Consequently, it is to find a breakthrough to strengthen mutual understanding between these two civilisations and promoting the development of China-India economic relations.

8.1. Overall Economic Relations and Cultural Dimensions

Economic relations between China and India grew extremely fast in the last few decades. Although the growth speed was fast, the base was low, and the volume was small; the amount of bilateral goods exported and imported were $ 84.54 billion (MOCPRC: 2018), which is much lower than the trade volume of China with the USA and Japan.[26] The size of Bilateral Goods Export and Import (BGEI)

26 India has overtaken Japan as the world's third largest economy in terms of purchasing power parity (PPP) in 2014 (Panda 2014). Moreover, it was considered that "India is likely to surpass US to be world's second largest economy by 2030" (Curran 2019).

between the USA and China is $ 635.97 billion (MOCPRC: 2018c), and between Japan and China $ 297.28 billion (MOCPRC: 2018d). These are 7.5 times and 3.5 times more than the volume of trade between India and China.

Although the economic relations of China-India have been continuously developing in the last two decades, it is deemed that "the level of China-India economic relations development is not high and not commensurate with the scale of the China-India economy" (Wen 2015:47). The constraints are related to asymmetric political mutual trust that caused problems such as the strict visa policy of India towards China, the difference of their economic systems that leads to different development planning and the like. These apparent hard factors are difficult to change in the short term. Comparatively, the role of culture as an invisible influence or soft power is imperceptible. It is true that the change in culture is slower. Still, if the similarities and differences of culture are well recognised, it is highly conducive for mutual understanding and respect while increasing the attractiveness towards each other. There is a need to reduce the negative impact caused by sketchy perceptions and promote the development of economic relations in the nearby future.

Although there is much room for improvement in the total economic output, if we look back at the changes in China-India economic relations from 2000 to 2017, it will be found that there are significant developments in the three aspects of total import and export, direct investment, and economic cooperation. By comparing the data of the year 2000 and 2017, the first part will examine the changes in China-India economic relations.

8.1.1. China-India Trade

China's total import and export volume (foreign trade volume, also known as "total import and export of customs goods") in 2000 was $ 474.29 billion, including total exports of $ 249.20 billion, and total imports of $ 225.09 billion (NBS 2001a). The total import and export volume of China with India is $ 2.91 billion, including $ 1.56 billion in exports and $ 1.35 billion in imports (MOCPRC 2011:472). In 2017, China's total import and export volume was $ 4,107.16 billion, an increase of eight times compared with the year 2000; the total export amount was $ 2,263.37 billion, and the total import value was $ 1,843.79 billion (NBS 2018a), which increased by eight times and seven times, respectively. The total import and export volume of goods of China with India was $ 84.39 billion, an increase of about 28 times compared with 2000, including total exports of $ 68.04 billion and imports totalling $ 16.35 billion (NBS 2018c), respectively, which increased by 43 times and 11 times. From 2000 to 2017, the growth multiple of China's import and export total amount with India (28 times) far exceeded the growth multiple of total import and export amount of China (eight times). Besides, China's total exports to India reached four times the total amount of imports from India in 2017; and in 2000, the total volume of imports and exports between China and India was flat.

China's main imports from India are minerals, base metals and related products as well as chemical products, while China's main exports to India are mechanical and electrical products, chemical products and base metals and related products (MOCPRC 2018). It seems that the items of bilateral trade could not be directly affected by culture. In the actual trade process, there would be the influence of culture. In addition to the lack of political mutual trust, high tariffs, and trade channels (more than 90 per cent of which are by marine transport), cultural concepts are also considered to be factors that directly or indirectly affect China-India trade relations and require sufficient attention (Ni and Wang 2006:97). The mutual understanding between the two countries at various levels is still far from enough. Indian culture, religion, language and the like are the content of the market environment that requires in-depth analysis and investigation in order to find suitable goods and services for local needs and promote marketing, and then promote the effective operation of China-India trade relations (Yang and Ni 2007:23).

Scholars realised the cultural influence on trade as mentioned above. Moreover, the influence of Hindu culture has an impact on trade policy. Hindu culture, according to Lu Xin (2013:205-208), has formed the characteristics of India's foreign trade policy summarised as follows: foreign trade policy has a delay and incompleteness in evolution, puts economic interests in a secondary position, presents forceful introversion, and regularly draws on traditional consciousness to obtain reasonability. This insightful summary has provided an outline for observing the trade policy of India. With the attention on it, it would improve the situation of China's trade with India.

8.1.2. FDI in China and India

In the world's top ten foreign-invested inflow countries (regions) of 2017, China's foreign investment flows were $ 136 billion, accounting for 9.5 per cent of the global total (MOCPRC 2018a:16), ranking second, after the USA ($ 275 billion); India with $ 40 billion, accounted for 2.8 per cent of the global total, ranking tenth (UNCTAD 2018:4). The FDI outflow of China in 2017 was $ 124.6 billion, accounting for 8.7 per cent of the total global outflow; India's was $ 11.3 billion, accounting for 0.8 per cent of the global total, and the investment amount for China from India was $ 0.16 billion (MOCPRC 2018b:28), accounting for 14 per cent of India's foreign investment.

Cultural differences exist between China and India influences attracting FDI (Jiang et al. 2008:33-39). It is difficult to sum up in one sentence that Confucianism and Hinduism are attractive or exclusive to FDI. However, it is easy to understand that the same cultural environment would be more attractive to investors. A considerable part of China's FDI comes from the Chinese economic circle, which is considered to be a unique advantage that China enjoys over most developing countries (Han and Chen 2007:49). Investment from Hong Kong ranked first in 2017 with the actual amount of foreign investment in the mainland of China of 69.3 per cent, second was from Singapore with 3.5 per cent, and ninth is from Taiwan region (MOCPRC 2018b:6).

Mauritius takes the largest share of 34 per cent of all the FDI in India from the years 2000 to 2017. Given that 48.5 per cent population of Mauritius is Hindu according to the 2011 Census and that Hinduism is the largest religion in that country, it seems cultural connection plays a role in attracting FDI. However, Mauritius is called a tax haven for facilitating treaty shopping, round-tripping, tax evasion and black money,"which has been highlighted in various reports including by government agencies and news outlets" (Jaiswal 2017:7).[27] It is considered that Hong Kong and the mainland of China are similar cases (Ibid: 11). Still, except that it is a free economic zone, Mauritius has always been the most significant source country of India's FDI because it has many Indian immigrants (Shi 2010:17).

Culture is considered a factor to attract FDI, especially in the initial stages of a company's overseas investment. Investing in the same cultural area is a supporting condition for reducing risks and smoothly carrying out business. Conversely, the more significant the cultural difference, the lower the attractiveness of the investment. The unique Indian culture is relatively weak to attract ordinary Chinese investors who are often discouraged from visiting India unless it is an entrepreneur, who fully understands the potential of the Indian market and would overcome culture difficulties. Whether economic potential is the primary consideration for investment or not can be viewed from the analysis of the next section. Only a particular field among China's investment in India can account for the top 25 investments in India.[28] It shows Chinese investment in India to be relatively small. In 2017, China's investment in India was nearly twice that of India's investment in China, showing that India also has less investment in China. The top foreign-invested countries in India mostly have similarities with India on culture (Hindu) or language (English). At the same time, Hong Kong and Taiwan, which have similar levels of Chinese culture, are the main source for investment in Mainland China. Although economic factors and tax considerations are crucial aspects, attention is needed to be paid to the influence of culture as well.

8.1.2.1. FDI to China

The number of registered foreign-funded enterprises in China at the end of the 2000 was 203,208, with a total investment of $ 824.68 billion (including FDI

27 The Government of India has amended treaties with Mauritius and "the full applicable tax rates will apply from 1 April 2019" (Jaiswal 2017:7,33).

28 It is from Indian sources, which shows the data of China includes the Mainland of China.

$ 62.38 billion) and 22,347 foreign direct investment contract projects. In 2017, the number of registered foreign-funded enterprises at the end of the year was 539,345 (the number of registered households at the end of the year includes branches since 2008), the total investment was $ 6,899.24 billion (including FDI $ 131.04 billion), and the number of foreign direct investment contract projects were 35,652. In 2000, the actually used amount of foreign investment (foreign direct investment) was $ 40.72 billion (NBS 2001a); FDI from India was $ 0.01 billion (NBS 2001f)), accounting for only 0.02 per cent of the total FDI of China in 2000. In 2017, the FDI and actual use of foreign investment in China was $ 131.04 billion (NBS 2018a); FDI from India was $ 0.16 billion (NBS 2018b), accounting for 0.12 per cent of the total FDI of China in 2017. It increased 15 times from 2000 to 2017, and its share increased fivefold. In 2017, US investment in China was $ 2.65 billion, and Japan's was $ 3.26 billion (NBS 2018b), which was respectively 17 times and 20 times of India's investment in China.

Manufacturing, information transmission, software and information technology services, real estate, lease and business services, and wholesale and retail are the top five industries attracting foreign investment in China, respectively accounting for 25.6 per cent ($ 33.51 billion), 16 per cent ($ 20.92 billion), 12.9 per cent ($ 16.86 billion), 12.8 per cent ($ 16.74 billion), and 8.8 per cent ($ 11.48 billion) in 2017 in actual use of foreign investment (MOCPRC 2018a:91). In addition, the financial industry (excluding banking, security and insurance), scientific research and technical services, transportation, warehousing and postal services, electricity, heat, gas and water production and supply, construction industry severally accounted for 6.1 per cent ($ 7.92 billion), 5.2 per cent ($ 6.84 billion), 4.3 per cent ($ 5.59 billion), 2.7 per cent ($ 3.52 billion), and 2.0 per cent ($ 2.62 billion) of actually used foreign investment in 2017 (MOCPRC 2018a:92).

The number of India's direct investment projects in China in 2000 was five with a contractual value of $ 7.44 million and an actual investment of $ 10.44 million (MOPRC 2001:678). India's investment in China mainly involves information technology, pharmaceutical products and biotechnology (Zhao 2006:203). Indian pharmaceutical companies have entered China for investment since 1993. Ranbaxy Laboratories Ltd. first established a joint venture with a Chinese pharmaceutical company; besides, Indian pharmaceutical companies such as Wockhardt, Dr. Reddy's Laboratories and Aurobindo Pharmaceuticals have invested in joint ventures in China (Zhang Minqiu 2004:209). In information technology education, Indian educational institutions, information technology companies, and software companies have successively invested, cooperated or established development centres in Shanghai and Beijing China in 2000 including the National Institute of Information Technology, Aptech Ltd., Asian Institute of Information Technology (AIIT), Satyam Computer Services Ltd., Tata Consultancy Services (TCS), Infosys Limited, etc. (Ibid. 209-210). Moreover,

Indian packaging company, Essel, and refractory company Grind and Diamond Company have established wholly-owned companies, joint ventures or invested in Guangzhou, Dalian and other cities of China.. Since 2000, Indian entrepreneurs have established more than 100 companies and factories in the Pearl River Delta (Ibid.)

In 2017, India established 281 new foreign-invested enterprises in China, accounting for 7.4 per cent, ranking fifteenth among the top 20 FDI countries (regions) in China, and third among countries along the BRI after Singapore (706 enterprises) and Malaysia (329 enterprises). Actual Indian investment in China amounted to $ 160 million, accounting for 2.9 per cent and ranking second among countries along the Belt & Road Initiative (BRI), after Singapore ($ 4.76 billion) (MOCPRC 2018a:89). It shows that India's ranking among the top FDI countries in China is not high, but India has become a critical FDI source among the states along with China's national initiative in 2017.

8.1.2.2. FDI to India

The policy of India's FDI had three strategic transformative processes since independence: prudent use of FDI, utilising and restricting FDI and positive encouragement (Li 2010:66). From 2000 to 2017, the four Indian governments implemented nearly 100 reforms; PM Atal Bihari Vajpayee implemented 29 reforms in the six years from 1998 to 2004, and PM Manmohan Singh (2004-2014) implemented 37 reforms (Wang 2018:44), PM Narendra Modi has implemented 37 reforms from 2014 to 2017 (Rossow 2017). Despite the rapid development of FDI in India, China's FDI in India accounts for only a small proportion, and the top 25 of FDI in India in the top ten sectors has almost no presence of China.

The FDI inflows received in India was $ 43.6 billion in 2017; FDI that flowed from Mainland China to India in 2017 was $ 0.2 billion and cumulative total from January 2000 to December 2017 was $ 1.8 billion (DIPP 2018a). FDI flows from Hong Kong to India was $ 1.0 billion and the cumulative total from 2000 to 2017 was $ 3.0 billion; FDI flows from Taiwan to India in 2017 was $ 0.1 billion and the cumulative total from 2000 to 2017 was $ 0.3 billion (Ibid.). Mainland China's FDI to India in 2017 took 0.5 per cent, Hong Kong 2.3 per cent, and Taiwan 0.2 per cent. According to data from China, cumulative FDI from China to India was $ 4.7 billion by the end of 2017 (MOCPRC 2019). Data from India mentioned the above-listed to Mainland China, Hong Kong and Taiwan separately. By adding up the cumulative total of Hong Kong and Taiwan, the cumulative total FDI from China to India was $ 5.1 billion from 2000 to 2017.

The top investing country into India was Mauritius with $ 16.3 billion accounting for 37 per cent share in the total FDI equity inflows from January to December 2017; Singapore, The Netherlands, the USA, and Japan were listed as the second to fifth-ranked countries with 25 per cent ($ 10.8 billion), 7 per cent

($ 3.3 billion), 5 per cent ($ 2.2 billion), and 4 per cent ($ 1.7 billion), respectively (DIPP 2018b). By adding up the FDI of Hong Kong and Taiwan, China would be the sixth-ranked country ($ 1.3 billion) on the list of 2017 and the eleventh-ranked country ($ 5.1 billion) on the list of cumulative total from January 2000 to December 2017 after Mauritius ($ 125.2 billion), Singapore ($ 63.8 billion), Japan ($ 27.0 billion), United Kingdom ($ 25.3 billion), The Netherlands ($ 23.1 billion), USA ($ 22.2 billion), Germany ($ 10.7 billion), Cyprus ($ 9.5 billion), France ($ 6.2 billion), and UAE ($ 5.3billion).[29]

China's foreign direct investment in 2017 was $ 158.29 billion, and the net amount of foreign direct investment was $ 1,809.04 billion by the end of 2017; which of the net direct investment to India was $ 0.29 billion in 2017, and the overseas direct investment stock to India was $ 4.75 billion at the end of 2017 (NBS 2018d). In 2017, China's investment in India was 1.8 times that of India's investment in China.

Computer software and hardware, telecommunications, services sector (financial and non-financial), construction (infrastructure) activities and trading are the five sectors that attracted the highest inflows in India in 2017, and shared 16 per cent ($ 7.0 billion), 14 per cent ($ 6.2 billion), 13 per cent ($ 5.8 billion), 7 per cent ($ 3.0 billion) and 6 per cent ($ 2.6 billion), respectively (DIPP 2018b). Besides, construction development (townships, housing, built-up infrastructure), automobile industry, drugs and pharmaceuticals, chemicals (other than fertilisers) and power were the other five sectors that attracted the highest FDI equity inflows from April 2000 to March 2018 (DIPP 2018c).

Among these sectors, FDI equity inflows from China to India occupied the top 25 only in the automobile industry[30] (DIPP 2018d). The remittance of SAIC General Motors Investment Ltd. of China through General Motors India Pvt. Ltd. occupied No. 8, 21 and 23 with the amount of FDI inflows respectively being $ 229.38 million, $ 117.74 million and $ 118.42 million from January 2000 to December 2017, while the items of manufacture of all were passenger cars (DIPP 2018e). Passenger cars, a sub-sector of FDI equity inflows in the automobile industry, accounted for 2.01 per cent with the total FDI inflows (Ibid.). Besides, China's investment contract projects for India include electricity, telecommunications, metallurgy and infrastructure (Xiao 2015:28). The top ten investing countries in India are Mauritius, Singapore, Japan, United Kingdom, The Netherlands, USA, Germany, Cyprus, France and UAE. Although China occupied the top 25 in the automobile industry sector, it is behind the top five

29 The twelfth is Switzerland ($ 4.2 billion).

30 The top five countries that attracted FDI equity inflows for the automobile industry were Japan, USA Germany, The Netherlands and Mauritius (DIPP 2017e). Again, the Indian resource shows the data of China only including the Mainland of China and the same below.

countries, i.e., Japan, USA, Germany, The Netherlands and Mauritius which severally occupied 27.21 per cent, 12.14 per cent, 12.07 per cent, 8.39 per cent and 7.43 per cent respectively, with total FDI inflows for the automobile industry and 67.24 per cent in total (Ibid.).

8.1.2.3. Cultural Constraints

8.1.2.3.1. Cultural Constraints of China on Investing in India

Both the "organisational entity" and "civilisational entity"of India limit China's investment in India. Those entities are considered as two parts of the functioning nation (Shang 2013:5). In "organisational entity", China's investment in India is constrained by:

> "[...] restrictive FDI regime, high import tariffs, exit barriers for firms, stringent labour laws, poor quality infrastructure, centralised decision-making processes, and very limited scale of export processing zones" (Bajpai and Sachs 2000).

In "civilizational entity", investment from China to India could be influenced by Indian living habits, such as food, cultural environment (less recreational facilities than in China), "doing things with delays", (Ibid: 31), non-punctuality, taking verbal commitments seriously and the like. Various investment restrictions have caused Chinese companies to invest in India with a small amount and slow growth. Comparing the economic aggregates and geographical advantages of the two countries, direct investment of Chinese enterprises in India is obviously very low (Li 2015:28). In addition to the constraints mentioned above that every investor has to face, India"is almost the country with the most anti-dumping investigations and litigation against China among developing countries" (Ibid: 29). There were 144 Anti-Dumping Cases involving China from 1 January 2000 to 31 December 2017 according to the Ministry of Commerce and Industry, India (DGTR 2019). Due to "security threats", India had repeatedly rejected investment of Chinese companies in India (Ibid: 32). The Indian government listed China as a "sensitive country" twice in 2002 and 2006 and temporarily suspended 25 Chinese telecom equipment suppliers in 2010 (Chen 2010). However, according to two international political economy scholars,

> "[...] people throughout history have often chosen other values, including nationalism and tariff protection of its domestic industry, over *laissez-faire* policies as the most efficient guarantor of prosperity. Participatory democracies by their very nature generate policies designed to protect the special interests of sub-national groups. Politicians whose livelihoods depend on the favour of voters are forced to make political choices, which liberal free trade economists often consider irrational." (Dougherty and Pfaltzgraff 2000:476)

This point would be conducive to understand why a nation like India imposes anti-dumping duties.

In addition to the institutional constraints of the organization, the role of civilization, that is, cultural aspects, also limits China's investment in India, especially economic nationalism; the emergence of economic nationalism is considered to be related to factors such as the level of economic development, national strategy, and historical and cultural traditions (Zhang Li 2007:12). It was pointed out that,

> "India's long-term colonial process and the nationalist trend of thought in the national independence movement have become increasingly high and have evolved into powerful economic nationalism. Indian nationalism has two distinctive features: First, the influence of religion, especially Hinduism, is far-reaching; Second, since India's independence, India's nationalist trends and policies have been evolving constantly." (Li 2015:24)

The Bharatiya Janata Party is an advocate of Indian economic nationalism; the Modi government has formulated a series of policies to develop Indian manufactures that is particularly obvious. The relevant policies would certainly increase the ability of India on related industries but reduce the advantage relatively for China's industries that are complementary to India such as infrastructure and manufacturing to play its most significant role in India.

> "The Bharatiya Janata Party has proposed three nationalisms, namely, cultural nationalism, political nationalism and economic nationalism. Among them, economic nationalism is more deeply rooted in the hearts of the people. That is to achieve industrialization and modernization in the way of the Indians themselves, without excessive dependence on foreign capital and technology, and selectively attract foreign direct investment, mainly to introduce foreign capital in high-tech fields, rather than low-level foreign investment, and even put forward the slogan of 'old computer chips yes, potato chips no'." (Murlidharan 2014 Wu 2010:29-30)

India's resistance to foreign goods has existed since long. This kind of influence is far-reaching. Chinese enterprises must be psychologically prepared to formulate effective measures to deal with their counterparts, fully understand the motives behind them, and be more conducive to adapting to the local investment environment. The ban on Pepsi and Coca-Cola in India reflects this kind of "national goods complex", i.e., in favour of domestic goods and the rejection of imported goods, which led to "more than a million shopkeepers expecting to comply with the ban" (BBC 2017). The economic nationalist sentiment is considered a problem that cannot be ignored in the studies of China-India relations, especially economic relations (Li 2015:25). India's "unique religious culture" is also considered an essential factor for Chinese investors in India to consider (MOCPRC 2015).

Moreover, it was held that the impact of nationalism and religion on China's overseas investment was thus,

> "[...] Religious beliefs often lead to fierce conflicts, and ethnic departmentalism (*minzu benwei zhuyi*, or ethnicism) is often popular. [...] To achieve political goals, political groups in some countries often use ethnicism to make a fuss, encourage national sentiment to trigger social unrest, and increase the risk of direct investment of Chinese companies." (Zhang Shucun 2017:7)

Further, some overseas organisations and politicians have stirred up anti-China sentiments to achieve their goals:

> "There are organisations within the countries along the 'Belt and Road' that have a resistance towards China. These organisations use various means to propagandise China, and oppose and undermine investment from China negatively. Some politicians also use people's resistance emotions on China for seeking personal political interests, such as constantly exaggerating China's 'political presence' and 'economic interests' in their country, and attributing its economic policy failures to Chinese factors" (Ibid.).

"Negative propaganda" has a major impact on people who do not have a deep understanding. Religion and nationalism will especially magnify this sentiment, which will undoubtedly have a huge negative impact on China's investment. Chinese overseas companies should pay attention to the establishment of a favourable image, respond by participating in public welfare undertakings and adopt "localisation"measures.

Meanwhile, an understanding of economic nationalism restrictions from a historical perspective is not blindly negative. Compared to Nehru's "closed economic nationalism", the economic nationalism advocated by the Bharatiya Janata Party is considered to be "open economic nationalism" (Li 2015:25). Overall, the Indian investment environment is still developing. Adapting to the environment would be conducive for investment.

The indicators, which could bring risks for China's investment abroad in general, include signing of the Bilateral Investment Treaty (BIT),[31] the level of obstacles for investment, bilateral political relations, the degree of trade and

---

31 China and India signed a Bilateral Investment Treaty (BIT), i.e., *Agreement between the Government of the Republic of India and the Government of the People's Republic of China for the Promotion and Protection on Investments*, on 21 November 2006 in New Delhi. It came into force on 1 August 2007 and ended on 3 October 2018 (DEA 2006).

investment dependence and the visa-free situation (CSSN 2019). The International Monetary Fund (IMF) reported that the rise and long-term existence of nationalism is one of the main factors for economic development (MOFCOM 2018:19). From the above, it is clear that Hindu economic nationalism influenced China's investment in India by influencing the risk indicators such as the level of obstacles for investment, bilateral political relations, the degree of trade and investment dependence and the visa-free situation. Most of the indicators are restricting China's trade and investment in India. The specific performance is the alertness of India to China. These fears and restrictions on Chinese investment have greatly restricted China's presence in India. It is an essential factor that investment "is extremely incompatible with the status of the two great powers" (Zhang 2007:13). At the same time, this kind of thought limits India's openness. It is considered that "one of the important reasons for the closed-door policy that restricts India's development is not another factor but highly correlated with the nationalist consciousness of constant flow in their blood" (Zhang 2007:12). Indians are also aware of these problems. A former Indian Congress spokesman once pointed out,

> "in addition to the socialist economic policy, nationalist sentiment has also seriously hindered India [...], this kind of seclusion under the nationalist sentiment that rejects the West leads to India's economic development being very slow. There is no real market, no competition, and economic efficiency is naturally low." (Zhang 2007:13).

In India, Chinese companies should consider how to integrate into local society and reduce "destroying local culture and environment, and ruining the business of the local enterprise", carefully caring for local interests and customs, and exerting influence on local business communities overseas (Zhang 2007:89). Meanwhile,

> "Chinese companies investing and operating in India must combine Indian cultural and institutional characteristics, [...] deal properly with the relationships within the enterprise and religious issues of local labourers, [...] The process of 'Indianization' of Chinese business operations is vital and urgent." (Li 2015: 42).

For Chinese companies in India, the religious concern is continuously highlighted, the research on these particular issues should unfold relevantly; it is a long and arduous task.

8.1.2.3.2. Cultural constraints of India to invest in China

In the cross-cultural management of foreign investors in China, there would also be cultural conflicts caused by cultural differences. For instance, when an Indian manager manages Chinese employees with his cultural concept, there was customer loss because problems could not be solved, employee loyalty reduction, and hostile employees and uncooperative sentiment due to disrespect to their "*mianzi*" (face) (Chen et al. 2004:73). These phenomena would inevitably hinder the development of Indian companies in China. It requires a high degree of emphasis on corporate culture, effective communication, mutual respect, and a corporate culture that integrates both the cultures for mutual benefit (Ibid: 74-75).

The specific cultural conflicts are manifested by, firstly, "serious quality defects, which are considered by Chinese customers but not considered by Indian customers". Because Chinese employees cannot apply for funds to solve quality defects, and this leads to customer loss (Ibid: 73). Similar issues involve the Chinese attaching importance to external packaging and the like, while Indians pay more attention to the inherent practicability and low price; besides, their requirements towards externals are not like the Chinese, which is related to their spiritual approach and frugal spirit.

Secondly, the Chinese like to "beat about the bush", i.e., not speaking directly, which makes it difficult for Indians to grasp their real intentions (Chen et al. 2004:73). The root of such behaviour is related to "*li*" (ritual) and "*mianzi*" (face) (See 6.2.2.2). Besides, not paying attention to establishing relationships and developing friendships with customers are also likely to cause loss of customers in China (Chen et al. 2004:73). It is also necessary to correctly and fully understand the situation of the *guanxi* concept in China.

Thirdly, India has a hierarchy, and people are also treated hierarchically, especially between the upper and lower levels. It is different from China's superior and subordinate concept and leads to differences in wage levels, employee development, and behavioural attitudes (Chen et al. 2004:73). It is different from the cultural and psychological expectations of Chinese employees and creates conflicts in attitudes of communication and towards work, which harms the business. The roots of these cultural factors are discussed in the second chapter, which is deeply related to the critical foundations of the traditional cultures of the two countries, especially Confucianism and Hinduism.

As mentioned above, there are many cultural factors that hinder India's investment in China. The differences in culture, living habits of residents, and thinking patterns all have a certain degree of adverse impacts on communication and operation. Lack of understanding on these aspects has led to the emergence of "inadaptability" for Indian companies in China, which has prevented full access to the Chinese market (Yang 2017:53-54). Therefore, "strengthening Sino-Indian cultural exchanges and fully understanding each other's market" is considered to be one of the essential aspects of promoting Sino-Indian investment cooperation (Ibid: 55). Only a full understanding of culture can create conditions for investment cooperation and increase the possibility of investment success (Ibid.)

Along with the active promotion of the two governments, cultural exchanges between China and India have continued and deepened based on the dialogue over the past 2,000 years. There is still a considerable gap to be filled, especially the lack of understanding of the Chinese on Hinduism, the belief of 79.8 per cent of India's population. India's lack of general understanding of Chinese traditional culture is worse. The lack of mutual understanding is a crucial factor to be considered for improving the development of investment cooperation.

8.1.3. Economic Cooperation

In the year of China's foreign economic cooperation in 2000, the contractual value was $ 14.943 billion (including foreign contracted projects, foreign labour cooperation and external design consultation) with a turnover of $ 11.325 billion (NBS 2001a). The turnover of $ 13.18 million with India's economic cooperation (including contracting projects $ 9.19 million, labour cooperation $ 3.95 million, design consultation $ 0.04 million) (NBS 2001e) accounts for 0.12 per cent (Ibid.). In China's foreign economic cooperation in 2017, the contract value of foreign contracted projects was $ 265.28 billion, and the value of turnover fulfilled of foreign contracted projects was $ 168.59 billion ("The Ministry of Commerce has incorporated external design consultation into the consolidated statistics of foreign contracted projects since 2009") (NBS 2018a).

There are two parts, "Contracted Projects" and "Labour Services"[32] in "Economic Cooperation with Foreign Countries or Regions" in *China Statistical Yearbook 2018*. The total number of despatched labour for contracted projects was 222,135 persons, the total number of persons abroad on contracted projects by the end of the year 2017 was 376,827 persons; the total number of persons despatched for labour services was 300,249, and the number of person abroad for labour services by the end of 2017 was 602,342 persons. The value of turnover fulfilled of contracted projects with India was $ 2.46 billion (It was more than 200 times the value for the year 2000) (NBS 2018e). Nearly 797 labour (contracted projects) were despatched, 1,279 persons (contracted projects) were in India by the end of 2017; 31 labour (labour services) were despatched to India, and 165 labour (labour services) were in India at the end of 2017 (Ibid.).

The higher the cultural differences between the two cultures, the more likely it is to increase the psychological distance. Culture differences could also affect economic cooperation between the two countries,

32 "Overseas Contracted Projects" refer to "activities of contracting overseas construction projects by Chinese enterprises or any other units, which are stipulated in the Regulations on Administration of Foreign Contracted Project". "Overseas Labour Services" refer to "operational activities of organizing the labour force to go abroad providing services to foreign enterprises or agencies"(NBS 2018f).

> "The lack of cultural exchanges has reduced the understanding and communication between the two peoples and increased the psychological distance between them. It makes the lack of a cultural basis for the establishment of an economic cooperation mechanism between China and India, which is not conducive to the deepening of China-India economic cooperation" (Xie 2017:38).

Although the turnover of economic cooperation between China and India has increased by more than 200 times from 2000 to 2017, the number of despatched labourers, as well as persons in India under contracted projects and labour services, is still small. Incompatibility towards Indian culture and the environment could cause Chinese employees to resist being sent to India. Even if psychological resistance is not their idea, they may be influenced by the impression of their families in India. Except for the concern of personal safety and environmental sanitation, the image of Indian culture in the Chinese media has not been fully demonstrated, especially the essence of Indian culture.

Even the Chinese, who have an understanding of India, will be criticised, when they praise Indian culture, by their compatriots who consider that the beautiful part of Indian culture does not need deep exploring. For example, the protection of animals in India would be criticised as ignorance. The *Jugaad* spirit of Indians could lead to them being considered poor and stingy. The emphasising of a spiritual approach could be ridiculed as the reason for poverty and not seeking development. The vegetarian culture would be linked to the fact that a large country has few Olympic champions. The thought of *manthan* is considered as gaining extra advantage by unfair means. The concept of unique time and reincarnation is considered as laziness and superstition. The care of the poor such as India's universal health insurance would be criticised due to lack of adequate facilities and many more.

In short, the inner part of Indian culture is considered to be inferior and backward by most people who do not fully understand its intrinsic value. Hinduism is especially perceived very often by people outside India "as a baffling tangle of myths" (Iyer 2018:3). The negative perceptions caused the unwillingness to step up the culture of India, and the complexity of Indian culture made the process of understanding it a difficult task.

Both China and India are ancient civilisations with large populations. Those two nations are always compared because of their different political systems and similar national conditions. The defence of their superiority has evolved into unyielding and conceited psychology. There are visible manifestations among intellectuals in China and India. To a certain extent, this kind of psychology has formed a restraining force that hinders the profound exchange of culture. China and India are more than willing to communicate based on their historical legacy, i.e., Buddhism, resulting in a lack of understanding of contemporary culture. It is realised that,

> "The lack of cultural exchanges, which affected the establishment of an economic cooperation mechanism, is not conducive to creating a new type of big country cooperation model for mutual benefit and win-win situation." (Xie 2017:38).

China and India need to fully understand the differences in culture and deepen cultural exchanges for the "mutually beneficial and win-win new model of cooperation of big countries". Cultural exchanges, from this perspective could also improve the economic cooperation between China and India. History and culture are considered to be favourable factors for the development of China-India economic and trade cooperation: "In the historical exchanges between China and India, culture is the most important bridge and plays a leading role" (Li 2004:108). Culture normally is not valued in economic research, so the obstacles that took shape by culture are even less fully understood. In a way, culture could be a breakthrough in improving economic and even other areas of cooperation. It is also slowly becoming a far-sighted consensus of the two national leaders during the Wuhan summit in April 2018. The establishment of China-India High-Level Mechanism on Cultural and People-to-People Exchanges is an important measure to reduce the psychological distance caused by cultural differences and "to build greater synergies in the people to people area" (MEA 2018).

8.2. Cultural Dimension of Companies' Business

8.2.1. Chinese Companies in India

There are more than 1,000 Chinese companies (Luo 2018) ranging from large-scale multinational corporations to small and medium-scale enterprises and traders that belong to various sectors such as power, steel, construction/engineering, energy, manufacturing, equipment, heavy industry, banking, electricity, telecom, mining, healthcare, consumer goods, transport, automobiles, media, consultations, etc., located in "Delhi, NCR Region, Mumbai, Gujarat, Pune"and other parts of India (CCCI 2013). Chinese companies are from different parts of China, i.e., Beijing, Tianjin, Shanghai, Guangdong, Jiangsu, Shandong, Hunan, Shenzhen, Sichuan, Zhejiang, Harbin, Hebei, Henan, Hubei (Wuhan), Guizhou, Hong Kong, Taiwan and other regions (Ibid). Some cultural elements could influence economic relations in the level of the companies. For instance, the cultural elements in advertisements, cultural taboos and the like.

8.2.1.1. Advertisements

To know the local culture well would be beneficial for businesses. Here the culture includes pop culture. For instance, the advertisements of a TV company could add an Indian cultural element, for instance, cricket and Indian drama to make them more attractive to Indian customers. The Indian characters in the advertisement are a vital strategy.

There are some Chinese companies that do not use Indian cultural elements in their advertisements. Without knowing customer psychology influenced by cultural characteristics, it would be difficult for the company to make its product accessible. Famous brands that understand the cultural features and their importance in society will survive. Meanwhile, to respect the local culture is also an important skill for companies. The offence of the cultural taboo could cause a ban of the company with serious conflicts.

8.2.1.2. Cultural Taboo for Doing Business in India

Given that leather products are part of the exports from China to India, cultural taboos should be seriously considered by Chinese companies in India. Aokang is a famous brand for shoes and other leather products from China. The first manufacturing facility of Aokang in India was commissioned in Manesar industrial town, Gurgaon district, Haryana, with "a production capacity of 200 pairs of shoes per day" (PTI 2008). It is reported that "Aokang set up the factory with a total investment of Rs. 2 crore over an area of 20,000 square feet, which could accommodate 200 employees and produce 1,000 pairs daily by 2009". Aokang planned to invest "Rs. 500 crore over the next five years to strengthen its footprint in the Indian leather market" (Ibid.). In 2017, Aokang International had its plants in Himachal Pradesh, Uttarakhand and Uttar Pradesh in India (Roy 2017). For this scale of investment, the source of leather could be a crucial consideration for the company. Meanwhile, respect for the local belief should be sincerely followed by the leather company; for instance, the worship of cows by the majority of Hindus.

The Una incident has relevance here. Four Dalits, who claimed that they were skinning dead cows, were beaten by cow protectors who were Shiv Sena members (TNN 2016). A colossal protest rally was held the next day led by Dalit leaders in which "more than 2,000 Dalits attended and blocked the state highway. The issue was discussed in the upper house of Parliament (Rajya Sabha). Two people had died, a policeman and a Dalit, and five people from the Dalit community attempted suicide during the protest against the Una incident (IANS 2016). Around 20,000 Dalits attended the protest, which ended after ten days, and they pledged to give up their traditional jobs of "removing cow carcasses and cleaning gutters" (Sharma 2016). Other accidents (Harshey 2017) related to cow protection happened in 2002 when newspaper headlines read as follows: "5 Dalit men killed in Haryana", "Murder of Mohd Akhlaq in Dadri, Uttar Pradesh" (in which a Muslim man was killed by a mob as he was accused of consuming beef (PTI 2015), "Murder of Praveen Poojary by gaurakshaks" (Swamy 2016), "Murder of 15-year-old Junaid Khan on a train between Delhi and Mathura" (Lakhani 2017). It should be noted that in some of the cases, the Dalits claimed they were selling the cowhide to the leather factory. Carefulness by the company would have helped to avoid such conflicts.

The diverse food culture of India should also be noted. There are some parts of India like Hyderabad where the habit of eating beef prevails; meanwhile, there are always protests to stop related activities such a beef festival in the city (Anita 2012). Not only cows, the killing of frogs and consumption of eggs was also banned in some states of India, for example there were headlines like "ban on frog dissection in Gujarat" in 1991, and Chhattisgarh HC has proposed that "eggs should not be sold in public places" in 2005 (Harshey 2017).

Given that the violation of cultural taboos could cause riots and their adverse effects on economic growth (Collier 1999), the macroeconomic consequences of riots could "include a reduction in consumption, business confidence, investment, and the possibility of greater state borrowing and higher budget deficits" (Iyer 2018:25-26). Although there is no direct or obvious influence on the business of Chinese companies, cultural taboos need careful attention, as their violation is a potential risk for doing business in India.

8.2.1.3. The Reason for Cow Protection and Market for Cow Leather

The cow was mentioned in the manifesto of the Bharatiya Janata Party's Lok Sabha election in 1999,

> "It is listed under 'good governance', a subsection under 'economy', which outlines the economic importance of the cow and its progeny for animal husbandry and dairying." (Harshey 2017)

In 2004, the cow was mentioned again in the BJP's manifesto under "animal husbandry and fisheries" and "talks of improving livestock breeds" (Ibid). The cow was listed under 'Preserving Cultural Heritage' in 2009 and 2014,

> "The language of the debate changes. For the first time, the cow was listed under 'Preserving Cultural Heritage' alongside topics like Ram Mandir, Ram Setu, and the river Ganga." (Ibid.)

As mentioned above, the cow was protected as an important part of husbandry and later as part of the cultural heritage at the government level. The policy of the government, especially the BJP government, is triggered by the cultural belief at the national level. It was argued that the BJP had done,

> "a rampant imposition of bans on the sale of cattle for slaughter, on the sale and consumption of beef, and a dramatic increase in vigilantism targeting marginalised and minority groups whose food cultures and livelihoods depend on the cow." (Ibid.)

The ban on cow slaughter was done in several states, i.e., Uttar Pradesh in 1955, Bihar in 1956, Odisha in 1960, Karnataka in 1964, Maharashtra in 1976, Andhra Pradesh in 1977, ("the President's Assent to the 1976 cow slaughter ban"), and

Daman and Diu district in 1978. "The politics of food by banning beef" was considered as "a new ploy by Hindutva groups" (Adhikari 2016). Although legislation of the beef ban by the Maharashtra government"has evoked a range of responses" and was"ridiculed, discussed and debated on social media sites", the implementation of the ban presented "a potent moment", and the only rallying cry came from the beef traders (Nair 2016:14, 16).

The condition of the cows, which were sold to the leather trader, needs to be considered. Vaidyanathan (2015:48) has pointed out that,

> "A large proportion of deaths among adult animals is due to poor care and disease. However, some, not insignificant, part consists of dysfunctional and unproductive animals that are abandoned or sold off. It is mostly this category of animals that traders buy and then send to abattoirs mainly to produce skins for which there is a lucrative market and incidentally for other byproducts, including meat".

It shows the condition of cows sold for their skins is "some, not insignificant" and "dysfunctional and unproductive animals"; meanwhile, the market is "lucrative" (Ibid.). The main contradiction here that caused conflict was the different appeals of belief of cow worship and the market demand. Although the cow is "dysfunctional and unproductive", it does not mean its slaughter would not harm religious emotions. How to balance this is a hard task for policymakers and traders.

> "The cow is protected under Article 48 of the Constitution, which says that the State shall endeavour to organise agriculture and animal husbandry on modern and scientific lines and shall, in particular, take steps for preserving and improving the breeds, and prohibiting the slaughter of cows and calves and other milch and draught cattle." (Harshey 2017)

The gap between the Constitution and the ground situation can be easily seen. It is a great example to know the complexity of the Indian market under the influence of its unique culture. As foreign investors, the Chinese should be more wary regarding the taboos of Indian culture.

8.2.1.4. Charity Spirit of Chinese Companies: the giving Back to Society

The difference in attitudes towards charity between the Chinese and Indians can be seen as a result of their cultural differences. The spirit of charity is reflected in Chinese companies, for instance, the Tiens Group,

> "Contributing to China through industrialization, and striving for higher goals through harmonious teamwork and genuine dedication. [...] Tiens Group has adhered to its charitable philosophy of 'originating from society and therefore contributing to society' and has been actively taking on corporate social responsibility. Tiens Group

has donated thus far more than RMB 1.5 billion to public welfare and social charities." (Tiens 2018)

This example shows that the Chinese character of charity is to give back to society after creating wealth. Indian companies tend to consider the poor at the outset of their businesses. China promotes poverty alleviation and lifts the poor out of poverty. As the goal of the Chinese government, poverty alleviation and reduction has pulled more than 850 million people out of poverty in China (The World Bank 2019). The idea of creating wealth in Confucianism encourages the Chinese to aspire for wealth while Hinduism tends to adapt to the current state, whatever poverty or wealth, instead of changing the status quo. Therefore, many people in India bow to their fate and devote themselves to spirituality and do not place the economy as the primary goal of development. This is the difference between Chinese and Indian traditions. It should be considered that Chinese companies in India adapt to the cultural environment instead of judging the situation from the viewpoint of Chinese culture or attempt to change the situation in short order.

8.2.2. Indian Companies in China

Indian companies in the mainland of China are located mainly in four cities and nine provinces (EOI 2018a). From information provided by the Embassy of India in Beijing, there are around 20 Indian companies in the capital of China, Beijing, one company in Fujian province (Xiamen city), 10 in Guangdong province (Shenzhen and Guangzhou cities), two in Hebei province (Shijiazhuang and Sanhe cities), one in Hongkong, two in Liaoning province (Dalian and Yingkou cities), one in Jilin province (Changchun city), three in Shangdong province (Qingdao city), 54 in Shanghai, three companies in Zhejiang province, five in Jiangsu province (Wuxi, Yancheng, Suzhou and Nanjing cities), one in Sichuan province (Zigong city), and six in Tianjin city (EOI 2018b).

8.2.2.1. Indian Caste System and Chinese Equality

The caste system exists even today, which profoundly influences the social order of India (Iyer 2018:43). An example of a driver and a leader sitting together to eat, it shows the differences between Chinese and Indian society (Mishra 2017). Caste prohibits them sitting together in this manner. One feature of caste is that normally "food is to be received and eaten only in the presence of members of the same or higher group" (Basham 1954:149). Besides, another two facets of caste are "marriage being legitimate only within the group" and "each man to live by the trade or profession of his own group, and not take up that of another" (Ibid.).

In traditional values, Vaishya is the caste that does business. In modern times, many people still pursue the traditional business of this caste in India. Although it does not mean that the relative caste has to do business for ever, caste is still a major influential factor to choose an occupation. The caste system could influence the career of the relative group of people, yet, it is not everlasting. For example, the caste of *Tanti* (which is a Hindi word and means a 'loom') was "traditionally weavers" and "traditionally associated with this craft" (Singh 2008:914-916). The founder of Suzlon Energy Ltd., Tulsi Tanti, started his business with a textile company in 1995; he moved into wind energy production for "fuelling his business' need for power" and exited from the textile business (Suzlon 2018). Tulsi Tanti is ranked as the eighth richest person in India, and his "group's $ 8 billion market cap [market capitalisation] makes it the world's most valuable wind company (Karmali 2006). As mentioned above, people may set up their businesses according to the tradition of their caste, but can change if they want to.

Caste also influences the business of Chinese companies in India due to its influence on professional skill. Initially, Chinese companies delightedly discovered the vast potential of developing the Indian market; yet, the cultural difference is one factor that raises barriers for them. An Indian journalist who worked in China observed that Indians prefer "a straight-talking no-nonsense approach" while the Chinese adopt an "indirect and subtle approach" (Patil 2017). The differences in their approaches emerge the sharpest during negotiations and probably led to "a never-ending loop or fail" (Ibid.). Except for the points mentioned above, the speed of Indian worker to learn new skills also troubles Chinese engineers to come to India for the same training repeatedly (Pan 2018).[33] It is probably not the intelligence of Indian workers but the influence of their family occupational heritage culture based on caste, i.e., members of an Indian family might continue to do the same job from generation to generation, and thus do the "family work" very masterly (Mao 2015), but probably will not be able to adapt to a new skill.

8.2.2.2. Cultural Initiatives and Spirit of a Leading Indian Group

Sub-units of the enterprise show its ambition not only about the business but also the value to the poor, culture and history of the nation. As a leading multi-mineral solutions provider, the global group of industries, Ashapura, also carries out cultural developmental activities through its non-profit organisation, Ashapura Foundation (Ashapura Group 2016a). Ashapura Foundation supports "aesthetic and cultural initiatives such as restoration of monuments, and patronage of local arts and crafts through the Hiralaxmi Craft Park" (Ashapura Group 2016b). The vision of Hiralaxmi Craft Park (HCP) is to "preserve, restore and promote the arts of Kutch (Gujarat) and make them accessible to the masses" (HCP 2008a). To protect the arts that "were on the verge of extinction", the Hiralaxmi Craft Park, which is "spread over 10 acres of land", was founded to "exhibit their artifacts

33 According to the Annual Employability Survey 2019 report by Aspiring Minds, Indian engineers are more capable than their Chinese counterparts but both are far behind their American peers (BT 2019).

and [provide] financial support" in December 2015 (Ibid.). The park "receives on an average 4,000 visitors every week" and "evolved into a learning centre and a source of information for students, surveyors and NGOs", and produces textile crafts and non-textile crafts (HCP 2008b). Besides, the Ashapura Group owns a non-profit institution, Vande Mataram Memorial (VMM), which "seeks to immortalize the most momentous episodes in India's freedom struggle from the revolt of 1857 right up to the country's independence in 1947" (VMM 2018). Carrying the culture of the enterprise forward while dealing with them could be a benefit for the business by knowing and understanding the whole picture.

8.2.2.3. For the Poor: Affordable Price and "Upliftment of Weak and Backward"

To take care of the poor is a feature of Indian enterprises. In the introduction of the founder of the global pharmaceutical conglomerate, Dr. Reddy's, it is mentioned that the founder Dr. K. Anji Reddy was born "in a well-to-do farming family" and "grew up watching his father make herbal pills that he distributed free. Little did he realize the prophetic significance of what he saw" (Dr. Reddy's 2018a). Since 1973, he has the vision "to bring new molecules into the country at a price the common man can afford". He established Dr. Reddy's Laboratories in 1984 and set up a business school to "help young people from disadvantaged backgrounds to learn skills [...] and become contributing members of society" (Ibid.). "[M]edicines to be useful must be affordable" is the conviction of Dr. Anji Reddy (Ibid.) and "Good Health Can't Wait" is the slogan and belief of his group (Dr. Reddy's 2018b).

Om Prakash Jindal (1930-2005), Founder-Chairman of the Jindal Group, a global industrial powerhouse, which has twenty factories and is worth over $ 10 billion (OP Jindal 2018), was born in 1930 to a farmer in Nalwa village of Hisar district in Haryana (JSPL 2014). With this background, Jindal was concerned about the poor. He "believed that without the upliftment of the weak and backward sections of society, a nation could never prosper" and "spent a lot of time in taking steps to alleviate poverty and boost the backward sections of society". He "envisioned a self-reliant India in every sector of industry" (Ibid.).

Besides, Jindal's political vision is also to contribute to society. "He was above caste politics and wanted to ensure a rightful place for every individual in politics, regardless of his caste, colour or creed" and "firmly believed that all differences could be amicably resolved through meaningful dialogues" (JSPL 2014). He was elected Member of the Haryana Legislative Assembly three times, Member of Parliament in the 11th Lok Sabha in 1996 and served as Minister of Power, Government of Haryana (Ibid.).

There is a slight difference between Chinese and Indian enterprises on charity; the former donate their wealth to society, while the latter works for the poor. With deep insight, it is related to the thoughts of Confucianism and Hinduism, respectively. Confucianism emphasises "*qiong-ze du-shan qi-shen, da-ze jian-shan tian-xia*" (*Meng Zi*) which means "If poor, they attended to their own virtue in solitude; if advanced to dignity, they made the whole land under heaven virtuous as well". Hinduism emphasizes to care for the weak and the poor at the very beginning. So the Chinese tend to reduce the poor, and Indians tend to care for them. At the government level, it is a target to reduce the poor, and policies and plans are formed in China. However, in India, the government makes policy to take care of the poor. The influence on the market is that there are many products in India specially made for the poor (See 6.3.2.3).

Moreover, in China, products do not have any unique feature for the poor but to motivate the poor to become rich. The Chinese are keen on increasing wealth, but Indians have a different view. This difference produces challenges for their general economic philosophy. It hinders development in the foreign market by using domestic economic strategy. Therefore, there should be a strategic adjustment to adapt the market towards outsiders where different cultures exist.

8.2.2.4. Less Cultural Influence and Reduction

For enterprises in steel, energy and so on, culture seems to have less influence on cross-nation business [except for enterprises involved in the cultural sector such as the Ashapura Group (See 8.2.2.2)]. Regarding information collected from businessmen of heavy industry, the cultural influence has hardly been mentioned or made aware of. Obviously, along with the improvement of the commercial mechanism and the relative rule of law, the economic interaction could be institutionalised and economised, and the cultural influence reduced.

Chinese businessmen pay more importance on verbal promises. In other words, the Chinese generally would strictly adhere to what they have said no matter whether it was formal or informal. However, when the *lun-ren* deal with Homo Hierarchicus, they belatedly found the latter do not attach more importance to what has been written (Pan 2018). With the normalisation of China-India economic interaction, this scenario of cultural conflict could be reduced. China and India signed the Agreement for the Promotion and Protection of Investments on 16 November 2006 (DEA 2006) (date of enforcement 1 August 2007, date of termination Wednesday, October 3, 2018) and amended the bilateral tax treaty in order to prevent tax evasion by allowing the exchange of information in November 2018 (PTI 2018).

8.2.2.5. Contradiction of Cognition

Indian national leaders have a high development goal for India's global positioning. Former PM Jawaharlal Nehru had stated that,

> "India, constituted as she is, cannot play a secondary part in the world. She will either count for a great deal or not count at all. No middle

> position attracted me. Nor did I think any intermediate position is feasible." (Nehru 1946:56).

Indian companies are also very ambitious. "At JSW Steel, we believe that India's journey to becoming a superpower is almost complete". This is written on the website of JSW Steel Limited which shows the national pride of "India's leading manufacturer of value-added and high-end steels" with "a total capacity of 18 million tons per annum (MTPA)" and a target of 40 MTPA by "scaling up existing plants and opening new ones" (JSW Steel 2018). JSW Steel was founded in 1982 and has "partnered the country in its journey to self-reliance" for "the last 35 years"; it is "India's largest exporter of steel with a presence in more than 100 countries" (Ibid.).

The Chinese government respects the positioning of India, but the voices that disapprove this are in the majority. Although India is growing very fast and recognised as a BRICS country, many Chinese do not treat India as a major power. It was said the "Chinese never care about Indians, but only for people from the USA, UK [...] and their view on Indians is very negative" [because of social issues such as numerous rape cases] (Sarma 2017). It is a big problem for people-to-people contacts between China and India and probably will last for the next few years. Still, the perception at the national level is much better. The governmental perception, in this sense, is a positive factor in economic relations.

8.2.2.6. Guanxi for Indian Companies and Chinese Skill

After engaging with the Chinese, Indians could see the importance of the business culture, especially *guanxi,* in the economic field. A graduate of Harvard Business School and Chairman of Metallon Holding Limited (MHL) Rajeshwar Mishra is described as "an expert on Indo-China business and culture" in a brochure of the group (MHL 2017:4). Interestingly, it was mentioned that they "have had presence in Asia Pacific for over a decade and due to '*guanxi*', [and] are in a position to arrange funds for promising projects" (Ibid: 3). The managing director of this group "has been in China since 1997 and has developed an in-depth understanding of China Business Culture" (Ibid: 5). Meanwhile, an excellent skill in Mandarin and fondness to "listen to Chinese music" could also be positive factors while doing business with the Chinese (Ibid: 6). It is seen as the strength to develop contacts in China by the Indian director (Mishra 2017). "*Guanxi*" and "loss of face" are seen as two important aspects in Chinese business culture. *Guanxi* is recognized as friendship.

> "In China's culture of doing business, *guanxi* is very important, if they are friends, they do lots of business together, they help each other, and they don't want to have any loss of face in business or even in personal life, which is not the case in...I think I must not say this as an Indian but...some of these attributes are missing in Indian business culture. Not everybody is proactive, the reflection of Chinese business culture

> is, I don't want to say totally missing but little less than the Chinese in India. Maybe that is the reason they are lagging behind, but they are picking up gradually [...] (Mishra 2017).

By having a deep insight into China's culture, the businessman of India in China is comfortable and professional in the market. In the same way, it would also be meaningful for Chinese businessmen to understand Indian culture.

8.2.2.7. Environmental Concern and Hindu Values

Environmental concern, which is a precious quality, is one feature of an Indian group, especially for a heavy industry company. It is mentioned in the mission statement of iron and steel products producer Rashmi Group that,

> "We are committed to work in the true spirit of entrepreneurship by making optimum utilization of resources, using environment friendly procedures and practices, maintaining highest work ethics, hiring the best people and providing them with a safe and healthy working environment."

While this healthy approach is not found only in Indian companies, Chinese groups are also highlighting "green development and a circular economy" (SDSTEEL 2010; HZSTEEL 2016). Although the environment is a global challenge, concern for it has Indian characteristics about the market; Chinese investors are surprised that assessment of environmental impacts is the top priority instead of profit, in an infrastructure project in India (Gu 2017). Except for the exclusion caused by the mistrust of India towards China, it becomes an obstacle for Chinese investors when Indian enthusiasm waned while protection of the ecological environment was discussed (Ibid.).

Concern for the environment is probably not only because of the internationalisation and the relative transparency of the Indian market but also influenced by Indian values, especially Hinduism values. For instance, "one of the major teachings" *ahimsa* (no violence, no killing to all living beings), and *karma* which "determines an individual's status within the cycle of rebirth" (Budhraj et al. 2014:65), *dharma* ["In Hinduism, protecting the environment is an important expression of *dharma*. Safeguarding the environment is an integral part of Hindu '*Dharma*' and often termed as a duty, virtue, cosmic order, and faith." (Budhraj et al. 2014: 69)]. In the spiritual texts of Hinduism such as the *Vedas*, *Puranas*, *Upanishads*, *Sutras*, and various sacred texts, , "the worship of the divine in nature" is directed and "millions of Hindus recite Sanskrit chants daily to venerate their mountains, rivers, trees, animals, and the earth" (Budhraj et al. 2014: 64). Those values influence the people greatly in India. This kind of environmental concept has become the habitual thought processes of Indians, internalising into ways of thinking and affecting external behaviours. For instance, in daily life, Indians naturally do not intentionally kill animals, insects or other living beings. They protect trees and plants and even worship trees. It is held that Indians consider should be merited for this even though the outside world considers it feudal and superstitious. The behaviour of Indians to worship nature, animals and trees could be mysterious for others.

Certainly, Hinduism's protection of the environment is a paradox. There is sincere love for nature and non-malicious destruction on the one hand, and on the other, the widespread bursting of firecrackers during Deepawali, the ancient festival of celebration. (This is also done during the Chinese New Year, though the government of China has controlled the activity strictly.) There is also the tradition of dumping cremation residue and statues of effigies in Indian rivers during Ganesh Chaturthi and Durga Pooja. Such practices still prevail. Considering the destruction of the environment through cherished rituals and ceremonies, it is also realised that "the effect of Hinduism on the environment is debatable" (Budhraj et al. 2014: 69-70).

8.2.2.8. Reliance: Cultural Principle and Gita Wisdom

Although they have split from the same Reliance Group that was founded by Dhirubhai Ambani, comparing the Reliance Anil Dhirubhai Ambani Group and Reliance Industries Limited, shows the latter more in line with the cultural principle behind its business (RADAG 2008; RIL 2018). Taking "Growth is Life" as their motto, and "to touch the lives of people in a positive way" as their ultimate aim, and adopt the ethos of its founder "to create India's largest company" by "converting adversity into opportunity and making the possible by challenging conventional wisdom", Reliance Industries Limited, a "Fortune 500 company and the largest private sector corporation in India", shows its modern spirit very clearly (RIL 2018a).

Still, there is a quotation at the top of Founder-Chairman Dhirubhai Ambani's introduction from the *Bhagavad Gita* (3:21), "Whatever action a great man performs, common men follow. And whatever standards he sets by exemplary acts, the entire world pursues" (RIL 2018b). These words from a classic Indian work are probably an important source that encouraged Dhirubhai, "from being a school teacher's son in the village of Chorwad to an unparalleled creator of wealth" (RIL 1998), to follow his corporate philosophy, "Think big. Think differently. Think fast. Think ahead. Aim for the best." (RIL 2018b). The value of Hinduism is an important source for ideas for this business mogul. Even though it is a large modern enterprise, the origin of its organisational thought is still related to the classic philosophy of Hinduism.

It is hard to say that this company is related to Hinduism in every respect, or that it does not fully show the characteristics of Hinduism (moreover, other cultures may have similar ideas), yet it can be inferred from the tip of the iceberg that Hindu values are influential to the leaders of this enterprise. As an important source of guiding thoughts, this aspect shows that enterprises growing up in an

Hindu environment attach importance to and apply traditional ideas, and, more importantly, such ideas coming from the *Bhagavad Gita* could become something for the employees to imitate, that is, continue to draw from Hinduism in work and life.

Although Hinduism is comprehensive and profound, with various ideas that are different or similar to other ideas, it is difficult to avoid observing the situation of development in this cultural background through an in-depth analysis of Hinduism. In particular, the community of different cultures in the process of evolving in India cannot ignore the characteristics of Hindu culture that permeate various fields.

8.2.2.9. Canara Bank: from the Pai Custom to Remove Superstition and Ignorance

Canara Bank was named Canara Bank Hindu Permanent Fund when it was founded in 1906, and renamed Canara Bank Limited in 1910, and nationalised in 1969. The founder, the late Sri Ammembal Subbarao Pai, took the following lines as "founding principles" of the bank. "A good bank is not only the financial heart of the community; but also one with an obligation of helping in every possible manner to improve the economic conditions of the common people" and "to remove superstition and ignorance", "to spread education among all, to sub-serve the first principle", "to inculcate the habit of thrift and savings", "to develop a concern for fellow human beings and sensitivity to the surroundings with a view to make changes/remove hardships and sufferings" (Canara Bank 2018). Concern for the poor was the main motivation to set up the bank,

> "Shri Pai's concern for the poor and illiterate inspired the formation of the bank and a group of educational institutions. Seeing the problems faced by poor, helpless people who had to pay exorbitant rates of interest charged by private moneylenders, Shri Pai was firm in his desire to establish an institution to render assistance to the community" (Madhukar and Prabhu: 108).

Besides, the motivation related more to culture regarding the establishment of the bank was recorded by M.V. Kamath in his book *A Banking Odyssey: The Story of Canara Bank*,

> "[...] the Gowd Saraswat Brahmins had a custom wherein on the birth of a child in the family, a certain sum of money was deposited with wealthy persons called 'Pattan Shetties' on the understanding that the same would be paid back to the beneficiary when the child became an adult. The money deposited carried no interest. The trouble was that the 18-year span was too long and there was no written understanding. This led to disputes and many widows reportedly went to Subba Rao

seeking redress in courts. This, it is believed, prompted him to start a bank." (*The Hindu* 2005).

The Gowd (also spelt Goud or Gawd) Saraswat Brahmins are a community which the founder of Carana Bank Ammembal Subbarao Pai belonged to, and Pai is a surname found among Hindus of this community. From the case of Canara Bank, it shows the connection of the custom of a Hindu community with the economy in India. Compared to the influence of religious or cultural rituals, the influence of Hinduism on this concept has been related to modern elements in external performance. However, an in-depth exploration of the source is conducive to understanding and analysing the motives behind it, so that the source of far-reaching influence can be included in the important factors of the overall performance of the analysis. By an analysis of the source, it is not difficult to understand its appearance. Understanding it becomes the basis for further mutual understanding and even mutual respect.

8.2.2.10. Summary

It can be seen that Hindu philosophy is an important source for many Indian corporate cultures. Meanwhile, open sources show that the cultural influence is easier to find among Indians. With the governance of a strong central government, Chinese commercial units have become more identical and modernised when compared with Indian ones. It reflects that on the one hand, transparency is more emphasised in India, society, which made India companies show all necessary information in the open. On the other hand, the pluralism and meticulous diversity in India made Indian commercial units need to show their identity in a more clear way to attract potential customers. In summary, Confucianism and Hinduism more or less influenced the business of companies. The cultural differences between these two have created some misunderstandings, even conflicts. More important is that there were serious conflicts that happened in Indian society related to the cultural differences between different faith groups in India. It forces Chinese companies in India to pay high attention to cultural taboos. The neglect of Chinese culture by Indian companies also created certain problems. Meanwhile, to be conversant with Chinese culture made it more expedient for Indian companies to do business in China.

8.3. Culture, Disputes and Economic Relations

8.3.1. Border Dispute

One of the direct influences of border tensions on economic relations is that India restricts visitors from China. Visa approval is a great hindrance for Chinese businessmen to come to India; it normally takes three months or more. Meanwhile, the rise of an anti-Chinese products movement is also an outcome of the dispute along with the rise of nationalism in India (Anderson and Geiger 2010:125). It was pointed out "the sale of Chinese goods declined by 30 per cent to 50 per cent during Diwali in 2016 caused by the boycott of Chinese goods in India (Mahajan 2017:10). Although it was claimed to be "not the only reason behind the campaign against Chinese goods", the Doklam standoff that took place in June 2017 provided "more fire" to the economic wing of the Rashtriya Swayamsevak Sangh (RSS) Swadeshi Jagran Manch's boycott Chinese movement (Mahajan 2017:10). Behind the fears of India towards China caused by the border dispute, there are cultural factors that play crucial roles.

From a cultural perspective, to analyse economic relations, border disputes are placed in the position of intermediate variables, that is, culture affects the strategy on border disputes, which, in turn, affect economic relations. Given the fact that there is also a dispute over the border between China and Bhutan which did not cause excessive conflict, the conflict between China and India is undeniably related to Indian strategic thought including strong cultural values. It was pointed out that the Doklam/Donglang confrontational crisis had a profound influence on Indian strategic culture, including "'the Mandala concept in Indian traditional culture' (from the Kautilya's *Arthashastra*) and 'Brahman supreme thought' (from the ideological base of the Hinduism caste system)..." and so on (Hu 2017:13). The conflict of territorial interests between India and China is also closely related to the "continuous development of Hindu nationalism in India" (Ibid: 15, 17). It can be seen that some ideas in Hinduism have led to India's mighty psychology, especially in the dispute with China. The influence of territorial disputes is a major issue in economic relations, which limits Chinese investment in India, and trade and economic cooperation.

8.3.2. Boycotting Chinese products in India: Swadeshi, SJM and Dharma

Boycotting Chinese products is also influencing Chinese business in India, which has a cultural root. A campaign to "promote domestic goods across the nation" launched by the Swadeshi Jagran Manch (SJM) was kicked off at New Delhi's Ramlila Maidan on 29 October 2017 in which boycotting Chinese goods was part of a nationwide campaign. It was claimed the Sangh Parivar's top brass, representatives from civil society, and outfits would participate; 75 lakh people pledged to reject "substandard" Chinese products, the "swadeshi" message would be spread to "two crore households", in order to "safeguard the interests of the nation", "create job opportunities", "promote a market for produce indigenously produced [indigenously]" instead of "depending on China or any other country" (Gusai 2017).

The Swadeshi Jagran Manch (SJM) was founded on 22 November 1991 at Nagpur; today more than 15 organisations are associated with it, [...] having an all-India network of sub-units up to district or block levels across the country (SJM 2017a). It is believed that Swadeshi is a "living tradition of India" (SJM 2017b), which is "via Hindi from Sanskrit 'of one's own country', reference to a nationalist movement advocating Indian-made products" (OD 2017). It was pointed out that "Swadeshi life is based on *Dharma*" (SJM 2017b). The SJM claimed it is,

> "actively coordinating with all those people and organizations that believe in the Swadeshi viewpoint, and in the process have become an important link between the lowest strata of society and policy planners and opinion makers at the national level" (SJM 2017a).

Its vision and action plan are "for a truly self-reliant *Bharat* [India] and equitable world order that nobody can afford to ignore" (Ibid.). In this sense, compared with the behaviour to oppose products of other countries, the ideology of the SJM, in the terms of an "equitable world order that nobody can afford to ignore", seems a positive value as it helps to protect the interests of the weak. Nevertheless, the interests of the other side could be threatened.

The Swadeshi Jagran Manch has been "time and again" cautioning that "China is the biggest threat to our [Indian] economy, employment of our [Indian] youth, our [India] national security and our [India] national integrity" (SJMNC 2017). The SJM made the year 2017 a year of "a campaign against Chinese goods, Chinese investments and Chinese companies, to save the nation from the Chinese onslaught". The logic was to "make ordinary people realize the need to buy Indian goods so that our [Indian] workers get jobs". The SJM claimed they had got signatures of one crore people who had pledged to boycott Chinese and other foreign-made goods. It showed that Chinese products were not the only target of its agenda but all foreign goods. The SJM works for the 'sole' interests of the nation. It should be noted that this resolution of the SJM was announced on 20-21 May 2017 before the Doklam standoff (June 2017). The campaign was not directly linked with the standoff with China but influenced more by its philosophy. It is part of a move to promote anti-China emotions in India and improve the popularity of native enterprises that could be a challenge towards foreign enterprises including Chinese. The reasons why the SJM organised the boycott were openly stated. It sees China as the biggest threat to India due to the following situations: 78 times increase of import ("almost all types of manufactured products") from China in the last 19 years since from 1996 to 1997, equivalent to about 22 per cent of Indian domestic manufacturing; and Chinese employment of Indians "fast increasing employable youth employment and our [Indian] demographic dividend" which the SJM considers as "being squandered into the hands of China" (Ibid.).

After the Doklam standoff, it was said by the national spokesperson of the BJP (Economic Affairs) Gopal Krishna Agarwal that "India and China will be working together to do away with the growing trade deficit in the country", which was claimed by Agarwal to be mainly because of the "import of manufactured goods from China" and "mainly affecting small and medium scale industries", and that "the government is doing its best to help domestic industries to flourish amidst competition from Chinese goods." (ANI 2017). It is noticeable that the SJM was deemed as a supporter of small and medium-scale industries in India by leading the "voluntary campaign", the 'Swadeshi Abhiyan' (mission) which was emphasised and compared to "Mahatma Gandhi's Swadeshi movement" (Ibid.). The consistency of opinion is clearly shown in the information above. Thus, to ignore the force of the SJM may cause huge hidden trouble.

8.3.3. The Attitude of Individual and Organisational Levels on Disputes

The influence of culture on economic relations during the border dispute can be examined by how the two sides faced the conflict at three levels. Firstly, the individual level, i.e., people's commercial behaviour; secondly, the organisational level, given that the SJM is the economic wing of the RSS so that it will be considered as an organisation here; and thirdly, at the national level, i.e., the government's attitude. In the first level, commercial behaviour was mainly reflected in the form of a boycott of the other side. It is a reasonable or understandable reflection to withstand the other country when one's own country is facing a severe problem, especially on the issue of territory. This is like the Chinese did when they held anti-Japanese products protests during the *Diaoyu* Island dispute when China claimed that Japan's had illegally occupied the Island.

One thought-provoking phenomenon regarding the Doklam standoff is why Indians protested against Chinese products when China claimed that India had intruded into its territory. Meanwhile, the Indian government said it was to help Bhutan as Bhutan has a treaty with India. Why then did not a similar boycott happen in China? This was discussed by Chinese netizens online to boycott Indian products when the news of anti-Chinese products in India was reported in the Chinese media. However, one of the conclusions could be that it would be difficult for Chinese netizens to find an Indian product to boycott except for spices and essential oils (WB 2017). Although the origin of Yoga is Indian, it was not discussed because it is quite popular to the Chinese who are too sinicised to think it is from India. It also reflected the real problem of the trade deficit between China and India, that is, extremely less imports from India to China. There is no such organisation like the SJM based on its culture in China.

On the Indian side, the sizeable boycott was taken seriously. The Swadeshi Jagaran Manch (SJM) held its anti-Chinese product campaign from 9 August 2017. Its aim was to oppose all the products made by foreign countries and "attempt to tap into the bitter border tussle" on Doklam (Maitra 2017). The organisers wanted the government to "scrap all contracts with Chinese companies setting up manufacturing units in India" and "sought prohibition of any new venture by Chinese firms setting up manufacturing facilities here in the light of the 'continued transgression and intimidating activities at the border'." (Maitra 2017). When China-India economic relations are examined, historical cases could remind one of the importance of the SJM and the Sangh Parivar. The first massive campaign of the SJM was on 12 January 1992, the birth anniversary of Swami Vivekananda, against the economic policy of the Central Government as well as "economic imperialism" (Swadeshionline 2017). The SJM has boycott McDonald in religious places and made it open completely vegetarian restaurants. The supervising authority of the SJM, i.e., the Sangh Parivar, had destroyed the British by boycotting their products (Maitra 2017).

8.3.4. The Attitude at the National Level towards Disputes

However, the approach of the Indian government was openly different. It suggested, on 15 July 2017, to party leaders to ensure that India would be "patient and peaceful" in dealing with its neighbouring countries (ENS 2017). It is reported that the then Defence Minister Arun Jaitley and External Affairs Minister Sushma Swaraj had mentioned that they would not act rashly "despite provocations" (Ibid.). The consensus at the meeting was to resolve the issue through negotiations with China. D. Raja of the Communist Party of India suggested that the government use existing mechanisms and consultations to deal with disputes. He pointed to the growing Sino-Indian trade relations and that both China and India are members of the Shanghai Cooperation Organization and BRICS. "China must be equally concerned about the standoff with India. Both countries should talk to resolve it (Ibid).

The China Railway Major Bridge Engineering Group Ltd. planned to construct a proposed 22-km sea-link in Navi Mumbai, but clearance was denied by the Home Ministry of India. Indian Foreign Minister Sushma Swaraj said in response to a question from members of the Congress Party in the Rajya Sabha (Council of States, the upper house of the Parliament of India) on 28 July 2017 that there was no policy to veto the security permission to the Chinese company (SC 2017). Later, the Indian government, under the tension of the border between the two countries, reasserted that the Chinese investment security clearance had not affected India. A spokesperson of the Ministry of Home Affairs (which is "the nodal authority for giving security go-ahead to foreign investments under the National Security Clearance Policy") declared "the issue of putting on hold security nods given to Chinese investment proposals was 'not under any consideration'" and "clearance to investment proposals is given on the basis of a well-established procedure laid down in the past. There is no change in the policy." (TNN 2017).

It seems the border dispute has not significantly affected China-India economic relations at the national level from the Indian side. Despite spurring by the RSS and social media and voices of boycotting Chinese goods in India had gradually increased, Chinese products are still in an advantageous position, whether in household goods, market supply or commercial trade. Chief Economist D. K. Joshi of the global analytical company Crisil pointed out that despite the imbalance in China-India trade, bilateral trade continues to grow and political differences have not affected trade between the two countries. China is India's largest trading partner; bilateral trade has reached US$ 71.5 billion and the trade deficit has reached $ 51.1 billion in 2016-17 from $ 37.2 billion in 2011-12 (Goyal 2017).

Although the Indian government has shown rationality and restraint towards China-India economic relations during the period of tension between the two countries, Hindu culture affects the attitude of the individuals and organisations in India along with the Modi government's hardball attitude in handling disputed territorial affairs. Further, it affects the economic relations between the two countries in some respects. The solidification of border issues and territorial disputes has been long-pending which leads low trust among the two countries and hinders the development of their relations" (Zhou Shuai 2016:24). India's strong concepts, including Hindu cultural ones, is brewing resistance to China in Indian society. In this sense, the border dispute is a challenge for bilateral economic relations as it influences the perception towards each other. Although India is the biggest trading partner of China in South Asia, it was considered that India has,

> "limited economic interdependence with China", and "Unlike China's East Asian neighbours, India has the capacity to absorb pressures from Beijing [...] Delhi can bear the costs of a severed commercial relationship. If India could turn its back on the dominant powers of the West for many decades during the Cold War, it could do that with China again." (Mohan 2017).

The Indian elite has a different understanding of economic development with China, which believes economic development is the most crucial target in the last few decades. The small scale of the China-India bilateral trade volume might also be a reason to make India consider "limited economic interdependence with China". Meanwhile, as a society with diverse voices, it is argued in India that "China's massive infusion of finished goods, such as mobile phones and others, are the core drivers of the Indian economy and impossible to substitute." (Iyer-Mitra, 2017). This reasonable comment is based on Indian interests in another aspect, as it is believed that,

> "[...], if we choose to go against China, we might as well kiss goodbye to any chance of UN Security Council and Nuclear Suppliers' Group (NSG) membership. In this situation, Doklam is a win, an emphatic win, the best possible under the circumstances, marking the first serious Indian (and arguably global) pushback to Chinese salami tactics." (Iyer-Mitra 2017)

Besides, the other negative element in China-India economic relations is the competition of these two nations in South Asia. The economic cooperation of China with other South Asian countries has always been observed and compared in India. It was pointed out that China lends $ 301 million at an interest rate of 6.3 per cent to Sri Lanka, while the interest of the World Bank and Asian Development Bank is only 0.25-3 per cent. India's Line of Credit to neighbouring countries is as low as 1 per cent,

> "China's strategy to grab land is simple: it gives them loans on high rates for infrastructural projects, and when the country is unable to repay the loan, it gets ownership of the project." (ET 2017)

The views of the Indian media on China are unique and critical. It should be noted that without knowing the traditional values of China on peace and the economy (2.4.2), it is difficult to understand the initiatives proposed by the Chinese government.

It should also be highlighted that the influence of traditional culture is not easy to detect, but the influence is enduring. In the *Organizer*, the mouthpiece of the Rashtriya Swayamsevak Sangh (RSS), an article said that India should form the "One Culture One Region" (OCOR) for the Eurasian countries like the South Asian Association for Regional Cooperation (SAARC) to respond to China's "imperialistic concept" (Shankar and Mishra 2017). It was said that the "One Belt and One Road" (OBOR) could not fulfil the current "cultural vacuum" in Europe and Asia. This cultural gap needs a "human and philosophical approach" to fulfil, "Only India has the past of doing so" and history is not enough to support China's initiative (Ibid.),

> "Hindu traders were at the heart of Eurasian economics. It was India, not China, that developed the region as a trading hub, contributed culturally in the form of ancient Hindu and Buddhist thoughts to make this region a peaceful place [...]" (Ibid.).

The RSS is influenced by Hinduism. Moreover, it has an impact on the Bharatiya Janata Party. This cultural inheritance and competitive attitude need to be given enough attention.

Given that improvement of Comprehensive National Power (CNP) is the first and most important task for both India and China and the quite low volume of economic activity between these two neighbouring countries, the border dispute should not be developed to be a significant constraint for relations of the two countries. It would be a more significant loss for both sides. It was believed that it would be regretful if the development of relations in other areas is hijacked by the border dispute between these two Asian giants (Lu 2017). The mechanism of dialogue should be promoted more strongly and effectively. Moreover, the different aspects of bilateral relations could not become a massive influence on the others.

8.4. Conclusion

8.4.1. Cultural Dimensions of Trade, Investment and Economic Cooperation

Firstly, in trade aspect, it was found that the trading items of China and India are not influenced by culture. Yet, the trade relations are affected by cultural concepts and the trade policy of India is influenced by Hindu culture. Culture is also influencing market demands. For example, Hindu culture creates the demand for statues of deities that are mainly imported from China to India.

Secondly, in the cultural dimensions of investment, the characteristics of the Indian "civilizational entity" have many factors to influence Chinese investments. The cultural factors influence potentially in terms of economic nationalism, which has a connection with Hinduism, especially under the governance of the Bharatiya Janata Party. The economic nationalism of India caused a movement against foreign products in Indian society. Chinese products were also targeted not only during the border disputes. For India, cultural differences with China have hindered the development of its investment in China. It caused cultural conflicts that hindered business by India in China. Noticeably, the influence of cultural factors is related to Confucianism and Hinduism.

Thirdly, the economic cooperation has also been affected by cultural differences that increased the psychological distance. The number of despatched labourers from China to India has shown considerable scope for bilateral economic cooperation. Culture is not well understood by the other side, although the negative perceptions of the Chinese to India is reducing along with the deeper interaction between these two old civilisations. Still, to create a new type of a big-nation cooperation model for mutual benefit and a win-win situation needs the efforts of generations. The China-India High Level Mechanism on Cultural and People-to-People Exchanges is an excellent starting point for a new era of bilateral relations. It would promote economic relations along with the enhancement of mutual understanding if the mechanism could function effectively.

8.4.2. Cultural Dimensions of Companies

For the Chinese companies in India, culture plays a role in the advertising of their businesses. Better knowledge of the culture leads to better business. Meanwhile, culture could influence particular businesses such as dealing in leather products and food. There are some bans on food relating to frogs, eggs, beef and so on by central or local governments in India. Among these, the most severe taboo is cow slaughter. Conflicts caused by cow protectors have erupted many times in India. Although they happened among Indians, it needs to a matter of great concern for Chinese companies and individuals in India especially considering that three Chinese employees of China Coal India were arrested under the Maharashtra Animal Preservation Act for possessing 10 kg beef at Khapa (Dabas 2019).

Besides, the different attitudes towards poverty caused different performances by the two governments and companies from the two civilisations. China works on the basis of poverty alleviation, while in India, emphasis is laid on caring for the poor and producing cheap products for them.

The caste system has influenced the choice of occupations for Homo Hierarchicus to a certain extent; it more or less influences the speed of learning a new skill for Homo Hierarchicus and could influence the business of the Chinese in India by reducing efficiency. Enterprises have shown their sense of duty towards the poor, and towards the culture and history of the nation. It is reflected more obviously in Indian enterprises. It might be summarised that Indian successful enterprises are not merely focusing on economic benefits for themselves and that comparatively, Chinese companies might be more concentrated on business and developing their commercial empires. (Certainly, there are many Chinese entrepreneurs who are very keen on charity.) The concept towards the poor has influenced the policy of government and companies. It also made for different performances of the two nations and could be used as a factor to explain the economic development of the two civilisations. In short, economic benefit is not the only concern for Indians but is a core concern for the Chinese too.

It seems there is a less cultural influence on the business of heavy industry, but in actual implementation, cultural differences could cause misunderstandings in any industry. For instance, the different attitudes towards verbal promise, which is part of the *xin* (trust) culture, especially in China, has consistently caused negative perceptions towards Indians among the Chinese who are not aware of their cultural differences. A certain extent of asymmetric perceptions towards each other, especially at the people's level is obstructing the growth of economic interaction. Meanwhile, an understanding of the culture of the other side could be a positive element to improve business. For example, the understanding of *guanxi* would help Indians to be more comfortable and confident in the Chinese market.

Indeed, there are similarities in the different civilisations, but in performance, there are different reasons for commercial thought and behaviour. Like the attitude towards the environment. The Hindu philosophy on nature influences their concerns on the environment which ideally could be beyond the expectations of their Chinese counterparts who could be discouraged after knowing the different priorities and tedious approval procedure in economic activities. Moreover, it shows that the Hindu classic work, the *Bhagavad Gita,* still influence a large business group of India. It can be seen in the vitality of traditional values. Although the traditional cultural characteristics of the business group could be reduced in modern society, it cannot be denied that some Hindu traditions have been the incentive for setting up businesses that could influence the choices of customers.

8.4.3. Cultural Dimension of Disputes in Economic Relations

Hindu thought influences Indian strategic thought in terms of cultural value. It led to the strong position of India on the border issue with China, which is a fundamental factor that affects bilateral economic relations. The boycotting of Chinese products in India is a specific manifestation of the conflict. The Hindu concept of *dharma* is an essential motivation for protecting the small industries of India through boycotting Chinese goods. Given that it could be developed in a more severe form from historical experience, its influence on economic relations could not be avoided although it is not extremely subversive yet.

Although this influence of cultural difference is rarely analysed, particularly in the available literature and especially in the field of China-India economic relations, the impact of the cultural difference has been gradually recognised by researchers. Yet, there is a gap between recognising the difference and shaping mutual understanding. Exploring the root cause is a way to lessen this gap. In addition to some cultural roots discussed above, combined with the particular cultural analysis of the third chapter, the cultural influence network behind the superficial phenomenon in the economy could be gradually constructed. The cultural influence network behind the economy could play an important auxiliary role in creating a way to weaken the negative impact of issues on the economic relations mentioned in this chapter. By understanding and applying the culture influence network, it could be beneficial for promoting economic relations between China and India.

CHAPTER 9

ASSESSING THE IMPACT OF CULTURE ON CHINA-INDIA ECONOMIC RELATIONS

9.1. Introduction

This research compares the differences between Chinese traditional culture (Confucianism) and Indian traditional culture (Hinduism)[34] and assesses the influence of the differences on the economic relations of the two countries. Data from the "Global Leadership and Organizational Behavior Effectiveness" (GLOBE) Research Project (hereinafter referred to as GLOBE) is used to support the analysis of the previous three chapters. Although the samples chosen by GLOBE could not cover all the people influenced by Confucianism or Hinduism, it is a strong support to manifest the differences between the two dominant cultures. The seven cultural dimensions out of nine have been selected for this research, i.e., Performance Orientation, Power Distance, Future Orientation, Assertiveness, Humane Orientation, Uncertainty Avoidance, and Collectivism.[35] The two manifestations of the each dimension, i.e., cultural attributes ("Should Be") and cultural practices ("As Is"), respectively, represent "values, beliefs, schemas, and implicit theories commonly held among members of a collectivity (society or organization)" and "common behaviors, institutional practices, prescriptions, and proscriptions" of "entities such as families, schools, work organizations, economic and legal systems, political institutions, and the like" (Chhokar et al. 2007:4). The score (0-7) of each dimension of the project from

---

34 The two concepts of Psycho-Culturology, i.e., the *Lun-ren* and Homo Hierarchicus, are used to refer to Chinese or Indian individuals influenced by Confucian culture or Hindu culture, respectively. On the one hand, it narrows the scope of this research. On the other, it emphasises that the analysis of objects are individuals who are deeply influenced by Confucianism or Hinduism.

35 The original In-Group Collectivism and Institutional Collectivism have been combined under Collectivism. The dimension of Gender Egalitarianism is not quoted, as this research does not involve gender material.

low to high shows the degree of the culture of inhibiting or contributing to a person from being or not being an outstanding leader. It is relevant to the degree of managerial ability in an organisation from the cultural perspectives.

Given the limitation of the data quoted from GLOBE for this research, the cultural influence on economic relations could explore deeper. However, in addition to the reference to the GLOBE's cultural dimension concept, this study also carried out a creative sublimation, that is, based on the exploration of cultural roots in the previous chapters and an analysis of the influence of culture on economic thought and behaviour, to extend the depth and breadth of the concepts of the GLOBE cultural dimension. Meanwhile, it is to be noted that the analysis of Chinese and Indian culture in the GLOBE is not limited to the relevant leadership, but also the relationship between culture and the behaviour of the individual or national. On this basis, this chapter makes up for the content that is not explicitly expressed in the words (some findings only showed the data but without a detailed explanation in GLOBE), and more clearly shows the impact of culture on the economy at different levels, i.e., individual, organisational, and national, as well as the cultural conflicts caused by cultural differences. This chapter also classifies the degree of cultural conflicts and the extent of their impact on economic relations based on descriptions of the phases of cultural conflicts in Intercultural Communication. The combination of the analysis among the cultural factors in economy the (Chapter 6), the cultural origin of behavioural characteristics (Chapter 7), and the influence of culture on economic relations (Chapter 8) with the quantitative culture dimensions of the GLOBE research project could demonstrate the cultural dimensions of China-India economic relations qualitatively and quantitatively to a certain extent.

9.2. Seven Cultural Dimensions

9.2.1. Performance Orientation

It has been shown in Chapter 8 that there are apparent traditional factors in the establishment of Indian companies and management concepts, and Chinese companies are more modern and less affected by tradition. It has selected Indian companies in China, which are influenced by many cultural factors, such as caste, earlier occupation, and working skills of Homo Hierarchicus, which leads to different Performance Orientations with the *Lun-ren*. The difference in Performance Orientations affected the fluency of economic cooperation to a certain extent. Performance Orientation refers to "the extent to which high-level members of organizations and societies encourage and reward group members for performance improvement and excellence" (Chhokar 2007:4).

> "According to House, Javidan, Hanges, and Dorfman (2002) and House et al. (2004), GLOBE's Performance Orientation is similar to Hofstede and Bond's (1988) Confucian work dynamism, which

focuses on social hierarchy, protecting the status quo, and personal virtue. The Chinese score was among the higher ranking countries on "As Is" (4.45, Rank 13), which is supportive of the traditional Chinese culture in which hard work and diligence were highly praised and appreciated." (Fu et al. 2007:886-887)

GLOBE scholars explained the possible reasons of the low score of "Should Be" for Chinese-speaking societies as , firstly, "the tendency of the Chinese to score toward the mean as a result of the influence of the 'doctrine of mean' [*zhong-yong*]"; secondly, "the Chinese think good performance is already highly encouraged", and thirdly, "the Chinese, being more collectivistic, may not like extreme emphasis on encouraging individual performances" (Fu et al. 2007:888).

The cultural attribute of India's Performance Orientation is much higher than China's score and rank, but the cultural practice is lower than China's. In Chapter 7's tracing of the core values of Chinese and Indian traditional culture, it can be seen that *karma* emphasises duty as an essential concept in Hinduism, which in turn emphasises performance of duty without attachment. It helps to understand the reason for the higher cultural attribute and lower cultural practice. In actual economic relations, according to the experience of Chinese business managers and related observations, the following comments can be stated: the mental state of Indian employees is always spirited and responsive, they always make managers comfortable in communication and have expectations of good results, but the results sometimes appear to be unsatisfactory. This is related to the emphasis on duty and the absence of attachment to the result in the culture of Homo Hierarchicus. Chinese managers who are unfamiliar with this cultural feature have a great psychological letdown. After experiencing high expectations and low actual reality, the Chinese have experienced disappointment and helplessness, which could hinder the development of relations. In cross-cultural management, this constitutes a cultural conflict or cultural shock (Oberg 1951), that is, people lose the familiar social communication signals or symbols, he/she is unfamiliar with the other's social symbols, so he/she has deep anxiety disorder psychologically. Intercultural Communication scholars point out that cultural conflict or shock involves four stages: honeymoon, depression (or hostility), adjustment and adaptation (Guan 1995:340-341). With in-depth interpretation and understanding of culture, cultural conflicts can be mitigated to a certain extent and then promote the development of relations.

Based on the description of the cultural conflict process in Intercultural Communication, this study classifies the degree of cultural conflict and the degree of its impact on economic relations, i.e.,

(1) Zero degree—the psychological manifestation is that cultural differences can be felt, but no influence on economic relations.

(2) Primary degree—the psychological manifestation is that the individual can feel depression because of the cultural differences and have a negative perception towards the other culture. It may hinder the smooth development of economic relations.
(3) Middle degree—the psychological manifestation is hostility; it can cause an attitude of passive cooperation towards the other culture and slow down the development of economic relations.
(4) Intermediate degree—the behavioural manifestation is a counterbalance,[36] the possible result is the limitation of or cancellation of the cooperation or even no cooperation. It could restrict the development of economic relations.
(5) High degree—the behavioural manifestation is aggressive action,[37] the possible result is boycotting the other's products or even indulge in trade war.
(6) Superlative degree—the behavioural manifestation is severing of diplomatic relations. Economic relations could also be severed.

Every society has incentives for excellent performance, and performance is an essential indicator of promotion. At the same time, every society has its traditional concept that could restrict or promote performance orientation. For example, the concept of *guanxi* in Chinese society is an important reference factor in personnel appointment and promotion, and it could also assist business expansion. Indian society is also constrained by traditional professional ideas, including the influence of caste on occupations. Of course, traditions also keep on changing in the process of cultural modernisation[38] such as entrepreneurial activities confined to specific community groups in Indian society, but "has started becoming more widespread" in the past few years, "and entrepreneurs have started attracting increasing social recognition" (Chhokar 2007:990). Tradition and modern concepts are intertwined in the process of modern development, and the interpretation of traditional ideas is still an indispensable factor of understanding modernity. Because the conventional concept of influence on people's deep thoughts, and as it is an essential factor to reflect national identity, it is continuously expanded and utilised. Traditional culture has a strong vitality. The influential German philosopher, Immanuel Kant, said that the core of culture is ultimately tied to the historical traditions and philosophical concepts of each nation. It has noted stability and will not change simply with

36 This can also be based on other considerations such as national interests or perceived imbalance in trade.

37 This can also be based on other reasons, such as no measures undertaken to reduce the existing trade deficit.

38 Cultural modernisation refers to the process of transforming the cultural model under conditions of traditional agricultural civilisation into a cultural model under the conditions of industrial civilisation (Xing 2011: 71).

changes in history (Xing 2011:75). It can be seen that culture affects performance, and the difference between cultural attributes and cultural practices of Performance Orientation will cause problems and even primary cultural conflict in economic interaction, which, in turn, will affect the development of economic relations. The gradual deep understanding and adaptation of cultural differences will shorten the stage of depression (hostility) and adjustment in cultural conflicts, thereby accelerating the development of economic relations.

9.2.2. Power Distance

Differences in the Power Distance dimensions of China and India also affect economic relations. Power Distance refers to "the degree to which members of an organization and society encourage and reward unequal distribution of power with greater power at higher levels" (Chhokar 2007:4). According to Jagdeep S. Chhokar (2007:991), Indian society is "quite structured and stratified" due to "the centuries-old caste system and almost 200 years of British rule" and the "Indian Civil Service, [...] was a very hierarchical and formal structure that has had a widespread impact on Indian organizations." [...] Eating places for workers and managers are often different". In the management processes of Chinese-funded companies in India, management personnel realised the different Power Distance in India. There are different counter-measures in various industries. Chinese manufacturers and builders have two different views on how Indian subordinates obey superior management. The builders pointed out that management could weaken the conflicts caused by cultural distinctions because Indian employees can implement rules and regulations more seriously (Bi 2019). Therefore, writing about the problems brought about by cultural differences (such as latecoming caused by the concept of time) into the rules and regulations can considerably reduce the negative impact (Ibid.).

However, Chinese manufacturers believe that when managing Indian employees, it is needed to "*gong-xin*" (play mind games) and fully take care of the feelings of Indian employees to make them better obey the management; otherwise, it may lead to loss of personnel (Hu 2019). This seems to contradict the characteristics of Indian "Power Distance". Theoretically, India's hierarchical concept is stronger, and subordinates are more likely to obey the leadership; but in practice, if without full consideration of the feelings of Indian employees, it may lead to employee turnover. Developing the analysis in detail, it can be found that different business situations and employee levels will have different phenomena. For example, the majority of employees of Chinese manufacturers who own factories are Indian technical workers. Chinese builders mostly face Indian management and service personnel. (Although there are many skilled workers at construction sites, they are managed by local people.)

Moreover, according to Chinese builders, Indian workers are much less efficient than Chinese workers; this includes factors such as cultural environment (time concept) and natural environment (hot summer climate). An analysis of culture can be said to be a macroscopic interpretation perspective at this level, and some specific issues require specific examination. In combination with the views of different industry personnel, the cultural characteristics of Indian employees should be considered in some matters; for example, in addition to maintaining the leadership image, managers should show respect to Indian employees, as well as honour their food culture in order to avoid discomfort or even depression, which may cause a tendency of diminishing of Indian staff. The following is an in-depth analysis of Power Distance in conjunction with the GLOBE data.

According to the outcome of the GLOBE project, the two Chinese scores on Power Distance are 5.04 ("As Is", cultural practices) and 3.10 ("Should Be", cultural attribute) (3.10) and the two Indian scores are 5.47 ("As Is") and 2.64 ("Should Be") (Fu et al. 2007:891,993).[39] The data shows the Indian cultural attribute of Power Distance (Should Be, 2.64) is lower than that of the Chinese, but the cultural practice ("As Is", 5.47) is higher than that of the Chinese (5.04). Chinese scholars pointed out that "Indian subordinates tend to be very respectful to their superiors", but if the superior "expresses arrogance or pays too much attention to his power status, he will be resented rather than respected by Indian subordinates"; for instance, "a company headed by a superior from the USA[40] has twice employee turnover rate than an Indian team headed by an Indian. One possible reason is that people are not happy with a manager who places too much emphasis on power distance." (Jiang Lu et al. 2008:37).

Compared with the Chinese, perhaps the higher "cultural practice" (As Is) score of Indians could prove they tend more to have a hierarchical distance (5.47>5.04), but their cultural attribute is less when the superior is arrogant or pompously self-important compared to the Chinese (2.64 <3.10). Chinese managers should pay attention to maintaining Power Distance with their Indian subordinates, but at the same time, they should not be too arrogant. When Indian superiors manage Chinese subordinates, perhaps Indians are more inclined to have a sense of being respected in reality, and their cultural attribute (Should Be) is not as concerned about Power Distance as the Chinese and hope to mingle with the employees. The Indian financial industry manager who was interviewed in Beijing told the author,

> "I feel that Chinese people are more reserved [than Indians], they never allow their personal relations beyond (in) work, whereas in India,

---

39 It was pointed out that "In fact, the scores of all countries on "Should Be" were lower than "As Is", showing a common desire that people in all these countries [25 societies] aspire for more equality than they currently have." (Fu et al. 2007:891)

40 The US cultural property of Power Distance (2.85) is higher than India's (2.64), while the team of USA with cultural practice (4.88) lower than India (5.47) (Jiang Lu et al 2008:37).

> colleagues or superiors are well aware of the family and family relations. This sort of belongingness is lacking in Chinese culture. For example, my staff member, when she is celebrating her daughter's birthday, never intended to invite us because we are alien people. This maybe because of a fear of cultural differences or maybe because of Chinese culture, their relationships are not extended outside, whereas in Indian culture, the office is always like an extended family, and people share their family problems and celebrations. I feel that here such attitude prevails even during marriages. [...]I was not aware of this but was told by my superior once that she had invited him with a wedding card, but told him that it was a personal ceremony, so close family members would be invited. I am giving this card to you just [for] intimation, later I may give a party to you, but you are not required to attend the marriage." (Sarma 2017).

The Indian manager was disappointed and thought that the Chinese were not very close to their colleagues. It caused the primary degree of cultural conflict.

This seems to confirm that the cultural attribute score (Should Be) of India is lower because Indian superiors want to shorten the distance from their employees in the company. This may be due to the concept of caste, and India has a higher score (5.47>5.04) in the cultural practice of Power Distance than the Chinese. Numerically, Chinese values respect leadership more than Indians, but in reality it seems the opposite. Although the gap between China and India on the data is subtle, Indians show a more prominent "Power Distance" and juniors show more respect to their superior. The difference in the data shows that in reality there are differences in attitudes towards the problem. If the differences are not handled properly, the cognitive conflict will increase the attrition rate and hinder the smooth operation of economic cooperation to a certain extent. Therefore, Chinese employees should show more respect to Indian superiors and are expected to narrow this Power Distance according to Indian cultural attributes and maintain a close relationship with Indian superiors outside working hours.

It can be seen that culture affects the management of enterprises and the operation of the investment. Cultural differences lead to some primary cultural conflicts in individual and organisational levels. It is necessary to increase mutual understanding and respect among cultures. On this basis, transpositional consideration is conducive to reducing or avoiding these conflicts. At present, the counter-measure of enterprises responds to cultural differences that may cause management problems, including localisation by increasing local management staff. Chinese companies in India propose to achieve full localisation, that is, no employees from China in the future. These initiatives can effectively reduce problems in cross-cultural management, but in the long run, cultural differences need to be understood genuinely and managed effectively.

9.2.3. Future Orientation

Future Orientation refers to "the degree to which individuals in organizations or societies engage in future-oriented behaviours such as planning, investing in the future, and delaying individual or collective gratification" (Chhokar et al. 2007:3). In GLOBE's assessment of China, Future Orientation "Should Be" (4.73) with a rank of 60 is second lowest among the 61 societies (Fu et al. 2007:888). However, according to Cheung (Cheung et al. 1996), there is planning of long-term thought in traditional Chinese society to "save as much as you can" and "thriftiness was a virtue cherished [...]" (Ibid.).[41] It seems there is a contradiction between planning long-term thought tradition and the lower score of Future Orientation. The understanding of GLOBE by a Chinese scholar about this incompatibility in Future Orientation is because the research of GLOBE does not concern "thriftiness" , but refers to "conscientiously planning for the future" , so it concludes that the Chinese are not concerned too much about planning (Ibid.). Meanwhile, it is also pointed out in the GLOBE research on China that

> "Unlike most religious societies, Chinese society does not have a dominant religion, but was exposed to multiple schools of thought in ancient times and people have the habit of using often seemingly contradictory principles to rationalize their thinking when necessary".

The analysis by GLOBE scholars also pointed out that Taoism[42] emphasises "let things take their natural course", while the author believes that Confucianism pays more attention to "the present". Influential ideas such as "when you are poor, just improve yourself, when you are rich, then help the world", "When one does not occupy a position, one does not plan its governance" (14.26), are emphasis on present identity. Besides, the analysis of "*zhi*" in Chapter 7 points out that the *Lun-ren* is more concerned about the present. It is, therefore, possible to understand the cultural reasons why China scored lower in Future Orientation.

At the same time, the influence of the political system also needs to be considered. The Chinese Communist Party attaches importance to the national development plan and has formulated it as the five-year plan and the hundred-year plan, which have accelerated China's development. State-owned enterprises are affected by national policies, but ordinary private enterprises, especially ordinary small and medium-sized enterprises and ordinary people, pay more attention to short-term benefits and are more likely to follow the market, rather

41 In the analysis of Chapter 6 (6.2.4), according to Chen Huanzhang (2009), it does not encourage extreme frugality in Confucianism but values the pursuit of wealth. These two views are not contradictory, as "thriftiness" and "extreme frugality" are two different concepts.

42 It was pointed out "the founder of Taoism, Lao Zi, opined that the cosmos is uncertain, and therefore we had better leave things alone, letting things take their natural course. To him, planning was both unnecessary and against nature" (Fu et al. 2007:888). Taoism is not the main analysis object of this research, so it will not be discussed in detail.

than having a rational long-term plan. The reasons behind this include that the country is also in a period of constant reform, and the policy is constantly improving and developing. Therefore, there are some speculations in society. Considering the benefits in the short term seems to be more obvious at the individual level. Given that the long-term economic environment is not affected by individual will, and that the central government plays a great role, it is likely to ban some industries in the process of regulating the market in a certain period. In addition, laws and regulations are in the process of continuous improvement, which causes business people to walk on the edge of the law, that is, to use the blank space and imperfections of the law to develop their business. In short, at the government level, there are relatively long-term goals, while Future Orientation is weaker at the organizational and individual levels. The Confucian doctrine emphasises respect for government and authority, and is more conducive to the implementation of government policies, which means that organizations and individuals are more likely to follow the government's policies, rather than make overly ambitious business plans. Certainly, this is a relative concept and not an absolute one, which means that there are people with high Future Orientation in Chinese society. An analysis of this dimension can only show one general feature, that is, more people among the Chinese tend to have short-term benefits rather than long-term planning orientation. As mentioned in one of the interviews in the GLOBE Research Project, a middle-level manager in a U.S.-owned Chinese company who was getting on-the-job training in the USA said,

> "Americans pay a lot of attention to individual development. They have 'road maps' for individuals and try to lay [plan] ahead where you are going to be in the next five years. We Chinese don't do that at all. We watch our steps as we walk along. How can we plan ahead when we don't even know which company we'll be working for in the next five years?" (Li, 1997, personal communication) (Fu et al. 2007:888).

Certainly, this data can only serve as a reference for cultural roots, and China's cultural characteristics are constantly evolving.

Besides, the explanation from the GLOBE research project is conducive to understanding the reasons behind India's higher score and rank than China, according to Chhokar (2007:990), "Historically and traditionally, Indian society has emphasized the 'hereafter' in preference to the 'here and now', and therefore has been generally future oriented." The cultural root is related to the concept of *karma*.

> "The concept of providing for the 'hereafter' at times extends to even providing for after death, with some people engaging in actions, ceremonies, and rituals that they hope will improve their lot in their next lives following [in keeping with] the doctrine of *karma*. These

> sometimes take the form of contributions to charitable and religious activities and institutions" (Ibid.).

Comparatively, *lun-ren* emphasised more on the present life, and Homo Hierarchicus emphasised more on the afterlife. It would be helpful to understand that the Indian characteristics of "spiritual exploration" and "time concept" have an impact on the economic development of India.

The differences between the Chinese and Indians on the influence of Future Orientation on the economic relations of these two nations through its impact on economic thought are clear. While the *lun-ren* pay more attention to the present, Homo Hierarchicus pays more attention to the future, even afterlife in the manifestation of spiritual exploration. It made the *lun-ren* keen on economic development while Homo Hierarchicus is not concerned only with economic growth. In other words, the way of Chinese development is challenging to be practiced in India. It might cause a feeling of depression of the Chinese towards the Indian market and so had to harden their patience to do business in India. Meanwhile, the time concept of the Homo Hierarchicus has created a negative perception of the *lun-ren* towards India. The different concerns about present life and the supernatural may cause a negative perception of Homo Hierarchicus and the Lun-ren towards each other.[43]

Moreover, as mentioned in Chapter 7, 7.2.12, the concept of *karma* might enhance the strain of the historical memory of Homo Hierarchicus, and the concept of *yi* could promote the *lun-ren* to seek common ground while reserving their differences. The different cultural attitudes towards the settlement of disputes could influence the policies of these two in the form of cancelling the cooperation or not cooperating at all. Thus, the Chinese and Indians might have a primary or intermediate degree of cultural conflict in the dimension of Future Orientation.

9.2.4. Assertiveness

In the analysis of Chapter 6, it was pointed out that cultural confidence is a factor that influences India's national policy. In particular, India's cultural status in South Asia has made India tend to form a leadership position and limit China's economic influence in the region. It can be said that at the national level, India is "engaged in conscious opposition to" China because China is pursuing what "appear to be incompatible goals" (Dougherty and Pfaltzgraff 2000:189). India balances China's economic activities in South Asia, and the progress is relatively slow in the multilateral economic cooperation with China in South Asia, such as the Bangladesh-China-India-Myanmar Economic Corridor, resulting in the

43. The *lun-ren* have the tradition of ancestor worship (See Chapter 6, 6.6.2.3), yet, Homo Hierarchicus spend much resources on the supernatural.

intermediate degree of culture conflict with the influence of different cultural concepts, and limiting the development of economic relations.

Assertiveness in the GLOBE Research Project refers to "the degree to which individuals in organizations or societies are assertive, confrontational, and aggressive in social relationships" (Chhokar et al. 2007:3). From the data of GLOBE, it can be seen that the cultural attribute and cultural practice of Indian Assertiveness are lower than Chinese. Besides, what is valuable to this research is that the cultural practices of China and India are much lower than their cultural attributes, no matter what score or rank. The explanation of a Chinese scholar of the GLOBE on the large discrepancy in cultural practices and cultural attributes is that the unique Chinese cultural concepts "constrain the behaviours of Chinese individuals and discourage them from behaving assertively", such as "*mianzi* (face; maintaining the respect of others as well as respecting others), *renqing* (being kind or respecting the feelings of others), and *guanxi* (relatedness or connections among individuals)" (Fu et al. 2007:889). A "plausible reason" for the high level of assertiveness on cultural values "could be due to the fact that rapid changes in society created an extremely high level of uncertainty, urging the Chinese to become increasingly aggressive in order to protect themselves".

In the dimension of assertiveness, the Chinese are more assertive than Indians in the cultural attribute (although both of them are lower in actual cultural practice), and as a reference, it can be concluded that the Chinese may have some conceit when they interact with other cultures. Combined with the case of Indian financial industry managers and Chinese employees in the survey, it shows that the common Chinese sometimes neglect Indians. An Indian financial industry manager feels that they are not made light of when they get along with the Chinese,

> "Chinese laymen are very cooperative, and they are very friendly and helpful. However, popular belief in India is that they do not care for Indians; they give respect only to Westerners like from the USA and the UK. However, in reality, laymen love Indians, and they are very fond of them, but the only hindrance is that because of communication incapability, they do not come forward to mingle with Indians" (Sarma 2017).

Several studies found the "Chinese more masculine and assertive than Americans" (Schmit and Yeh, 1992; Shermerhorn and Bond, 1991). Perhaps the gap in the strength with the USA has caused China's cultural attribute to be suppressed. However, to countries with weaker comprehensive national strength, the Chinese might be inevitably showing assertive psychology. The high cultural attribute of the Chinese in the Assertiveness dimension during interactions with the Indians could cause the depression among them. It is a primary cultural conflict manifestation, and has caused a certain degree of hindrance to the development of relations at the individual level.

9.2.5. Humane Orientation

Humane Orientation refers to "the degree to which individuals in organizations or societies encourage and reward individuals for being fair, altruistic, friendly, generous, caring, kind to others, and exhibiting and promoting altruistic ideals" (Chhokar et al. 2007:3).

China shows the large gap between the scores of cultural attribute and cultural practice in the Humane Orientation dimension of the GLOBE research project, while the cultural practice rank is lower than India's. The link in the traditional culture could be found both in China and India. The concept of "*ren*" in Confucian culture promotes the quality of kindness of the *lun-ren* (mainly towards human beings). It is believed that,

> "A person high on Humane Orientation would be described as having a strong sense of *renqing* in China, which implies an *"implicit set of rules"* that involve reciprocation in the form of money, goods, information, status, service, and affection (Cheung et al. 1996). Under these rules, two basic kinds of social behaviour are expected: (a) ordinarily, one should keep in contact with acquaintances in one's social network, exchanging gifts, greetings, or visits with them from time to time, and (b) when a member of one's network gets into trouble or faces a difficult situation, one should sympathize, offer help, and "do a *renqing*" for that person (Hwang, 1987: 954). All these expectations urge Chinese individuals to be kind and considerate to others."

It was pointed out in Chapter 6 that although *renqing* began to fade in the concept of some modern individuals, it still has a significant influence on *lun-ren*'s exchange mode and regional organisational culture. Meanwhile, the concept of *renqing* has a different manifestation at different levels of relationship, and with modern people's attention to interests along with changes in moral values, the thought of *ren* is also fading in society, as pointed out by GLOBE scholars,

> "[...] society is going through so much change and the ways in which things used to get done are all being reformed, creating an extreme amount of uncertainties. Many traditional values are also being challenged by realities and people there find it increasingly important to be assertive and aggressive in order to survive. Therefore, the notion of being kind and maintaining harmony with others is not as important as it used to be. Maybe that is why the score on Humane Orientation "Should Be" dropped quite a lot from the "As Is" score." (Fu et al. 2007: 892)

This can also be considered as a manifestation of China's transition from an acquaintance society to a non-acquaintance society. People who are acquainted with each other (relatives, friends) will still practice the moral values of *ren*, but probably not those not familiar with, or do not in the third layer of PSH (the so-called "*sheng-ming-bao*"or life pack(Shang 2013:54). Homo Hierarchicus is different from the *lun-ren* at this point. Although the Hindu concept analysed in this study does not directly express the values of humane behaviour, the concept of attaching importance to behavioural results in *karma* is to encourage Homo Hierarchicus to attach importance to and be kind to all living beings. Because of Homo Hierarchicus's religious view, they believe that doing good deeds is also beneficial to the afterlife. Just as Indian GLOBE scholars mentioned that "Being altruistic and charitable is also considered to help in improving one's lot after life" (Chhokar 2007: 991). Therefore, the cultural difference at this point probably causes Homo Hierarchicus to form a negative perception of the *lun-ren*, which is the formation of primary degree cultural conflict, as the *lun-ren* may not show kindness to strangers at times. Indeed, this is not common, but it happens from time to time. For example, the *lun-ren* is kind over a slight request, but there are also many *lun-ren* who mind their own business and do not get involved in other people's matters. Besides, the *lun-ren* will have different levels of performance in the "differential pattern" according to the closeness. Also, in the last decade of Chinese society, there had been many cases of helping strangers and then encountering "*peng-ci*" (fraud), resulting hesitation to help strangers. This is more frequent in cities that tend to be a non-acquaintance society than in an area or region dominated by acquaintances.

For Homo Hierarchicus, it happens that even if it is for a stranger and does not relate to him/her in any, they do provide help believing in the beneficial for afterlife concept. Also, in the analysis of "*ren*" (benevolence) in Chapter 7, it was pointed out that the idea of "*ren*" tends to be "*fu*" (rich) first and then practice "*ren*". Moreover, "*ren"* emphasises "*zhong*" (loyalty), which makes the *lun-ren* different from Homo Hierarchicus. The latter is relatively more tolerant and kind to poverty, more loyal to the supernatural than to lay people. This difference affects the exchange mode between the two cultures. The relative *maya* ("an illusion where things appear to be present but are not what they seem to be") (Shang 2013:178) towards human relations made Homo Hierarchicus not to pay as much attention to the verbal commitment as the *lun-ren*, which causes a negative perception of the *lun-ren* on Homo Hierarchicus, that is, the primary degree of cultural conflict. Besides,"*ren*" emphasises "*shen-yu-yan*" (talk with caution), but Homo Hierarchicus is argumentative. The "showoff" characteristic of the latter is probably natural to cause a negative perception (at least one can feel the difference) of the *lun-ren* who emphasises on the "*zhong-yong*" (doctrine of the mean) and is not inclined to express their own, that is the zero or primary degree cultural conflict. The concept of "against excessive frugality" (Chapter 6,

6.2.4) of the *lun-ren* and the frugal spirit of Homo Hierarchicus is another difference. It might cause a negative perception of the former towards the latter, given that frugal behaviour was called "*kai-gua*" (unbelievably good in using specialized software used to cheat in online games) (Mao K. J. 2015) by Chinese citizens, that is not a positive word.

The kindness towards the nature of Homo Hierarchicus is also expressed in their food culture. Indians believe the Chinese eat anything and everything, which is incredible for the people of India many of whom are vegetarians. It is likely to make Indians have a slightly negative perception of the Chinese. Meanwhile, the lack of meat in India has also caused problems for Chinese employees in India. The Chinese business people bought beef in some areas of India, leading them to detention (Dabas 2019). It caused a relatively negative social impact.

Moreover, some Chinese business people in India observed, "without Chinese chefs, the annual employee turnover rate is 40 per cent, and after getting Chinese chefs, the employee turnover rate dropped to 5 per cent" (Zhang C. 2019). In addition, as pointed out in Chapter 7, the *dharma* concept of Homo Hierarchicus has made Indians "tend to protect the interests of the weak and against foreign interests", specifically manifesting in the boycotting of Chinese products by the SJM, the economic branch of the Hindu right-wing organization RSS, which has had a heavy impact on one of India's main ruling parties. This aggressive action already belongs to the high degree cultural conflict, which hurts economic relations and is a potential danger that causes more severe results. It can be seen that the differences between the Chinese and Indians on Humane Orientation dimensions have caused primary and high degree influence on economic relations.

9.2.6. Uncertainty Avoidance

Uncertainty Avoidance refers to,

> "the extent to which members of an organization or society strive to avoid uncertainty by relying on established social norms, rituals, and bureaucratic practices to decrease the probability of unpredictable future events that could adversely affect the operation of an organization or society, and also to remedy the potential adverse effects of such unpredictable future events" (Chhokar 2007:4).

A GLOBE scholar considered "The high Chinese scores are consistent with the traditional Chinese value of order" (Fu et al. 2007:891). It is considered that the history and traditional values of order shaped the current Chinese society that has "a high intolerance for uncertainty". Meanwhile,

> "[...] all the Chinese people enjoy the better living they have now and welcome change in that sense, but many of them are worried about the

loss of 'order', therefore longing [they long] for more rules and regulations to reduce uncertainties" (Fu et al. 2007:891).

Notably, the thoughts of *li* (rites) and *yi* (righteousness) in Confucianism make the *lun-ren* tend to respect authority and order. In Confucian thought, *li* means different treatments for different positions. If a junior enjoys superior treatment, it is against *li*. This also affects the order concept of the *lun-ren*, and this is contrary to the Western pursuit of freedom. A Chinese scholar believes that based on *li* values, it is conducive to the establishment of civilized world order, and the values of freedom will lead to chaos in the world. The concept of order for the *manthan* of Homo Hierarchicus is even more different, which considers the world to be inherently chaotic. This helps to understand that India's score in Uncertainty Avoidance [4.73 (29), 4.15 (29)] is lower than that of China [5.28 (9), 4.94 (10)]. Because the world is considered chaotic, the uncertainty may be a normal state for Homo Hierarchicus, without the need for avoidance. In Chapter 6, it was pointed out that *manthan* influences the economic thoughts of Homo Hierarchicus and business behaviours. The concept of righteousness and benefit (*yi-li-guan*) of Confucianism emphasises on only striving for one's interests but not to obtain the interests that belong to someone else. It is different from the view of the Hindu"to absorb the negative and adapt to take advantage of the positive" (Sinha and Sanyal 2016). It is easy to cause a sense of aversion among the *lun-ren* who do not know the concept of Hindu values. It falls in the middle degree of cultural conflict.

Besides, at the national level, from the summary of Chapter 6, it can also be seen that the concept of "Great Harmony" in Confucianism, economic equality for world peace as well as the extensibility of *guanxi* are all about creating stability. Even the "Differential Pattern" is to avoid uncertainty. Meanwhile, an Indian GLOBE scholar mentioned, "Religious beliefs and practices arising out of them are a major source of attempts to reduce the uncertainty of the future" (Chhokar 2007:991). Also, for the Avoidance Uncertainty, India has shown a balance towards China due to the growing influence of China in its cultural sphere (civilisational entity), especially in South Asia. In Chapter 6, it was pointed out that the cultural confidence of India gave it a strong sense of autonomy and contained the influence of foreign forces. China's *guanxi* infinite extensibility, as well as the economic development philosophy vis-a-vis protectionism in India in its cultural circle as well as its Swaraj thought, have already caused hostility on the Indian side, that is, middle degree cultural conflict. Moreover, the conflict of interests in India's perspective and India's checks and balances against China have caused this cultural conflict to rise to intermediate degree conflict, which is reflected in India's non-cooperative attitudes[44] towards China including India's

44 This is from the Chinese perspective. In the Indo-foreign concept, China probably is also not cooperating with India in some aspects.

clear indications that it will not participate in China's multiple invitations to join its economic initiative, the BRI. It is a manifestation of non-cooperation in intermediate degree cultural conflicts behind the territorial dispute concern.

9.2.7. Collectivism

Collectivism is divided into "Institutional Collectivism" and "In-Group Collectivism" in the GLOBE research project. The former reflects "the degree to which organizational and societal institutional practices encourage and reward collective distribution of resources and collective action" and the latter reflects "the degree to which individuals express pride, loyalty, and cohesiveness in their organizations, families, circle of close friends, or other such small groups" (Chhokar et al. 2007:3).

Although the "joint" or "extended" family has been weakening for some time in urban areas, the family is still an essential unit in Indian society for life (such as board and lodging, child care and arranging marriage) and problems and crises sharing (Chhokar 2007:991). Meanwhile, there are lots of family-controlled and managed business organisations in India—some of the largest business organisations are controlled by families of their founders such as Tata, Birla, Ambani, Mahindra, and Shriram (Ibid: 992). Professional managers often dilute family control by the third generation after the founder (Ibid.)

The society of the *lun-ren* pays more attention to collectivism than the society of Homo Hierarchicus. Although it has been challenged by Western individualism, the "equality" of collectivist-oriented extreme individualism that has been chased after in China is now being replaced by "equity" (Fu et al. 2007:889-890). This is related to the traditional Chinese thought *li* (rites) that has the meaning of a hierarchical order. The characteristics of Chinese Collectivism can be seen in the following points: "the differential pattern" is gradually weakening outwards, patriarchal sentiment caused by filial piety and the patriotic sentiment of the concept of the family country. Moreover, for Homo Hierarchicus, In-Group collectivism is stronger than that of the *lun-ren*. India's score and rank are higher than China's in the dimension of In-Group Collectivism (lower than China in the dimension of Institutional Collectivism). Because of the divisions in solidarity in Indian society, each ethnic group has its centripetality and has a sense of boundaries with other ethnic groups. National leaders who can unite India, such as Patel, are highly regarded by the Hindu tradition-oriented government. The collective of the *lun-ren* is continuously expanding to form a larger circle. Comparatively, Homo Hierarchicus is more inward, each group is closed and is distanced from other groups, or other groups are placed in different sequences. It is performed at the national, organizational, and individual levels (Chapter 6). The people of different classes probably could flow into a different class as the concept of *li* is based on strength, while the class of Homo Hierarchicus is unchangeable as the hierarchy is based on birth.

Meanwhile, at the national level, India's sense of Collectivism is based on the cultural frontier, that is, South Asia, which makes it show a "strong civilisational entity and weak organisational entity" with a distinction between enemy and friend influenced by the concept of the *mandala*. According to a survey by Pew Research Centre (2017),[45] 41 per cent of Indians hold negative views on China and only 26 per cent have positive views. Meanwhile, a 56 per cent majority in India considered "China's growing military power is bad for India" (even before the "summer's military standoff", i.e., Doklam standoff) (Stokes, Manevich and Chwe 2017). Fifty-one per cent believed "China's growing economy, with which India runs a trade deficit, does not bode well for their country" while 44 per cent Indians feel very threatened by China's power and influence (Ibid.). Indian vigilant or hostile attitude towards China has formed a cultural conflict from the middle degree to the intermediate degree. Undoubtedly, India also has substantial autonomy (independent pursuit) and will not blindly follow another country's strategy to check and balance China. This will enable India to cooperate with China while facing different interests.

9.3. Summary

Table 1: Assessment Cultural Dimensions of Three Levels and Cultural Conflict in Economic Relations

	Cultural Dimensions	**Individual level**		LCC	**Organisation level**		LCC	**National level**		LCC
		Lun-ren	**Homo Hierarchicus**							
		China	**India**		**China**	**India**		**China**	**India**	
1	**Performance Orientation**	*Li*	*Karma*	P	*Yi*	*Karma*	P			
2	**Power Distance**	*Li*	*Karma* Caste	P	*Li (mianzi)*, *Yi*	*Karma*	P			
3	**Future Orientation**	*Yi*	*Karma*	P	*Yi*	*Karma*	I	*Yi*	*Karma*	I
		Xin	*Karma*	P						
		Zhi	*Jnana*	P						
		Time concept		P						
4	**Assertiveness**	*Li*	*Dharma*	P				*Li*	*Dharma*	I
5	**Humane Orientation**	*Ren*	*Karma*	Z-P	*Yi*	*Dharma*	H			
6	**Uncertainty Avoidance**	*Li, Yi*	*Manthan*	M				*Li, Yi*	*Manthan*	M
								Guanxi	*Swaraj, Manthan, Karma*	M-I
7	**Collectivism**							*Guanxi*	*Mandala*	M-I

Note: "LCC" refers to the level of cultural conflict. "P" refers to the primary degree of cultural conflict. "M" refers to the middle degree of cultural conflict. "I" refers to an intermediate degree of cultural conflict. And "H" refers to the high degree of cultural conflict.

45 Pew Research Centre survey was conducted among 2,464 respondents in India from 21 February to 10 March 2017 (Stokes et al. 2017).

In summary, the analysis of Chapter 6 is conducive to linking culture with economic performance. The analysis of cultural core values in Chapter 7 helps to trace the root of behavioural thinking, while the analysis of Chapter 8 is more conducive to meticulously observe the specific role of culture in economic relations and the mechanism of interaction between culture, conflict and economic relations. The last three chapters laid the foundation for assessing the impact of culture on China-India economic relations. This chapter combines the content of the first three chapters with the concept of the cultural dimension of the GLOBE Research Project and uses the scores of GLOBE to demonstrate the differences between Chinese and Indian cultures visually and to interface with their cultural roots, thus deeply explaining the behavioural phenomena caused by culture. The cultural factors, the core value of culture, culture in economic relations and the GLOBE cultural dimension are combined to form a network that explains the cultural impact on economic relations, cultural conflicts caused by cultural differences, and the degree of its influence on economic relations (Table 1). As shown above, the analyses of each chapter is connected to the others. In Table 1, the manifestations of economic behaviours are categorised based on the cultural dimensions of GLOBE and connected with the core value of the culture or the similar core value that directly or indirectly affects the economic performances, thus facilitating the comparison of the two cultures. Cultural concepts that specifically influence economic behaviour can be found correspondingly in each section of this chapter.

By assessing the impact of culture on China-India economic relations, it can be seen that the core cultural concepts of China and India have an impact on the economy, and the differences in cultural concepts between China and India have caused different degrees of cultural conflicts, which have affected economic relations with different degrees. According to the current research and analysis, the following conclusion can be made. Firstly, in the Performance Orientation dimension, the gap between the cultural attribute and the cultural practice of Homo Hierarchicus at the individual level shows the influence of the *karma* concept that made Homo Hierarchicus pay attention to responsibility without attachment to the result. The feature of Homo Hierarchicus in the dimension of Performance Orientation is easy to cause a feeling of depression for the *lun-ren*, which forms the primary degree of cultural conflict, and has a particular hindrance for the smooth development of economic cooperation. Secondly, the differences between China and India in the dimension of Power Distance have formed a primary degree of cultural conflict among individuals, which has formed a relatively negative perception in economic relations and delayed the development of economic relations. Thirdly, in the Future Orientation dimension, at the individual level, the influence of the different traditional ideas of China and India on future concepts and time concepts formed different attitudes on economic development and disputes and caused a feeling of depression towards each other, resulting in a primary degree of cultural conflict. At the organisational and national levels, the difference between Chinese and Indian culture formed an intermediate degree of cultural conflict, which caused the cancellation of economic cooperation or caused economic non-cooperation. Fourthly, the difference between China and India in the dimension of Assertiveness caused the arrogance of the *lun-ren* and depression of the Homo Hierarchicus, thus forming the primary degree of cultural conflict. At the national level, because of the regional leadership of India caused by its cultural confidence, India has balanced the influence of China in South Asia, and the progress of China's multilateral economic cooperation with South Asian countries such as BCIM has been slowed down. In regional cooperation, it has formed the intermediate degree cultural conflict, and the development of the economic relations is limited.

Fifthly, in the Humane Orientation dimension, the differences of humane-derived qualities between China and India, such as loyalty, wealth concept (the attitude towards the rich and the poor), the way of expression, and dietary habit, has caused zero to primary degree cultural conflict at the individual level. At the organisational level, the high degree cultural conflict was formed due to the different attitudes and behaviours towards the interests of the weak; boycotting Chinese products that appeared in India can be attributed to aggressive action. Sixthly, in the Uncertainty Avoidance dimension, the different concepts of order in China and India caused a middle degree of cultural conflict at the individual level. At the national level, the middle to intermediate degree cultural conflict was created. To avoid uncertainty and enhance stability by strengthening the relations with surrounding countries, China's *guanxi* expansion in South Asia has shaken India's leading position, causing an unfriendly or even hostile attitude in India towards China, and the implementing equilibrium of India to China formed a situation of passive cooperation or non-cooperation in economic relations. Seventhly, in the Collectivism dimension, the difference between the concept of *guanxi* expansion of China and the *mandala* concept of India made India adopt a vigilant and even hostile attitude toward China, forming an intermediate degree cultural conflict, which has hindered and restricted economic relations.

In brief, culture has an impact on the individual, organisational, and national levels of Chinese and Indian economies, and cultural differences between China and India have formed obstacles in the development of economic relations in different degrees. Only by strengthening the understanding of cultural roles and cultural differences, would it be conducive for the benign development of China-India economic relations.

CHAPTER 10

CONCLUSION

This research is to examine the influence of culture[46] on the economies of China and India economy respectively at three different levels, i.e., individual, organisational and national, and explore the impact of culture on China-India economic relations, cultural conflicts caused by cultural differences between them, and how cultural conflicts have hindered China-India economic relations.

10.1. Culture Influence on Economy on Three Levels

This research reveals that culture has an impact on the three levels of individual, organisational and national in the economy, and cultural differences have caused different degrees of cultural conflicts in the interaction between the Chinese and Indians, which in turn affects the development of economic relations in varying degrees.

10.1.1. Culture at Individual Level

The influence of culture can be seen on China-India economic relations, especially in terms of commercial behaviour, organisational culture, and trade policy. At the individual level, Confucian culture influences the *lun-ren*'s interpersonal relationships (*guanxi*, *mianzi*, *li* and gift-giving), family concept (ancestor worship and filial piety), concept of wealth (emphasising wealth), attitude towards poverty (against extreme frugality), exchange mode (exchange as trustworthiness credit). In India, Hinduism influences the mindset on

46 This study selected Confucian culture and Hindu culture, which occupy dominant positions in China and India, respectively and separately, as the primary analysis object. Although these two cultures are not considered to represent the whole contemporary of China and India, Confucian culture is always dominant to analyse while to concern the traditional Chinese thoughts. Hinduism is followed by 79.8 per cent of India's population (GoI 2011). Indeed, it does not mean that other cultures are not significant. Buddhism has much influence on Chinese business people. Indian Muslims have many influential figures in the economic field. However, beyond Confucian and Hindu cultures is out of the scope of this study.

stratification of Homo Hierarchicus, which limits free competition and economic mobility (Harriss-White 2003:134), and affects wealth flow in society (the gap between the rich and the poor). To a certain extent, it made Homo Hierarchicus look at light material wealth, pay attention to frugality, and attach importance to spiritual exploration, thus affecting attitude of Indians towards the outside world.

In the dimension of Assertiveness, the primary degree of cultural conflict is formed due to the cultural differences at the individual level, while the neglect of *lun-ren* to Homo Hierarchicus has caused depression of the latter. It hindered the smooth development of people-to-people interaction. Besides, the food culture of India has caused the Chinese to stick to a limited diet in India leading to a depressed mood, which is prone to the primary degree of cultural conflict. It could affect the attrition rate of employees, which is the factor hindering the smooth development of economic relations.. Moreover, the Hindu view of order reflected in the *Manthan* concept affects the exchange mode of Homo Hierarchicus and could cause the *lun-ren* with different exchange modes to be frustrated or even hostile while during negotiations or other forms of interaction. This belongs to the primary to middle degree of cultural conflict. Hindu ideology influences Homo Hierarchicus's concept of time, thus forming a primary cultural conflict in the Future Orientation dimension with the *lun-ren*, which cultural conflict could slightly hinder the development of relations.

In short, the influence of culture at the individual level led to differences in Performance Orientation, Power Distance, Future Orientation, Assertiveness, Humane Orientation, Uncertainty Avoidance, and Collectivism between the *lun-ren* and Homo Hierarchicus, which caused different levels of cultural conflict with a corresponding impact on economic relations.

10.1.2. Culture at Organisational Level

At the organisational level, Confucian culture influences the structure of commercial organisations or, say, strengthens the formation of these organisations in the form of Patrilinealism or Patriarchicalism. That is to say, it provides an environment for these organisations to survival and affects the attitude towards employees in this form of business organisation. Family enterprises influenced by Confucian culture treat employees as family members. However, in Hindu culture, it is hard to treat employees as such because of the caste concept (Chapter 6, 6.3.1). Even, traditionally, employees from different castes do not eat together.

Besides, Patriarchicalism could be called a unique organisational form influenced by Confucianism, and the concepts influenced by Confucianism such as *guanxi*, *mianzi*, *renqing* that have influenced the operation of state-owned enterprises. The Chinese characteristics of interpersonal relationships within state-owned enterprises have been strengthened. However, these concepts are challenged by implementation of national laws and provincial regulations.

Moreover, the ability of the *lun-ren* to form a regional group is better than in other cultures. There were many regional groups based in cities or provinces in China. In India, groups or provinces have mainly taken language as a reference, while China's provinces are mostly named after geographical features (Shang 2013). These are some of the manifestations in the Collectivism dimension. India also has family-based business organisations, but as mentioned above, the *lun-ren*'s management of employees is different.

Hinduism has an impact on the motivation, purpose, and organisational culture of an economic organisation. Firstly, the founders of many business organisations in India have traditionally belonged to the trading caste or mercantile communities (Kudaisya 2009:85). Secondly, the Hindu classic work, *Arthasastra,* is also the source of some aspects of corporate organisational culture. Thirdly, several Hindu-inspired business organisations have been formed in India, offering products with religious characteristics such as Patanjali, Khadi, Good Earth, Saravana Bhavan, and Mother Dairy. The founder of Patanjali also publicly stated that India should ban Chinese products and companies; in this concept of friends and foes, China is a non-friend (Mitra 2017). Swadeshi Jagaran Manch (SJM), the economic wing of the Hindu nationalist organisation, the Rashtriya Swayamsevak Sangh (RSS), launched a campaign boycotting Chinese products in 2017. This is different from the Chinese *guanxi* expansion concept. The difference forms the middle to high degree of cultural conflict, and could slow down or even restrict the development of economic relations.

10.1.3. Culture at National Level

Confucianism has an impact on the choice of a national development route, economic development concept, and strategic thinking of China at the national level. Confucianism is considered associated with China's choice of Socialism (Wang 1995:53). Communist society and Confucian "*Shi-jie da-tong*" (Great Unity or Universal Harmony) have similarities in the Chinese perception (Shang 2013:275) (Marx 1875). The Chinese government emphasises "harmonious society" and "harmonious world", two concepts that are derived from Confucianism. The idea of promoting peace through economic development of Confucianism is the cultural heritage of modern China. It is also a significant development guiding the ideology of the Chinese government after reaffirming the value of traditional culture and a value concept accepted by the Chinese people. China's economic initiative, the BRI, is considered by national leaders to be consistent with Confucian ideology "*Tian-xia Da-tong*" (*CCTV News* 2018). However, economic determinism has been pointed out as challenging to continue to benefit China's diplomacy in the future because conflicts of economic interests will hinder China's diplomatic relations (Yan 2013). This has reflected in China-India relations, such as India's refusal to participate in the BRI because of territorial disputes along the China-Pakistan Economic Corridor. Pursuing only economic interests would inevitably violate the interests of other countries.

Sometimes, it does not necessarily directly affect China's interests while conflict violates the interests of other countries. Even for China's more significant interests, it is non-subjective for it to threaten the interests of other countries. In other words, being harmful to the interests of other countries (India) does not necessarily harm the interests of the beneficiary party (China). In such a situation, it is difficult for the beneficiary party (China) to make changes, making the conflict difficult to eliminate.

Conflict is Good or Bad

As an IR theorist pointed out, conflicts are good or bad,

> "[...] some [social scientists] regard violent conflict as irrational, while others judge it to be good or bad, depending on the context in which it arises; the political, economic, or social values at stake; the costs incurred in comparison with anticipated gains; and the net outcome for the group, the nation, or the international system" (Dougherty and Pfaltzgraff 2001:194).

What benefits does the conflict bring to the nation? Combined with Table 1 in Chapter 9, the primary degree of cultural conflict in this study has less impact on economic relations and is not conducive to the interests of both the countries. The middle, intermediate or high degree of cultural conflict, to a certain extent, is to protect the inherent interests of one side, probably by sacrificing the "anticipated gains" (e.g., the possibility of economic cooperation) or specific aspects of interests (such as economic interests). For instance, with the cultural concept influence, such as attaching importance to the strain of historical memory (*karma*), India did not cooperate with China in economic initiatives over territorial disputes. From the perspective of India, this kind of conflict with China is more significant for its "net outcome". The main initiator[47] of the high level of cultural conflict (India) considers that the conflict is for protection of its inherent interests, although it will lose the "anticipated gains" (e.g., possibility of economic cooperation with China). From the Chinese perspective, the conflict has damaged China's economic interests, and India abandoned its economic interests. Therefore, the "net outcome" for the Chinese side is small, which means that the conflict is more harmful to the loss of Chinese interests. Alternatively, it can be said that the initiator of a conflict is the party that benefits when the conflict is within the controllable range. In a word, conflict is not always bad. It could bring benefit or "net outcome" for the initiator.

47 The main initiator of conflict refers to the party that makes the conflict inevitable. For example, if Party A first makes a provocative action that could cause but did not cause conflict, and Party B does not respond, the conflict will not occur. If Party A provokes and Party B responds (the response includes non-cooperation gestures), then conflict occurs. Then, Party B is the initiator of the conflict, and Party A is the sponsor of the conflict.

This conflict of national interests is also shown in the cultural dimension of Uncertainty Avoidance. India has set up checks and balances against China and refuses to cooperate with China on its economic initiatives. There are different cultural concepts behind this situation, such as the "deifying wealth" thoughts of Confucianism (Weber 1951), the extensibility of *guanxi* in the cultural dimension of Collectivism, vis-à-vis the spirit of a "strong civilisational entity", cultural confidence, the classification of friends and foes for surrounding countries in the *mandala* concept of Hinduism. The above-mentioned differences of cultural concept limit the economic cooperation in the bilateral and multilateral form, which caused the intermediate degree of cultural conflict.

Although the self-centred exclusivity and "Central Plains Centralism" of Confucianism influenced by the concept of *li* (Zhao 2016) is similar to the spirit of the strong civilisational entity of Hinduism, the conflicts formed in the confrontation between the two civilisations are also reflected in the Assertiveness dimension. In the GLOBE Research Project survey, China scored higher than India in this dimension. In the individual interactions between China and India, the ordinary *lun-ren* often have an arrogant mindset towards Homo Hierarchicus, which causes a primary degree of cultural conflict and somewhat hinders economic relations. At the national level, the attitude of India's regional leadership based on the spirit of a "strong civilisational entity" and cultural confidence has restricted China's activities in South Asia. Besides, the hierarchy of Hindu castes and the "Differential Pattern" in Confucianism are related with the stratification of people. However, the former hierarchy is more solidified, and the concept evened. Though India's relations with China are continually improving and strengthening, it will still tend to balance China's influence. In other words, it is hard for India to treat China completely as a friend influenced by its *mandala* concept in the contemporary situation and in the same way for China because of the synergy. These factors limit cooperation and restrict the development of economic relations.

In addition to the above, the impact of Hinduism on the state has also risen through the influence of the leading individual to the influence of the state, such as the "self of independent type" of the political leader. This makes it hard for India to follow other countries blindly. Some scholars have pointed out that India will not bandwagoning towards China like other Asian countries but balance China (Huntington 1996). This is reflected in the balance of India towards China in the South Asia region and the motivation of the Quadrilateral Security Dialogue (QUAD) of India with the USA, Japan, and Australia. From the perspective of Psycho-Culturology, unlike the *lun-ren* which belongs to the "self of mutual reliance type" (Chapter 6, 6.4.3), the leading Homo Hierarchicus is inclined to pursue "autonomy" instead of "bandwagoning". This psychological and cultural difference has caused the intermediate degree of cultural conflict, and the behavioural manifestation, as mentioned above, is India's balance towards China. It restricts the development of economic relations.

Moreover, the caste concept of Hinduism influences the hierarchy view of Homo Hierarchicus. This includes acknowledging the status of the upper caste or the authority, which evolved into faithful follow-up support for a goal, especially when combined with religion (Shang 2013). Considering the link of the Indian government with the philosophy of reviving Hindutva, the national power that the country may unite cannot be ignored. The boycott of Britain in the history of India is enough to make people beware. The Indian attitude against foreigners has also had an impact on China at the individual, organisational and national levels. The representative one is the Swadeshi Jagran Manch (SJM), the organisation that led the campaign to boycott Chinese goods. It can be said that the cultural difference has formed a high degree of cultural conflict towards China-India economic relations. This high degree of cultural conflict is reflected in the dimension of Humane Orientation, which can be classified as a difference between the *yi* of Confucianism and the *dharma* of Hindu culture. The former tends to create a win-win situation, while the latter tends to protect the interests of the weak. The conflict arises when one side uses its cultural concept to request others. In the context of the increasing influence of Chinese companies in the Indian market, a Hindu organisation has launched aggressive action, which has impacted China-India economic relations in a specific range. It is a force that cannot be ignored, although it is a single spark that maybe could start a prairie fire.

10.2. China-India Economic Relations and Culture

In this study, China-India economic relations mainly covered trade, investment (FDI), and economic cooperation. Culture has large or small impacts on these three macro-areas, and the different cultural concepts caused different degrees of conflict, which, in turn, has hindered economic relations.

10.2.1. China-India Trade and Culture

From 2000 to 2017, the total import and export volume of China with India jumped from $ 2.91 billion, including $ 1.56 billion in exports and $ 1.35 billion in imports (MOCPRC 2011:472) to $ 84.39 billion including total exports $ 68.04 billion and imports totalling $ 16.35 billion (NBS 2018c). The total import and export volume between China and India has increased by about 28 times from 2000 to 2017, including about 43 times increase in imports and 11 times in exports from China to India. Notably, total exports from China to India was four times the total imports from India to China in 2017, while the total volume of imports and exports between these countries was almost identical.

The main imports from India to China comprise minerals, base metals and related products as well as chemical products, while the main exports from China to India are mechanical and electrical products, chemical products, base metals and related products (MOCPRC 2018). The cultural influence on trade is mainly manifested in the market environment, trade operations and policy, as Hindu culture has an impact on India's trading policy such as putting economic interests in a secondary position, presenting forceful introversion, and drawing on traditional consciousness to obtain reasonability (Lu 2013:205-208).

10.2.2. China-India Investment and Culture

China was ranked second with $ 136 billion of foreign investment flows among the world's top ten foreign-invested inflow countries of 2017 and accounted for 9.5 per cent of the global total (MOCPRC 2018a:16). India was ranked tenth with $ 40 billion of foreign investment flows accounting for 2.8 per cent of the global total (UNCTAD 2018:4). The FDI outflow from China was $ 124.6 billion that accounted for 8.7 per cent of the total global outflow in 2017 while India's was $ 11.3 billion and accounted for 0.8 per cent of the global total (MOCPRC 2018b:28). The amount of FDI that China received from India was $ 0.16 billion in 2017, which accounted for 14 per cent of India's foreign investment (Ibid.). According to Indian data (DIPP 2018a), the FDI flow from China to India in 2017 was $ 1.3 billion and was ranked sixth with a share of 3 per cent of the total FDI inflows to India. Based on Chinese sources, the cumulative FDI from China to India was $ 4.7 billion by the end of 2017 (MOCPRC 2019).

The main field of India's investment in China involves information technology, pharmaceuticals, biotechnology, infrastructure, manufacturing, steel, minerals, commodities, banking, and energy. China invested in India in the following areas, i.e., automobiles, electricity, telecommunications, metallurgy infrastructure, energy, manufacturing, banking, healthcare, and consumer goods.

Cultural similarity could be a crucial factor to attract FDI while the influences of cultural differences are more dominant between China and India in the economic field. Economic nationalism of India, which is influenced by religion, especially Hinduism (Li 2015:24), restricted Chinese investment in India. It is also a significant potential hidden danger for Chinese investors in India. While analysing the impact of culture on investment, especially cross-cultural management, managers in both countries face apparent or potential problems with cultural differences. In combination with *mianzi*, which extends from *li* to *yi* (Chapter 8, 8.1.2.3.2) (Chapter 6, 6.2.2), unlike the *karma* of Hinduism, it can be concluded that Confucian culture emphasises *li-xian xia-shi* (be considerate and kind to people of talent), cares for the *renqing* (favour), *ge-jin qi-ze* (each one does his/her duty), while Hindu culture emphasises responsibility without attachment, and leaders and employees deal with their problems, respectively, on their own. Chinese employees consider that Indian managers have the responsibility to improve the quality of service and products, and need to pay attention to their *mianzi* (favour). While Indian managers believe that employees have responsibilities towards them, and when managers perform their duties and neglect or ignore the results (such as product quality), it is easy to cause problems such as Chinese employee dissatisfaction, hostility and even attrition.

Meanwhile, Chinese managers face time concept problems of Indian employees, strong spiritual exploration, and related market characteristics. Confucian culture and Hindu culture made individuals have different language expression characteristics, interpersonal relationship treatment and attitude, and thinking patterns. It is natural to create discomfort between each other. It reflects in the dimensions of Performance Orientation, Power Distance, and Future Orientation, which forms the primary degree of cultural conflict, i.e., feel depression or hostility, and thus hinder or slow down the development of economic relations.

Moreover, the *lun-ren* emphasis on the present and tend to seek common ground while reserving the differences. Homo Hierarchicus emphasises on the future (afterlife) and tends to labour under the strain of historical memory (*karma*). These differences caused different ways of understanding and managing disputes at the national level. It made India vigilant towards China and tends to restrict its economic influence in India and the South Asian region. It formed a middle degree (hostility) and even intermediate degree (balance) of cultural conflict, and delayed or restricted the development of economic relations.

10.2.3. China-India Economic Cooperation and Culture

The economic cooperation turnover of China and India was \$ 13.18 million in 2000, including \$ 9.19 million contract projects, \$ 3.95 million labour cooperation, and \$ 40,000 design consultations (NBS 2001e). It accounted for only 0.12 per cent of China's total turnover of foreign economic cooperation of \$ 11.325 billion (NBS 2001a). The turnover of China's contracted projects of \$ 2.46 billion with India increased more than 200 times in 2017 as compared with the year 2000. The number of despatched labour was only 797 for contracted projects and 31 for labour services at the end of 2017. There were only 1,279 Chinese labourers in India for contracted projects and 165 for labour services at the end of 2017.

The cultural differences have created a psychological distance between China and India. The small number of labour from China to India could be seen as signalling attractiveness. Except for the limitation of India's overseas labour policy, the lack of people-to-people and cultural contacts could be a crucial element to limit the exchanges. While it is realised that cultural exchanges could affect the establishment of an economic cooperation mechanism, promoting cultural exchanges and mutual understanding could be conducive for creating "a new type of big-country cooperation model for mutual benefit and win-win situation" (Xie 2017:38). The establishment of the China-India High-Level Mechanism on Cultural and People-to-People Exchanges is a significant step to improve mutual cultural understanding towards a new era of China-India relations with "greater synergies".

10.3. Summarise the Main Findings

The main findings of this research are based on the influence of culture on three levels (individual, organisational and national) in the economy, cultural conflicts caused by cultural differences and the impact of culture and cultural conflicts on economic relations. It can be summarised as below. Firstly, the cultures of China and India have respectively influenced the three different levels, which has made economic relations between China and India also being influenced by it. This has been explained elaborately in the previous section and will not be repeated here.

Secondly, culture has different degrees of influence on the seven major cultural dimensions (i.e., Performance Orientation, Power Distance, Future Orientation, Assertiveness, Humane Orientation, Uncertainty Avoidance, and Collectivism) at the individual, organizational and national levels, and the cultural conflicts formed by cultural differences have different degrees of influence on economic relations (See Chapter 9, Table 1). In the dimension of Performance Orientation, the difference between concepts such as *li* and *karma* have caused a primary degree cultural conflict at the individual level, namely, negative perception, and microscopically hinders the smooth development of economic relations. At the organisational level, the differences between the concepts such as *yi* and *karma* promoted different levels of performance and caused management problems. At the national level, although the expression of Performance Orientation characteristics is not as evident as at the individual level, there are specific manifestations. For example, an official Indian statement expressed support for the development of China-India economic relations, but it limits China's economic activities in India and South Asia. The influence of culture on the dimension of Power Distance is mainly caused by the primary degree of cultural conflict at the individual and organisational levels due to different concepts such as *li* and *karma*, and caste, which raise problems in business organisation management and affect the smooth operation of the business. In the dimensions of Future Orientation, the primary degree of cultural conflict is reflected at the individual level, including the management difficulties of the manager caused by different cultural thinking and behaviour, and the decreasing of investor confidence due to the market characteristics caused by the different cultures. The cultural differences at the organisational and national levels have formed an intermediate degree of cultural conflicts and led to restrictions on China's economic activities in India. The differences in the Assertiveness dimension caused primary and intermediate degrees of cultural conflicts at the individual and national levels, respectively, due to different concepts such as *li* and *dharma*. For instance, Indian individuals are frustrated when they come in contact with Chinese individuals, and China's economic activities in South Asia are restricted.

In the dimension of Humane Orientation, the zero or primary degree of cultural conflicts at the individual level were caused due to the different concepts of Confucianism and Hinduism such as *ren* and *karma*. Due to the different concepts of *yi* and *dharma*, they caused a high degree of cultural conflicts at the organisational level, including the boycott of Chinese products in India by a Hindu economic organisation. In the dimension of Uncertainty Avoidance, because of the different values of Confucianism and Hinduism such as *li*, *yi* and *manthan*, the middle degree of cultural conflict was caused at the individual level, that is, due to different understandings on order and the way of pursuing interests; negative and even hostile emotions are formed that hindered cooperation by the two sides. The middle to intermediate levels of cultural conflicts were formed at the national level due to differences such as *li*, *yi* and *manthan*, *guanxi* and *swaraj*, *manthan*, *karma*, including India on its own or jointly cooperating with other countries, resulting in checks and balances on China's economic development in the South Asian region. Besides, India does not participate in some of the economic projects of China. In the dimension of Collectivism, mainly due to the difference between the *guanxi* and *mandala* concepts, it led to the middle to intermediate level of cultural conflicts at the national level, that is, due to the hostile attitude of some of the Indian forces towards China, the development of economic relations slowed down. Besides, the summary described the impact of culture in all the seven main dimensions and all the three levels with emphasis depending on the degree of impact. Still, specific effects at different levels concerning each dimension can be further analysed in greater detail.

Thirdly, cultural differences do not necessarily lead to cultural conflicts, and some are also conducive to the development of economic relations. For example, Chinese and Indian companies have slightly different understandings and performances in terms of charity, protection and promotion of their cultural heritages, treatment of the poor (Chapter 8, 8.2), and protection of the environment. However, these different attitudes are suitable for companies to build positive images in their local areas through various approaches, and then promote economic relations. Also, although there are asymmetrical perceptions within a specific range at the organisational level, the mutual recognition at the national level is relatively rational. Although these are the differences in the dimension of Assertiveness for these two cultures, emphasising each other's roles in bilateral and multilateral cooperation makes these two countries put in more effort for interacting rationally with each other.

Fortunately, the economic relations of China and India in 2000-2017 did not occur in a superlative degree of cultural conflict even during the confrontation between two neighbouring countries in the border area. There were a series of problems in some fields, especially the losses suffered by small and medium enterprises, such as the suspension of the projects due to the increase of security concerns in India. The tension of political relations undercut some investment projects because the confidence of Chinese investors was frustrated, which led to credit losses of banks and later divestment. Still, there was no complete termination of economic exchanges between China and India. Moreover, the follow-up actions of the two governments through diplomatic channels such as high-level consultations and informal meetings of the two national leaders have resolved the dispute and slowly improved the situation for economic relations.

Fourthly, the increase of mutual cultural understanding could promote economic exchanges. In other words, improving the understanding of each other's culture could promote the development of economic relations. As Indian culture became more popular in China, India's attractiveness to China is also increasing. It is observed that "Watching Bollywood movies, tasting Darjeeling tea and practising Yoga" has become "three fashionable things among the urban youths in China" (Luo 2019). Indian films have been introduced through the official channel (although films had been informally introduced to China and spread on Chinese websites). It made Chinese audiences gradually understand Indian culture. More people want to know about India, and Indian products such as Assam tea and yoga are fast becoming popular in China. This is not unrelated to the promotion of the two governments and civilian forces. The "Visit India Year" in China (2015) and "Visit China Year" in India (2016) designated by the two governments, the annual youth exchange programmes initiated in 2006 and exchange of students have increased the number of people who visit each other. The Indian market has also attracted more and more Chinese companies to invest. The popular culture output of the Indian side seems stronger than China's. However, the translation project based on a Memorandum of Understanding (MoU) signed by China and India in 2013 made the classic Confucian books *Si Shu* (*Four Books*) be translated into Hindi for the first time in the entire history of China and India, along with other classics and recent literary works (Wang 2019). It is more profound in terms of influence. Likewise, most Hindu classics such as the *Mahabharata* and the *Ramayana* have already been translated into Chinese and published in 1999 and 2005. However, maybe due to the length of the two epics and difficulty in understanding them, they have not had a significant impact on the Chinese population. It can be seen that the exchange of popular culture seems to be more immediate than that of the classics. Yet, it is needed to understand the profound concepts of culture and return to the classics. How culture spreads in foreign countries and how to spread it more effectively is also an area that needs to be analysed in depth.

In short, the cultural exchanges between the two countries have promoted mutual understanding between them and created a foundation for eliminating the negative impressions. Meanwhile, they have increased the mutual attractiveness between the two countries, which is conducive to shortening the psychological distance and promoting economic interaction between them.

10.4. Implications of the Study

This study profoundly explored the cultural factors behind the economic phenomenon and cultural differences that influenced the economic relations of China and India. It provided a prerequisite for effectively solving the problems brought about by cultural differences. Although previous research has included comparison of cultural differences between China and India, analysis of China-India economic relations, and the impact of culture on the economy, this study linked these separate research units and traced the cultural differences from the classics of the two civilisations. Based on combing the diverse fields in the economic relations of China and India (trade, investment, economic cooperation), it has deepened the explanation of the factors in economic relations that are influenced by culture. Moreover, the cultural values that influenced the economy are connected with ideological roots, thus fundamentally interpreting the sources of the thought and behaviour in economic activities.

It needs to be pointed out that culture is one of the factors in economic relations and conflict and culture cannot represent the whole cause of economic performance and conflict. There are many other essential dimensions in economic relations. This study looks at it only from a cultural perspective. Since the method of this research is inductive, there are still many worthy cases for further exploration, especially the small and medium-sized business organisations, which are closely related to the daily life of the general public. The influence of traditional thought can be seen even more. In a sense, this research has carried out a particular vital analysis of some representative Chinese and Indian companies. In the future, it can also combine with the theory of International Political Economy (IPE) to gain an insight into the role of enterprises in the economic relations of the two countries. Besides, in the course of this research, it combined with Psycho-Culturology to analyse the behavioural characteristics of the two countries at the national level but failed to fully develop them in this research. Research on the characteristics of national behaviour can also be integrated with more actual cases in the history of China-India economic relations.

The single core value of each culture deserves to be explored in depth and linked to the behavioural characteristics of the individual, organisation and nation. Existing literature has the interpretation of the single classic concept such as the *lun* of Confucianism with an attitudinal generalisation of the particular cultural feature. Moreover, there is a recent trend in Chinese and Indian academic circles to study the relationship between classical values and diplomatic thoughts (Song 2013; Xu and Sun 2014; SIRPA 2018; SIRPA 2019; Bourne 2018). This part can also be further explored, especially an analysis of Indian traditional values and the comparison of traditional values between China and India.

Besides, this study mainly focuses on the BJP government of India, which is more influenced by Hinduism, and also covers the analysis of religious concepts and practices of the other main political party, the Indian National Congress. Future research can deepen the interpretation of the influence of Hinduism at different levels in India under the leadership of the Indian National Congress. There are more Chinese companies complaining of doing business in India that Indian companies doing the same in China. This needs further exploration.

The outcome and research frame of the GLOBE research project could be used in the interdisciplinary field. One of the main objects of the GLOBE research project is to interpret leadership and its differences among 61 societies, with the main research level of analysis being the individual. Although some scholars have pointed out that individuals can influence organisations and nations and the three levels of behavioural characteristics have some similarities, further study can cover the characteristics of a nation (government) or organisation in each cultural dimension. This could be exploring the performances of China and India in multilateral cooperation to show the characteristics of Collectivism of China and India at national levels. This study ranked cultural conflicts and the associated impacts on economic relations. The conflict theory in international relations theory and the international political economy still are of valuable reference to improve and upgrade related research, especially how political tensions impact the business of enterprises as well as coping strategies during and after a conflict.

EPILOGUE

The publication of a book requires the author's day and night efforts as well as courage and pressure. There is always space for improvement in writing, and it takes courage to keep moving forward. There are always pressures from all kinds of work chasing, and need to complete the final draft as soon as possible. Let these words go out of my computer and learn to face more challenges and opportunities.

My passion for Chinese traditional culture, especially Confucianism, started around 2005. My college teacher Yang Chunming aroused my great interest in it. My mentor Ma Hongyi encouraged me to study in India and provided many insightful suggestions in this long journey. The enthusiasm and confusion about the cultural differences between China and India stem from the misunderstandings and contradictions that occurred around me during my study in India. When facing with the same problem, people in different cultures will have very different reactions and understandings. Constantly improve myself, gain energy from learning, and get out of the predicament. With the continuous advancement of thesis writing, I gained energy from books, teachers and friends, and gradually realized the influence of culture on people, and those confusions were gradually resolved. In the process of writing, I got help from many teachers and friends, and it was difficult to write down their names one by one, but when I looked back at the text, their words and faces came to my mind.

For the publication of this book, in addition to the teachers and friends who helped and mentioned in the acknowledgement and above, I would also like to thank Rajan Arya from Pentagon Press for his hard work, patience and suggestions, and editor Jeevan Nair for his meticulous editing of manuscripts. Many thanks to Dr Li Jieruo and Dr Tian Yun, they helped me constantly improve the quality of the manuscript.

I am especially grateful to the guidance and support of my leaders and colleagues from National Museum of China and Chinese Academy of Social Sciences. Many thanks to China Postdoctoral Science Foundation for support me for my research, especially on the project "A Study on the Interaction and Mutual Perception of China and India Based on the Collections of National Museum of China (1912-1949)". They provided me with a better working environment and allowed me to achieve a greater accessibility in book purchases, which was a great joyous thing.

Appendix
Cultural Exchanges between China and India Despite Pandemic

The year 2020 is the 70th anniversary of the establishment of diplomatic ties between China and India, as well as the Year of China-India Cultural and People-to-People Exchanges. The two sides have agreed to host a number of celebratory activities. However, the rampant spread of the coronavirus worldwide has held back these celebrations. In spite of the situation, people from both sides are still enthusiastic about participating in bilateral cultural and people-to-people exchanges. Various academic activities and cultural activities went hosted online. With rich and in-depth content, these activities drew massive attention.

The accumulated experience of organizing activities during the COVID-19 pandemic has built a new arena and explored new possibilities for cultural and people-to-people exchanges between China and India. In early May, there was an online event to commemorate the 159th birthday of Rabindranath Tagore (1861-1941). This event to remember the Indian iconic luminary was organized by an Indian cultural organization and attended by participants from both China and India. Although it was an online activity, participants made full preparations and were formally dressed to show their respect. "Even after 79 years since he breathed his last, Tagore has been standing tall as the most prominent and pioneering cultural ambassador between the current Sino-Indian interaction and has still been playing a pivotal role in consolidating the timeless bridge of friendship", remarked the Indian organizers.

Former Chinese and Indian diplomats, scholars, and artists from 15 cities in 10 countries, all admirers of Tagore and his works, participated in the online event. It was evident that they had made elaborate preparations. For example, on-site simultaneous interpretation service by Indian professors who know the Chinese language was available, providing Chinese participants who did not know Hindi or Bengali or were not proficient in English with an opportunity to understand the great poet better.

During the event, Indian participants gave wonderful performances. Among them were a group of dancing sisters performing in full costume and singers sitting on a balcony rendering a lighthearted song to the accompaniment of a guitar. There was also a family performing an Indian dance in their simple living room, and a scholar explaining the philosophy of Tagore to his online audience in front of a portrait of Swami Vivekananda, a key figure in the introduction of the Indian philosophies of Vedanta and Yoga to the Western world. Students from Visva Bharati University, which was founded by Tagore in 1921 in Santiniketan, West Bengal, India, sang with great passion some songs written by Tagore.

Former diplomats from both China and India delivered speeches full of good wishes, bringing the activity to a climax. Then, Chinese performers went on "stage" one after another, and artfully presented the audience with classical Chinese music performances with traditional Chinese instruments. Pipa, a four-stringed and pear-shaped Chinese musical instrument, and the tabla, and sitar together produced pure and naturally harmonious tones, resonating with each other. Through internet, the music was sent to audiences across the globe.

I love Tagore's poems and admire his literary achievements as well as his intellectual wealth. I even produced a ballad, using a poem from his *Stray Birds* as the lyrics. Out of respect for the great poet, I contacted the Indian organizers over internet, and asked them if I could give a performance. I received a warm response and the news about me performing an original song was immediately announced in the virtual "meeting room."

After my presentation, I saw many positive online comments made by Indian participants. The performance was a spontaneous decision. Thus, I was quite proud and secretly rejoiced because of the smooth performance and the positive feedback I received.

An Indian university student from Santiniketan asked me for my contact details. He told me that he admired Tagore so much that he wanted to grow up like the multi-faceted polymath. He also told me he was a big fan of music, and hoped to engage in more dialogues with me in the future in the form of music and art creation.

This online activity reawakened the memory of my days in India as an international student. I made many new friends during the event, and even got in touch with a few old Indian friends whom I had not heard from for quite some time. Cultural and people-to-people exchanges are communications between peoples and dialogues between cultures. The content of the exchanges are the best parts of the best things among the two nations and peoples. The process of the exchanges has invisibly planted many seeds of friendship that will sprout and bear abundant fruit for the two sides in the future.

If it were not for the COVID-19 pandemic, there would have been a great deal of cultural celebrations for the 70th anniversary of the establishment of China-India diplomatic ties. The outbreak of the coronavirus forced many events to be cancelled. Moreover, the recent border tensions between China and India have put a stop to some cultural and people-to-people exchange activities.

Nationalistic sentiments were on the rise in both countries, with radical and aggressive stories and voices becoming common on the internet and in the media coverage. However, even under such circumstances, many people from both sides still called for a peaceful settlement of disputes in the border areas, and at the same time, continued to conduct bilateral cultural and artistic exchanges.

When we are not blessed with the right time and right place, the right people are vital to promote the development of important bilateral activities. The experience of online communication accumulated during the COVID-19 pandemic has provided more possibilities and reference points for future China-India cultural and people-to-people exchanges. The border clashes between the two countries posed new challenges for bilateral cultural and people-to-people exchanges. Globally, many potential risks and uncertainties are in play due to the pandemic. Only by shaking off excessive caution, enhancing bilateral cultural and people-to-people exchanges, and acting prudently can a better future be created for both countries. It is expected that the cultural and people-to-people exchanges between China and India will be more diversified and carry more features of the times in the future, regardless of the current state of the bilateral relationship. (This original text was published in the bimonthly magazine *China-India Dialogue*, Vol. 21, No. 3, May-June 2020, pp. 37-39.)

BIBLIOGRAPHY

(* indicates a primary source)

Acharya, Alka and Deshpande, G. P. (2003), "Taking of and with China", *Economic and Political Weekly*, 38(28): 2940.

Acharya, Alka (2005), "India-China Relations, Beyond the Bilateral", *Economic and Political Weekly*, 40(14): 1421.

—— (2006), "India-China Relations, A Partnership of 'Global Significance'." *Economic and Political Weekly*, 41(48): 4934.

Adhikari, Harasankar (2016), "Hindutva and Cow Protection", *Economic and Political Weekly*, Vol. 51(12), 19 March 2016, URL: https://www.epw.in/journal/2016/12/letters/hindutva-and-cow-protection.html

Agence France-Presse (2005), "US Unveils Plans to Make India 'Major World Power'," (available at www.afp.com) in Varun Sahni (2006), "India's strategic programs and India-US strategic trade" in Ganguly, etc. (eds.), *US-Indian Strategic Cooperation into the 21st Century*, London: Routledge (Taylor & Francis E-Library): 173.

Agreement with China", *Xinhua Net*, 17 August 2017, accessed 20 September 2018, URL: http://www.xinhuanet.com/silkroad/2017- 08/17/c_1121500544.html.

Amos, Jonathan (2014), "Why India's Mars mission is so cheap—and thrilling", 24 September 2014, accessed 8 March 2017, *BBC News*, URL: http://www.bbc.com/news/science-environment-29341850.

Anand, Vinod (2015), "Impressions from a visit to China: Part II", *Vivekananda International Foundation*, 29 June 2015, accessed 9 July 2019, URL: https://www.vifindia.org/article/2015/june/29/impressions-from-a-visit-to-china-part-ii.

Anderson, David A. and Geiger, Isabel (2010), "Sino-Indian Trade Relations and the Ongoing Border Dispute", *China and Eurasia Forum Quarterly*, Vol. 8(4): 125-141.

Anita (2012), "After bloody 'beef festival'; more such festivals planned", *One India News,* 17 April 2012, accessed on 13 April 2018, URL: https://www.oneindia.com/2012/04/17/after-beef-festival-in-hyd-more-such- festivals-planned.html.

ANI (2017), "Trade imbalance with China is cause of concern: BJP", *Business Standard*, accessed 13 September 2017, URL: http://www.business- standard.com/article/news-ani/trade-imbalance-with-china-is-cause-of-concern-bjp-117 091300108_1.html.

An Pei (2017), "69 Countries and International Organizations have signed Cooperation Agreement with China", *Xinhua Net*, 17 August 2017, accessed 20 September 2018, URL: http://www.xinhuanet.com/silkroad/2017- 08/17/c_1121 500544.html.

Aneja, Atul and Haidar, Suhasini (2014), "Xi's visit a defining moment in India-China ties", *The Hindu*, accessed on 8 July 2015, URL: http://www.The hindu.com/news/national/xis-visit-a-defining-moment-in-indiachina-ties/article 6416751.ece.

Aneja, Atul (2019), "Xi Jinping rejects 'clash of civilisations' theory", *The Hindu*, 15 May 2019, accessed 7 July 2019, URL: https://www.thehindu.com/ news/ international/xi-jinping-rejects-clash-of-civilisations-theory/article27141289. ece.

Apparasu, Srinivasa Rao (2018), "Telangana man worships photo of Donald Trump every day", *Hindustan Times*, 21 June 2018, accessed 30 October 2018, URL: https://www.hindustantimes.com/india-news/telangana-man-worships-photo-of-us-president-everyday-gives-aarti/story-lu3kt2rHjHj9xbvwzA8DiO.html.

Audretsch, David B. and Meyer, Nancy S. (2009), "Religion, Culture, and Entrepreneurship in India", IPAA 2009 International Public Affairs Conference Indiana University, URL: http://www.indiana.edu/~iunews/IPAAAudretsch.pdf.

Ashapura Group (2016a), "About us", accessed on 17 May 2018, URL: http://www. ashapura.com/fulfilling-aspirations.php.

Ashapura Group (2016b), "Sustainability", accessed on 17 May 2018, URL: http:// www.ashapura. com/ashapura-foundation.php.

Basham, A. L. (1954), *The Wonder that was India*, Delhi: Rupa/Fontana Books, reprinted in 1967. Quoted in Chhokar, Jagdeep S. (2007), "India: Diversity and Complexity in Action" in Chhokar, Jagdeep S.; Brodbeck, Felix C. and House, Robert J. (2007) (eds.), *Culture and Leadership Across the World: The GLOBE Book of In-Depth Studies of 25 Societies*, Mahwah, New Jersey/London: Lawrence Erlbaum Associates: 974.

Babu, Venkatesha (2017), "How Gen 5 is reimagining the 117-year-old Murugappa Group", *Business Today*, 18 June 2017, accessed 14 June 2018, URL: https://www.businesstoday.in/magazine/features/how-gen-5-is-reimagining-the -117-year-old-murugappa-group/story/253135.html.

Bansal, Samarth (2016), "More Indians eating beef, buffalo meat", *The Hindu*, 29 October 2016, accessed 16 August 2018, URL: https://www.thehindu.com/ news/national/'More-Indians-eating-beef-buffalo-meat' /article16085248.ece.

Banerjee, Sumanta (2005), "Civilising the BJP", *Economic & Political Weekly*, Vol. 40(29): 3116.

Banerjee, Avijit (2015), personal interview, Zhang Yang, Visva-Bharati University, Santiniketan, 30 January, 2015.

Bai Yunyi (2017), "India wants to boycott Chinese goods? Chinese business people: we don't want to deal with Indian business people at all!" [yin-du hai-xiang di-zhi zhong-guo-huo? zhong-guo shang-ren:wo-men gen-ben bu-yuan-yi he yin-du shang-ren da-jiao-dao!], *Shanghai Observer*, 22 July 2017, accessed 10 June 2019, URL: https://www.jfdaily.com/news/detail?id=59928.

Bajpai, Nirupam and Sachs, Jeffrey D. (2000), "Foreign Direct Investment in India: Issues and Problems", Development Discussion Paper, Harvard University, URL: https://academiccommons.columbia.edu/doi/10.7916/D8F195J2.

Baruah, Amit (2006), "Pranab: nuclear issue may figure in talks with Hu", accessed 26 May, 2015, URL http://www.thehindu.com/todays-paper/pranab-nuclear-issue-may-figure-in-talks-with-hu/article3050301.ece.

Basu, Mihika (2013), "Chinese Premier Li to meet Kotnis kin today", accessed 17 June, 2015, URL: http://archive.indianexpress.com/news/chinese-premier-li-to-meet-kotnis-kin-today/1118408/.

Bagchi, Indrani (2013), "Depsang Bulge Incursion Accidental, Chinese Military Thinktank Says", *Times of India*, 15 July 2013, accessed 16 July 2013.

Bayne, Nicholas; Stephen, Woolcock and Nicholas, Bayne (eds.) (2011), *The New Economic Diplomacy: Decision-Making and Negotiation in International Economic Relations*, Farnham (England): Ashgate Publishing Limited.

BBC (2015), "Indian man lynched over beef rumours", 30 September 2015, accessed 17 October 2018, URL: https://www.bbc.com/news/world-asia-india- 34398433.

—— (2016), "India Muslim couple attacked over rumours of carrying beef", 15 January 2016, accessed 17 October 2018, URL: https://www.bbc.com/news/world-asia-india-35320637.

—— (2017), "Tamil Nadu: Traders ban Pepsi, Coca-Cola to support local products", *BBC News,* 1 March 2017, accessed 8 April 2019, URL: https://www.bbc.com/news/world-asia-india-39124767.

Bendix, Reinhard (1997), *Max Weber: an Intellectual Portrait*, Berkeley: University of California Press: 196.

Berry, John W. (2005), "Acculturation: Living successfully in two cultures", *International Journal of Intercultural Relations*, Vol. 29(6), Nov. 2005: 697-712.

Bhasin, Avtar Singh (2013), *India's Foreign Relations-2012 Documents*, New Delhi: Geetika Publishers.

Bhatt, Sheela (2010), "Wen visit: At least the Chinese are willing to talk now", accessed 12 June 2015, URL: http://www.rediff.com/news/special/wen-trip-at-least-chinese-are-willing-to-talk-now/20101217.html.

Bhoothalingam, Ravi (2015), "BCIM-Economic Corridor and India-China Relations", In Bhatia, Rajiv K. and Mishra, Rahul (eds.) (2015), *BCIM-Economic Corridor: The Road Ahead*, New Delhi: Pentagon Press: 119.

Bhatia, Rajiv K. and Mishra, Rahul (eds.) (2015), *BCIM Economic Corridor: The Road Ahead*, New Delhi: Pentagon Press.

Biswas, Soutik (2012), "India's billionaires and the wealth of the nation", *BBC NEWS*, 12 October 2012, accessed 14 August 2018, URL: https://www.bbc.com/news/world-asia-india-19921501.

Bi N. (2019), personal interview at Vasant Kunj, New Delhi, 26 May 2019.

Bose, Nirmal Kumar (1967), *Culture and Society in India*, Bombay: Asia, 9. Quoted in Chhokar, Jagdeep S. (2007), "India: Diversity and Complexity in Action" in Chhokar, Jagdeep S.; Brodbeck, Felix C. and House, Robert J. (2007) (eds.), *Culture and Leadership Across the World: The GLOBE Book of In-Depth Studies of 25 Societies*, Mahwah, New Jersey/London: Lawrence Erlbaum Associates: 971.

Bose, Adrija (2016), "Vegetarian India A Myth? Survey Shows Over 70% Indians Eat Non-Veg, Telangana Tops List", *Huffpost*, 14 June 2016, accessed 16 August 2018, URL: https://www.huffingtonpost.in/2016/06/14/how-india- eats_n_1043 4374.html.

Bowles, Samuel (1998), "Endogenous Preferences: The Cultural Consequences of Markets and Other Economic Institutions", *Journal of Economic Literature*, 36(1): 75–111.

Bourne, Jennifer (2018), "Classical Indian and Chinese World Views on Global Order: A Comparison, A Berggruen China Centre Workshop", 13 February 2018, accessed 6 July 2019, URL: https://www.berggruen.org/activity/classical-indian-chinese-world-views-on- global-order-a-comparison/.

*BRICS, "Joint Statement, 2009-2016", URL: http://brics2016.gov.in/content/.

Braudel, Fernand (1980), *On History*, University of Chicago Press: 210-211, 226. Quoted in Huntington (1996), *The Clash of Civilizations and the Remaking of World Order*: 45.

Bukhari, Fayaz and Bhattacharjya, Satarupa (2013), "India and China Withdraw Troops from Himalayan Face Off", *Global Post*, 7 May 2013, accessed 11 May 2013.

Business Dictionary (2018), "Organizational Culture", URL: http://www. Business dictionary.com/definition/organizational-culture.html.

—— (2018b), "Trade policy", URL: http://www.businessdictionary.com/defini tion/trade-policy.html.

Bu Yidao (2017), "印度，你到底拿什么跟中国比" [India, What can you compare with China], *Global Times,* 14 February 2017, accessed 14 October. 2018, URL: http://world.huanqiu.com/weinxingonghao/2017- 02/10121954.html.

Business Today (2019), "80% of Indian engineers not fit for jobs, says survey", *Business Today*, 25 March 2019, accessed 9 July 2019, URL: https://www. businesstoday.in/current/corporate/indian-engineers-tech-jobs-survey-80-per-c ent-of-indian-engineers-not-fit-for-jobs-says- survey/story/330869.html.

Casson, Mark (2006), "Culture and Economic Performance", in Victor A. Ginsburgh & David Throsby (2006) (eds.), *Handbook of the Economics of Art and Culture*, Vol. 1, Chapter 12: 359-397.

Cao Pengcheng (2008), "温家宝与印度总理辛格举行会谈" [Wen Jiabao meets Indian PM Singh], *People's Daily* Online, URL: http://paper.people.com.cn/ rmrb/html/2008-01/15/content_38667906.html.

Cai Feng (ed.) (2007), "中印交往大事年表" [Chronology of Events between China and India], in Tan Chung, Liu Chaohua and Huang Rong (eds.) (2007), *Chindia—Idealism and Realization*, Yinchuan: Ningxia People's Press: 472.

Cai Jing (2017), "'The Hierachicus' Model—View of Indians based on the psycho-culturology research method", *International Journal of English Language, Literature in Humanities,* Vol. 5(7): 263-271.

Cai Wu (2009), "新中国 60 年对外文化工作发展历程" [The 60 years of foreign cultural work of New China], accessed 1 May 2015, URL: http: //culture.people. com.cn/GB/22226/154984/155051/9820259.html.

CCTV News (2014), "习近平在印度世界事务委员会发表重要演讲" [Xi Jinpin's speech in ICWA], accessed 4 July 2015, URL: (News) http://news.cntv.cn/

2014/09/19/VIDE1411125298287798.shtml; (Speech) http://news.cntv.cn/2014/09/18/VIDE1411050642620838.shtml.

—— (2018), "Belt and Road Initiative in five years, what are the achievements? What to do in the future? Xi Jinping emphasized" "一带一路" 5 周年取得哪些成果？未来怎么干？习近平这样强调, *CCTV News*, 27 August 2018, accessed on 14 September 2018, URL: https://www.weibo.com/ttarticle/p/show?id= 2309404277755951887989.

Chandra, Satish (2004), *Medieval India: From Sultanat to the Mughals–Delhi Sultanat (1206-1526)*–Part One, New Delhi: Har-Anand Publications: 41.

Chai Sun-ki (2003), "Culture, Rationality and Economic Institutions in East Asia: The Chinese Family Firm", URL: https://pdfs.semanticscholar.org/f460/801bda7dbd66d54fc8873e7a659060b5cf 4c.pdf.

Chawla, Prabhu (2003), "Dancing with the dragon, Historic visit to China by Prime Minister Vajpayee brings Beijing and Delhi closer", *India Today*, accessed on 18 March 2015, URL: http://indiatoday.intoday.in/story/historic-visit-to-china-by-prime-minister-vajpayee-brings-beijing-and-delhi-closer/1/206119.html.

Chandra, Lokesh and Ikeda, Daisaku (2011), *Buddhism A Way of Values: A Dialogue on Valorisation Across Time and Space*, New Delhi, Motilal Banarsidass: 175.

Chakraborty, S. K. (1997), "Business ethics in India", *Journal of Business Ethics,* Vol. 16: 1529-1538.

Chand, Manish (2014), "India-Myanmar ties: Buddha, Business and Bollywood", accessed on 20 July 2015, URL: http://mea.gov.in/in-focus-article.htm?23881/IndiaMyanmar+ties+Buddha+Business+and+Bollywood.

Chai, Winberg (2012), "Communist Ideology and Chinese Foreign Policy", in Emilian Kavalski (ed.), *The Ashgate Research Companion to Chinese Foreign Policy*, Surrey (England): Ashgate Publishing Limited: 89-101.

Cheng Zhongying (1991), 论中西哲学精神 [On the Spirit of Chinese and Western Philosophy], Shanghai: Orient Publishing Centre, Chapter 3, Quoted in Qin Yaqing (2015), "Relational Theory of International Politics", *World Economics and Politics*, No. 2: 9.

Chen Nan (2010), "印度：遥远的邻邦" India: Distant Neighbour, *Business Weekly,* URL: http://www.p5w.net/news/gjcj/201008/t3172947.htm.

Chen Chunhua; Jin Zhihui, and Jiang Zixue (2004), "Research on Cross-Culture Management of Developing Country Invested Joint Ventures in China: A Case Study of India K Company (China)", *China Soft Science*: 73-75.

Chen Fei (2015), On Strategic Connectivity between the OBOR Initiative and India's Mausam Project ["一带一路" 与印度" 季风计划" 的战略对接研究], *Global Review*, 2015, Vol. 6: 15-32.

Chen Jian (2011), "The New Explanation of *ren yi li zhi xin*", ['仁义礼智信' 新解], *People's Daily*, 15 July 2011: 7.

Chen Jihui (2007), "Half of Hundred Million Indians Rely on Tourism" [印度半亿人 靠旅游吃饭], *Global Times*, 13 February 2007, URL: http://world.people.com.cn/GB/14549/5401350.html.

Cheung, F. M.; Leung, K.; Fan, R. M.; Song, W. Z.; Zhang, J. X.; & Zhang, J. P. (1996), Development of the Chinese personality assessment inventory. *Journal of Cross-Cultural Psychology*, 27(2): 181-199. Quoted in Chhokar, Jagdeep S.; Brodbeck, Felix C., and House, Robert J. (eds.) (2007), *Culture and Leadership Across the World: The GLOBE Book of In-Depth Studies of 25 Societies*, London: Lawrence Erlbaum Associates: 888.

Chhokar, Jagdeep S. (2007), "India: Diversity and Complexity in Action", in Chhokar, Jagdeep S.; Brodbeck, Felix C., and House, Robert J. (eds.) (2007), *Culture and Leadership Across the World: The GLOBE Book of In-Depth Studies of 25 Societies*, London: Lawrence Erlbaum Associates: 990.

Chindia Chamber of Commerce and Industry (2013), "Our Members", accessed 4 April 2018, URL: http://en.ccei.org.in/Our-Members.html, http://www.ccei.org.in/3. The list of Chinese companies in India has also been updated following information from different channels.

Chhokar, Jagdeep S. (2007), "India: Diversity and Complexity in Action", In Chhokar, Jagdeep S.; Brodbeck, Felix C., and House, Robert J. (eds.) (2007), *Culture and Leadership Across the World: The GLOBE Book of In-Depth Studies of 25 Societies*, London: Lawrence Erlbaum Associates: 971-972, 992.

Chhokar, Jagdeep S.; Brodbeck, Felix C., and House, Robert J. (eds.) (2007), *Culture and Leadership Across the World: The GLOBE Book of In-Depth Studies of 25 Societies*, London: Lawrence Erlbaum Associates: 20.

China Global Television Network (2017), "Beyond political rift: How Asia's two oldest civilizations are filling the exchange gap", *The Point*, 9 August 2017.

Chen Honggen (2003), "中印古老文明交往的见证——记瓦杰帕伊访问洛阳" [Vajapayee visit Luoyang], accessed 3 March 2015, URL: http://news.xinhuanet.com/newscenter/2003-06/26/content_937984.htm.

Chen Ming-Jer (2001), Inside Chinese Business: A Guide for Managers Worldwide, Boston: Harvard Business School Press.

Chong Xuyi (2012), "The Political Economy of SOEs in China and India", cited in Chong Xuyi (ed.) (2012), *The Political Economy of State-owned Enterprises in China and India*, Basingstoke: Palgrave Macmillan.

Chen Huanzhang (2009), *The Economic Principles of Confucius and His School,* Translated by Zhai Yuzhong, Beijing: Central Compilation & Translation Press, Chapter 10, Chapter 15, No. 3, Chapter 16, Kindle eBook.

—— (1911), *The Economic Principles of Confucius and His School*, Treatise for Doctor of Philosophy, New York: Columbia University.

Chen Jiexuan (1994), *Cooperation Network and Life Structure: Social and Economic Analysis of Taiwan Small and Medium Enterprises*, Taipei: Linking Publishing: 59-60. In Huang Guangguo, Hu Xianjin et al. (2010), *Favour and Face: Power Game of Chinese,* Beijing: China People's University Press: 248.

Chen Jihui and Fu Chen (2003), "Indian PM and Poet: Vajpayee", accessed on URL: http://news.xinhuanet.com/book/2003-06/25/content_934496.html.

Chen Qinan and Qiu Shuru (1984), Fundamental Form of Business Organization and Traditional Family System: Comparative Studies of China, Japan and Western Society 企业组织的基本形态与传统家族制度——中 国、日本和西方社会的比较研究, *Chinese Style Management* in *Commercial Times*《工商时报》编《中国式管理》, *Taipei Times*: 459-484. In Huang Guangguo, Hu Xianjin *et al.*

(2010), *Favour and Face: Power Game of Chinese*, Beijing: China People's University Press: 247.

Chen Ruisheng (2006), "外交官看世界：睦邻外交四十年 (Diplomatist Worldview: Good Neighbour Diplomacy in Forty Years)", Cheng Dong: *Sichuan People's Publishing House* in Qiu Yonghui (2006), "Sino-Indian Cultural Communication in Globalization", *Journal of Sichuan University* (Social Science Edition): 4.

Chen Xiaoru (2013), "印度总理访华有稳定边界势态作用" [Indian PM's visit to China will be beneficial for stability of border], accessed 17 June 2015, URL: http://news.ifeng.com/mainland/special/xingefanghua2013/content-5/detail_2013_10/23/30582606_0.shtml.

Chen Ziming (2010), "Indian Music and Dance: Their Dissemination and Influence in China", *South Asian Studies*, 4: 145-153.

Cheng Chung-ying (1986), "The concept of face and its Confucian roots", *Journal of Chinese Philosophy*, 13: 329-348. In Huang Guangguo, Hu Xianjin et al. (2010), *Favour and Face: Power Game of Chinese*, Beijing: China People's University Press: 76.

Cheng Wei Yuan (2003), "Traditional Solidarity, Market and the Specialties and Generalities of the Employer-employee Relations in the East Asian Firms", *Journal of Labour*, Institute for Labour Research, National Chengchi University, Taipei, Taiwan: 22. In Huang Guangguo, Hu Xianjin et al. (2010), *Favour and Face: Power Game of Chinese*, Beijing: China People's University Press: 246-252.

Cheng Yan (2013), "印媒：习近平为辛格设宴是罕有礼遇" [Indian Media: Xi Jinping treats Singh with special courtesy], accessed 17 June 2015, URL: http://newspaper.jfdaily.com/xwcb/html/2013-10/23/content_1103790.html.

Chengappa, Raj and Shukla, Saurabh (2005), "The New Bhai Bhai", *India Today*, 30(15): 48-51.

Cheena Bhavana (2015), "Visva Bharati Complex", accessed 25 March 2015, URL: http://www.visva-bharati.ac.in/map/contents/cheenabhavan.html.

China Religion (2007), "中印友好交流的新篇章" [New chapter of China-India friendly exchanges], Reports, *China Religion* 3: 13-15.

Collier, P. (1999), "On the Economic Consequences of Civil War." *Oxford Economic Papers,* 51(1): 168-183; Collier, P.; V.L. Elliott, H. Hegre, A. Hoeffler, M. Reynal-Querol and N. Sambanis. (2004). *Breaking the Conflict Trap: Civil War and Development Policy*, Oxford: Oxford University Press.

Condoleezza Rice (2005), "Remarks en route to India", Archive of Department of State, USA, accessed 6 June 2015, URL: http://2001-2009.state.gov/secretary/rm/2005/43465.htm.

CPC (2017), *Constitution of the Communist Party of China*, Beijing: People's Press: 2-4, 13.

CSSN (2019), *"Main views of 2019 China Overseas Investment Country Risk Rating Report"* [《2019 中国海外投资国家风险评级报告》主要观点], *Chinese Social Sciences Net*, 16 January 2019, accessed 4 July 2019, URL: http://www.iwep.org.cn/xscg/xscg_sp/201901/t20190116_4811983.shtml.

Cyrus, Teresa L. (2015), "Culture and Trade in the European Union", *Journal of Economic Integration*, Vol. 30(2): 206-239.

Dabas, Maninder (2019), "Nagpur Police Arrest Five Including Three Chinese Nationals For Possessing Beef", *India Times*, 2 February 2019, accessed 20 April 2019, URL: https://www.indiatimes.com/news/india/nagpur-police- arrest-five-including-three-chinese-nationals-for-possessing-beef-361469.html.

Dai Yonghong, Qin Yonghong and Yi Xiang (2011), *The Behaviour Rule of Multinational Enterprise: India's Practice and Revelation,* Chengdu: Sichuan Publishing Group.

Damodaran, Harish (2008), *India's New Capitalist: Caste, Business and Industry in a Modern Nation*, Delhi: Palgrave Macmillan: 1-7, in Medha Kudaisya and Ng Chin-keong (eds.) (2009), *Chinese and Indian Business: Historical Antecedents*, Leiden: Brill NO: 85-86.

Deng Xiaoping (1988), "以和平共处五项原则为准则 建立国际新秩序" (To use Panchsheel as the norm to build new international order) in Deng Xiaoping (1993), *Deng Xiaoping Wenxuan* (Selected Works of Deng Xiaoping), 3, Beijing: People's Publishing House, 281; Dasgupta, A.K. (2006), "India- China Border War", *Economic and Political Weekly*, 25: 4834.

Dasgupta, Ajit K. (1993), *A History of Indian Economic Thought,* London: Routledge: 132, 185-189.

—— (1974), *Economic Theory and the Developing Countries*, London: Macmillan: 116.

Darbey, Abhishek Kr. (2018), "China-Africa Relations: Political, Defence and Security Aspects, 1996-2013", Ph.D. Thesis, Jawaharlal Nehru University.

*DEA (2006), "Bilateral Investment Treaties (BITs)/Agreements", Department of Economic Affairs, Ministry of Finance, Government of India, URL: https://dea.gov.in/bipa?page=5.

—— (2006), "Agreement between the Government of the Republic of India and the Government of the People's Republic of China for the Promotion and Protection of Investments", Department of Economic Affairs, Ministry of Finance, Government of India, 21 November 2006, URL: https://dea.gov.in/sites/default/files/China.pdf.

Dehejia, Rajeev H. and Dehejia, Vivek H. (1993), "Religion and Economic Activity in India", *American Journal of Economics and Sociology*, Vol. 52(2): 145-153.

Deepak, B.R. (2007), "中印大同' 要求中印边界纠纷早日解决" [Early Solution to the Border Dispute is the Prerequisite for 'CHINDIA'] in Tan Chung, Liu Chaohua and Huang Rong (eds.) (2007), *Chindia—Idealism and Realization*, Yinchuan: Ningxia People's Press: 348.

—— (2013), "Prof. B. R. Deepak on the panel of India-China Joint Working Group on Translation and Publication of Classic and Contemporary Works", *CCSEAS Newsletter*, 1(1): 2.

Dereesky, Helen (2011), *International Management: Managing Across Borders and Cultures Text and Cases*, Translated by Song Picheng, Beijing: Tshinghua University Press.

*DGTR (2019), "Anti-Dumping Cases", Directorate General of Trade Remedies, Department of Commerce, Ministry of Commerce and Industry, Government of India, accessed 28 May 2019, URL: http://www.dgtr.gov.in/anti-dumping-cases?title=&field_cn_code_value=&field_case_country_value=China&field_t

ype_of_proceeding_value=All&field_case_status_value=All&date_filter%5Bmin%5D%5Bmonth%5D=1&date_filter%5Bmin%5D%5Bday%5D=1&date_filter%5Bmin%5D%5Byear%5D=2000&date_filter%5Bmax%5D%5Bmonth%5D=12&date_filter%5Bmax%5D%5Bday%5D=31&date_filter%5Bmax%5D%5Byear%5D=2017&save=Search.

Dikshit, Sandeep (2013), "We're determined to talk it out, say India & China", accessed 17 June 2015, URL: http://www.thehindu.com/todays-paper/tp-national/were-determined-to-talk-it-out-say-india-china/article4737873.ece

—— (2013), "Ties hinge on peaceful border, Manmohan tells Li", accessed 17 June 2015, URL: http://www.thehindu.com/todays-paper/ties-hinge-on-peaceful-border-manmohan-tells-li/article4731730.ece.

Dikshit, Sandeep and Krishnan, Ananth (2013), "India plays down omission of 'Tibet' from joint statement", accessed 17 June 2015, URL: http://www.thehindu.com/todays-paper/tp-national/india-plays-down-omission-of-tibet-from-joint-statement/article4734561.ece.

Dikshit, Sandeep (2013), "Li may raise Depsang incident in talks", accessed 17 June 2015, URL: http://www.thehindu.com/todays-paper/li-may-raise-depsang-incident-in-talks/article4728967.ece.

*DIPP (2017a), "Foreign Direct Investment in India—Annual Issue 2017, Chapter – 3, Cumulative FDI equity inflows data statements, 3.2 Statement on country-wise /year-wise FDI equity inflows between January 2000 and December, 2017", URL: https://dipp.gov.in/sites/default/files/FDI_AnnualIssue_2017_Chapter3.2.pdf.

*—— (2017b), "Foreign Direct Investment in India—Annual Issue 2017, Focus Year 2017", Department of Industrial Policy & Promotion, Ministry of Commerce and Industry, Government of India, URL: https://dipp.gov.in/sites/default/files/FDI_AnnualIssue_2017_Focusyear.pdf.

*—— (2017c), "Foreign Direct Investment in India—Annual Issue 2017, Chapter – 1, Foreign Direct Investment (FDI) in India, 3. Investment Scenario, (A) 4. Sectors attracting highest FDI equity inflows", Department of Industrial Policy & Promotion, Ministry of Commerce and Industry, Government of India, URL: https://dipp.gov.in/sites/default/files/FDI_AnnualIssue_2017_Chapter1.3.A.iv.pdf.

*—— (2017d), "Foreign Direct Investment in India—Annual Issue 2017, Chapter 6, FDI synopsis on country, sector & RBI's regional offices (with state covered) received highest FDI equity inflows, 6.2 Sector profile: sector specific brief of top sectors attracting FDI inflows", Department of Industrial Policy & Promotion, Ministry of Commerce and Industry, Government of India, URL: https://dipp.gov.in/sia-newsletter/foreign-direct-investment-india-annual-issue-2017.

*—— (2017e), "Foreign Direct Investment in India—Annual Issue 2017, Chapter 6, 6.2 (v) Automobile Industry", URL: https://dipp.gov.in/sites/default/files/FDI_AnnualIssue_2017_Chapter6.2.v.pdf.

DNA (2014), "Did Arun Jaitley delete his blogpost on the India-China war report from his website?" accessed 5 June 2015, URL: http://www.dnaindia.com/india/report-did-arun-jaitley-delete-his-blogpost-on-the-india-china-war-report-from-his-website-2000849.

Dougherty, James E. and Pfaltzgraff, Robert L. Jr. (2001), *Contending Theories of International Relations: A Comprehensive Survey*, Boston: Addison Wesley Longman: 476.

Dong Juan (2007a), "薄伽梵歌与孙子兵法" [Bhagavad Gita and Sun-Tzu Art of War], *Business* (China Business Review), Vol. 1.

—— (2007), "从《孙子兵法》到《薄伽梵歌》"[From Sun-Tzu Art of War to Bhagavad Gita], *Corporate Culture* , Vol. 3: 80.

Doniger, Wendy (ed.) (1999), *Merriam-Webster's Encyclopedia of World Religions*, Merriam-Webster, Springfield: Incorporated Springfield: 186.

Dougherty, James E. and Pfaltzgraff, Robert L. Jr. (2001), *Contending Theories of International Relations: A Comprehensive Survey*, Boston: Addison Wesley Longman: 189.

Dr. Reddy's (2018a), "Our Founder", URL: http://www.drreddys.com/our-story/our-heritage/our-founder/.

—— (2018b), "Featured Stories", URL: http://www.drreddys.com/our-story/featured-stories/.

Dumont, Louis (1966), *Homo Hierarchicus: Essai sur le systeme des castes*, translated by Mark Sainsbury, Louis Dumont and Basia Gulati (1980), *Homo Hierarchicus: The Caste System and Its Implications*, Chicago: The University of Chicago Press.

Dutta, Vishal and Dave, Sachin (2017), "After yoga, PM Narendra Modi now wants to make khadi an international brand", *The Economic Times*, 23 May 2017, accessed on 23 May 2017, URL: http://economictimes.indiatimes.com/industry/cons-products/garments-/-textiles/after-yoga-modi-now-want-to-make-khadi-an-international-brand/articleshow/587 97198.cms.

EB (2019), "Jnana" (Indian Religion), *Encyclopaedia Britannica*, accessed 30 April 2019, URL: https://www.britannica.com/topic/jnana.

Economic Times Online (2017), "For Pakistan, a grim reminder from Sri Lanka: China gives loan, then grabs land", *The Economic Times*, 29 July 2017, accessed on 29 July 2017, URL: http://economictimes.indiatimes.com/article show/59822644.cms?utm_source=contentofinterest&utm_medium=text&utm_campaign=cppst.

Ellinger, Herbert (1996), *Hinduism*, London: Bloomsbury Academic: 69–70.

Embassy of the P. R. of China in India (2004), "Cultural Relations Between China and India Strengthened", accessed on 18 March 2015, URL: http://in.chineseembassy.org/eng/wh/t61253.html.

—— (2006), "China-India Joint Declaration", 30 November 2006, accessed on 18 March 2015, URL: http://in.china-embassy.gov.cn/eng/embassy_news/ 2006en/2 00611/t20061130_2375141.htm.

Embassy of India in Beijing, China (2016), "Economic and Trade Relations", accessed 21 April 2016, URL: http://www. indianembassy.org.cn/Dynamic Content.aspx?MenuId=97&SubMenuId=0.

*Embassy of India, Beijing, China (2018a), "Trade & Commerce, Indian Companies in China, Beijing", accessed 9 April 2018, http://indianembassybeijing.in/beijing.php.

*—— (2018b), "Indian Companies in China", accessed 9 April 2018, URL: http://indianembassybeijing.in/indian-companies-china.php.

Engels, Frederick (1914), *The Principles of Communism*, *Vorwärts!* (*Forward*), "Section 18", URL: https://www.marxists.org/archive/marx/works/1847/11/prin-com.html.

Express News Service (2017), "India will be 'patient, peaceful' in dealing with neighbours: Government", Express News Service, *The Indian Express*, 16 July 2017, accessed 16 July 2017, URL: http://indianexpress.com/article/india/india-will-be-patient-peaceful-in- dealing-with-neighbours-government-4752514/.

Express News Service (2008), "Pranab admits Chinese incursions, but says no need to panic", accessed 9 June 2015, URL: http://archive.indianexpress. com/news/pranab-admits-chinese-incursions-but-says-no-need-to-panic/260907/0.

Fan Zhonghui (ed.) (1993), "The Policy of New China's Foreign Cultural Exchanges", An Overview of China's Foreign Cultural Exchange (1949-1991), Beijing: Guangming Daily Press.

Fang Shuangjian (2009), "文化交流立丰碑—白马寺印度风格佛殿建设始末", accessed on 19 July 2015, URL: http://news.lyd.com.cn/content/2009/8/7/603471.shtml.

Fei Xiaotong (1988), *Fei Xiaotong Academic Excerption*, Beijing: Beijing Normal University Press: 359. In Shang Huipeng and You Guolong (2010), *Psycho-Culturology: The Research and Application of Francis L. K. Hsu,* Taipei: SMC Publishing Inc.: 324.

Feng Bing (2006), "重走"玄奘之路"回归人生精神 弘扬民族之魂" [Return to the road of Xuan Zang], accessed 19 April 2015, URL: http://news.sina.com.cn/o/2006-11-24/024210581220s.shtml.

Feng Zhongping (2004), "An Analysis of China's EU Policy Paper", *Journal of China Foreign Affairs University*, 75: 49.

Fishman, Ted C. (2005), *China, INC.: How The Rise of The Next Superpower Challenges America and the World*, New York: Scribner.

Fukuyama, Francis (1995), *Trust: the social virtues and the creation of prosperity*, New York: Simon & Schuster.

Fu Ping Ping, Wu Rongxian, Yang Yongkang, and Ye Jun (2008), "Chinese Culture and Leadership", in Jagdeep S. Chhokar, Felix C. Brodbeck and Robert J. House (eds.), *Culture and Leadership Across the World: The GLOBE Book of In-Depth Studies of 25 Societies*, Lawrence Erlbaum Associates: 884.

Fukuyama, Francis (1995), 信任：社会美德与创造经济繁荣 [Trust: The Social Virtues and The Creation of Prosperity], New York: Simon & Schuster, Chinese edition (2016), Guangxi Normal University Press, Kindle eBook.

Francis, L. and K. Hsu (1981), *Americans and Chinese: Passage to Differences,* University Press of Hawaii.

Gage, Richard L. (ed.) (1976), "*One World- East Asian role", Arnold Toynbee and Daisaku Ikeda Choose Life: A Dialogue,* London: Oxford University Press (Printed in Japan), 230.

Gandhi, Mahatma (1947), *India of My Dreams*, Ahmedabad: Navajivan Publishing House: 284, URL: http://www.mkgandhi.org/indiadreams/chap17.html.

Gao Yu (2013), "印度总理辛格结束访问回国 高度评价访华成果 http://news.ifeng.com/mainland/special/xingefanghua2013/content-5/detail_2013_10/25/30659184_0.shtml.

Gao Yang and Hu Ruifa (2017), "中印贸易变化原因及其发展策略分析" [Analysis of the Causes of China-India Trade Change and Its Development Strategy], *Foreign Economic Relations & Trade*, No. 6: 34.

Gay, Paul du and Pryke, Michael (eds.) (2002), *Cultural Economy: Cultural Analysis and Commercial Life*, London: Sage Publications Inc.: 1.

Gehrke, Joel (2019), "State Department preparing for clash of civilizations with China", *Washington Examiner*, 7 July 2019, accessed 7 July 2019, URL: https://www.washingtonexaminer.com/policy/defense-national-security/state-department-preparing-for-clash-of-civilizations-with-china.

Ge Weijun (2014), "Kochi", in Ministry of External Affairs (2014), Government of India, *Encyclopedia of India-China Cultural Contacts,* New Delhi: 792.

Ghosh, Abantika and Singh, Vijaita (2015), "Census: Hindu share dips below 80%, Muslim share grows but slower", URL: http://indianexpress.com/article/india/india-others/census-hindu-share-dips-below-80-muslim-share-grows-but-slower/99/#sthash.DDrh1Q02.dpuf.

Global Times (2013), "环球时报社评：总理" 首访 "印度 中国社会应当跟上"，*Global Times*, accessed 17 June 2015, URL: http://cpc.people.com.cn/n/2013/0520/c78779-21537374.html.

* Government of India (2008), "A Shared Vision for the 21st Century of the Republic of India and the People's Republic of China", Ministry of External Affairs, New Delhi.

—— (2011), "Census of India Organisation", URL: http://www.censusindia.gov.in/2011-common/aboutus.html.

—— (2011), "Distribution of Population by Religions", Census of India 2011, Ministry of Home Affairs, New Delhi, accessed 8 June 2015, URL: http://censusindia.gov.in/Ad_Campaign/drop_in_articles/04-Distribution_by_Religion.pdf.

*—— (2011), Census Data-Religion, Office of the Registrar General & Census Commissioner, India, Ministry of Home Affairs, Government of India, http://censusindia.gov.in/Census_And_You/religion.aspx.

*—— (2018), "Indian Meat Industry Red Meat Manual", Agricultural & Processed Food Products Export Development Authority, Ministry of Commerce & Industry, Government of India, URL: http://apeda.gov.in/apedawebsite/six_head_product/animal.html.

Goswami, Namrata (2013), "China's Incursions Show Strategic Blindness". *Asia Times* Online. 9 May 2013. Retrieved 11 May 2013.

Gouldner, Alvin (1960), "The Norm of Reciprocity: A Preliminary Statement", *American Sociology Review*, 25:1976-1977. In Huang Guangguo, Hu Xianjin et al. (2010), *Favour and Face: Power Game of Chinese*, Beijing: China People's University Press: 15.

Goldstein, Judith and Keohane, Robert O. (1993), *Ideas and Foreign Policy: Beliefs, Institutions, and Political Change*, Ithaca and London: Cornell University Press.

Goyal, Malini (2017), "How China beats India hollow in trade and dominates Indian homes, markets and economy", *Economic Times*, 16 July 2017, accessed 10 June 2019, URL: https://economictimes.indiatimes.com/news/economy/foreign-trade/china-dominates-indian-homes-markets-and-economy-as-trade-deficit-widens/articleshow/59611452.cms?from=mdr.

Goff, Patricia M. (2013), "Cultural Diplomacy" in Andrew F. Cooper, Jorge Heine, and Ramesh Thakur (eds.), *The Oxford Handbook of Modern Diplomacy*, Oxford: Oxford University Press.

Gransow, Bettina (1993), "Gifts and Corruption" 送礼与腐败——中国送礼形式和功能的转变, *Sociological Research* 社会学研究, 1993, No. 6: 9, 11.

Grewe, Alexander (2005), "'I'm sick to death with you...' or External Character Conflicts in Fawlty Towers", Seminar Paper, Passau: University of Passau. U R L: https:/ /books.google.co.in/books?id=wRnUcigKzqEC&pg= PA10&redir_esc=y#v=onepage&q&f=false.

Guan Shijie (1995), *Intercultural Communication* [*kua-wen-hua jiao-liu-xue:ti-gao she-wai jiao-liu neng-li de xue-wen*], Beijing: Peking University Press: 340-341, reprinted in 2012.

—— (2015), "中华文化国际影响力评估体系初探" [The Primary Study of the International Influence of Chinese Culture], Duiwai Chuanbo [International Communications], 1: 45-48.

Guiso, Luigi; Sapienza, Paola and Sapienza, Luigi (2006), "Does Culture Affect Economic Outcomes?", *Journal of Economic Perspectives*, Vol. 20(2): 23.

Gupta, Anil K.; Pande, Girija and Wang Haiyan (2014), *The Silk Road Rediscovered: How Indian and Chinese Companies are Becoming Globally Stronger By Winning in Each Other's Markets,* San Francisco: Jossey-Bass.

Gupta, Anil Kumar (2016), *Grassroots Innovation: Minds on the Margin Are Not Marginal Minds*, Gurgaon: Penguin Random House India, "Introduction", Kindle eBook.

—— (2016), personal interview, Indian Institute of Management, Ahmedabad, India, 17 December 2016.

Gupta, Bina (2006), "Bhagavad Gita as Duty and Virtue Ethics", *Journal of Religious Ethics*, 34(3): 385-386.

Gu B. (2017), personal interview, The Third Construction & Engineering Company, Hebei, China, 1 February 2017.

Guo Dan (2018), "中印贸易发展现状及前景分析" [Analysis of the Status Quo and Prospects of Sino-Indian Trade Development], *Business Story*, No. 2: 197.

Gusai, Yojna (2017), "SJM steps up drive to target Chinese goods", *The Asian Age*, 3 July 2017, accessed 19 April 2019, URL: https://www.asianage.com/india/all-india/030717/sjm-steps-up-drive-to- target-chinese-goods.html

Hanban (2017), "About Confucius Institutes", Hanban/Confucius Institute Headquarters, Chinese Ministry of Education, URL: http://www.hanban.edu.cn/confuciousinstitutes/node_10961.html.

Han Qi and Chen Xingyu (2007), "中国与印度利用 FDI 比较分析" [Comparative Analysis of Using FDI in China and India], *International Economic Cooperation*, No. 9, 2007: 49.

Hangzhou Iron & Steel Group Co., Ltd. (2016), "Introduction" 公司简介, URL: http://www.hzsteel.com/jx//gywm/gsjj.html.

Harshey, Sohnee (2017), "Man Vs Cow: Solve the Puzzle, 7. What does the Constitution say about the cow?", *Economic and Political Weekly*, accessed 13 April 2018, URL: http://www.epw.in/man-versus-cow-solve- puzzle?0=ip_login_no_cache%3D7ba1bf0bf287f44ef325e387246bddc7.

Harriss-White, Barbara (2003), *India Working: Essays on Society and Economy*, Cambridge University Press: 133-136.

He Youhui, Chen Shujuan and Zhao Zhiyu (1989), "Rational orientation: Seeking answers to the Chinese social psychology methodology" [guan-xi qu-xiang: wei zhong-guo she-hui xin-li fang-fa-lun qiu-da-an]; Yang Guoshu and Huang Guangguo (1989) (eds.), *Psychology and Behaviour of Chinese* [zhong-guo- ren de xin-lin yu xing-wei], Taipei: Guiguan Tushu Company: 49-66.

He Xinhua (1996), "试评甘地的反工业主义思想" [Evaluation of anti-Industrial ideology of Gandhi], *Zhangye Shizhuan XueBao*, Vol. 13(1): 22-27.

Heim, Maria (2005), "Differentiations in Hindu Ethics", in Schweiker, William (2005) (ed.), *The Blackwell Companion to Religious Ethics*, Oxford: Black Publishing: 350.

Henrich, Joseph et al. (2005), "'Economic Man' in Cross-Cultural Perspective: Behavioural Experiments in 15 Small-scale Societies", *Behavioural and Brain Sciences*, 28(6): 795-815.

Hiralaxmi Craft Park (2008a), "About us", URL: http://www.hmcraftpark.co.in/aboutus.html.

—— (2008b), "Craft", URL: http://www.hmcraftpark.co.in/leather.html

Hilton, William (2013), "Gifts Economy and the Reform of China Economic System" 送礼经济和中国经济体制改革, *China Today*, 15 March 2013, accessed 8 September 2018, URL: http://www.chinatoday.com.cn/ctchinese/economy/article/2013- 03/15/content_527523.html.

Hoppe, Michael H. (2007), "Culture and Leader Effectiveness/The GLOBE Study", URL: http://www.inspireimagineinnovate.com/pdf/globesummary-by-michael-h-hoppe.pdf.

Holisti, K. J. (1992), *International Politics: A Framework for Analysis*, 6th edn., Englewood Cliffs: Prentice Hall: 9-10.

Hsu, Francis L. K. (1963), *Clan, Caste and Club*, New York: Van Nostrand Reinhold.

—— (1973), "亲属之钥", *Center Magazine*, Vol. 6(6), November/December 1973: 4-14.

—— (1981), *American and Chinese: Passage to Difference*, Honolulu: University Press of Hawaii.

—— (1985), "The self in cross-cultural perspective", in Marsella, A.J.; DeVos, G. and Hsu, F.L.K. (1985) (eds.), *Culture and Self: Asian and Western Perspectives*, New York: Tavistock Publications: 32-35.

Huaxia Xinghuo (2007), "Huaxi Village: A Model of Building a New Socialist Countryside", *Huaxia Xinghuo*: 47-53.

Hu, H. (2019), personal interview, Taj Palace, New Delhi, 27 May 2019.

Hu, Pingsheng and Zhang Meng (2017), *Li-Ji (*Book of Rites), Zhong Hua Book Company: 419-441.

Hu Shisheng (2015), The Space to connect Maritime Silk Road and Project Mausam [“海上丝路”与“季风计划”的对接空间], *Xinhua Net*, 16 March 2015, accessed 30 November 2017, URL: http://news.xinhuanet.com/globe/2015-03/16/c_134064582.html.

Hu Xu (2018), “How do local State-Owned Enterprises take the road of reform?” *Economic Information Daily*, 2 July 2018, accessed 21 September 2018, URL: http://jjckb.xinhuanet.com/2018-07/02/c_137294536.html.

Hu Jintao (2006), “携手拓展合作 共创美好未来” [Deepen Mutually Beneficial Cooperation for a Better Future], Ministry of Foreign Affairs of the People’s Republic of China, accessed 18 March 2015, URL: http://www.fmprc.gov.cn/mfa_chn/ziliao_611306/zyjh_611308/t281240.shtml.

Huan Pingqing (2017), “A Study of Confucius Idea of Nationalities from ‘Rarely Speaking of the Barbarians”: With a Discussion of the Theoretical Consciousness in Ethnic Studies”, *Journal of Chinese Humanities*, No. 1 (Serial No. 358): 113-115, URL: http://ethn.cssn.cn/mzx/yysx/201709/t20170911_3636165.shtml.

Huang Guangguo (1987), “Face and Favour: The Chinese Power Game”, *American Journal of Sociology*, Vol. 92(4), January 1987: 944-974.

—— (2010), “儒家关系主义与华人企业的组织文化” (Confucian relationships and organizational culture of Chinese enterprises), in Huang Guangguo, Hu Xianjin et al. (2010), *Favour and Face: Power Game of Chinese* 人情与面 子：中国人的权力游戏, Beijing: China People’s University Press: 245, 247.

Huntington, Samuel P. (1993), “The Clash of Civilizations?”, *Foreign Affairs*, Vol. 72(3): 22.

—— (1996), *The Clash of Civilizations and the Remaking of World Order*, New Delhi: Random House India, reprinted 1 January 2016: 45, 209.

—— (1996), *The Clash of Civilizations and the Remaking of World Order*, Translated by Zhou Qi et al. (2013), Beijing: Xinhua Publishing House.

Hussain, Mehdi (2017), “Cultural Foundation of India’s Look East Policy: A Critique”, *Journal of South Asian Studies*, 5 (03): 147-155.

Hymer, Stephen Herbert and Rowthron, Robert (1976), “Multinational Corporations and International Oligopoly: The Non-American Challenge”, in Stephen Herbert Hymer, *The International Operations of National Firms: A Study of Direct Foreign Investment,* Cambridge: MIT Press, 1976: 183-207.

IANS-Indo-Asian News Service (2008), “119 get Padma awards”, *Hindustan Times*, accessed 9 June 2015, URL: http://www.hindustantimes.com/india-news/119-get-padma-awards/article1-271820.aspx.

ICBCMB (2016), “Chinese company India Survival Report” [中资企业印度生存报告], Industrial and Commercial Bank of China Limited, Mumbai Branch, 3 October 2016, accessed 1 May 2018, URL: https://mp.weixin.qq.com/s? __biz = MzA4MjI3NTg5Nw==&mid=2652612183&idx=1&sn=1dc11f9f5db6fa772c65fe9c121155e6&chksm=84673d01b310b417b0b404c1290bbdccfc84040b928e9 1fce540bcdd242d75f1915c947e7a71&sc ene=38#wechat_redirect.

ICS (2017), “Third Bangladesh-China-India-Mynamar Economic Corridor Joint Study Group Meeting”, 25-26 April 2017; Kolkata, Institute of Chinese Studies, 25 April 2017, accessed 24 October 2018, URL: https://www.icsin.org/third-bangladesh-china-india-mynamar-economic-corridor-joint-study-group-meetin g 25-26-april-2017-kolkata.

Indian Council for Cultural Relations (2015), "Constitution: The Objects of the Council", accessed 20 July 2015, URL: http://iccr.gov.in/content/constitution.

Iyer, Sriya (2018), *The Economics of Religion in India*, Cambridge, Massachusetts: The Belknap Press of Harvard University Press: 25, 43.

Iyer-Mitra, Abhijit (2017), "A Molehill Out of a Mountain", *The Economic Times*, 11 August 2017, accessed 11 August 2017: 20, URL: http://blogs.economictimes.indiatimes.com/et-commentary/a-molehill-out-of- a-mountain/.

Iyengar, Rishi (2015a), "India Stays World's Top Beef Exporter Despite New Bans on Slaughtering Cows", *Time*, 24 April 2015, accessed 17 October 2018, URL: http://time.com/3833931/india-beef-exports-rise-ban-buffalo-meat/.

—— (2015b), "Indian Prime Minister Narendra Modi Is Now Being Worshipped Like a God", *Time*, 12 February 2015, accessed 30 October 2018, URL: http://time.com/3706501/india-narendra-modi-temple-god/.

Jacob, Jabin T. (2008), "Manmohan Singh's Visit to China: New Challenges Ahead", *China Report*, 44(1): 63-70.

Jaiswal, Suraj (2017), "Foreign Direct Investment in India and Role of Tax Havens", New Delhi: Centre for Budget and Governance Accountability (CBGA), URL: http://www.cbgaindia.org/wp-content/uploads/2017/12/Foreign-Direct-Investm ent-in-India-and-Role-of-Tax-Havens.pdf.

JCCEICCC (2014), *Encyclopedia of India-China Cultural Contacts*, Joint Compilation Committee for the Encyclopedia of India-China Cultural Contacts, New Delhi: MaXposure Media Group (I) Pvt. Ltd.: 3.

Ji Xianlin (1986), "交光互影的中外文化交流", in Ji Xianlin (2008), *The History of China and India Cultural Exchanges*, Beijing: China Social Sciences Press: 153.

—— (1998), *A History of Sugar*, Nanchang: Jiangxi Educational Press.

—— (2008), *The History of Sino-Indian Cultural Exchanges*, Beijing: China Social Sciences Press: 145.

Jiang Lu, Wang Hong and Dong Yudong (2008), "The Cultural Difference of China and India and Its Influence on Attracting FDI", *International Economic Cooperation*, Vol. 11: 33-39.

Jiao Liwei and Stone, Benjamin M. (2014), *500 Common Chinese Proverbs and Colloquial Expressions: An annotated frequency dictionary*, New York: Routledge: 13.

Jindal Steel & Power Limited (2014), "About Us, O.P. Jindal—A Tribute", accessed 25 May 2018, URL: http://www.jindalsteelpower.com/o-p-jindal-a- tribute.html

Jin Canrong and Zhang Kunpeng (2018), "The world trend and China's strategic choice in the next ten years under the background of New Era", *Northeast Asia Forum*, 2018, Vol. 1, URL: https://mp.weixin.qq.com/s/V8x-by1-mXFCvDeie OlAWw.

Johnston, Alastair Iain (1995), *Cultural Realism: Strategic Culture and Grand Strategy in Chinese History*, New Jersey: Princeton University Press: 39-40.

Jose, P. Chacko, Rajan, K. and Krishnan, C. (2011), *History of Economic Thought (BA Economics)*, University of Calicut: 175-176, URL: http://www.univer sityofcalicut.info/SDE/Economic_thought.pdf.

JSW Steel (2018), "About Us", URL: http://www.jsw.in/steel/about-us

Kane, Pandurang Vaman (1941), *History of the Dharmasastra (Ancient and Medieval Religious and Civil Law)*, Vol. II, Part I, Poona: Bhandarkar Oriental Research Institute: 696-698.

Kapp, William H. (1963), *Hindu Culture, Economic Development and Economic Planning in India*, New York: Asia Publishing House; In Kudaisya, Medha (2009), *Marwari and Chettiar Merchant's, c. 1850s-1950s: Comparative Trajectories*; in Medha Kudaisya and Ng Chin-keong (eds.) (2009) *Chinese and Indian Business: Historical Antecedents*, Leiden: Brill NV: 85-86.

Karmali, Naazneen (2006), "India's 40 Richest", *Forbes*, accessed 4 June 2018, URL: https://web.archive.org/web/20120727215554/http://www.forbes.com/global/2006/1127/039.html.

Kaynak, Erdener; Wong, Y.H. and Leung Thomas (2012), *Guanxi: Relationship Marketing in a Chinese Context*, New York: Routledge.

Kazi, Reshmi Fatima (2002), "Chronology of India-China relations (1947-2002)", rediff.com, URL: http://www.rediff.com/news/chtime.html.

Ke Zhiming (1993): *The Entrepreneurship, Management and Production Organization of Taiwan's Urban Small Manufacturing Industry: A Case Study of Wufenpu Garment Manufacturing Industry,* Taipei: Institute of Ethnology, Academia Sinica; In Huang Guangguo, Hu Xianjin et al. (2010), *Favour and Face: Power Game of Chinese*, Beijing: China People's University Press: 248.

Khera, Reetika (2017), "What Explains the Popular Support for Demonetisation?" *The Wire*, 27 February 2017, accessed on 20 October 2018, URL: https://thewire.in/uncategorised/what-explains-the-popular-support-for- demonetisation.

Kondapalli, Srikanth (2008), "PM in China: Stability in times of turmoil", accessed 5 June 2015, URL: http://www.rediff.com/news/2008/jan/09guest1.html.

—— (2010), "Dr Manmohan Singh and Wen Jiabao can use their great personal rapport to enhance relations between India and China", accessed 12 June 2015, URL: http://www.rediff.com/news/column/column-what-to-expect- from-wen-jiabaos-visit/20101210.html.

Koehn, Daryl (2001), "Confucian Trustworthiness and the Practice of Business in China", *Business Ethics Quarterly*, Vol. 11(3), (July 2001): 415-429.

Krishna, S.M. (2012), "Address by External Affairs Minister on 'India's External Environment and Current Foreign Policy Challenges' at the Institute of South Asian Studies, Singapore", in Bhasin, Avtar Singh (2013), *India's Foreign Relations-2012 Documents*, New Delhi: Geetika Publishers: 23.

Kristoff, Nicholas and Wudunn, Sheryl (1994), *China Wakes: The Struggle for The Soul of A Rising Power*, New York: Vintage Books.

Krishnan, Rishikesha (2010), *From Jugaad to Systematic Innovation: The Challenge for India*, Bangalore: Amazon Asia-Pacific Holdings Private Limited.

Kudaisya, Medha (2009), Marwari and Chettiar Merchant's, c. 1850s-1950s: Comparative Trajectories, in Medha Kudaisya and Ng Chin-keong (eds.) (2009), *Chinese and Indian Business: Historical Antecedents*, Leiden: Brill NV: 85-86.

Kugler, Jacek; Ronald L. Tammen and Siddharth Swaminathan (2001), Power Transitions and Alliances in the 21st Century, *Asian Perspective*, Vol. 25: 5-29.

Kumar, Rajesh and Worm, Verner (2011), International Negotiation in China and India: A Comparison of the Emerging Business Giants, London: Palgrave Macmillan.

Kumar, Ranjit (2013), "बॉर्डर विवाद को लेकर चीन से कोई ठोस समझौता होने की उम्मीदें कम नवभारत टाइम्स" (Border dispute with China to lower expectations of a firm agreement), accessed 17 June 2015, URL: http://navbharattimes.indiatimes.com/india/Li-Keqiangs-visit-to-India/articleshow/20130868.cms.

Kunkel, John H. (1965), "Values and Behaviour in Economic Development", *Economic Development and Cultural Change*, Vol. 13(3): 257-277.

Kurz, Heinz D. (2013), *Geschichte des okonomischen Denkens*, Muchen: Verlag C.H. Beck oHG, Translated by Li Han (2016), 经济思想简史 [The Brief History of Economic Thought], Beijing: China Social Sciences Press, Chapter III, Marx and Socialist Scholars.

Krishnan, Ananth (2013), "Chinese State media sees Li visit as marking 'new chapter'," accessed 17 June 2015, URL: http://www.thehindu.com/todays-paper/tp-national/chinese-state-media-sees-li-visit-as-marking-new-chapter/article4728974.ece.

Khanna, Tarun (2005), "Climb Over the Great Wall", *India Today*, XXX (15): 58.

Krishnan, Ananth (2013), "Li visit 'strong boost' to ties, say Chinese media", accessed 17 June 2015, URL: http://www.thehindu.com/todays-paper/tp-national/li-visit-strong-boost-to-ties-say-chinese-media/article4737871.ece.

Laalit (2014), "Bharat Ratna Atal Bihari Vajpayee's 1977 UN General Assembly Speech Still Makes Us Proud", *Times of India*, accessed 18 March 2015, URL: http://www.indiatimes.com/news/india/bharat-ratna-atal-bihari-vajpayees-1977-un-general-assembly-speech-still-makes-us-proud-229059.html

Lakhani, Somya (2017), "On Mathura-bound train, 15-year-old killed, brother says were called beef eaters", *The Indian Express*, 24 June 2017, accessed 13 April 2017, URL: http://indianexpress.com/article/india/18-year-old-stabbed-to-death-they-flung-our-skull-cap-pulled-beard-ballabhgarh-mathura-bound-train-4719096/.

Lala, R.M. (1981), *The Creation of Wealth: The Tatas from the 19th to the 21st* Century, Bombay: IBH Publishers Pvt. Ltd.: 3, reprinted 2004.

Lam, Kit-Chun Joanna (2003), "Confucian Business Ethics and the Economy", *Journal of Business Ethics*, Vol. 43(1/2): 153.

Landes, David S. (1998), *The Wealth and Poverty of Nations: Why Some are So Rich and Some So Poor*, New York: W. W. Norton & Company: 516.

Lan Jianxue (2006), "中印文化交流：意义、特点及问题" [China-India cultural exchanges: significance, characteristic and issues], CASS Academic Report: 2.

Li F. (2017), personal interview, Tata Sons Office, Beijing, 24 February 2017.

Li Junyong and Liu Enwei (2008), "中印关系：认知与理解——解读中国高校学生眼中的印度" [China-India relations: knowing and understanding—a perception from a Chinese University student], *South Asian Studies*, 1: 36-41.

Li Jianping (2013), "中印学者称辛格访华将实现" 龙象合作 "新突破", accessed 17 June 2015, URL: http://www.chinanews.com/gn/2013/10-19/5400407.shtml.

Li Li (2017), "Analysis of India's Deviation from Non-Alignment and its Motivation", *Quarterly Journal of International Politics*, Vol. 2(1): 8, 34.

Li Peilin, Jiang Xiaoxing and Zhang Qizai (1992), *Chinese Enterprises in Transition: Organizational Innovation of State-owned Enterprises*, Jinan: Shandong People's Press; In Huang Guangguo, Hu Xianjin et al (eds.) (2010) *Favour and Face: Power Game of Chinese*, Beijing: China People's University Press: 249-250.

Li Xiao (2015), "The Belt and Road Initiative and China's Investment in India", *International Economic Review*: 19-42.

Li Xiang (2004), "Sino-Indian Trade and Economic Cooperation Status Quo and Prospect", *South Asian Studies Quarterly*: 108.

Li Wengui (2010), "On the Economic Effects of FDI in India and its Revelation for China", *South Asian Studies Quarterly*, Sum No. 140, No. 1, 2010: 66.

Li Zhiquan (2010), "印度佛殿" 落户"洛阳白马寺　印度总统揭碑题献", accessed 19 July, URL: http://www.chinanews.com/gn/news/2010/05-29/2311825.shtml

Li Zhifeng and Le Aiguo (2014), "Thoughts on the Evolution of Chinese Communist Party's Attitude towards Traditional Culture and Policy" [*zhong-guo gong-chan-dang dui-dai chuan-tong wen-hua tai-du yu zheng-ce yan-bian si-kao*], *People's Tribune*, Sum. 460, No. 32: 9.

Li Zhongping (2016), "China's Top Ten Business Groups", *China Social Science Net (CSSN)*, URL: http://www.cssn.cn/zt/zt_zh/zhgshdshb/.

Lieberthal, Kenneth G. (2014), *Managing the China Challenge: How to Achieve Corporate Success in the People's Republic*, translated by Wei Xing el na, Bejing: China Social Sciences Press.

Lin Minwang (2017), "中巴经济走廊建设应考虑第三方参与吗?" [Should the construction of the China-Pakistan Economic Corridor consider third-party participation?], *World Affairs*, Vol. 10.

Lin Justin Yifu (2011), "China's Economic Development and Cultural Renaissance in the Multipolar Growth World of the 21st Century", URL: http://siteresources.worldbank.org/DEC/Resources/84797-1104785060319/598886-1104852366603/599473-1223731755312/Lin-Chin a_Economic_Development_and_Cultural_Renaissance_in_the_Multipolar_Gr owth_World-Beijing_Forum.pdf.

—— (2012), 解读中国经济 *Demystifying the Chinese Economy*, Beijing: Peking University Press: 30-31.

Liu Dongkai (2010), "胡锦涛同印度总统帕蒂尔举行会谈" [Hu Jintao meets Indian President Patil], *Xinhua Net*, accessed 12 June 2015, URL: http://news.Xinhuanet.com/politics/2010-05/27/c_12150540.html.

Liu Weijia (2006), "Will Uncle Die if Have Hair Cut in the First Month of the Year? Nonsense" '正月剪头死舅舅'? 扯!, *Huashang Chenbao,* 14 March 2006, accessed on 8 September 2018, URL: http://news.sina.com.cn/o/2006-02-14/08008198187s.shtml?from=wap.

Liu Yang (2016), "The Cooperation and Double-Win Situation of BRI to Fast Develop", *People's Daily*, 31 October 2016, accessed 20 September 2018, URL: http://www.gov.cn/xinwen/2016-10/31/content_5126297.html.

Lebow, Richard Ned (2008), *A Cultural Theory of International Relations*, Cambridge: Cambridge University Press: 69.

—— (2015), *A Cultural Theory of International Relations*, translated by Chen Kai, Shanghai Academy of Social Sciences Press.

Lee, Lavina (2015), "India as a nation of consequence in Asia: The potential and limitations of India's 'Act East' policy", *The Journal of East Asian Affairs*, Vol. 29(2): 67.

Lee, Peter (2013), "China's Border Rows Mirror Grim History", *Asia TimesOnline*, 3 May 2013. Retrieved 11 May 2013.

Lei Ming (2015), e-mail to the author, 29 April 2015.

LeBaron, Michelle (2003), "Culture and Conflict", Beyond Intractability (eds.) Guy Burgess and Heidi Burgess. Conflict Information Consortium, University of Colorado, Boulder. Posted: July 2003, URL: http://www.beyondintract ability. org/essay/culture-conflict

Levi-Strauss, Claude (1965), "The Principle of Reciprocity", in *Sociological Theory*, edited by L.A. Coser and B. Rosenberg, New York: Macmillan: 61-70.

Long Xingchun (2016), *India Major-Power Diplomacy*, Beijing: China Social Sciences Press: 3.

Lu Xin (2013), *Research on India's Foreign Trade Policy*, Dalian: Dongbei University of Finance and Economics Press: 205-208.

Lu Yang (2017), "Doklam standoff: China's understanding of India has increased", *The Indian Express*, 1 September 2017, accessed on 1 September 2017, URL: http://indianexpress.com/article/opinion/doklam-standoff-china- understanding-of-india-has-increased-4823264/.

Luo Yadong (2007), *Guanxi and Business*, Singapore: World Scientific Publishing: 1.

Luo Zhaohui (2017), "In My Eyes: India, Indians and India-China Relations—Remarks by H.E. Ambassador Luo Zhaohui at the United Service Institution of India", Embassy of the People's Republic of China in the Republic of India, 5 May 2017, accessed 29 November 2017, URL: http://in.china-embassy.org/eng/embassy_news/t1459430.htm. Also see Luo Zhaohui (2017), "Turn the Old Page to a New Chapter for a Promising Future of Sino-India Relations", 22 September 2017, URL: http://in.china-embassy.org/eng/ gdxw/t1496066.html.

—— (2018), "Remarks by Ambassador Luo Zhaohui at China-India Youth Dialogue 2018", Chinese Embassy, 16 November 2018, accessed 9 July 2019, URL: http://in.chineseembassy.org/eng/dsxxs/dshdjjh/t1613935.html.

—— (2019), "Remarks by Ambassador Luo Zhaohui at Farewell Reception", Embassy of the People's Republic of China in the Republic of India, 27 May 2019, accessed 5 July 2019, URL: http://in.china- embassy.org/eng/gdxw/t1667032.html.

Luthans, Fred and Doh, Jonathan P. (2012), *International Management: Culture, Strategy and Behavior*, New York: McGraw-Hill, translated by Zhao Shuming and Cheng Dejun (2009), Beijing: China Machine Press.

Lv Pengfei (2013), "首届中印媒体高峰论坛开幕", URL: http://paper.people.com.cn/rmrb/html/2013-09/17/nw.D110000renmrb_20130917_10-03.html.

Ma Jiali (2005), "两个亚洲巨人的握手" [The handshake of the two giants], 《崛起中的巨象——关注印度》 [The Rising Elephant: India]: 199-201.

—— (2008), "学学印度的文化自信" [To learn cultural confidence from India], *People's Daily* Online, accessed 5 March 2015, URL: http://world.people.com.cn/GB/1030/6775782.html.

Ma Xueling (2013), "印度总理今起访华 "龙" "象" 频密互动谋新局" [Indian PM started his visit to China today], accessed 17 June 2013, URL: http://www.chinanews.com/gn/2013/10-22/5406408.shtml.

Ma Xiaoning, Ren Yan and Chen Jihui (2005), "温家宝在印度德里理工大学发表演讲" [Wen Jiabao's speech in IIT, New Delhi], accessed 18 March 2015, URL: http://news.xinhuanet.com/newscenter/2005-04/13/content_2821642.html.

Madhukar, R.K. and Prabhu, A. K. (1996), "Canara Bank: Case I", in Budhiraja, S.B. and Athreya, M.B., *Cases in Strategic Management*, New Delhi: Tata McGraw-Hill Publishing Company Limited: 108.

Mahajan, Ashwani (2017), "Boycott China: Interview with Dr. Ashwani Mahajan", *Swadeshi Patrika*, August 2017: 10-12, URL: https://www.swadeshion line.in/category/english-patrika?page=1.

Maitra, Pradip Kumar (2017), "'Total boycott': RSS affiliate up in arms against Chinese goods", *Hindustan Times,* accessed 1 August 2017, URL: http://www.hindustantimes.com/india-news/total-boycott-rss-affiliate-up-in- arms-against-chinese-goods/story-2pdjBwq5QnPIpwdGrUfu4O.html.

Malinowski (1926), Bronislaw, "Reciprocity as the Basis of Social Structure", in *Crime and Custom in Savage Society*, London: Routledge: 46-49; Kegan Paul, in Huang Guangguo, Hu Xianjin et al (eds.) (2010), *Favour and Face: Power Game of Chinese*, Beijing: China People's University Press: 15.

Mankiw, N. Gregory (2012), *Principles of Economics*, translated by Liang Xiaomin and Liang Xiaoli, Beijing: Peking University Press: 10.

Mao Keji (2015), "严肃地探讨为什么印度人爱 '开挂'"? [Seriously Discuss why Indians like 'kai gua' (unbelievably good in using special software used to cheat in an online game)?], URL: http://www.guancha.cn/MaoKeJi/2015_06_11_322915.shtml.

Mao Shichang and Liu Xuelan (eds.) (2011), 辉煌灿烂的印度文化的主流——印度教 [The glorious and splendid mainstream of Indian culture—Hinduism], Beijing: China Social Sciences Press, "前言 印度教——印度主流文化 以 及认识印度的一把钥匙" [Preface, Hinduism—India's mainstream culture and a key to know India], Kindle eBook.

Marques, Joan (2014), "The Caribbean Community: A Promise yet Unfulfilled", in Christiansen, Bryan (2014) (ed.), *Handbook of Research on Economic Growth and Technological Change in Latin America*, Pennsylvania: IGI Global. URL: https://www.igi-global.com/dictionary/economic-relations/41234.

Mashelkar, R. A. (2017), President, Global Research Alliance, Chairman, National Innovation Foundation, "From Incremental to Disruptive Innovation", Lecture in Seminar Hall, Indian Institute of Technology, New Delhi, 10 January 2017, URL: http://www.iitd.ac.in/content/lecture-dr-r-mashelkar-frs.

March, Robert M. and Wu Su-hua (2007), *The Chinese Negotiator: How to Succeed in the World's Largest Market*, Tokyo: Kodansha International Ltd.: 127. Mencius, *Mencius*.

Marx, Karl (1970), *Critique of the Gotha Program*, Moscow: Progress Publishers.

McLane, John R. (2002). "Land and Local Kingship in Eighteenth-Century Bengal", *Cambridge South Asian Studies,* Vol. 53, Cambridge University Press: 131.

Meng Jie (ed.) (2014), "Chinese President Confers Friendship Award in India", *Xinhuanet*, New Delhi, 19 September 2014, URL: http://news.xinhuanet.com/english/china/2014-09/19/c_133656854.html.

Mencius (c.300 BC), *The Mencius*, Book 6, Gaozi, Part A, 6A.6.

Mente, Boye Lafayette De (1994), *Chinese Etiquette and Ethics in Business*, New York: NTC Publishing Group: 121. Quoted from Koehn, Daryl (2001), "Confucian Trustworthiness and The Practice of Business in China", *Business Ethics Quarterly*, Vol. 11(3) (July 2001): 429.

Menon, Ramdas (1985), "Banking and Trading Castes in the Colonial Period: The Case of the Nattukotai Chettiars of Tamil Nadu", *South Asia Bulletin*, Vol. 5(2): 19-26. Quoted in Kudaisya, Medha (2009), "Marwari and Chettiar Merchant's, c. 1850s-1950s: Comparative Trajectories", in Medha Kudaisya and Ng Chin-keong (eds.) (2009), *Chinese and Indian Business: Historical Antecedents*, Leiden: Brill NV: 85-86.

*MEA (2018), "Transcript of Weekly Media Briefing by Official Spokesperson (20 December 2018)", 20 December 2018, accessed 20 December 2018, Ministry of External Affairs, Government of India, URL: https://www.mea.gov.in/media-briefings.htm?dtl/30808/Transcript_of_Weekly_Media_Briefing_by_Official_Spokes person_December_20_2018.

MFAPRC (2018), "Deputy Minister of Foreign Affairs Le Yucheng accepted an interview with the Financial Times of UK" [外交部副部长乐玉成接受英国《金融时报》专访实录], Ministry of Foreign Affairs of the People's Republic of China, 10 September 2018, accessed 2 October 2018, URL: https://www.fmprc.gov.cn/web/wjbxw_673019/t1598794.shtml

MHL (2017), "Brochure", Metallon Holding Limited, URL: http://www.metallon corporate.com/about-mhl-group.php: 3-6.

Miao Ru (2015), Personal interview by Zhang Yang, 27 January 2015.

Mishra, N. (2017), personal interview, Beijing, China, 1 March 2017.

Mitra, Sounak (2017), "Baba Ramdev's Patanjali eyes two-fold rise in sales at Rs. 20,000 crore in FY18", *Livemint*, 4 May 2017, accessed 9 August 2018, URL: http://www.livemint.com/Industry/cjCMZnD0eGkYOMjayFuUVN/Patanjali-eyes-2fold-rise-in-revenue-at-Rs-20000-crore-in.html?from=timeline&isappinstalled=0.

Ministry of Home Affairs (2005), "Padma Awards", Government of India, URL: http://www.mha.nic.in/sites/upload_files/mha/files/Scheme-PadmaAwards-050514.pdf.

Ministry of Education of the P. R. of China (2014), "郝平会见印度驻华大使对中印教育合作交流" [Hao Ping meets Indian Ambassador to China for China-India education cooperation exchanges], accessed 4 July 2015, URL: http://www.jsj.edu.cn/news/1/489.shtml.

—— (2014), "2014 年全国来华留学生数据统计" [The analysis of a foreign student in China in 2014], accessed 4 July 2015, URL: http://www.jsj.edu.cn/news/1/579.shtml.

—— (2014), "为帮助自费出国留学人员正确选择国外学校教育部公布 46 个国家学校名单" [The list of Universities from 46 Countries from Ministry of

Education for helping students choose the right universities], accessed 4 July 2015, URL: http://www.jsj.edu.cn/news/1/414.shtml.
—— (2014), "外国高等学校名单" [List of foreign universities], accessed 4 July 2015, URL: http://www.jsj.edu.cn/n1/12018.shtm.
*Ministry of Development of North Eastern Region (2015), Government of India, "Restricted/Protected Area Permit", accessed 21 July 2015, URL: http://www.mdoner.gov.in/content/rappap-restrictedprotected-area-permit.
*Ministry of Foreign Affairs of the People's Republic of China (2003), "China's Policy Paper on the EU", accessed 18 July 2015, URL: http://www.fmprc.gov.cn/mfa_chn/ziliao_611306/tytj_611312/zcwj_611316/t27700.shtml.
—— (2006), "China's Policy Paper on Africa", accessed 18 July 2015, URL: http://www.fmprc.gov.cn/mfa_chn/ziliao_611306/tytj_611312/zcwj_611316/t230612.shtml.
—— (2008), "China's Policy Paper on Latin America and the Caribbean", accessed 18 July 2015, URL: http://www.fmprc.gov.cn/chn//pds/ziliao/tytj/zcwj/t521016.html.
—— (2014), "China's Policy Paper on the EU", accessed 18 July 2015, URL: http://news.xinhuanet.com/world/2014-04/02/c_1110054550.html.
Ministry of External Affairs, Government of India (2015), "Indian Foreign Service", accessed 18 July 2015, URL: http://www.mea.gov.in/indian-foreign-service.htm.
—— (2015), "India and Neighbours", accessed 20 July 2015, URL: http://mea.gov.in/india- and-neighbours.html.
—— (2012), "India-China bilateral relations", accessed 20 July 2015, URL: http://mea.gov.in/Portal/ForeignRelation/China-January-2012.pdf.
Ministry of Finance, Government of India, "Annual Report 2015-2016", URL: http://finmin.nic.in/reports/AnnualReport2015-16.pdf.
Ministry of Commerce and Industry, Government of India, "Annual Report 2009-2010: Commercial Relations and Trade Agreement", URL: http://commerce.nic.in/publications/anualreport_chapter8-2009-10.asp.
——, "Annual Report 2009-2015", URL: http://commerce.nic.in/publications/contents-PDF-2010- 11.asp.
——, "Outcome Budget2010-2011", URL: http://commerce.nic.in/publications/Outcome_budget201011.pdf?id=19.
*——, "Outcome Budget 2013-2014", URL: http://commerce.nic.in/publications/outcome_budget_2013_14.pdf?id=27.
——, "Foreign Trade Policy 2004-2005", URL: http://dgft.gov.in/exim/2000/policy/contents.html.
——, "Foreign Trade Policy [1 April 2015-31 March 2020]", URL: http://dgft.gov.in/exim/2000/ Updated_FTP_2015-2020.pdf.
——, "Foreign Trade Policy Statement (2015-2020)", URL: http://dgft. gov.in/exim/2000/FTPstatement2015.pdf.
—— (2003), "Conference of Commercial Representatives of India Based in Select WANA Countries, Final Report", URL: http://commerce.nic.in/publications/conf_wana.pdf.

—— (2008), "Strategy for Increasing Exports of Pharmaceutical Products, Report of the Task Force", URL: http://commerce.nic.in/publications/Report%20Task%20Force%20Pharma%2012th%20Dec%2008.pdf?id=16.

Ministry of Culture, Government of India, "Cultural Agreement Between the Government of the Republic of India and the Government of the People's Republic of China", URL: http://www.indiaculture.nic.in/sites/default/ files/Cultural %20Agreement/170.pdf.

*——, "Chinese delegation headed by Minister of Religious Affairs of China calls on Union Tourism and Culture Minister", URL: http://www.indiaculture.nic.in/sites/default/files/press _ release/chinese%20delegation.pdf.

Ministry of External Affairs,Government of India (2003), "Declaration on Principles for Relations and Comprehensive Cooperation Between the Republic of India and the People's Republic of China", URL: http://www.mea.gov.in/in-focus-article.htm?7679/Declaration+on+Principles+for+Relations+and+Comprehensive+Cooperation+Between+the+Republic+of+India+and+the+Peoples+Republic+of+China.

—— (2005) "Joint Statement of the Republic of India and the People's Republic of China", URL: http://www.mea.gov.in/bilateral-documents.htm?dtl/6577/Joint+Statement+of+the+Republic+of+India+and+the+Peoples+Republic+of+China.

—— (2005), "Report of the India-China Joint Study Group on Comprehensive Trade and Economic Cooperation", URL: http://www.mea.gov.in/Uploads/PublicationDocs/6567_bilateral-documents-11-april-2005.pdf.republic_of_India _and_Beijing_Peoples_Republic_of_China.

*—— (2015), "Business MoU/Agreements signed at India-China Business Forum during PM's visit to Shanghai (16 May 2015)", URL: http://www.mea.gov.in/bilateral-documents.htm?dtl/25248/.

—— Business_MoU_Agreements_signed_at_ India_China_Business_Forum_during_PMs_visit_to_Shanghai_May_16_2015.

—— (2016), "Agreed Minutes of 4th India-China Strategic Economic Dialogue", URL: http: //www.mea.gov.in/bilateral-documents.htm?dtl/27478/ Agreed_Minutes_of_4th_IndiaChina_Strategic_Economic_Dialogue.

*—— (2017), "Official Spokesperson's response to a query on participation of India in OBOR/BRI Forum", 13 May 2017, accessed 2 October 2018, URL: https://mea.gov.in/media-briefings.htm?dtl/28463/Official%2BSpokespersons%2Bresponse%2Bto%2Ba%2Bquery%2Bon%2Bparticipation%2Bof%2BIndia% 2Bin%2BOBORBRI%2BForum.

*—— (2018), "Official Spokesperson's response to a query on media reports regarding possible cooperation with China on OBOR/BRI", 5 April 2018, accessed 2 October 2018, URL: https://www.mea.gov.in/media- briefings.htm?dtl/29768/Official%2BSpokespersons%2Bresponse%2Bto%2Ba%2Bquery%2Bon%2Bmedia%2Breports%2Bregarding%2Bpossible%2Bcooperation%2Bwith%2BChina%2Bon%2BOBORBRI.

Ministry of Foreign Affairs of the People's Republic of China (2016), "China-India Relations" [中国同印度的关系], February 2016, accessed 23 July 2016, URL: http://www.fmprc.gov.cn/web/gjhdq_676201/gj_676203/yz_676205/1206_677220/ sbgx_677224/.

*Ministry of Commerce of the People's Republic of China (2001), 中国商务年鉴 China *Commerce Yearbook*, http://history.mofcom.gov.cn/book/book.asp?p=677&bid={1379CEEB-C429- 4D18-90B9-150AA29EA1CE}.

*—— (2006), "Foreign Market Access Report: 2006", URL: http://images.mofcom.gov.cn/trb/accessory/ 200603/2006en.PDF.

*—— (2014), China Foreign Trade and Economic Cooperation Gazette, No. 51.

*—— (2015), "Country Trade Report: The main origin of India trade deficit", URL: http : //countryreport.mofcom.gov.cn/record/view110209.asp?news_id=48163.

*—— (2015), "五、印度与中国的经贸关系" [Fifth Economic and Trade Relations between India and China], accessed 4 March 2019, URL: http://history.mofcom.gov.cn/?bandr=ydyzgdjmgx.

—— (2018), *Country Report*, "2017 India Goods Trade and China-India Bilateral Trade Survey," 13 March 2018, accessed 5 April 2018,URL: https://countryreport.mofcom.gov.cn/record/view110209.asp?news_id=58276.

—— (2018a), "Report of Foreign Investment in China 2018": 91-92, URL: http://images.mofcom.gov.cn/wzs/201810/20181009090547996.pdf.

—— (2018b), "Statistical Bulletin of FDI in China": 91-92, URL: http://images.mofcom.gov.cn/wzs/201811/20181113170135971.pdf.

—— (2018c), Country Report, 2017, "The United States Goods Trade and China-US Bilateral Trade Survey", 7 March 2018, accessed 5 April 2018, https://countryreport.mofcom.gov.cn/record/view110209.asp?news_id=58151.

—— (2018d), Country Report, 2017, "Japan Goods Trade and China-Japan Bilateral Trade Survey, 13 February 2018, accessed 5 April 2018, URL: https://countryreport.mofcom.gov.cn/record/view110209.asp?news_id=57703.

*—— (2018), "Report on Development of China's Outward Investment", URL: http://images.mofcom.gov.cn/fec/201901/20190128155348158.pdf: 19.

Ministry of Culture, PRC (2015), "Bureau for External Cultural Relations", accessed 10 July 2015, URL: http://www.chinaculture.org/2015-02/02/content_595553.html and http://www.mcprc.gov.cn/gywhb/jgsz/bjg/201111/t20111121_278092.html.

—— (2015), "Department of Policies and Regulations", accessed 10 July 2015, URL: http://www.chinaculture.org/2015-02/02/content_595546.html.

Ministry of Foreign Affairs, PRC (2015), "China's Foreign Policy", accessed 10 July 2015, URL: http://www.fmprc.gov.cn/mfa_chn/ziliao_611306/tytj_611312/zcwj_611316/t24782.shtml.

*Ministry of Culture, Government of India (2015), "Mission Statement", accessed 20 July 2015, URL: http://www.indiaculture.nic.in/mission-statement.

Mohan, C. Raja (2017), "Raja Mandala: Doklam's unintended consequence", *The Indian Express*, URL: http://indianexpress.com/article/opinion/columns/doklams-unintended-consequence-sikkim-standoff-china-india-narendra-modi-xi-jinping-4786837/

Morris, Morris David (1995), "Book Reviews: Dwijendra Tripathi and Makrand Mehta, *Business Houses in Western India: A Study in Entrepreneurial Response*, 1850-1956, New Delhi: Manohar, 1990: 223, Rs. 175; *Economic Development and Cultural Change*, Chicago: The University of Chicago Press: 900.

Myrdal, Gunnar (1972), *Asian Drama: An Inquiry into the Poverty of Nations*, Middlesex: Penguin Press.

Mohan, C. Raja (2014), "Chinese takeaway: String of Pearls", accessed 8 July 2015, URL: http://indianexpress.com/article/opinion/columns/chinesetakeaway-string-of-pearls/99/.

Movchan, Andrey (2015), "5 factors limiting the impact of the BRICS nations", URL: https://www.weforum.org/agenda/2015/07/5-factors-limiting-the-impact-of-th e-brics-nations/.

Mohapatra, Amulya and Mohapatra, Bijaya (1993), *Hinduism: Analytical Study*, New Delhi: Mittal Publications.

Muniapan, B. and Dass, M. (2008), "Corporate social responsibility: A philosophical approach from an ancient Indian perspective", *International Journal of Culture and Business Management*, 1(4): 408-420. Quoted in Balakrishnan Muniapan and Biswajit Satpathy (2013), "The 'Dharma' and 'Karma' of CSR from the Bhagavad Gita", *Journal of Human Values*, 19(2): 177.

Muniapan, Balakrishnan and Satpathy, Biswajit (2013), "The 'Dharma' and 'Karma' of CSR from the Bhagavad-Gita", *Journal of Human Values,* 19(2), (2013): 173-187.

Munshi, Kaivan (2016), "Caste and the Indian Economy", URL: http://www.histe con.magd.cam.ac.uk/km/Munshi_JEL1.pdf.

Murphy, I.P. (1996), "It Takes *Guanxi* to Do Business in China", *Marketing News,* 30(22), 12, quoted in Fu Ping Ping, Wu Rongxian, Yang Yongkang, and Ye Jun (2008), *Chinese Culture and Leadership*; in Jagdeep S. Chhokar, Felix C. Brodbeck and Robert J. House (eds.), *Culture and Leadership Across the World: The GLOBE Book of In-Depth Studies of 25 Societies*, Lawrence Erlbaum Associates: 884.

Murugappa (2018), "About Us", Murugappa Group, accessed 14 June 2018, URL: http://www.murugappa.com/about-us/.

Murlidharan, S. (2014), "Modi's 'first develop India' slogan may actually shoo foreign investors away", *Firstpost*, 25 September 2014, accessed 8 April 2019, URL: https://www.firstpost.com/business/economy/modis-first-develop-india-slogan-may-actually-shoo-foreign-investors-away-1992015.html.

Mulgan, G. (ed.) (1997), *Life After Politics*, London: Fontana. In Gay, Paul du and Pryke, Michael (eds.) (2002), *Cultural Economy: Cultural Analysis and Commercial Life*, London: Sage Publications Inc.: 2.

Myrdal, Gunnar (1968), *Asian Drama: An Inquiry into the Poverty of Nations*, Vol. I, Middlesex (England): Penguin Press.

Nadkarni, M.V. (2017), *The Bhagavad-Gita for the Modern Reader: History, interpretations and philosophy*, New York: Routledge: 266.

Nanda, Meera (2009), "Hindu Triumphalism and the Clash of Civilisations", *Economic and Political Weekly*, Vol. 44(28): 108.

National Bureau of Statistics of the People's Republic of China (2003), *China National Conditions and Strength*, URL: http://www.stats.gov.cn/tjzs/tjsj/tjcb/ zggqgl/200312/t20031219_37428.html.

—— (2012), "Statistical Communiqué on the 2011 National Economic and Social Development", URL: http://www.stats.gov.cn/english/NewsEvents/201202/t20120222_26575.html.

Narayanan, Dinesh (2016), "Pakistan, terrorists & China: Read how India's superspy Ajit Doval wants to tackle all 3", *The Economic Times*, 27 September 2016, URL: http://economictimes.indiatimes.com/news/politics-and-nation/pakistan-terrorists-china-read-how-indias-superspy-ajit-doval-wants-to-tackle-all-3/articleshow/54535404.cms, accessed on 27 September 2016.

Naisbitt, John and Naisbitt, Doris (2010), *China's Megatrends: The 8 Pillars of A New Society*, New York: Harper Collins.

Nair, Gayatri (2016), "The Bitter Aftertaste of Beef Ban 'Choice', Caste and Consumption", *Economic and Political Weekly*, Vol. 51(10), 5 March 2016, URL: https://www.epw.in/system/files/pdf/2016_51/10/The_Bitter_Aftertaste_of_Beef_Ban_0.pdf.

Nav Bharat Times (2010), "चीन ने तिब्बत में बनाई अहम सुरंग" (China made a key tunnel in Tibet), accessed 14 June 2015, URL: http://navbharattimes.indiatimes.com/world/asian-countries/-/yearendershow10/7107359.cms.

—— (2010), "चीन से रिश्ते" (Relationship with China), accessed 14 June 2015, URL: http://navbharattimes.indiatimes.com/opinion/editorial/-/articleshow/7118011.cms.

—— (2013), "चीन से बॉर्डर को लेकर समझौता होने की उम्मीदें कम" (The border agreement with China is in low expectations), accessed 17 June 2015, URL: http://navbharattimes.indiatimes.com/articleshow/20131155.cms.

Nalanda University (2014), "Nalanda's History", Rajgir, URL: http://www.nalandauniv.edu.in/abt-history.html.

* NBS (2001a), "17-1 Foreign Trade and Economic Cooperation", *China Statistical Yearbook 2001* 中国统计年鉴 (2001 年), National Bureau of Statistics, URL: http://www.stats.gov.cn/tjsj/ndsj/2001c/q1701c.html.

—— (2001b), "17-7 Value of Imports and Exports by Country (Region)", *China Statistical Yearbook 2001*, National Bureau of Statistics, URL: http://www.stats.gov.cn/tjsj/ndsj/2001c/q1707c.html.

—— (2001c), "17-13 Utilized Foreign Investment", *China Statistical Yearbook 2001,* National Bureau of Statistics, URL: http://www.stats.gov.cn/tjsj/ndsj/2001c/q1713c.html.

—— (2001e), "17-22 Turnover of Economic Cooperation with Foreign Countries or Regions", *China Statistical Yearbook 2001,* National Bureau of Statistics, URL: http://www.stats.gov.cn/tjsj/ndsj/2001c/q1722c.html.

—— (2001f), "17-15 Foreign Direct Investment Actually Utilized and Other Investment Amount (by Countries or Regions)" [*shi-ji li-yong wai-shang zhi- jie he qi-ta tou-zi e (an guo-bie, di-qu fen*], *China Statistical Yearbook* 2001, URL: http://www.stats.gov.cn/tjsj/ndsj/2001c/mulu_q.htm.

—— (2018a), "11-1 Foreign Trade and Economic Cooperation", *China Statistical Yearbook 2018*, National Bureau of Statistics, URL: http://www.stats.gov.cn/tjsj/ndsj/2018/indexch.html.

—— (2018b), "11-14 Foreign Direct Investment Actually Utilized by Countries or Regions", *China Statistical Yearbook 2018*, National Bureau of Statistics, http://www.stats.gov.cn/tjsj/ndsj/2018/indexch.html.

—— (2018c), "11-5 Value of Imports and Exports by Country (Region) of Origin/Destination (2017), *China Statistical Yearbook 2018*, National Bureau of Statistics, URL: http://www.stats.gov.cn/tjsj/ndsj/2018/indexch.html.

— (2018d), "11-19 Overseas Direct Investment by Countries or Regions", *China Statistical Yearbook 2018*, National Bureau of Statistics, URL: http://www.stats.gov.cn/tjsj/ndsj/2018/indexch.html.

—— (2018e), "11-22 Economic Cooperation with Foreign Countries or Regions (2017)", *China Statistical Yearbook 2018*, National Bureau of Statistics, URL: http://www.stats.gov.cn/tjsj/ndsj/2018/indexch.html.

—— (2018f), "11-23 Explanatory Notes on Main Statistical Indicators", *China Statistical Yearbook 2018*, National Bureau of Statistics, URL: http://www.stats.gov.cn/tjsj/ndsj/2018/indexch.html.

*NCERT, "Policies, Programmes and Schemes for Educational Development of Children from Scheduled Castes", National Council of Educational Research and Training: 7-9, URL: http://www.ncert.nic.in/departments/nie/degsn/pdf_files/degsnmodule6.pdf.

Needle, David (2004), *Business in Context: An Introduction to Business and Its Environment*, London: Thomson Learning: 239. https://books.google.com/books?id=jP6OngEACAAJ&printsec=frontcover&source=gbs_ge_summary_r&cad=0#v=onepage&q=organizational%20culture %20&f=false.

Nehru, Jawaharlal (1946), *Discovery of India*, (Centenary Edition), New Delhi: Oxford University Press: 56.

NNM (2014), Nava Nalanda Mahavihara (Deemed to be University), Ministry of Culture, Government of India, "Xuan Zang Memorial Hall", accessed 2 February 2015, URL: http://www.nnm.ac.in/xuanzang_memorial_hall.html.

Ni Xiangqin and Wang Xiaoying (2006), "A Trail Discussion on Developing Characteristics of Sino-Indian Trade Cooperation and Its Influential Factors", *South Asian Studies Quarterly*, No. 4: 97.

Nie Yun (2008), "印度官员说将与中国加强文化交流" [Indian official said they will strengthen cultural exchange with China], *People's Daily* Online, URL: http://world.people.com.cn/GB/10540026.html.

Nie Zhihong (2012), 中国经济思想史撷要 [Research on the History of China's Economic Thought], China Minzhu Fazhi Press: 70-71.

Niu Donghao (2010), "外交部就温家宝访印度、巴基斯坦举行媒体吹风会" [MFA media meeting before Wen Jiabao's India Pakistan visit], accessed 11 June 2015, URL: http://www.china.com.cn/policy/txt/2010-12/14/content_21536557.html.

Nuri, Maqsudul Hasan (2016), "China's economic development: Confucian values", *Business Recorder*, 2 April 2016, accessed 12 October 2018, URL: https://fp.brecorder.com/2016/04/2016040332073/.

—— (2017), "Confucian values and China's development trajectory", *Shanghai Daily*, 14 March 2017, accessed 15 November 2018, URL: https://archive.

shine.cn/opinion/foreign-perspectives/Confucian-values- and-Chinas-developm ent- trajectory/shdaily.shtml.

Oberg, Kalvero (1951), "Cultural Shock", Institute of International Education: Chicago, Talk delivered on 28 November 1951, URL: http://citeseerx.ist. psu.edu/viewdoc/download?doi=10.1.1.461.5459&rep=rep1 &type=pdf.

O'Neil, Jim (2001), "Building Better Global Economic BRICs", Goldman Sachs Global Economics Paper, No. 66, November 2001.

—— (2011), *The Growth Map: Economic Opportunity in the BRICs and Beyond*, London: Portfolio Penguin.

O.P. Jindal (2018), "About Bauji", accessed 25 May 2018, URL: http://opjindal.com/ about_bauji.html.

Oxford University Press (2017), "Swadeshi", Oxford Living Dictionaries, URL: https://en.oxforddictionaries.com/definition/swadeshi.

Orru, M.; Biggart, N. W. and Hamilton, G. G. (eds.) (1997), *The Economic Organization of East Asian Capitalism*, Thousand Oaks, CA: Sage. In Huang Guangguo, Hu Xianjin et al. (2010), Favour and Face: Power Game of Chinese, Beijing: China People's University Press: 247.

Pan Song (2010), *What Should We Learn from India: the Rise and Revelation of India's Super-premium Enterprises*, Beijing: China Machine Press.

People's Daily (2004), "UN report: China becoming major investor abroad", URL: http://en.people.cn/200401/07/eng20040107_132003.shtml.

Pan, S. S. (2018), personal interview, I.G.I Airport, New Delhi, India, 6 May 2018.

Pant, Harsh V. (2014), "觀點：習近平印度之行為何意義重大" [Why Xi Jinping's visit to India is significant], accessed 5 March 2015, URL: http://www. bbc.com/zhongwen/trad/china/2014/09/140917_analysis_china_india_relation.

Parsai, Gargi (2013), "India, China renew flood data pact on Brahmaputra", accessed 17 June 2015, URL: http://www.thehindu.com/todays-paper/tp-national/india-china-renew-flood-data-pact-on-brahmaputra/article4734680.ece.

Patil, Reshma (2017), "More Chinese Cos Investing In India, But Political & Cultural Barriers Remain", *India Spend*, 10 April 2017, accessed 9 July 2019, URL: https://archive.indiaspend.com/cover-story/more-chinese-cos-investing-in-indi a-but-political-cultural-barriers-remain-45078.

Patanjali (1998), *Yoga: Discipline of Freedom, the Yoga-sutra attributed to Patañjali*, Translated by Miller, Barbara Stoler (1998), Berkeley: University of California Press: 2, 31, 35-39, 53-54.

Patricia M. Goff (2013), "Cultural Diplomacy" in Andrew F. Cooper, Jorge Heine, and Ramesh Thakur (eds.), *The Oxford Handbook of Modern Diplomacy*, Oxford: Oxford University Press.

People's Republic of China (1982), Constitution of the People's Republic of China, accessed 10 July 2015, URL: http://www.gov.cn/gongbao/content/2004/ content_62714.html.

People's Daily (1990), "China will never allow other countries to interfere in its internal affairs", 11 July 1990, accessed 9 July 2019, URL: http://en.people.cn/dengxp/vol3/text/d1150.html.

—— (2013), “汇聚战略共识、构建战略互信” [Unity, the strategic consensus to build strategic mutual trust], accessed on 17 June 2015, URL: http://politics.people.com.cn/n/2013/0522/c1001-21579355.html.

Pew Research (2020), “Top 10 Countries with the Highest Number of Buddhists”, accessed 22 March 2022, URL: https://worldpopulationreview.com/country-rankings/buddhist-countries#:~:text=Buddhist%20Countries%202021%20%20%20%20Country%20,%20%20779%2C898%20%2054%20more%20rows%20.

Phoenix TV (2013), “温家宝中午以老朋友身份宴请印度总理辛格” [Wen Jiabao treats Indian PM Singh to lunch as old friend], accessed 17 June 2015, URL: http://news.ifeng.com/mainland/special/xingefanghua2013/content-5/detail_2013_10/24/30623314_0.shtml.

PMO (2014), Prime Minister’s Office, “PM: Buddhism is a very strong bond between China and India”, accessed 20 February 2015, URL: http://pmindia.gov.in/en/news_updates/pm-buddhism-is-a-very-strong-bond-between-china-and-india/.

Pokharel, Sugam and George, Steve (2018), “China and India agree to maintain border peace, as summit ends”, *CNN*, 29 April 2018, accessed 11 June 2018, URL: https://edition.cnn.com/2018/04/28/asia/modi-xi-summit- statement/index.html.

Pratt, Andy C. (2007), “Cultural Economy”, An entry (MS 146) in *The International Encyclopaedia of Human Geography,* Kitchen and Thrift (eds.), URL: http://www.andycpratt.info/andy_c_pratt/Research_Writing__Downloads_files/cultural.pdf.

* Press Information Bureau (2015), “RGI releases Census 2011 data on Population by Religious Communities”, Press Information Bureau, Government of India, Ministry of Home Affairs, 25 August 2015, URL: http://pib.nic.in/newsite/PrintRelease.aspx?relid=126326.

PM India (2018), “Major Initiatives: Swachh Bharat Abhiyan”, URL: http://www.pmindia.gov.in/en/major_initiatives/swachh-bharat-abhiyan/.

Press Trust of India (2006), “Guarded Chinese support to nuclear energy quest”, accessed 26 May 2015, URL: http://www.thehindu.com/todays-paper/guarded-chinese-support-to-nuclear-energy-quest/article3050300.ece.

—— (2006), “Visa norms for Chinese liberalised”, *The Hindu*, accessed May 2015, URL: http://www.thehindu.com/todays-paper/tp-national/visa-norms-for-chinese-liberalised/article3050817.ece.

—— (2008), “Aokang opens first manufacturing facility in India”, *The Economic Times*, 28 July 2008, accessed 10 April 2018, URL: https://economictimes.indiatimes.com/industry/cons-products/durables/aokang-opens-first-manufacturing-facility-in-india/articleshow/3298993.cms.

—— (2010), “Wen quotes Upanishads, praises Mahatma”, *Times of India*, accessed 12 June 2015, URL: http://timesofindia.indiatimes.com/india/Wen-quotes-Upanishads-praises-Mahatma/articleshow/7113101.cms.

—— (2010), “Wen Jiabao sets positive tone, calls India ‘great neighbour’,” *Times of India*, accessed 12 June 2015, URL: http://timesofindia.indiatimes.com/

india/Wen-Jiabao-sets-positive-tone-calls-India-great-neighbour/articleshow/7110215. cms.

—— (2013), "Chinese Premier Li Keqiang arrives to hold talks with PM on boundary, water issues", accessed 17 June 2015, URL: http://archive.indianexpress.com/news/chinese-premier-li-keqiang-arrives-to-hold-talks-with-pm-on-boundary-water-issues/1117844/0.

—— (2013), "83% Indians view China as major security threat: Poll", accessed 17 June 2015, URL: http://archive.indianexpress.com/news/83-indians-view-china-as-major-security-thr/1118252/.

—— (2013), "India and China ink eight agreements on trade, water resources", accessed 17 June 2015, URL: http://archive.indianexpress.com/news/india-and-china-ink-eight-agreements-on-trad/1118220/.

—— (2013), "Li Keqiang's visit: Tibetan groups threaten protest, security stepped up" accessed 17 June 2015, URL: http://archive.indianexpress.com/news/li-keqiangs-visit-tibetan-groups-threaten-protest-security-stepped-up/1118170/0.

—— (2014), "Modi, Xi hold talks; India conveys concern over incursions", *The Hindu*, accessed 8 July 2014, URL: http://www.thehindu.com/news/national/modi-xi-hold-talks-india-conveys-concern-over-incursions/article6422361. ece.

—— (2014), "Chinese Army pushes in more troops into Indian territory", *The Hindu*, accessed 8 July 2014, URL: http://www.thehindu.com/news/national/chinese-army-pushes-in-more-troops-into-indian-territory/article6422339.ece.

—— (2014), "Keeping a tradition alive, Xi meets family of Dr. Kotnis", *The Hindu*, accessed 8 July 2014, URL: http://www.thehindu.com/news/national/chinese-president-xi-jinping-meets-family-of-dr-dwarkanath-kotnis/article6426545.ece.

—— (2014), "Amarinder Singh wants disclosure of Henderson Brooks Report on '62 War", *Times of India*, accessed 5 June 2015, URL: http://articles.economictimes.indiatimes.com/2014-11-16/news/56137327_1_national-war-memorial-great-war-henderson-brooks-report.

—— (2015), "India, China bound by 'unbreakable bond": PM Narendra Modi" , *The Indian Express*, New Delhi, 3 February 2015 , accessed February 3, 2015, URL: http://indianexpress.com/article/india/india-others/india-china-bound-by-unbreakable-bond-pm-narendra-modi/.

—— (2015), "Dadri: Outrage after mob lynches man for allegedly consuming beef", *The Indian Express*, 25 December 2015, accessed 13 April, URL: http://indianexpress.com/article/india/india-others/outrage-after-man-lynched-over-rumour-of-storing-beef-in-house/.

—— (2016), "GST bill taken up in Rajya Sabha, most parties support except AIADMK", *Press Trust of India*, 3 August 2016, accessed 30 October 2018, URL: https://yourstory.com/2016/08/rajya-sabha-takesup-gst/.

—— (2017), "Doklam Standoff ends: MEA says Modi to attend BRICS summit in China", Press Trust of India, 29 August 2017, accessed 11 June 2018, URL: https://www.hindustantimes.com/india-news/day-after-doklam-standoff- ends-mea-says-pm-modi-to-attend-brics-summit-in- china/story- hscMDwatFd2nEC3D5nucBK.html.

—— (2018), "India-China amends double taxation avoidance treaty", *The Economic Times*, 26 November 2018, accessed 22 May 2019, URL: https://eco nomictimes.

indiatimes.com/news/economy/policy/india-china-amends-double-taxation-avoidance-treaty/articleshow/66811070.cms.

—— (2018), "India should join BRI, says Chinese expert", *Times of India*, 31 January 2018, accessed on 2 October 2018, URL: https://timesofindia.indiatimes.com/india/india-should-join-bri-says-chinese- expert/articleshow/62726558.cms.

Qian Tong (2013), "习近平会见印度总理辛格 就中印关系提出四点建议" [Xi Jinping met Indian PM Singh and made four propositions], accessed 3 March 2015, URL: http://news.ifeng.com/mainland/special/xingefanghua2013/content-5/detail_2013_10/23/30596912_0.shtml.

Qiao Taiping (2006), "《西游记》暑假热播值得深思" [It is worth to think deeply that Xiyouji (Journey to the West) is popular in summer vacations], 中华读书报 (China Reading Weekly), Beijing, 23 August 2006, URL: http://www.gmw.cn/01ds/2006-08/23/content_469025.html.

Qin Yaqing (1998), "Level-of-Analysis Method and Scientific International Relations Research", *Europe*, Vol. 3; In Qin Yaqing (2005), *Power, Institutions and Culture: Anthology of International Relations Theory and Methodology*, Beijing: Peking University Press: 243-255, reprinted in 2016.

—— (2012), **"**Relations and Processes: Cultural Construction of Chinese International Relations Theory**"**, Shanghai: Shanghai People's Publishing House, Quoted in Qin Yaqing (2015), "Relational Theory of International Politics", *World Economics and Politics*, No. 2: 6.

—— (2015), "Relational Theory of International Politics", *World Economics and Politics*, No. 2: 6.

Qiu Yonghui (2007), "The Creation of A New Cultural World of 'CHINDIA'," in Tan Chung, Liu Chaohua and Huang Rong (eds.) (2007), *Chindia—Idealism and Realization*, Yinchuan: Ningxia People's Press.

Qu Tingyi (2017), "中国赴印度旅游客人同比增长 24%" [Chinese tourists to India increased by 24% year-on-year], *The Beijing News*, 21 June 2017, accessed 9 September 2018, URL: http://epaper.bjnews.com.cn/html/2017- 06/21/content_685838.htm?div=-1.

Radjou, Navi; Prabhu, Jaideep and Ahuja, Simone (2012), *Jugaad Innovation: A Frugal and Flexible Approach to Innovation for the 21st Century*, Gurgaon: Random House India: 3-5.

Rahul Saraogi (2014), *Investing in India: A Value Investor's Guide to the Biggest Untapped Opportunity in the World*, translated by Zheng Lei and Yuan Guiguan (2015), Beijing, China Machine Press.

Ramakrishnan, Venkitesh (2004), "The Hindutva road", *Frontline*, 4 December 2004, accessed 30 October 2018, URL: https://www.frontline.in/static/html/fl2125/stories/20041217006712900.html.

Ramesh, Jairam (2005), *Making Sense of Chindia: Reflections on China and India*, New Delhi: India Research Press.

Ram. N. (2004), "The most important event on my agenda", says Chinese Premier about India visit", *The Hindu*, accessed 10 June 2015, URL: http://www.thehindu.com/2004/12/01/stories/2004120106480100.html.

Ren Jia and Li Li (2016) (eds.), *India*, Beijing: Social Sciences Academic Press: 89.

Reliance Anil Dhirubhai Ambani Group (2008), "About Us, Overview", accessed 30 May 2018, URL: http://www.relianceadagroup.com/ada/overview.html.

Reliance Industries Limited (1998), "Wharton Dean's Medal for Dhirubhai Ambani", URL: http://www.ril.com/DownloadFiles/Founder%20Chairman/Awards/Whar tons %20Dean.pdf.

—— (2018a), "About Our Company", accessed 30 May 2018, URL: http://www.ril.com/OurCompany/About.aspx.

—— (2018b), "Founder Chairman", accessed 30 May 2018, URL: http://www.ril.com/OurCompany/Leadership/FounderChairman.aspx.

Rice, Condoleezza (2005), "Remarks en route to India", URL: http://2001-2009.state.gov/secretary/rm/2005/43465.html.

Roy, Abhik (2015), "How the Chinese view India", accessed 1 June 2015, URL: http://www.thestatesman.com/news/opinion/how-the-chinese-view-india/6507 7.html.

Rodrik, Dani and Subramanian, Arvind (2004), "Why India Can Grow at 7 per cent a Year or More: Projections and Reflections", *Economic and Political Weekly*, Vol. 39(16), (April 17-23, 2004): 1595.

Ross, Eleanor (2017), "Pollution in India kills more than in China, a new study finds", *Newsweek International*, 15 February 2017, accessed 18 February 2017, URL: http://europe.newsweek.com/pollution-india-kills-more-china-n ew-study-finds-556700?rm=eu.

Rossow, Richard M. (2017), "India's FDI Reforms Under Modi: Once a Fountain, Now a Drip", 15 August 2017, accessed 14 February 2019, URL: https://www.csis.org/analysis/india's-fdi-reforms-under-modi-once-fountain- now-drip.

Roy, Tasmayee Laha (2017), "Woodland coming to China with Aokang", *The Economic Times*, URL: https://economictimes.indiatimes.com/industry/cons-products/fashion-/-cosmetics-/-jewellery/woodland-coming-to-china-with-aoka ng/articleshow/57135793.cms

Roy, Shubhajit (2013), "India and China ask Special Representatives to work on more border steps", accessed on 17 June 2015, URL: http://archive.indianexpress.co m/news/india-and-china-ask-special-representatives-to-work-on-more-border-steps/1118270/0.

—— (2013), "India and China ask border envoys to work on more steps", accessed 17 June 2015, URL: http://archive.indianexpress.com/news/india-and-china-ask-border-envoys-to-work-on-more-steps/1118532/0.

—— (2013), "Chinese Premier Li Keqiang arrives today, PM to seek early revival of border talks", accessed 17 June 2015, URL: http://archive.indianexpress.com/news/chinese-premier-li-keqiang-arrives-today-pm/1117669/.

Samanta, Pranab Dhal (2010), "No mention of 'One China' is New Delhi reply to Beijing for its silence on J&K", 17 December 2010, accessed 3 March 2015, *Indian Express*, URL: http://archive.indianexpress.com/news/no-mention-of--one-china--is-new-delhi-reply-to-beijing-for-its-silence-on-j-k/725951/.

—— (2013), "Talkative Li quoted Weber, Hegel, Jobs, said PM is large-hearted", accessed 8 July 2015, *Indian Express*, URL: http://archive.indianexpress.com/news/talkative-li-quoted-weber-hegel-jobs-said-pm-is-largehearted/11185 44/0.

Sabharwal, G. (2015), personal interview, Zhang Yang, Nalanda University, Rajgir, 4 February 2015.

Saravana Bhavan (2012), "Vision and Mission", accessed 14 October 2018, URL: http://www.saravanabhavan.com/vision_mission.php.

Saraswati, Swami Satyananda (1969), *Asana Pranayama Mudra Bandha*, Munger: Yoga Publications Trust, "Introduction to Yoga": 2, reprinted in 2012.

Saraswat, Satya Prakash (2005), "Reflections on Spiritual Foundations of Human Values for Global Business Management", *The Journal of Business Perspective*, Vol. 9(3): 4-5.

Sarma, P. (2017), personal interview, a financial institution, Beijing Representative Office, 20 February 2017.

*SCPRC (2014), "Planning Outline for the Construction of a Social Credit System (2014-2020)", The State Council, The People's Republic of China, 14 June 2014, accessed 3 May 2019, URL: http://www.gov.cn/zhengce/content/2014-06/27/content_8913.htm.

SCIOPRC (2011), *China's Peaceful Development* 中国的和平发展, The State Council Information Office of the People's Republic of China, Beijing: People's Press: 24. Quoted in Yan Xuetong (2015), *The Transfer of World Power: Political Leadership and Strategic Competition* 世界权力的转移：政 治领导与战略竞争, Beijing: Peking University Press: 88; Also see The State Council Information Office of the People's Republic of China (2011), "IV. China's Path of Peaceful Development Is a Choice Necessitated by History", China's Peaceful Development, URL: http://www.scio.gov.cn/zfbps/ndhf/2011/Document/1000031/1000031.html.

Sebenius, James K. and Qian, (Jason) Cheng (2008), "Cultural Notes on Chinese Negotiating Behaviour", Working Paper 9-76, Harvard Business School, URL: http://www.hbs.edu/faculty/Publication%20Files/09-076.pdf.

Sen, Amartya (2005), *The Argumentative Indian*, New Delhi: Penguin Books: 166.

Sen, Tansen (2004), *Buddhism, Diplomacy and Trade: The Realignment of Sino-Indian Relations, 600-1400*, New Delhi: Manohar Publishers & Distributors: xii, 2.

—— (2007), From Buddhism to commerce: The transformation of Sino-Indian relations, Panchsheel and The Future, SAMSKRITI.

—— (2012), "Trust Deficit in India-China Relations", in *Emerging China, Prospects for Partnership in Asia*, New Delhi: Routledge: 295-296.

—— (2014), "中印研究的兴起、发展与现状" ,Wen Hui Bao, Shanghai, accessed 17 March 2015: URL: http://whb.news365.com.cn/mzjy/201405/t20140519_1050957.html.

—— (2014), "Hindi Chini Shy Shy", *The Times of India*, Mumbai, URL: http://blogs.timesofindia.indiatimes.com/toi-editorials/25828/.

—— (2014), "Silk Road Diplomacy—Twists, Turns and Distorted History", *Yale Global Online Magazine*, URL: http://yaleglobal.yale.edu/content/silk-road-diplomacy—-twists-turns-and-distorted-history.

—— (2014), "Introduction: Buddhism in Asian History", in Sen, Tansen (ed.), *Buddhism Across Asia: Networks of Material, Intellectual and Cultural Exchange*, New Delhi: Manohar Publishers & Distributors.

Shang Huipeng and You Guolong (2010), *Psycho-Culturology: The Research and Application of Francis L. K. Hsu*, Taipei: SMC Publishing Inc.: 18.

Shang Huipeng (2013), *An Outline of Psychoculturology, the Comparative Study of Literate Civilizations*, Beijing: Peking University Press: 54, 171-172, 177.

—— (2013), "Man, Civilizational Entity, and International Relations", *International Politics Quarterly*, Vol. 34(4): 3-19.

—— (2015a), 中国人与印度人：文化传统的比较研究 [Chinese and Hindus, A Comparative Study of Cultural Traditions], Beijing: Peking University Press: 254-257, 260, 271, 276-277.

—— (2015b), "The International System in Ancient South Asia: The Logic of the 'Dharma System'" , *The Journal of International Studies*, Vol. 36(5): 9-27.

Shandong Iron & Steel Group Co., Ltd. (2010), "Introduction" 集团介绍, URL: http://www.sdsteel.cc/page-412930076158.html.

Shankar, Ravi and Mishra, Newton (2017), "New paradigm/Opinion: Toppling OBOR with OCOR", *The Organiser*, 17 July 2017, accessed 16 April 2019, URL: https://www.organiser.org//Encyc/2017/7/17/New-paradigm-Opinion-Toppling-OBOR-with-OCOR.html.

Sharma, Arvind (2005), *Modern Hindu Thought: An Introduction*, Oxford University Press: 186.

Sharma, Betwa (2016), "The Leader of the Fledgling Dalit Uprising in Gujarat is Determined to Not Let it Die", *Huffpost India,* 4 August 2016, accessed on 10 April 2018, URL: https://www.huffingtonpost.in/2016/08/04/meet-the- face-of-the-rising-dalit-move ment-in-gujarat_a_21444800/.

Sharma, Dasharatha (1975), *Early Chauhān dynasties: a study of Chauhān political history, Chauhān political institutions, and life in the Chauhān dominions, from 800 to 1316 A.D.*, Delhi: Motilal Banarsidass: 279.

Sharma, Satya P. (1996), "The Cultural Costs of a Globalized Economy for India", *Dialectical Anthropology*, Vol. 21(3/4): 311, 312.

Sheff, David (2002), *China Dawn: The Storyof a Technology and Business Revolution*, New York: Harper Collins.

Shen Kaiyan and Xu Zhihua (2015), *The Analysis of India Economy: Comparative Perspective between China and India* 印度经济分析：中印比 较的视角, Shanghai: Shanghai Academy of Social Sciences Press; "Section I Indian urban form and related cultural connotations" [印度城市形态与相关 文化内涵], Kindle eBook.

Shi Lin (2010), "Comparative Studies of Using FDI between China and India", *Oriental Enterprise Culture*, No. 5, 2010: 7.

Shukla, Saurabh (2005), "The Dragon Smiles", *India Today*, 30(16): 48.

Sima Qian (2006), *Shiji* [*Records of the Great Historian*], "Huozhi liezhuan 69" [Merchants/Usurers Biographies 69], Beijing: Zhonghua Book Company: 752; Shiji was completed in 91 BCE during the Han Dynasty of China. This edition was published in 2006.

Sinha, Jayant and Sanyal, Sanjeev (2016), "Is it possible to build a framework for policy and governance based on our own civilisational values?" *TheEconomic Times*, 14 September 2016, accessed 14 September 2016, URL: http://blogs.

economictimes.indiatimes.com/et-commentary/is-it-possible-to-build-a-frame work-for-policy-and-governance-based-on-our-own- civilisational-values/.

Singh, Manmohan (2008), "印度总理辛格在中国社会科学院发表演讲 (全文)" [Indian PM Singh's speech in CASS], accessed 3 March 2015, URL: http://world.people.com.cn/GB/8212/114343/114344/6777082.html.

Singh, Pritam (2016), "How Centre-State Relations Have Shaped Punjab's Development Pattern", in L. Singh and N. Singh (2016) (eds.), *Economic Transformation of a Developing Economy*, New Delhi: India Studies in Business and Economics: 375; Quoted in Xie Chao, "Federalism and Domestic Peace: A Cursory Review of Indian Government Efforts to Respond to the Sikh Separatist Insurgency", *South Asian Studies*, 2016, Vol. 4: 86.

Singh, P. (2019), personal interview, School of Language, Literature and Culture Studies, Jawaharlal Nehru University, New Delhi, 1 May 2019.

Singer, Milton (1956), "Cultural Values in India's Economic Development", *Annals of the American Academy,* Vol. 305: 83; Quoted in Kunkel, John H. (1965), "Values and Behaviour in Economic Development", *Economic Development and Cultural Change*, Vol. 13(3): 268.

Singh, K.S. (2008) (ed.), *People of India: Volume XVI. Bihar Including Jharkhand, Part Two*, Kolkata: Seagull Books: 914-916.

Singh, K.; Suresh, Gopal, S. and Jha, Hetukar (2008), *People of India, Bihar, Volume XVI,* Calcutta: Seagull Books, Part Two: 914-916. JNUL: http://eds.b.ebscohost.com.ezproxy.jnu.ac.in/eds/detail/detail?vid=2&sid=a09 bcca5-ca77-4fac-a37c-615a05ebf90a%40sessionmgr104&bdata=JnNpdGU9ZWRzLWxpdmUmc2NvcGU9c2l0ZQ%3d%3d#AN=jnu.375264&db=cat00706a.

Singh, V.K. (2017), personal interview, Wanda Plaza, Beijing, 20 February 2017.

SIRPA (2018), Seminar on 'Chinese Classics International Political Concept Research', School of International Relations & Public Affairs, Fudan University, 23 November 2018, accessed 6 July 2019, URL: http://www.sirpa.fudan.edu.cn/?p=12461.

—— (2019), "Notice of Call for Papers for the Second 'Chinese Classical International Relations Concept Research' Theory Seminar of Fudan University", School of International Relations & Public Affairs, Fudan University, 20 May 2019, accessed 7 July 2019, URL: http://www.sirpa.fudan.edu.cn/?p=13622.

Sivananda, Sri Swami (2000), "The Yoga of Meditation", *Bhagavad Gita*, Tehri-Garhwal: The Divine Life Society: 53.

Sivaswamy, Saisuresh (2018), "Congress are better Hindus than BJP", *Rediff.com*, 9 July 2018, accessed 2 October 2018, URL: http://www.rediff.com/news/interview/shashi-tharoor-we-are-better-hindus- than-bjp/20180709.html.

SJMNC (2017), "Free Bharat from Chinese Influence", Guwahati National Council Meeting Resolution 1 (E), Swadeshi Jagaran Manch National Council, May 20-21, 2017, URL: http://www.swadeshionline.in/resolution/guwahati- national-council-meeting-resolution-1-e.

So Ying Lun and Walker, Anthony (2013), *Explaining Guanxi: The Chinese Business Network*, New York: Routledge.

Song Haixiao (2010), "印度民族性格及其对印度国家的影响—以印度教民族为中心" [Indian National Character and Its Influence on India—Focusing on the Hindu Nationality], *World Ethno-National Studies*, Vol. 1: 94.

—— (2011), *India's Foreign Policy: Processes and Models,* Beijing: World Knowledge Publishing House: 47-49.

Song Wei (2013), "A Summary of the Seminar on "Creation of Core Concepts and Development of China's International Relations Theory", *International Politics Quarterly*, 2013, Vol. 4: 175.

Special Correspondent (2017), "No ban on Chinese firms: Sushma", *The Hindu*, 28 July 2017, accessed 28 July 2017, URL: http://www.thehindu.com/todays-paper/tp-national/no-ban-on-chinese- firms-sushma/article19374178.ece.

—— (2017), "Asia-Africa corridor to respect sovereignty", *The Hindu*, 6 July 2017, accessed 28 November 2017, URL: http://www.thehindu.com/business/Industry/asia-africa-corridor-to-respect-sovereignty/article19225378.ece.

Streeten, Paul (2006), "Culture and Economic Development", in Victor A. Ginsburgh and David Throsby (2006) (eds.), *Handbook of the Economics of Art and Culture*, Vol. 1, Chap. 13: 399-412.

Sterckx, Roel (2019), *Chinese Thought From Confucius to Cook Ding*, Penguin Random House.

Stross, Randall E. (1990), *Bulls in The China Shop and Other Sino-American Business Encounters*, New York: Pantheon Books.

Stokes, Bruce; Manevich, Dorothy and Chew, Hanyu (2017), "Three Years In, Modi Remains Very Popular, '4. India and the world'", *Pew Research Centre,* 15 November 2017, accessed 6 July 2019, URL: https://www.pewresearch.org/global/2017/11/15/india-and-the-world/.

Subrahmanyan, Sanjay (1996), "Institutions agency and economic change in South Asia: A survey and some suggestions", in Burton Stein and Sanjay Subrahmanyam (eds.), *Institutions and Economic Change in South Asia*, Delhi, Oxford University Press; in Medha Kudaisya and Ng Chin-keong (2009) (eds.), *Chinese and Indian Business: Historical Antecedents*, Leiden: Brill NV: 85-86.

Sun Shihai (2000) (ed.), *Development and Foreign Strategy of India* 印度的发展及其对外战略, Beijing: China Social Sciences Press: 2, 204-205.

Sun Shihai, Kang Hui and Lin Yu (2007), "央视主持人谈印度印象： 繁华公寓与低 矮棚子共处" [Hosts of China Central Television talk about their impression of India: co-existence of prosperous apartment and low shack], accessed 17 February 2017, URL: http://news.sina.com.cn/c/2007-05-18/213013022272.shtml.

Suzlon (2018), "History", Suzlon Group, accessed 4 June 2018, URL: https://www.suzlon.com/in-en/about-suzlon/history#key.

Swamy, Rohini (2016), "BJP worker ferrying cows beaten to death by gaurakshaks in Karnataka", *India Today*, 18 August 2016, accessed 13 April 2018, URL: https://www.indiatoday.in/india/story/karnataka-bjp-worker-murdered-transporting-cows-335848-2016-08-18.

Swadeshi Jagran Manch (2017a), "Introduction", Swadeshi Jagran Manch, URL: http://www.swadeshionline.in/content/introduction.

—— (2017b), "Philosophy", Swadeshi Jagran Manch, URL: https://www.swadeshionline.in/content/philosophy.

Tagore International School, URL: http://www.tagoreint.com.

Tan Yun-Shan (1957), "Vide Visva-Bharati Bulletin No. 24, dated April, 1938", Its Aims and Objects, Twenty Years of The Visva-Bharati Cheena-Bhavana 1937-1957, The Sino-Indian Cultural Society of India: 18-20.

Tan Chung (2002), "India and China: A Saga of Sharing a Historical Heritage" in *History of Science, Philosophy and Culture in Indian Civilization,* Volume III, Part 2, *India's Interaction with China, Central and West Asia*, edited by A. Rahman, New Delhi: Oxford University Press, 133.

—— (2008a), "'Chindia' 中印大同前景光明" [Chindia has brilliant future], *People's Daily* Online, accessed 6 June 2015, URL: http://world.people.com.cn/GB/1030/6799884.html.

—— (2008b), "Rise of the Asian Giants", in *The Dragon-Elephant Tango*, New Delhi: Anthem Press India.

—— (2011), "加强中印两大文明国之间的 '恕道'" [Strengthening "Empathy" between the two great civilizations of China and India], *South Asian Studies*, 4, 146-155.

Tan Chung, Liu Chaohua and Huang Rong (eds.) (2007), 《中印大同 理想与实现》 [Chindia—Idealism and Realization], Yinchuan: Ningxia People's Press.

Tang Lu (2003), "重量级高官晤谈 特别代表拉开中印边界谈判序幕", accessed 9 July, 2015, URL: http://news.xinhuanet.com/world/2003-10/24/content_1140325.html.

—— (2010), "印度主流英文媒体报道与公众舆论对华认知", 南亚研究, http://study.ccln.gov.cn/fenke/zhengzhixue/zzzgwj/68424.shtml.

Tan Jie (2014), "Faxian", in *Encyclopedia of India-China Cultural Contacts*: 288.

Taneja, Nisha; Wadhwa, Deepika and Bimal, Samridhi (2015), "India's Trade Deficit with China: How to Bridge the Gap", *Economic & Political Weekly*, 11 July 2015, Vol. 50(28): 18.

Tang Zongli (1995), "Confucianism, Chinese Culture, and Reproductive Behaviour" *Population and Environment*, Vol. 16(3): 269-284.

Taylor, Jay (1987), *The Dragon and the Wild Goose: China and India with New Epilogue*, Westport: Praeger Publishers Inc.

Tao Liang (2015), "Project Mausam", India's Maritime Strategy and the "21st Century Maritime Silk Road" ["季风计划"、印度海洋战略与"21 世纪海上 丝绸之路"], *South Asian Studies*, 2015, Vol. 3: 95-110.

Tata (2018), "About us, Tata group profile", Tata Group, accessed 4 June 2018, URL: http://www.tata.com/aboutus/sub_index/Leadership-with-trust.

Tang Zhenquan (2011), "Indian Tourism Service Trade and the Emerging China-India Cooperation", *South Asian Studies Quarterly*, Sum No. 146, No. 3, 2011.

Tenkayala, Raghavendra; Radhika, P. and Radhika, Ashish (2014), "India: 4.2.3 Cultural/creative industries: policies and programmes", *World CP (Cultural Policies)*, URL: http://www.worldcp.org/india.php?aid=423.

The Washington Times (2005), "China builds up strategic sea lanes", *The Washington Times*, accessed 8 July 2015, URL: http://www.washingtontimes.com/news/2005/jan/17/20050117-115550-1929r/.

Thampi, Madhavi (2005), *Indians in China 1800-1949*, New Delhi: Manohar Publishers and Distributors.

—— (2007), in Tan Chung, Liu Chaohua and Huang Rong (eds.) (2007), 《中印大同 理想与实现》 [Chindia—Idealism and Realization], Yinchuan: Ningxia People's Press.

The Indian Express (2013), "Omar: India, China should fix boundary in Ladakh", accessed 17 June 2015, URL: http://archive.indianexpress.com/news/omar-india-china-should-fix-boundary-in-la/1118398/.

—— (2013), "India, China set to sign landmark pact on border cooperation", accessed 17 June 2015, URL: http://archive.indianexpress.com/news/india-china-set-to-sign-landmark-pact-on-border-cooperation/1185788/0.

Times of India (2015), "15 things you should know about Atal Bihari Vajpayee", *Times of India*, accessed 18 March 2015, URL: http://timesofindia.India times.com/india/15-things-you-should-know-about-Atal-Bihari-Vajpayee/artic le show/45627161.cms.

The Hindu (2013), "India, China take steps to reduce trade gap", accessed 17 June 2015, URL: http://www.thehindu.com/todays-paper/tp-business/india-china-take-steps-to-reduce-trade-gap/article4734522.ece.

—— (2013), "Dr. Kotnis is a symbol of friendship, says Li", accessed 17 June 2015, URL: http://www.thehindu.com/todays-paper/tp-national/dr-kotnis-is-a-symbol -of-friendship-says-li/article4737872.ece.

—— (2005), "Canara Bank going strong after 100 years in business", *The Hindu*, 2 July 2005, accessed 29 June 2018, URL: https://www.thehindu.com/2005/07/02/stories/2005070218720400.html.

The Indian Express (2010a), "India a great neighbour, says Wen Jiabao", accessed 14 June 2015, URL: http://archive.indianexpress.com/news/india-a-great-neighbou r-says-wen-jiabao/725543/.

—— (2010b), "Chinese Premier Wen critical of India's free media", accessed 14 June 2015, URL: http://www.rediff.com/news/report/chinese-pm-criticises-indian-media/20101217.html.

—— (2010c), "Karan Singh says no to China friendship award", accessed 14 June 2015, URL: http://archive.indianexpress.com/news/karan-singh-says-no-to-china-friendship-award/725358/.

—— (2010d), "China to provide flood data of Sutlej river to India", accessed 14 June 2015, URL: http://www.hindustantimes.com/newdelhi/china-to-provide-flood-data-of-sutlej-river-to-india/article1-639538.aspx.

The World Bank (2019), "The World Bank in China, Overview", 8 April 2019, accessed 22 April 2019, URL: https://www.worldbank.org/en/country/ china/overview.

Tian Zhenshan (2008), 中国辩证法： 从<易经>到马克思主义 [China's Dialectics: From *The Book of Changes (Yi Jing)* to Marxism], Beijing : China People's University Press; Quoted in Qin Yaqing (2015), "Relational Theory of International Politics", *World Economics and Politics*, No. 2: 9.

Tiens (2018), "About TIENS", accessed 10 April 2018, URL: http://www.tianshi india.co.in/About_TIENS.htm.

Times News Network (2013), "Ladakh crisis not our creation: Govt", *Times of India*, accessed 15 July 2015, URL: http://timesofindia.indiatimes.com/india/Ladakh-crisis-not-our-creation-Govt/articleshow/19812010.cms?referral=PM.

—— (2014), "INCH towards MILES: Modi's China mantra", *Times of India*, accessed 8 July 2014, URL: http://timesofindia.indiatimes.com/india/INCH-towards-MILES-Modis-China-mantra/articleshow/42670778.cms.

TNN (2015), "Sushil Modi vows cow slaughter ban in Bihar, Congress cites 1955 law", *The Times of India,* 6 October 2015, accessed 17 October 2018, URL: https://timesofindia.indiatimes.com/india/Sushil-Modi-vows-cow-slaughter-ban-in-Bihar-Congress-cites-1955-law/articleshow/49235945.cms.

—— (2016), "Over 93 percent support demonetisation in survey on PM Narendra Modi's app", *Times of India,* 27 November 2016, accessed 30 October 2018, URL: https://timesofindia.indiatimes.com/india/Over-93-percent-support-for-demonetisation-in-survey-on-PM-Narendra-Modis-app/articleshow/55584567.cms.

—— (2016), "4 Dalits stripped, beaten up for skinning dead cow", *Times of India,* 13 July 2016, accessed 10 April 2018, URL: https://timesofindia.indiatimes.com/city/rajkot/4-Dalits-stripped-beaten-up-for-skinning-dead-cow/articleshow/53184266.cms.

—— (2017), "China wants India to go slow on Asia-Arica corridor", *Times of India,* 2 September 2017, accessed 28 November 2017, URL: http://ris.org.in/aagc/sites/default/files/TOI-02-09-2017-China%20wants%20India%20to%20go%20slow%20on%20Asia- Africa%20corridor_0.pdf.

—— (2017), "Despite Doklam, no security hold on Chinese investments", *Times of India*, 18 August 2017, accessed on 18 August 2017, URL: http://timesofindia.indiatimes.com/business/india-business/despite-doklam-no- security-hold-on-chinese-investments/articleshow/60111128.cms. 62.

Toynbee, Arnold and Daisaku, Ikeda (1984), 《展望二十一世纪》 (Forecast 21st Century), Translated by Xun Chunsheng, Zhu Jizheng and Chen Guoliang, Beijing: International Cultural Press Limited.

Toynbee, Arnold Joseph (1986), *A Study of History*, Translated by Cao Weifeng, Shanghai: Shanghai People's Press; Quoted in Xing Yue (2011), *How Does Culture Affect Foreign Policy: A Case Study of U.S.A.*, Beijing: Peking University Press: 61.

Tong Chee-Kiong (2014), *Chinese Business: Rethinking Guanxi and Trust in Chinese Business Networks*, New York: Springer Publishing.

Tripathi, Dwijendra (2004), *The Oxford History of Indian Business*, Delhi: Oxford University Press.

Tripathi, Dwijendra and Mehta, Makrand (1990), *Business Houses in Western India: A Study in Entrepreneurial Response, 1850-1956*, New Delhi: Manohar Publication; in Medha Kudaisya and Ng Chin-keong (2009) (eds.), *Chinese and Indian Business: Historical Antecedents*, Leiden: Brill NV: 85-86.

Tsai, Kellee S. (2010), "Friends, Family or Foreigners? The Political Economy of Diasporic FDI and Remittances in China and India", *China Report* 46(4):387.

Turner, Jonathan H. (2005), *Sociology*, New Jersey: Prentice Hall: 87.

UNCTAD (2018), "World Investment Report 2018", United Nations Conference on Trade and Development: 4, URL: https://unctad.org/en/ PublicationsLibrary/wir2018_en.pdf.

Vaidyanathan, A. (2015), "Cow Slaughter Ban and the Welfare of Cattle", *Economic & Political Weekly*, 28 November 2015, Vol. 50(48): 48.

Vajpayee, Atal Bihari (2003), "Speech by the Prime Minister of India Shri Atal Bihari at Peking University, 23 June 2003", *China Report*, 39(4): 583-586.

Vande Mataram Memorial (2018), "About us", URL: http://vmm.ashapura.com/explore.php?section=tab1 (The year is not mentioned, typed year is the year accessed).

Vij, Shivam (2013), "India's Mars mission: worth the cost?" 5 November 2013, accessed 8 March 2017, *The Christian Science Monitor*, URL: http://www.csmonitor.com/World/Asia-South-Central/2013/1105/India-s-Mars-mission-worth-the-cost-video.

Virmani, Arvind (2005), "The New Tripolar World", *India Today*, XXX (16): 49.

VKO (2019), "Trivarga", Vedic Knowledge Online, accessed 4 May 2019, URL: http://veda.wikidot.com/trivarga.

Wabag (2018a), "Our philosophy", Va Tech Wabag Water Treatment Technology Co. Ltd., accessed 4 June 2018, URL: http://www.wabag.com/the-company/our-philosophy/.

—— (2018b), "History", Va Tech Wabag Water Treatment Technology Co. Ltd., accessed 4 June 2018, URL: http://www.wabag.com/the-company/history/.

Waltz, Kenneth N. (1959), *Man, the State and War*, New York: Columbia University Press, Chapters 6-7.

Wang Bangwei (2014), "Yijing", in *Encyclopedia of India-China Cultural Contacts*: 304.

Wang Chunyan (2018), "Modi Administration's Reform on Foreign Direct Investment Policy", *South Asian Studies Quarterly*, Sum No. 173, No. 2, 2018: 66.

Wang Dianqing (2015), "People's Daily Refuted Confucianism Impedes China's Development: Practice has proved that this understanding is not objective", *People's Daily* (Overseas Edition), 21 April 2015, accessed 30 September 2018, URL: https://www.thepaper.cn/newsDetail_forward_1323058.

Wang Dong (2013), "中印不再是"习惯性 "对手 边防协议签订最具意义" [China-India are no more 'traditional' competitors, to sign the border agreement will be most significant], accessed 8 July 2015, URL: http://www.chinanews.com/hb/2013/10-24/5418748.shtml.

Wang Huning (1995), *Political Life*, Shanghai People's Press: 53.

Wang Hongwei (2009), "胡锦涛主席访印与战略合作伙伴关系内涵的充实" [Hu Jintao's visit to India which fulfilled the context of strategic cooperation partnership], *A Critical Review of the Sino-Indian Relations of the Present Age*, Beijing: China's Tibetan Studies Press: 362, 366.

—— (2015), "温总理访印与中印关系的新发展" [Premier Wen's visit to India and the new development of China-India relations], *South Asia Studies*, 1(78): 3.

Wang Jun (2017), "On Confucius' View of 'Yi' and 'Li'", *Journal of Jiangsu University of Science and Technology* (Social Science Edition), Vol. 17(3): 14.

Wang Junling (2017), "State-owned enterprise reform boosts China's economic expectations", *People's Daily* (Overseas Edition), 9 October 2017, accessed 21 September 2018, URL: http://www.gov.cn/guowuyuan/2017-10/09/content_5230154.html.

Wang Jenn-Hwan and Hsung Ray-May (2016), *Rethinking Social Capital and Entrepreneurship in Greater China: Is Guanxi Still Important?* New York: Routledge.

Wang Lingqiang (2019), "Dong Zhongshu and the Formation of the Five Constant Virtues in Confucianism", *Journal of Dezhou University*, Vol. 35(1), February 2019: 41.

Wang Wei (2019), "China-India translation project facilitates sharing of ancient ideas", *China Global Television Network*, 10 May 2019, accessed 7 July 2019, URL: https://news.cgtn.com/news/3d3d674e3067544e34457a6333566d54/index.html.

Wang Xiaofeng (2014), "专家：习近平出访阐明南亚政策新思路", accessed 5 March 2015, URL: http://www.chinanews.com/gn/2014/09-17/6598170.shtml.

Wang Yahui (2006), "Cover the Integrity of Our Current Social Transformation with a Deficiency", Master's Dissertation, Dalian: Dalian Maritime University.

Wang Yi (2013), "Adhere to the correct view of righteousness and benefit, and actively play the role of responsible big country", *People's Daily*, 10 September 2013, accessed 16 May 2019, URL: http://opinion.people.com.cn/n/2013/0910/c1003-22862978.html.

Wang Yizhou (2018), "Move towards a wise and benevolent power: *ren* (benevolent) society and *zhi* (wise) diplomacy", 6 July 2018, accessed 30 April 2019, URL: https://wemedia.ifeng.com/67993506/wemedia.shtml.

Wang Yudan (2010), "印度总统抵京访华" [Indian President reaches Beijing and starts visit to China], *Xinhua Net*, accessed 12 June 2015, URL: http://news.xinhuanet.com/politics/2010-05/26/c_12145612.html.

Wang Zhengyi (2010), 国际政治经济学通论 [General Theory of International Political Economy], Beijing: Peking University Press: 437.

WB (2017), "Chinese netizens' comments", *SinaWeibo*, 6 July 2017, accessed 6 July 2017, https://www.weibo.com/1921495471/Fb9Yvl3DS?refer_flag=1001030106_&t ype=comment.

Weber, Max (1916), *The Religion of India: The Sociology of Hinduism and Buddhism*, New Delhi: Munshiram Manoharlal Publishers.

—— (1951), *The Religion of China: Confucianism and Taoism*, Translated and edited by Hans H. Gerth, Glencoe (Illinois): The Free Press: 237.

—— (2010), 儒教与道教 *Confucianism and Taoism*, translated by Yue Wen Xi'an: Shaanxi Normal University Press, Kindle E-book.

—— (1958), *The Religions of India: The Sociology of Hinduism and Buddhism*, translated and edited by H. H. Gerth and D. Martindale, Free Press.

Wen Jiabao (2010), "共铸东方文明新辉煌", Ministry of Foreign Affairs of the People's Republic of China, accessed 18 March 2015, URL: http://www.fmprc.gov.cn/mfa_chn/ziliao_611306/zyjh_611308/t778950.shtml.

Wen Xian and Wu Chengliang (2008), "踏着柯棣华的足迹走来——记中国印度联合医疗队成立仪式" [Following the footsteps of Kotnis—the opening ceremony of China-India Medical United Team], accessed 9 June 2015, URL: http://world.people.com.cn/GB/1029/42354/6773722.html.

Wendt, Alexander (1999), *Social Theory of International Politics*, Cambridge: Cambridge University Press.

Wei Xiaojun (2011), *Cross Cultural Business Cases* [跨文化管理精品案例], Shanghai: Shanghai Jiaotong University Press.

Wei W. (2017), personal interview, World Peace Forum (Sixth), Tsinghua University, Beijing, 24 June 2017.

World Trade Organization, *World Trade Report 2015*, URL: https://www.wto.org/english/res_e/booksp_e/world_trade_report15_e.pdf.pdf.

——, *International Trade Statistics 2015*, URL: https // www.wto.org/english/res_e/statis_e/its2015_e/its2015_e.pdf.

Wu Changqi (2014), *The Internationalisation Strategy of China's Enterprises: Theoretical Discussion and Empirical Study,* Beijing: Peking University Press: 7, 145.

Wu Lejun , Lv Pengfei and Li Ning (2013), "李克强会见柯棣华大夫亲属时强调让中印传统友谊薪火相传　生生不息" [Li Keqiang to highlight China-India traditional friendship when he meets the relatives of Dr. Kotnis], accessed 17 June 2015, URL: http://politics.people.com.cn/n/2013/0522/c1024-21565456.html.

Wu Lejun (2013), "印度主流媒体认为李克强访印非常及时　系里程碑式访问" [Indian mainstream media: Li Keqiang's visit is very timely and is a milestone visit], accessed 17 June 2015, URL: http://politics.people.com.cn/n/2013/0528/c1001-21649654.html.

Wu Qiang (2010), "看中印龙象共舞 60 年　中国网友集体误读印度?——中国印度：　龙象共舞 60 年" [60 years Dragon-Elephant Tango, are all the Chinese netizens misunderstanding India— —China-India: 60 years Dragon-Elephant Tango], accessed 11 June 2015, URL: http://world.people.com.cn/GB/11283254.html.

Wu Yongnian (2010), *The Changing India*, Beijing: People's Press: 29-30.

Xi Jinping (2014), "Towards an Asian century of prosperity", 16 September 2014, accessed 16 Sep 2014, *The Hindu*, URL: https://www.thehindubusinessline.com/opinion/towards-an-asian- century-of-prosperity/article64597597.ece.

—— (2014), "携手追寻民族复兴之梦", accessed 18 March 2015, URL: http://in.chineseembassy.org/chn/ssygd/xjp/t1192744.html.

—— (2017), "Secure a Decisive Victory in Building a Moderately Prosperous Society in All Respects and Strive for the Great Success of Socialism with Chinese Characteristics for a New Era", Speech delivered at the 19th National Congress of the Communist Party of China, 18 October 2017: 36.

—— (2019), "Full Text of President Xi Jinping's speech at the Opening Ceremony of the Conference on Dialogue of Asian Civilizations", 23 May 2019, accessed 7 July 2019, *CPEC*, URL: http://www.cpecinfo.com/news/full-text-of-president-xi-jinping-speech-at-the- opening-ceremony-of-the-conference-on-dialogue-of-asian- civilizations/NzE0MA==.

Xiao Jun (2015), "中国对印度投资态势及影响因素" [China's investment situation in India and its influencing factors], *Journal of Chengdu University (Social Sciences)*, Serial No. 161(5): 28-31.

Xiao Fang (2006), "中国公司印度频遇'安全门" [Chinese companies encountered 'safety gate' frequently in India], *Phoenix Weekly*, 34, accessed 27 May 2015, URL: http://phtv.ifeng.com/phoenixtv/73005390240940032/20070119/907749.shtml.

Xie Guoxiong (1989), "Class Mobility in Taiwanese Manufacturing", *A Radical Quarterly in Social Studies*, Vol. 2(2): 48; In Huang Guangguo, Hu Xianjin et al. (2010), *Favour and Face: Power Game of Chinese*, Beijing: China People's University Press: 248.

Xie Ting and Wei Siyuan (2014), "解读习近平出访印度成果" [An analysis of the achievements of Xi Jinping's visit], accessed 5 March 2015, URL: http://ft.people.com.cn/fangtanDetail.do?pid=3310.

Xie Xiangwei (2017), "An Analysis of Improving Sino-Indian Economical Cooperation Mechanism in the Context of the Belt and Road", *Southeast Asian and South Asian Studies*, No. 4: 38.

Xie Yizhe (2016), What Can China's Managers Learn from India's Managers? [中国经理可以向印度经理学什么], *Financial Times*, 26 February 2016, accessed 26 July 2016, URL: http://www.ftchinese.com/story/001066325?full=y.

Xinhua Net (2006), "印报论中国外交成就: 从'恐华症'到'中国热'" [India media comments on China's diplomatic achievements: from China's Threat to Sinomania], accessed 27 May 2015, URL: http://news.xinhuanet.com/world/2006-03/10/content_4283056.html.

—— (2013), "FM: China-India Border Troops Strictly Observe Agreements", *Xinhua*, accessed 5 May 2015, URL: http://news.xinhuanet.com/english/china/2013-04/24/c_132336965.html.

—— (2013), "China, India have enough wisdom to resolve differences: Premier", The State Council, The People's Republic of China, 28 June 2013, accessed 11 June 2018, URL: http://english.gov.cn/premier/news/2014/08/23/content_281474983009831.html.

—— (2013), "辛格访华将在中央党校演讲 印媒：少有的礼遇" [Singh is visiting China], accessed 17 June 2015, URL: http://news.xinhuanet.com/cankao/2013-10/18/c_132809420.html.

—— (2018), "Fifth Anniversary of BRI Initiative proposed by President Xi Jinping", 26 August 2018, accessed 20 September 2018, URL: http://www.xinhuanet.com/2018-08/26/c_1123330829.html.

Xing Yue (2011), *How Does Culture Affect Foreign Policy: A Case Study of U.S.A.*, Beijing: Peking University Press: 7-8, 61.

Xu Jin and Sun Xuefeng (2014), "The Tsinghua Approach and the Future Direction of Chinese International Relations Research", *Global Review*, 2014, Vol. 6, URL: http://www.siis.org.cn/shgjwt201512107417/UploadFiles/file/20161227/201406004%20徐%20%20%20%20进.pdf.

Xu Weihong (2010), "Brief account on the divergence of economic thought of Gandhi and Sun Yat-sen" [*lue-lun gan-di he sun-zhong-shan zai jing-ji-si-xiang shang de fen-qi*], *Anhui Literature*, 2010, Vol. 9: 254-255.

Xu Zhongqiang (2013), "How is the Family Hereditary System of Hua Xi Village formed?", *Times Figure*: 68.

Xue Cheng (2015), *Civilizational Dialogue: The Role of Chinese Buddhism as Cultural Tie on the One Belt One Road,* 文明的对话——中国佛教在 "一带一路" 中的文化纽带作用, Beijing: Ren Min Press: 144.

Xue Keqiao (2003), "Cultural changes after India's reforms and opening up" [印度改 革开放以后的文化变迁], *Journal of Contemporary Asia-Pacific Studies*: 8.

—— (2007), 《中印文化交流史话》 [The Historical Narrative of cultural exchanges between China and India], Beijing: American Presbyterian Mission Press: 60.

—— (2014), "Xuanzang", in *Encyclopedia of India-China Cultural Contacts*: 296.

—— (2017), 《中印文化交流史》 [A History of China-India Cultural Exchanges], Beijing: Encyclopedia of China Publishing House: 2, 29, 30.

Yan Xuetong (2013), *Inertia of History: China and the World in the Next Ten Years*, Beijing: China CITIC Press; "Chapter 5, *Great Power Diplomacy: The Diplomatic Strategy of China in Next Ten Years, Benevolent and Hegemony: What kind of Diplomatic Thought China Need,*" Kindle eBook.

—— (2015), 《世界权力的转移:政治领导与战略竞争》 [*The Transfer of World Power: Political Leadership and Strategic Competition*], Beijing: Peking University Press: 91.

—— (2017), "China should clearly prioritize national interests and prevent premature advance", *Journal of Strategy and Decision-Making,* 2017, Vol. 3, URL: http://www.uscnpm.com/model_item.html?action=view&table=article&id=13 803.

Yang Fengcheng (2014), "The Historical Review on the Traditional Culture of the Communist Party of China", *Teaching and Research*: 78.

Yang Wenwu, Wang Yan and Wen Shuhui (2017), "Sino-Indian Cooperation in Post-Financial-Crisis Era", *South Asian Studies Quarterly*, Sum No. 168, 2017, No. 1: 53-55.

Yang Wenwu and Ni Xiangqin (2007), "An Analysis of the Status Quo, the Existent Problems and the Countermeasures during the Process of Sino-Indian Economic Trade Cooperation", *Journal of Social Sciences,* No. 9: 23.

Yin Junling (2003), "A Commentary on the Studies in Shanxi Merchant of Ming and Qing Dynasties", *Journal of Shanxi Teachers University* (Social Science Edition), April 2003, Vol. 30(2): 74-75.

Yin Xinan and Zhang Li (2001), "泰戈尔 1924 年访华在中国知识界的反响" [The influence of Tagore's visit to China in 1924 in Chinese academic field], 南亚研究季刊, 4, URL: http://www.svabhinava.org/indochina/YinXinan/Tagore1924 ChinaVisit (泰戈尔 1924 年访华在中国).pdf.

Yin Xinan (2014), 《印度中国观演变研究》 [A Historical Study of Indian Perceptions of China], Beijing: Shishi Press.

Ye Hailin (2008), "为 Chindia 加油" [To support Chindia], *People's Daily* Online, URL: http://world.people.com.cn/GB/1030/6774300.html.

Ye Shengli (2004), 中国诚信经济思想研究 [China's *Chengxin* (Sincerity) Economy Thought Studies], Fudan University, Ph.D. Thesis.

Yeung, I.Y.M., and Tung, R.L. (1996), "Achieving business success in Confucian societies: The importance of *guanxi* (connections)", *Organizational Dynamics,* 25 (2), 58.

You Zhiwei (2013), "印度总理先访俄后访华 外界指其与中国较劲" [Indian PM visit to Russia and then China, It was Commented for Contesting with China], http://news.ifeng.com/mainland/special/xingefanghua2013/content-5/detail_2013_10/23/30589677_0.shtml.

Yuan Yuan (2013), "中印军队" 帐篷对峙 "已十日" [India and China militaries' "Tent Confrontation" has been ten days], accessed 24 June 2015, URL: http://paper.people.com.cn/gjjrb/html/2013-04/25/content_1230524.htm#.

Zeng Wei and Li Jingyu (2014), "习近平 '友情' 外交备受瞩目专家: 开启新时代" [Xi Jinping's friendship diplomacy was paid much attention, Expert: It is a starting of new age], accessed 3 March 2015, URL: http://politics.people.com.cn/n/2014/0919/c1001-25693297.html.

Zhai Xuewei (2011), *The Principles of Chinese Guanxi: Time-space Order, Life Desire and Their Changes,* 中国人的关系原理：时空秩序、生活欲念及其流变, Beijing: Peking University Press: 2-4, 103-104.

Zhao Lei (2016) (ed.), *The Annual Report on One Belt One Road,* "一带一路" 年度报告：从愿景到行动, Beijing: The Commercial Press.

Zhang C. (2019), personal interview, New Delhi, 18 March 2019.

Zhang Hanmo (2018), *Authorship and Text-making in Early China*, Boston: Walter de Gruyter Inc.: 95.

Zhang Li (2006), "中国与印度：相互再认识的必要" [China and India: the Necessity of Recognition of Each Other] in Zhang Minqiu (ed.) 《跨越喜马 拉雅障碍——中国寻求了解印度》 [Across the Himalayan Gap, A Chinese Quest for Understanding India], Chongqing: Chongqing Publishing Group, 350.

Zhang Li (2007), "India's Economic Nationalism: the Roots, Effects and Counter Measures China should Take", *South Asian Studies Quarterly*, No. 3: 12-14, 89.

Zhang Minyu (2014), "Awara", in Ministry of External Affairs (2014), *Government of India*, *Encyclopedia of India-China Cultural Contacts*, New Delhi, 721.

Zhang Pengxiong (2013), "外交部： 中印将签署一系列双边合作协议" [MFA: China-India will sign a series of bilateral cooperative agreements], accessed 17 June 2015, URL: http://news.xinhuanet.com/politics/2013-10/18/c_117781832.html.

Zhang Ran and Qiao Anquan (2014), "White Horse Temple", in Ministry of External Affairs (2014), Government of India, *Encyclopedia of India-China Cultural Contacts*, New Delhi, 173.

Zhang Shucun (2017), "The ideas and countermeasures for optimizing the layout of China's foreign direct investment under the "One Belt, One Road" strategy, *Management World*, No. 4: 7.

Zhang Sisi (2015), "Will Uncle Die for Hair Cut in First Month? The Reason of No Hair Cut in the First Month of the Year", 正月剃头死舅舅？为什么正月不 能剃头原因如此, *People's Net*, 28 February 2015, accessed 8 September 2018,

URL: https://web.archive.org/web/20150509140916/http://www.sn.xinhuanet.com/2015-02/28/c_1114465794.html.

Zhang Wenjuan (2018), "为什么中国人感觉印度人难打交道", [Why do Chinese people feel that Indians are difficult to deal with], *The Paper*, 18 April 2018, accessed 18 October 2018, URL: https://www.thepaper.cn/newsDetail_forward_ 2082989.

Zhang Yang (2019), "儒家文明和印度教文明核心价值观对比及其对经济关系影响分析： 冲突与合作" [Comparative Studies of the Core Values of Confucianism and Hinduism and Analysis of its Influence on China-India Economic Relations: Conflict and Cooperation], 东亚儒学研究 "一带一路" 儒家文明创新论坛 丛书 [*Confucianism Studies of East Asia "BRI" Confucian Civilization Innovation Forum Series*], Beijing: Thread-Binding Books Publishing House, 404-410.

—— (2017), "India's frugal innovation on China's Internet: Evaluation from a Cultural Perspective", conference paper presented at the conference of "India-China Cross Cultural Dialogues 2017: New Media, Transforming Societies and the Coming of the Information Age", organized by the Department of East Asian Studies, University of Delhi, in collaboration with Sun Yat-sen University, Guangzhou, China, 10-11 March 2017, at University Guest House, University of Delhi.

Zhao Cheng, Tan Jingjing and Du Shangze (2010), "龙象共舞, 从文化开始" ——温家宝总理与中印文化界人士座谈侧记, accessed 11 June 2015, URL: http://news.xinhuanet.com/world/2010-12/18/c_12892976.html.

Zhao Cheng and Mao Xiaoxiao (2010), "温家宝出席庆祝中印建交60周年活动暨" 中国节"闭幕式", *Xinhua Net*, URL: http://news.xinhuanet.com/world/2010-12/17/c_12889227.html.

Zhao Ligen (2003), "瓦杰帕伊诗意访中国 传递美好愿望促进经济合作" [Vajpayee's poetic visit to China conveys good wishes for economic cooperation], Ban Yue Tan, accessed 17 March 2015, URL: http://news.xinhuanet.com/world/2003-07/10/content_965556.html.

Zhao Jiayan (2006), "Dramatic Increase of Indian FDI in China", *South Asian Studies Quarterly*, No. 2: 203.

Zhou Jinglu (2013), "辛格中央党校演讲：印中两国不是命中注定的对手" [Singh's speech in Central Party School: India and China are not competitors], accessed 17 June 2015, URL: http://news.ifeng.com/mainland/special/xingefanghua2013/content- 5/detail_2013_10/25/30655767_0.shtml.

Zhou Shuai (2016), "Strategic Trust between China and India: Regime Type and Strategic Interests" [中印战略信任：国家类型与战略利益], *South Asian Studies*, 2016, Vol. 4: 24.

Zi Jin (2013), "印度人是'节俭式创新'的行家", [Indians are experts of 'frugal innovation'], *Southern Metropolis Daily*, 13 November 2013, accessed 10 February 2017, URL: http://news.ifeng.com/gundong/detail_2013_11/13/311925 52_0.shtml.

—— (2013), "印度人是'节俭式创新'的行家" [Indians are experts of 'frugal innovation'], *Southern Metropolis Daily*, accessed 10 February 2017, URL: http://news.ifeng.com/gundong/detail_2013_11/13/31192552_0.shtml.

Zong Qi (2013), "Wu Renbao: Disputed Legend", *Times Figure*: 69.

Zou Song et al. (2015), "印度劲吹 "中印暖风" 西方媒体渲染中印对抗" [Indian media shows positive information about China-India while Western media shows China-India confrontation], accessed 8 July 2015, URL: http://world.huanqiu.com/exclusive/2015-05/6429704.html.

Zuo Zhuan (2016), *Commentary on the Spring and Autumn Annals*, translated and annotated by Guo Dan, Beijing: Zhonghua Book Company.

INDEX

About the Author

Zhang Yang is a Post-Doctoral Research Fellow supported by the National Museum of China and the Chinese Academy of Social Sciences, Beijing, the People's Republic of China. He holds M.Phil. and Ph.D. degrees from the Centre for East Asian Studies, School of International Studies, Jawaharlal Nehru University, and Master from the Department of Buddhist Studies, University of Delhi. He has studied in Langfang Normal University, Capital Normal University and National Taiwan University. His research interests are cultural studies, IR theory and world history with a focus on China-India relations. His research has appeared in edited books and journals including *One Belt and One Road: China's Global Outreach* (Pentagon Press, 2017) and *China and the BRICS: Setting Up a Different Kitchen* (Pentagon Press, 2017). He is part of The Juxtapose Project, Oxford (A multi-disciplinary international annual forum on China-India comparative studies).

Email: zhangyang0086@qq.com, zhangyang0086@yahoo.com.